STAGE IT
WITH MUSIC

STAGE IT

WITH MUSIC

An Encyclopedic Guide to the American Musical Theatre

THOMAS S. HISCHAK

GREENWOOD PRESS
Westport, Connecticut • London

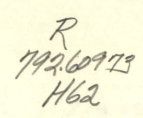
For my parents

Library of Congress Cataloging-in-Publication Data

Hischak, Thomas S.
    Stage it with music : an encyclopedic guide to the American
musical theatre / Thomas S. Hischak.
        p.   cm.
    Includes bibliographical references and index.
    ISBN 0–313–28708–2 (alk. paper)
    1. Musicals—Encyclopedias. I. Title.
ML102.M88H6   1993
792.6'0973—dc20   92–35321

British Library Cataloguing in Publication Data is available.

Library of Congress Catalog Card Number: 92–35321
ISBN: 0–313–28708–2

First published in 1993

Greenwood Press, 88 Post Road West, Westport, CT 06881
An imprint of Greenwood Publishing Group, Inc.

Printed in the United States of America

The paper used in this book complies with the
Permanent Paper Standard issued by the National
Information Standards Organization (Z39.48–1984).

10 9 8 7 6 5 4 3 2 1

Contents

187756

Musical play or opera? *Porgy and Bess* was atypical of Broadway; but what is the typical American musical like? Alternately grandiose and intimate, highly lyrical and conversational, *Porgy and Bess* still proves how flexible the rules of musical theatre are. (Billy Rose Theatre Collection, the New York Public Library for the Performing Arts, Astor, Lenox and Tilden Foundations.)

Preface

Whether one is studying the history and literature of the American musical theatre or one just enjoys Broadway musical shows, there are many books available filled with historical, critical, pictorial and even gossipy information. What has not existed for some time is a single-volume work that covers in encyclopedic form the subject of the American musical. This guide hopes to present general information as well as interesting details, raw data as much as subjective commentary, important concepts regarding musical theatre but also attempts to explain what makes Broadway musicals so terrific.

While many surveys or histories of the American musical tend to emphasize the composer, I have tried to give considerable attention to the other creative forces as well. In addition to the three hundred-some individual musical shows described, there are entries on directors, choreographers, producers, music directors, orchestrators, scenic–costume–lighting designers, actors, librettists, lyricists and, oh yes, composers. And, because the information could not be easily included in the above, there are separate entries for various musical genres, theatre organizations, subjects relating to the musical theatre and famous musical series. (See list of Subjects, Genres, and Musical Series following this Preface.)

Trying to be as comprehensive as any one-volume book can practically be, the decision has been made to include as many entries as possible and to not attempt to list every musical credit for every artist. For the same reason, not all the songs or actors are mentioned under each title listing. American works and artists are emphasized over foreign ones, but entries for British performers, authors and productions that have had a considerable impact on Broadway are included.

Some clarification on the entries: the indicated number of performances, always an item for debate, is the generally accepted number of New York performances starting with the official opening and does not include previews or tryout performances. Dates given refer to the Broadway opening date unless stated otherwise. Every effort has been made to keep the guide as up to date as possible. For the most part, the information contained herein covers events up through the 1991–1992 theatre season. More specifically, the cutoff date for artists' credits is September 1, 1992. All names, titles and subjects presented in UPPERCASE TYPE have an individual entry. The chronological list and index at the end of the book will also be helpful in locating more detailed information.

I should like to acknowledge the continued help of the staff at the Cortland Memorial Library at the State University of New York at Cortland as well as the assistance of Rosalie Kabana and Cathy Hischak in preparing the manuscript. My thanks also to Marilyn Brownstein, my editor at Greenwood Publishing Group. I also wish to acknowledge the work of two outstanding predecessors in the field: Gerald Bordman, whose detailed study of early musical works is unsurpassed, and the late Stanley Green, whose lifetime of musical theatre appreciation and scholarship gave the study of this uniquely American art form a respectability it so long deserved.

Subjects, Genres, and Musical Series

SUBJECTS AND GENRES

Anti-War Musicals
Biblical Musicals
Biographical Musicals
Black Musicals
British Imports
Business and Labor
Classical Music in Musicals
Comic Strip Musicals
Concept Musicals
Dance in Musicals
Flop Musicals
Goodspeed Opera House
Hollywood
Locations of Musicals
Music Directors
New York Shakespeare Festival
Operetta
Orchestrations
Original Cast Recordings

Pastiche Musicals
Playwrights Horizons
Politics
Pulitzer Prize Musicals
Revue
Rock Musicals
Shakespeare Musicals
Sports
Theatre Guild
Tony Awards

MUSICAL SERIES

Earl Carroll Vanities
The Garrick Gaieties
George White's Scandals
Greenwich Village Follies
The Mulligan Guard Musicals
Music Box Revues
Princess Theatre Musicals
Ziegfeld Follies

Musical comedy or musical play? *Pal Joey* may be a pre-*Oklahoma!* show but at times it sure doesn't feel like it. *Pal Joey* seemed abrasive when it opened in 1940; when it was revived fourteen years later it came close to being charming. Musical comedy encompasses much more than the name implies. (Billy Rose Theatre Collection, the New York Public Library for the Performing Arts, Astor, Lenox and Tilden Foundations.)

Encyclopedic Guide to the American Musical Theatre

A

ALEX A. AARONS (1891–1943) and his partner VINTON FREEDLEY were successful Broadway producers who were most often associated with the GERSHWINS' early shows. Aarons produced George Gershwin's first musical, *La La Lucille* (1919), and his later *For Goodness Sake* (1922) in which Freedley appeared as an actor. The two men formed a partnership and produced the Gershwin brothers' first show together, *LADY, BE GOOD!* (1924), as well as their subsequent *TIP-TOES* (1925), *OH, KAY!* (1926), *FUNNY FACE* (1927), *Treasure Girl* (1928) and *GIRL CRAZY* (1930).

GEORGE ABBOTT (1887–   ), the dean of American musical comedy directors, is also a successful playwright, producer and musical librettist. He holds the record for the longest career in the American theatre (1913–1987) and is certainly among the most prolific artists with over one hundred plays and musicals to his credit. However, Abbott's importance is more than a matter of longevity or statistics; as a director and librettist, he developed the fast-paced, tightly constructed form of musical comedy that dominated Broadway for over four decades. Abbott worked as a messenger boy, salesman, cowboy and sports coach before his Broadway debut as an actor in 1913. By 1925 he was writing plays and in 1935 he made his musical directing debut with *JUMBO*, co-directed by JOHN MURRAY ANDERSON; RODGERS and HART's *ON YOUR TOES* (1936) was his first musical libretto assignment. He would go on to direct the same team's *THE BOYS FROM SYRACUSE* (1938), *TOO MANY GIRLS* (1939) and *PAL JOEY* (1940). Over the next forty years Abbott would direct and co-author musicals with just about every major composer and lyricist of the Broadway theatre, from JULE STYNE to BOB MERRILL to FRANK LOESSER to STEPHEN SONDHEIM to IRVING BERLIN to LEONARD BERNSTEIN. Among the many memorable Abbott musicals were *ON THE TOWN* (1944), *HIGH BUTTON SHOES* (1947), *WHERE'S CHARLEY?* (1948), *CALL ME MADAM* (1950), *WONDERFUL TOWN* (1953), *THE PAJAMA GAME* (1954), *DAMN YANKEES* (1955), *FIORELLO!* (1959), *A FUNNY THING HAPPENED ON THE WAY TO THE FORUM* (1962) and *FLORA, THE RED MENACE* (1965). His last Broadway success was the long-running revival of *On Your Toes* (1983) and at the age of one hundred he directed a revival of his play *Broadway* in 1987. In addition to his numerous productions, Abbott was the mentor for dozens of performers, directors and songwriters whose careers would be greatly influenced by him.

THE ACT (1977) was a vehicle for LIZA MINNELLI who triumphed in the show but the libretto by George Furth, the direction by Martin Scorcese (later replaced by GOWER CHAMPION), and JOHN KANDER and FRED EBB's score were less than inspired. *The Act* was about a film star who loses her husband and watches her career falter, all told in the format of a Las Vegas nightclub act. There were two comic songs that pleased: the sexy romp "Arthur in the Afternoon" and "Little Do They Know," a satirical number sung by the disgruntled dancers who have to support the star. The "gypsies' " opinion notwithstanding, Minnelli kept *The Act* alive for 233 performances.

EDIE ADAMS (1927–), a singer-actress in films, on television and in nightclubs, originated two notable Broadway musical roles, the amorous Eileen in *WONDERFUL TOWN* (1953) and the ever-persistent Daisy Mae in *LI'L ABNER* (1956).

LEE ADAMS (1924–), the lyricist partner of composer CHARLES STROUSE, contributed lyrics for a number of notable musicals in the 1960s. Adams was born in Mansfield, Ohio, and studied journalism at Ohio State University and Columbia University. He worked as a writer and editor for *Pageant* magazine and later *This Week*. In 1949 he met Strouse and his hobby of writing songs grew into a career. The team scored some shows at the Green Mansions summer resort and for some BEN BAGLEY revues Off Broadway. Their first Broadway musical was *BYE BYE BIRDIE* (1960), and they followed it with *ALL AMERICAN* (1962), *GOLDEN BOY* (1964), *IT'S A BIRD, IT'S A PLANE, IT'S SUPERMAN* (1966) and *APPLAUSE* (1970). The team temporarily separated in 1972 after their London musical *Albert and I* and Strouse worked with other lyricists. Adams was reunited with his former partner for two notable flops, *A Broadway Musical* (1978) and *Bring Back Birdie* (1981), the latter an ill-conceived sequel to their 1960 hit. In the early shows with Strouse, Adams demonstrated an admirable talent for exuberant lyricwriting for young and idealistic characters. The Strouse–Adams musicals are decidedly

American in tone and subject matter and Adams' ear for the vernacular is impeccable.

BRUCE ADLER (1944–), a character actor in plays and musicals on and off Broadway since 1957, made his musical debut as Ali Hakim in the 1979 Broadway revival of *OKLAHOMA!* Adler's other musical credits include *Oh, Brother!* (1981), *Those Were the Days* (1990), and as the impressario Bela Zangler in *CRAZY FOR YOU* (1992).

RICHARD ADLER (1921–) and his collaborator JERRY ROSS are unusual in that both songwriters wrote both music and lyrics together for their musicals. Adler was born in New York to a musical family and studied playwriting at the University of South Carolina. While working as a copywriter for an advertising firm, he started writing songs, but he did not seriously pursue a musical career until he met Ross in 1950. FRANK LOESSER published some early works by the team and some of their songs appeared in *John Murray Anderson's Almanac* (1953). It was Loesser who recommended the young songwriters for *THE PAJAMA GAME* (1954) and their vivacious score for that musical hit secured their reputation. They followed it with the equally lively *DAMN YANKEES* (1955); but Ross died suddenly in 1955 and Adler's musical theatre career never fully recuperated. He provided the score for the challenging *KWAMINA* (1961) and collaborated on the unsuccessful *Music Is* (1976).

ADONIS (1884) and its score are long forgotten today but this extravagant musical burlesque ran an astonishing 603 performances, the longest Broadway run at the time. Edward E. Rice, of *EVANGELINE* (1874) fame, wrote the music and collaborated on the book with William Gill. The story of a sculptress who prays to the gods to bring her beautiful male statue to life was an interesting twist on the Pygmalion legend. But unlike George Bernard Shaw's later play and *MY FAIR LADY* (1956), *Adonis* concerned itself mainly with the misadventures the statue-turned-man encounters trying to win the love of the country lass Rosetta while all the adoring women in town are chasing him. Unlike Eliza Doolittle, he despairs and returns to stone.

GILBERT ADRIAN (1903–1959), a costume designer on Broadway and in films who was also a fashion designer known simply as "Adrian," did designs for *GEORGE WHITE'S SCANDALS* (1921) and a few other revues before going to Hollywood in 1925. He returned to Broadway in 1958 to design the costumes for *CAMELOT* (1960) but died before they were done so Tony Duquette completed the project.

MAX ADRIAN (1903–1973), a British character actor who performed in many London revues as well as classical pieces, made only one Broadway musical appearance, as the philosophic Dr. Pangloss in *CANDIDE* (1956).

AIN'T MISBEHAVIN' (1978) was arguably the finest musical revue seen on Broadway since the last holdouts of the genre in the 1950s. This sprightly entertainment had no original songs but instead celebrated the past works of Thomas "Fats" Waller by presenting thirty songs he either wrote or recorded. RICHARD MALTBY, JR., conceived the idea for the show with Murray Horowitz and they provided new lyrics for some instrumental pieces as well. The five performers—Nell Carter, ANDRE DE SHIELDS, Armelia McQueen, Charlaine Woodard and KEN PAGE—were dynamic individually and in unison and the sleek Harlem nightclub production directed by Maltby made *Ain't Misbehavin'* an audience favorite for 1,604 performances. The success of the show inspired a series of other revues saluting past black artists, but few had the dexterity of this original.

KAREN AKERS (1945–) is an exotic-looking cabaret singer who gave memorable performances as Luisa, the film director's wife, in *NINE* (1982) and as the confidante Raffaela in *GRAND HOTEL* (1989).

EDDIE ALBERT (1908–), a veteran actor of many films, plays and television, made two notable Broadway musical appearances: Antipholus of Syracuse in *THE BOYS FROM SYRACUSE* (1938) and Horace Miller in *MISS LIBERTY* (1949).

THEONI V. ALDREDGE (1932–), the prolific costume designer who has provided designs for over one hundred plays and musicals on and off Broadway, is known for her stunning sense of theatricality and her period costumes in many musicals. Aldredge began designing in New York in 1957 and made her Broadway musical debut with *I CAN GET IT FOR YOU WHOLESALE* (1961). Her most notable design credits include *Skyscraper* (1965), *A CHORUS LINE* (1975), *ANNIE* (1977), *Ballroom* (1978), *THE GRAND TOUR* (1979), *BARNUM* (1980), *42ND STREET* (1980), *DREAMGIRLS* (1981), *LA CAGE AUX FOLLES* (1983), *Chess* (1985), *Teddy and Alice* (1987), the 1990 black version of *OH, KAY!* and *THE SECRET GARDEN* (1991).

ALL AMERICAN (1962) was one of the later in a long line of musicals that used a college setting with the big football game to create its plot; but this effort was not one of the successful ones. Mel Brooks' libretto had a promising premise—a Hungarian refugee, Professor Fodorski, arrives at Southern Baptist Institute of Technology to teach and ends up coaching football—but the plotting thereafter was awkward and predictable. *All American* did boast a joyous performance by RAY BOLGER as Fodorski but even he could not keep the musical running for more than eighty performances. The score was by CHARLES STROUSE and LEE ADAMS and, although it was not up to their usual high standard, it did contain the lovely ballad "Once Upon a Time."

ALLEGRO (1947) was RODGERS and HAMMERSTEIN's first original musical and also their first effort to meet with mixed reviews and lukewarm audience response. Hammerstein's ambitious libretto attempts to explore the common man's loss of integrity because of worldly compromise. The plot follows the life of physician Joe Taylor from his birth to his success at thirty-five years of age. The story is told in expressionistic terms using a Greek chorus and extended stream of consciousnesslike musical numbers. The authors followed their own advice and did not compromise in telling their modern-day *Everyman* tale, even going so far as eliminating traditional scenery. But much of the musical was too numbing for audiences and only the large advance sale kept it running for 315 performances. The musical numbers were fully integrated into the plot, but "A Fellow Needs a Girl" and "The Gentleman Is a Dope" stand well on their own. *Allegro*, one of the first CONCEPT musicals, was a bold experiment and illustrated that the team was capable of hard-hitting, unsentimental, and even cynical writing.

DEBBIE ALLEN (1950–), a vibrant black actress-singer-dancer and sometimes choreographer, made her Broadway debut as Beneatha Younger in *RAISIN* (1973) before going on to a career in television and film. Allen played Anita in the 1980 Broadway revival of *WEST SIDE STORY* and the title role in the 1986 revival of *SWEET CHARITY*. She choreographed the short-lived horror musical *Carrie* (1988).

ELIZABETH ALLEN (1934–), an actress-singer intermittently in Broadway musicals, first gained attention as the gypsy Magda in *THE GAY LIFE* (1961) and went on to play the American spinster Leona in *DO I HEAR A WALTZ?* (1965). Allen was also featured in the short-lived musical *Sherry!* (1967).

FRED ALLEN (1894–1956) was a twangy-voiced vaudeville comic who appeared in a few musicals in the 1920s before going on to a celebrated career in radio. Allen's Broadway musicals include *The Passing Show* (1922), *Vogues of 1924*, *Polly* (1929), *THE LITTLE SHOW* (1929) and *THREE'S A CROWD* (1930).

ROBERT ALTON (1897–1957) was a Broadway choreographer who greatly affected the look of dancing in musicals. Some of his most famous credits include *ANYTHING GOES* (1934), *BETWEEN THE DEVIL* (1937), *LEAVE IT TO ME!* (1938), *TOO MANY GIRLS* (1939), *DuBARRY WAS A LADY* (1939) and *PAL JOEY* (1940). Alton was instrumental in replacing static chorus line choreography with an exciting new approach that featured solo dancers and put the chorus in groupings rather than strict regimented formations. Alton danced in or choreographed over thirty Broadway musicals as well as several Hollywood films.

DON AMECHE (1908–), a romantic leading man of many films, appeared in a handful of Broadway musicals in the 1950s and 1960s, most notably as Steve Canfield in *SILK STOCKINGS* (1955), the movie director Max Grady in *Goldilocks* (1958) and as the celebrity Henry Orient in *Henry, Sweet Henry* (1967).

JOHN MURRAY ANDERSON (1886–1954), the versatile director and some-time lyricist, had a career that covered Broadway musicals and revues, circuses, nightclub acts, films, pageants, movie house shows and even aquacades. Anderson's chief Broadway contribution was a series of revues that used the latest innovations in technical theatre, often coordinating lights and movement with spectacular effect. His most remembered revues include the *GREEN-WICH VILLAGE FOLLIES* (annual editions from 1919 through 1924), *John Murray Anderson's Almanac* (1929 and 1953), *Two for the Show* (1940) and *NEW FACES OF 1952*. Among Anderson's book musicals are *DEAREST ENEMY* (1925), *JUMBO* (1935) and *The Firebrand of Florence* (1945). In addition to the thirty-three Broadway musicals he directed, Anderson wrote the lyrics for most of the *Greenwich Village Follies* editions with composer Louis Hirsch and others.

MAXWELL ANDERSON (1888–1959), the renowned verse playwright who wrote history plays and social dramas, provided the librettos and lyrics for two unforgettable Broadway musicals with composer KURT WEILL: *KNICKER-BOCKER HOLIDAY* (1938) and *LOST IN THE STARS* (1949).

JULIE ANDREWS (1935–) is a British actress-singer who has spent only a small part of her career in the theatre yet Broadway has always considered her their own. Andrews first came to New York in 1954 with the BRITISH IMPORT *THE BOY FRIEND* but it was her incomparable performance as Eliza Doolittle in *MY FAIR LADY* (1956) that secured her fame. Her only other Broadway appearance to date was as Queen Guenevere in *CAMELOT* (1960).

ANIMAL CRACKERS (1928) was a wacky musical vehicle for the MARX BROTHERS with a libretto by GEORGE S. KAUFMAN and MORRIE RYSKIND. The story concerned a valuable painting that is stolen from Mrs. Rittenhouse's estate but the slight plot was forever being interrupted by the brothers' gags. The BERT KALMAR–HARRY RUBY score was pleasant but forgettable except for the daffy "Hooray for Captain Spaulding," which was thereafter associated with Groucho. Sadly, *Animal Crackers* was the Marx Brothers' last Broadway musical; in 1930 they went to Hollywood and never returned to the stage. (191 performances)

ANNIE (1977), the most successful musical ever made from a comic strip, took Harold Gray's satiric "Little Orphan Annie" and made it *the* family entertainment of the 1970s. Thomas Meehan wrote the tight libretto for CHARLES

STROUSE's music, and MARTIN CHARNIN provided the lyrics and directed the show. The musical utilized several of the comic strip's famous characters—the eleven-year-old foundling Annie and her dog, Sandy; billionaire Oliver Warbucks; the self-destructive Miss Hannigan and so on—and put them all together into a Depression-era tale that even involved FDR and the New Deal. With a gaggle of adorable moppets, a dog and a Christmas tree, *Annie* seemed marketed for success. But the musical was well crafted, expertly staged, and agreeable on several levels. Andrea McArdle as Annie led the cast that also included REID SHELTON, DOROTHY LOUDON, Sandy Faison, Robert Fitch and Barbara Erwin. The tuneful score featured the unabashedly optimistic hit "Tomorrow" as well as some fun 1930s-type songs such as "Easy Street," "It's a Hard-Knock Life" and "You're Never Fully Dressed without a Smile." (2,377 performances)

ANNIE GET YOUR GUN (1946) was IRVING BERLIN's greatest Broadway success and offered his most varied and engaging score. After composing for book musicals for over thirty years, Berlin finally got a sure-fire libretto to work with in *Annie Get Your Gun*. DOROTHY and HERBERT FIELDS wrote the competent, funny story about sharpshooter Annie Oakley from her back-woods days to international stardom in Buffalo Bill's Wild West Show. The romantic plot involving Oakley and Frank Butler was alternately sassy and tender, allowing for a variety of love songs. ETHEL MERMAN triumphed in the title role and RAY MIDDLETON had his finest moment as Butler. The superlative score included "There's No Business Like Show Business," "I Got Lost in His Arms," "They Say It's Wonderful," "Doin' What Comes Natur'lly," "The Girl That I Marry," "I Got the Sun in the Morning," "Moonshine Lullabye" and "Anything You Can Do." *Annie Get Your Gun* is Berlin's best score not because of the number of hits it contains but because its songs successfully combine character and plot development in a manner not evident in his other work. (1,147 performances)

ANTI-WAR MUSICALS were plentiful Off Broadway in the late 1960s and 1970s but Broadway, despite its inclination toward escapism, has seen a handful of musicals over the years that had very pacifist viewpoints. *JOHNNY JOHNSON* (1936) was as strong an anti-war piece as any non-musical play dealing with the crushed idealism of World War I. The wacky *HOORAY FOR WHAT!* (1937) was broad satire but there was no mistaking its creators' targets; the show featured a poison gas that made the enemy laugh and a prophetic atom bomblike device. Even in the midst of World War II, *BLOOMER GIRL* (1944) managed to remain palatable by applying its anti-war sentiments to the Civil War. Although such pacifist ideas were anathema in the 1950s and early 1960s, anti-war musicals flourished with the arrival of ROCK MUSICALS, guerrilla theatre, happenings and all the other experiments of the late 1960s and early 1970s. Most of these musicals were stronger in content and conviction than in craftsmanship but there were notable exceptions. *HAIR* (1968) unabashedly attacked the Vietnam War and the military along with its other establishment targets. *Now Is the Time for All Good Men* (1967) and *THE LAST SWEET DAYS OF ISAAC* (1970) were more subtle but just as potent. *TWO GENTLEMEN OF VERONA* (1971) found anti-war philosophy in Shakespeare and even the patriotic *1776* (1969) found room for an anti-war song. By the mid-1970s the whole subject had become safe enough that no one was bothered that the old-fashioned, conventional *SHENANDOAH* (1975) was actually a very pacifist musical, although setting it during the Civil War didn't hurt. During the last few decades of an economically floundering Broadway, anti-war musicals have been more a financial risk than ever but we have not seen the end of this very particular genre.

ANYONE CAN WHISTLE (1964) was a short-lived (nine performances), adventurous musical that featured a dynamic STEPHEN SONDHEIM score, a bold libretto by ARTHUR LAURENTS and a grand performance by ANGELA LANSBURY in her first Broadway musical. Because it was so offbeat, so ambitious and so unsuccessful, *Anyone Can Whistle* has risen to a cult status few FLOP MUSICALS can aspire to. The plot was about an impoverished industrial town that fakes a miracle to draw in the tourists. Added to the story are escaped inmates from the local mental institution, a fraudulent psychiatrist and a daffy nurse who is sometimes French. HARRY GUARDINO, Lee Remick and Gabriel Dell were also in the cast directed by Laurents, who took the show's ideas so far as to have the actors viciously laugh at the audience. "There Won't Be Trumpets," "Simple," "Me and My Town," "A Parade in Town" and the title song were notable in a score that ranged from sardonic to wistful. Although Laurents' quirky, dated libretto makes *Anyone Can Whistle* difficult to revive, it is still a unique and commendable work.

ANYTHING GOES (1934) stands as the most popular and often-revived 1930s musical today and it is not surprising. The show captures all the wit, romance and high spirits of that decade and the COLE PORTER score is one of the finest ever heard on Broadway. The original libretto, by GUY BOLTON and P. G. WODEHOUSE, was about a loveable group of eccentric characters on an ocean liner that is shipwrecked. When a fire destroyed an actual liner off the New Jersey coast and 125 people died, producer VINTON FREEDLEY halted production and asked his director HOWARD LINDSAY to come up with a new plot using the completed sets and score. Lindsay teamed up with press agent RUSSEL CROUSE and wrote the first of their many musical librettos together. Most of the story takes place aboard ship where Billy Crocker (WILLIAM GAXTON) has stowed away to be near his truelove, Hope (BETTINA HALL), who is slated to wed Sir Evelyn Oakleigh (Leslie Banic). Also on board is evangelist-singer Reno Sweeney (ETHEL MERMAN) with her chorus girls and the comic fugitive Reverend Dr. Moon

(VICTOR MOORE). From that point on anything goes as disguises, mistaken identity and surprise revelations keep the plot lively until the illogically contrived happy ending. Merman got to introduce three Porter standards—"I Get a Kick Out of You," "Blow, Gabriel, Blow" and the title song—and the score also contained "All Through the Night," "You're the Top" and "The Gypsy in Me." *Anything Goes* ran for 420 performances and has had several revivals, most notably a 1962 Off-Broadway production with HAL LINDEN, Eileen Rodgers and Mickey Deems that ran for 239 performances and a 1987 Broadway revival with PATTI LuPONE, HOWARD McGILLIN and Bill McCutcheon that ran 804 performances.

APPLAUSE (1970) was a musical version of the celebrated 1950 film *All About Eve* with LAUREN BACALL, in her musical debut, in the Bette Davis role of Margo Channing. Neither the libretto, by BETTY COMDEN and ADOLPH GREEN, nor the songs, by CHARLES STROUSE and LEE ADAMS, were any match for the original but Bacall's star performance and RON FIELD's masterful direction and choreography made the musical seem new and exciting. Also in the cast were LEN CARIOU, Penny Fuller, Bonnie Franklin, Brandon Maggart and LEE ROY REAMS. The title song became somewhat popular and there was pleasing work in "Who's That Girl?" "Fasten Your Seat Belts" and "Welcome to the Theatre." (896 performances)

THE APPLE TREE (1966) was an odd and somewhat unsatisfying show that consisted of three one-act musicals scored by JERRY BOCK and SHELDON HARNICK and based on three very different and unrelated sources: Mark Twain's "The Diary of Adam and Eve," Frank R. Stockton's "The Lady or the Tiger?" and Jules Feiffer's "Passionella." Bock and Harnick, with help from Jerome Coopersmith, adapted the tales and Mike Nichols, in his first Broadway musical, directed them with a flair. But the songs were forgettable and the characters poorly drawn and only the strong personalities of BARBARA HARRIS, Alan Alda and LARRY BLYDEN brought the musical to life. (463 performances)

EVE ARDEN (1912–1990), the droll, angular comedienne of many films and television, appeared in the 1934 and 1936 editions of the *ZIEGFELD FOLLIES* as well as in *VERY WARM FOR MAY* (1939), *Two for the Show* (1940) and *LET'S FACE IT!* (1941).

HAROLD ARLEN (1905–1986), one of Broadway's most unique composers, had a special talent for using blues and Negro rhythms to create his musical theatre scores. Arlen was born in Buffalo and started his career as a pianist and arranger for local bands. His dream was to become a singer on Broadway but that all changed when his song "Get Happy," with lyrics by Ted Koehler, was added to *9:15 Revue* (1930). Arlen and Koehler then wrote several songs for the Cotton Club revues, a handful of which have become standards: "I've Got the World on a String," "Between the Devil and the Deep Blue Sea," "I Love a Parade" and "Stormy Weather." In the 1930s Arlen contributed songs to Broadway revues and in 1937 he collaborated with E. Y. HARBURG on his first book musical, the ambitiously satiric *HOORAY FOR WHAT!* Arlen's Hollywood career began in 1932 and he would score some two dozen film musicals, most memorably *The Wizard of Oz* (1939) with Harburg. Back on Broadway, Arlen concentrated on book musicals and his projects were known for their unusual and often disturbing subject matter and themes. *BLOOMER GIRL* (1944) was a popular musical with strong anti-war and anti-slavery sentiments. *ST. LOUIS WOMAN* (1946), *HOUSE OF FLOWERS* (1954) and *JAMAICA* (1957) all dealt with Negro life. Arlen's most challenging undertaking was his last Broadway musical, *SARATOGA* (1959), an unsuccessful attempt to musicalize Edna Ferber's novel *Saratoga Trunk*. An Arlen song has a distinctive flavor to it that is rich and evocative. After GEORGE GERSHWIN, no other Broadway composer utilized blues and jazz as effectively as Arlen did.

WILL STEVEN ARMSTRONG (1930–1969), a scenic, lighting and sometimes costume designer on Broadway during the 1960s, designed sets and lights for *CARNIVAL* (1961), *I CAN GET IT FOR YOUR WHOLESALE* (1961), *KWAMINA* (1961), *SUBWAYS ARE FOR SLEEPING* (1961) and others.

BORIS ARONSON (1900–1979), one of the most experimental and influential scenic designers of the American theatre, designed several musicals and created some of Broadway's most distinctive and memorable visual images. Born the son of a rabbi in czarist Russia, Aronson studied art in Kiev and began designing for the theatre in Moscow where he was greatly influenced by the landmark productions of Myerhold and Tairov. He emigrated to Berlin and then later to New York in 1923, where he began designing for the Yiddish theatre. Aronson's first Broadway musical was *Walk a Little Faster* (1932) and he continued to contribute designs for musicals on an irregular basis for the rest of his career. His bold designs for the early CONCEPT MUSICAL *LOVE LIFE* (1948) and the expressionistic images for *DO RE MI* (1960) paved the way for his famous designs of the 1960s and 1970s. *FIDDLER ON THE ROOF* (1964) combined Aronson's memories of Russia with a Marc Chagall-inspired style and *CABARET* (1966) utilized his Berlin background. His crowning achievements were the four musicals Aronson did with HAROLD PRINCE and STEPHEN SONDHEIM: *COMPANY* (1970), *FOLLIES* (1971), *A LITTLE NIGHT MUSIC* (1973) and *PACIFIC OVERTURES* (1976). Aronson has been associated with the concept musical and the unconventional approach to scenery more than any other American designer.

MARTIN ARONSTEIN (1936–), a lighting designer on and off Broadway, lit the musicals *How Now Dow Jones* (1967), *GEORGE M!* (1968), *PROM-*

ISES, PROMISES (1969), *Ain't Supposed to Die a Natural Death* (1971), *SUGAR* (1972), *THE GRAND TOUR* (1979) and others.

BEATRICE ARTHUR (1926?–), the sharp-tongued comic actress known mostly for her television roles, appeared in a handful of musicals in the 1950s and 1960s, including the role of Lucy in the Off-Broadway *THE THREE-PENNY OPERA* (1954), *Shoestring Revue* (1955), *Seventh Heaven* (1955) and the 1960 revival of *GAY DIVORCE*. Arthur's most famous musical theatre roles were the meddling matchmaker Yente in *FIDDLER ON THE ROOF* (1964) and the acerbic actress Vera Charles in *MAME* (1966).

AS THE GIRLS GO (1948) was an old-style musical comedy built around the talents of its star, the inspired comic BOBBY CLARK. William Roos wrote the thin libretto about the first woman to become U.S. president and Clark played her daffy girl-chasing husband. JIMMY McHUGH (music) and Harold Adamson (lyrics) provided a sparkling score but because of an ASCAP strike at the time, the show's songs were not recorded and never got the attention they deserved. "You Say the Nicest Things, Baby," "I Got Lucky in the Rain" and "It Takes a Woman to Take a Man" were standouts in a fine score. MICHAEL TODD produced the show and Hollywood choreographer Hermes Pan did the dances. Despite a run of 420 performances, *As the Girls Go* didn't make a profit.

AS THOUSANDS CHEER (1933), probably IRVING BERLIN's finest musical revue, was one of the most popular examples of the genre during its golden age of the 1930s. MOSS HART wrote all the sketches, which were held together thematically by the device of newspaper headlines leading into each scene or song. Many celebrities, from Joan Crawford to Mahatma Gandhi, were satirized, as was high society, the theatre season and even the weather. The superb cast included CLIFTON WEBB, HELEN BRODERICK, ETHEL WATERS and, in her last Broadway appearance, MARILYN MILLER. The Berlin score was one of his best: "Heat Wave," "Easter Parade," "Lonely Heart," "How's Chances?" "Harlem on My Mind" and "Supper Time." The last, a haunting ballad about racial persecution, was unusually weighty for a musical revue but Waters' rendition of the song was so powerful that producer SAM HARRIS defied tradition and kept it in the show. (400 performances)

HOWARD ASHMAN (1950–1991), the lyricist-librettist who found success in the theatre and in films before his untimely death from AIDS, most often worked with composer ALAN MENKEN. The team's Off-Broadway musical *God Bless You, Mr. Rosewater* (1979) was an odd piece that attracted some attention but their camp musical *LITTLE SHOP OF HORRORS* (1982) became one of Off Broadway's longest-running hits. He next collaborated with composer MARVIN HAMLISCH on the short-lived Broadway musical *Smile* (1986), a show Ashman also directed. Menken and Ashman turned to films next and wrote the scores for Disney's *The Little Mermaid* (1989) and, released after his death, *Beauty and the Beast* (1991) and *Aladdin* (1992). Ashman was adept at writing parody, pop, character and traditional Broadway-style songs.

ASSASSINS (1990) was a daring and darkly comic Off-Broadway musical about the men and women who have killed or tried to kill U. S. presidents. JOHN WEIDMAN wrote the offbeat libretto that personalized the infamous figures without passing judgment on them, often capturing the bizarre fascination and even the comic aspects of these characters. John Wilkes Booth, Lee Harvey Oswald, "Squeaky" Fromme and others all met in this CONCEPT MUSICAL that embraced expressionism, surrealism and even vaudeville. STEPHEN SONDHEIM wrote a powerful score that was quite unlike anything he had attempted before, using American folk music, the narrative ballad form, 1960s pop and even turn-of-the-century cakewalk rhythms. At sixty years old, Sondheim was still the boldest and most innovative songwriter in the contemporary American theatre. JERRY ZAKS directed a talented cast that included VICTOR GARBER, JONATHAN HADARY, TERRENCE MANN, Debra Monk and Jace Alexander. *Assassins* played a limited engagement of eight weeks at the PLAYWRIGHTS HORIZONS, where it was greeted with mixed reviews and, facing a tide of patriotism due to the Gulf War, was considered too risky to move to Broadway. The show survives in its superb cast recording and in regional theatre productions.

ADELE ASTAIRE (1897–1981) was considered the more talented of the dancing–singing team of Adele and Fred Astaire and many, including her brother, felt Fred's career would be over when Adele retired in 1932 to marry Lord Cavendish. The team first became popular in vaudeville, then, starting in 1917, they appeared on Broadway and in London's West End in a dozen musical comedies. Her Broadway credits included *Over the Top* (1917), *The Passing Show* (1918), *Apple Blossoms* (1919), *For Goodness Sake* (1922), *The Bunch and Judy* (1922), *LADY, BE GOOD!* (1924), *FUNNY FACE* (1927), *Smiles* (1930) and *THE BAND WAGON* (1931). Besides being an accomplished dancer, Adele Astaire had a bewitching soprano singing voice and a droll sense of comedy.

FRED ASTAIRE (1899–1987), was a dancer-singer who had three distinct and successful careers: with his sister ADELE ASTAIRE he became a vaudeville favorite; on Broadway and the West End, the team appeared in a series of popular musical comedies; and then, with a variety of leading ladies, he starred in over thirty Hollywood film musicals. The Astaires were born in Omaha, Nebraska, and toured together from an early age. They made the transition from vaudeville to Broadway in 1917 with *Over the Top*. Subsequent musicals in which they appeared on Broadway and in London included *The Passing Show* (1918), *Apple Blossoms* (1919), *The Love Letter* (1921), *For Goodness Sake*

(1922), *The Bunch and Judy* (1922), *LADY, BE GOOD!* (1924), *FUNNY FACE* (1927), *Smiles* (1930) and *THE BAND WAGON* (1931). Many consider the team's variety of characters and innovative dance routines in this last revue as the highpoint of their stage careers. After Adele retired in 1932, he had a solo hit with *GAY DIVORCE* (1932) before going off to Hollywood. Fred Astaire's persona as an agile dancer and elegant leading man, known to millions because of his films, was developed and perfected on the stage where he got to introduce several memorable songs by the GERSHWINS and the team of HOWARD DIETZ and ARTHUR SCHWARTZ.

AT HOME ABROAD (1935) was a delightful musical revue that used the gimmick of a world cruise to loosely tie its songs and sketches together. From a London department store to the jungles of Africa to a Japanese garden, the whimsical tour kept running into the same delectable players on every continent: BEATRICE LILLIE, EDDIE FOY, JR., ELEANOR POWELL, Reginald Gardiner, ETHEL WATERS, Paul Haakon, John Payne, VERA-ELLEN and others. The HOWARD DIETZ–ARTHUR SCHWARTZ score included "Love Is a Dancing Thing," "Get Yourself a Geisha," "Farewell, My Lovely," "Paree," "Thief in the Night" and "Hottentot Potentate," the last two sung superlatively by Waters. VINCENT MINNELLI co-directed with Thomas Mitchell and the revue ran 198 performances.

RENE AUBERJONOIS (1940–), a durable character actor equally adept at plays, musicals and the classics, played Sebastian Baye in *COCO* (1969), the con man Duke in *BIG RIVER* (1985), the Samuel Goldwyn-like Hollywood producer Buddy Fidler in *CITY OF ANGELS* (1989) and other musical roles.

LEMUEL AYERS (1915–1955) was a scenic and costume designer who had a short but esteemed career on Broadway. He did both the sets and costumes for *ST. LOUIS WOMAN* (1946), *KISS ME, KATE* (1948), *KISMET* (1953) and the *PAJAMA GAME* (1954). Ayers also designed sets for *BLOOMER GIRL* (1944), *SONG OF NORWAY* (1946), *Out of This World* (1950) and *MUSIC IN THE AIR* (1951). His most famous design was the stylized prairie scenery for the original *OKLAHOMA!* (1943).

B

BABES IN ARMS (1937) produced more hit songs than any other RODGERS and HART musical and it also introduced a group of young actors-singers who would figure significantly in future Broadway endeavors: ALFRED DRAKE, Mitzi Green, RAY HEATHERTON, ROBERT ROUNSEVILLE, Dan Daily and Wynn Murray. Rodgers and Hart wrote their own libretto for this youthful musical about the teenage children of vaudevillians who put on a show to raise money and keep them all out of the work farm. The outstanding score included "Where or When," "I Wish I Was in Love Again," "My Funny Valentine," "Imagine," "All at Once," "The Lady Is a Tramp," "Johnny One-Note" and the title song. (289 performances)

BABES IN TOYLAND (1903) is perhaps the most widely known work by composer VICTOR HERBERT. Lyricist-librettist Glen MacDonough took several of the successful elements from that year's musicalization of *THE WIZARD OF OZ* and fashioned a fantastical tale about two children, set adrift by a wicked uncle, who are shipwrecked in the magical Toyland filled with Mother Goose characters. A series of spectacular scenes followed until the children arrive at the Toyland Palace of Justice, MacDonough's version of Oz's Emerald City. The Herbert score is unforgettable—"Toyland," "Never Mind, Bo-Peep," "I Can't Do the Sum," "Song of the Poet," "March of the Toys." The show has remained a favorite on stage and on film throughout the decades. (192 performances)

BABY (1983) is, to date, the only Broadway musical by the accomplished songwriting team of RICHARD MALTBY, JR., and DAVID SHIRE. The rest of their work together has been Off Broadway and, in retrospect, that was probably where this intimate little musical belonged. Sybille Pearson's libretto, about three very different couples expecting or hoping for a baby, was a bit too clinical for some tastes but the characters were vividly drawn and the show was more entertaining than it sounds. The Maltby–Shire score was topflight with the songs shifting from pop to rock to traditional Broadway, depending on which generation was singing. "I Want It All," "Fatherhood Blues," "The Story Goes On" and "Easier to Love" were the standouts in a consistently satisfying score. Despite favorable reviews, a likable cast and excellent word of mouth, *Baby* could not survive on Broadway and closed after a valiant 241–performance run. The show has since found new life in regional theatres and in smaller performing spaces.

LAUREN BACALL (1924–   ), the film star known for her angular beauty and deep, seductive voice, only appeared in two Broadway musicals but triumphed in both despite her obvious lack of singing and dancing talent. Bacall played the temperamental actress Margo Channing in *APPLAUSE* (1970) and the television celebrity Tess Harding in *WOMAN OF THE YEAR* (1981). Both musicals were based on popular movies (*All About Eve* and *Woman of the Year*) and the roles were created by distinctive actresses (Bette Davis and KATHA-RINE HEPBURN), but Bacall made them very much her own on the stage.

BEN BAGLEY (1933–   ) is a producer of Off-Broadway musical revues and record anthologies "revisiting" the famous and obscure songs of America's outstanding composers and lyricists. Bagley presented the *Shoestring Revue* (1955), *The Littlest Revue* (1956) and *Shoestring '57* (1956), which gave several later-famous performers and writers their professional debut. Bagley also produced *The Decline and Fall of the Entire World as Seen Through the Eyes of Cole Porter* (1965) and a compendium of his various revues was presented Off Broadway under the title *Ben Bagley's Shoestring Revues* (1970).

PEARL BAILEY (1918–1990), the popular singer and recording artist, turned in dynamic performances in two valiant but unsuccessful Broadway musicals: Butterfly in *ST. LOUIS WOMAN* (1946) and Madame Fleur in *HOUSE OF FLOWERS* (1954). The unique song stylist also appeared in *Arms and the Girl* (1950) and *Bless You All* (1950) but her greatest stage success came in 1967 when she played Dolly Levi in the all-black production of *HELLO, DOLLY!* Bailey's jocular recreation of the role helped that musical run long enough to break the standing record for most performances. She reprised the role again on Broadway in 1975.

THE BAKER'S WIFE (1976) never even made it to Broadway, closing in Washington, D.C., in 1976, but it has gotten much attention over the years due to its superb score by STEPHEN SCHWARTZ. The problematic libretto by JOSEPH STEIN was based on the 1938 French film by Marcel Pagnol about a provincial baker whose young wife runs off with a local chauffeur, causing the old husband such grief that he stops baking. The town is distraught and they try to locate the wife but she has tired of the affair and returns on her own. This rather thin and predictable story did not adapt itself well to the musical stage and the pre-Broadway touring show went through a series of directors, choreographers and actors before calling it quits. But Schwartz's score, arguably his finest, was recorded and interest in the musical would continue. It was produced Off Broadway in 1985 and in London in 1989, but neither production solved the book problems and both failed to run. Writing in a much more conventionally romantic style than was typical of him, Schwartz provided such beloved cult favorites as "Gifts of Love," "Meadowlark," "Chanson" and "Where Is the Warmth?" The story of *The Baker's Wife*, like its libretto, has yet to be completed.

GEORGE BALANCHINE (1904–1983), one of the giants of the world of international ballet, was also instrumental in bringing modern ballet to the Broadway musical. Born in St. Petersburg, Russia, Balanchine was associated with Diaghilev's ballet company before coming to America in 1934. He founded and directed the New York City Ballet Company for many years but found time to choreograph sixteen Broadway musicals. His shows include the four RODGERS and HART hits, *ON YOUR TOES* (1936), *BABES IN ARMS* (1937), *I MARRIED AN ANGEL* (1938) and *THE BOYS FROM SYRACUSE* (1938), as well as *LOUISIANA PURCHASE* (1940), *CABIN IN THE SKY* (1940), *SONG OF NORWAY* (1944) and *WHERE'S CHARLEY?* (1948). Balanchine's greatest accomplishment for the musical theatre was his celebrated "Slaughter on Tenth Avenue" ballet for *On Your Toes*, the first successful integration of modern ballet in a Broadway musical.

LUCILLE BALL (1910–1989), television's premiere comedienne, appeared in a handful of movie musicals in the 1930s and 1940s but only did one Broadway musical later in her career: *WILDCAT* (1960), in which she played the vivacious Wildcat Jackson and introduced the song "Hey, Look Me Over."

KAYE BALLARD (1926–), the versatile comedienne-singer who has made many nightclub and television appearances in her busy career, is most remembered by Broadway audiences for her languorous Helen of Troy in *THE GOLDEN APPLE* (1954) and as the magician's sly assistant Rosalie in *CARNIVAL* (1961).

LUCINDA BALLARD (1908–) was the first costume designer to win a TONY AWARD. Among her Broadway musical credits were *ANNIE GET YOUR GUN* (1946), *ALLEGRO* (1947), *LOVE LIFE* (1948), *SILK STOCKINGS* (1955) and *THE SOUND OF MUSIC* (1959).

THE BAND WAGON (1931) was the best of the HOWARD DIETZ–ARTHUR SCHWARTZ shows and, in the opinion of many, the greatest of all musical revues. Dietz and GEORGE S. KAUFMAN wrote the sketches, including the famous "The Pride of the Claghornes" playlet, and the stellar cast included FRED and ADELE ASTAIRE, FRANK MORGAN, HELEN BRODERICK, Tilly Losch, Philip Loeb and John Barker. The Dietz–Schwartz score introduced "New Sun in the Sky," "Dancing in the Dark," "I Love Louisa," "High and Low," "Sweet Music" and the comic "Hoops," in which the Astaires played two obnoxious French schoolchildren. Director HASSARD SHORT and choreographer Albertina Rasch staged the revue stunningly with twin revolving turntables, a full-sized merry-go-round and the dazzling use of mirrors and lights on a raked stage. *The Band Wagon* was on a larger scale than the earlier Dietz–Schwartz revues but it retained the intimate, engaging quality that their shows were known for. (260 performances)

BARNUM (1980) came nowhere close to capturing the audacious P. T. Barnum on stage, but it was a highly entertaining show and Jim Dale as the title character was as much fun as a three-ring circus so few seemed to mind this substandard musical biography. Mark Bramble's libretto used the framework of a circus to tell Barnum's story and the various events and characters in his life were introduced as big top attractions. This promising concept was deflated by the lack of strong characters and believeable conflict in the tale and the musical only came to life during the musical numbers. CY COLEMAN (music) and MICHAEL STEWART (lyrics) provided a merry score that rarely slowed down to anything less than a gallop: "Bigger Isn't Better," "The Museum Song," "Come Follow the Band," "Black and White" and the pretty but atypical ballad "The Colors of My Life." Dale not only sang and danced marvelously but also walked a tightrope, juggled and leapt about the stage to everyone's amusement. Among the supporting players in thankless roles were Glenn Close, as Barnum's long-suffering wife, Marianne Tatum as Jenny Lind, Terri White and Leonard John Crofoot. JOE LAYTON devised the inventive staging and dances and DAVID MITCHELL came up with the sets that were an attraction in themselves. (854 performances)

WATSON BARRATT (1884–1962) was a prolific scenic designer who did the sets for dozens of musicals for the SHUBERT BROTHERS. Among his many design credits were *BLOSSOM TIME* (1921), *THE STUDENT PRINCE* (1924) and several editions of *The Passing Show* and *Artists and Models*.

JAMES BARTON (1890–1962), a vaudeville comic actor seen in several Broadway musicals and plays from 1919 to 1951, is best remembered for his performance as crusty Ben Rumson in *PAINT YOUR WAGON* (1951). Barton's other musical credits included *The Last Waltz* (1921), *No Foolin'* (1926), *Sweet and Low* (1930) and editions of *The Passing Show* and *Artists and Models*.

HINTON BATTLE (1956–   ), an energetic dancer-actor who performed with the Dance Theatre of Harlem, made his Broadway debut in *THE WIZ* (1975) and was featured in *DANCIN'* (1978), *SOPHISTICATED LADIES* (1981) and *DREAMGIRLS* (1981). Battle's most notable roles were Uncle Dipsey in *THE TAP DANCE KID* (1983) and John in the Broadway production of *MISS SAIGON* (1991).

HOWARD BAY (1912–1986) was a much-acclaimed scenic and lighting designer whose most famous musical production was *MAN OF LA MANCHA* (1965), for which he did the sets, lights and, with Patton Campbell, the costumes. Other distinctive musicals that Bay designed include *CARMEN JONES* (1943), *ONE TOUCH OF VENUS* (1943), *UP IN CENTRAL PARK* (1945), *FLAHOOLEY* (1951) and *THE MUSIC MAN* (1957).

NORA BAYES (1880–1928), a popular singer in vaudeville and on Broadway, introduced "Shine On, Harvest Moon" in the *Follies of 1908*. Bayes was featured in several shows between 1901 and 1922, including *The Jolly Bachelors* (1910), *Little Miss Fix-It* (1911), *The Cohan Revue* (1917), *Ladies First* (1918) and *Queen o' Hearts* (1922).

ORSON BEAN (1928–   ), a character actor on stage and television, had featured roles in the Broadway musicals *John Murray Anderson's Almanac* (1953), *SUBWAYS ARE FOR SLEEPING* (1961) and *Illya, Darling* (1967).

CECIL BEATON (1904–1980), the famous London-born designer of costumes and scenery, created distinctive designs for the stage, opera and film and was also a renowned photographer. Beaton is best remembered for his costumes for *MY FAIR LADY* (1956) on Broadway, the West End and the film version. He also did both sets and costumes for *SARATOGA* (1959), *TENDERLOIN* (1960) and *COCO* (1969).

NORMAN BEL GEDDES (1893–1958), the innovative American designer whose productions around the world were very influential to modern scenic design, only did a handful of Broadway musicals but each was unique and memorable: *Five O'Clock Girl* (1927), *FIFTY MILLION FRENCHMEN* (1929), *FLYING COLORS* (1932) and *Seven Lively Arts* (1944).

BELLS ARE RINGING (1956) was a conventional musical comedy that was more than satisfying because of a lovely score by JULE STYNE (music) and BETTY COMDEN and ADOLPH GREEN (lyrics) and its radiant star performance by JUDY HOLLIDAY. Comden and Green wrote the original libretto about a telephone answering service operator who falls in love with one of her clients. In a comic subplot, a bookie utilizes the service to place racing bets using code words taken from classical music. Holliday was supported by SYDNEY CHAPLIN, JEAN STAPLETON and Eddie Lawrence, and JEROME ROBBINS directed and (with BOB FOSSE) choreographed. Two songs from the score became hits on the charts—"The Party's Over" and "Just in Time"—but also memorable were "Long Before I Knew You," "I'm Going Back," "I Met a Girl" and "It's a Perfect Relationship." (924 performances)

MICHAEL BENNETT (1943–1987) was one of the most theatrical and dynamic director-choreographers of the 1970s. Although he only directed four musicals before his untimely death at the age of forty-four, Bennett had a powerful effect on the Broadway musical. He conceived, workshopped, directed and choreographed his last shows and, consequently, they had a unity of vision not often seen on Broadway. Bennett started as a dancer in such musicals as *SUBWAYS ARE FOR SLEEPING* (1961), *HERE'S LOVE* (1963) and *Bajour* (1964). His career as choreographer started with two quickly forgotten shows, *A Joyful Noise* (1966) and *Henry, Sweet Henry* (1967), but Bennett's dances for the hit *PROMISES, PROMISES* (1968) put him in the spotlight. He staged some clever numbers for *COCO* (1969) and got involved with his first CONCEPT MUSICAL with *COMPANY* (1970). Bennett's dances for *FOLLIES* (1971) became so pervasive and integrated into the action that HAROLD PRINCE billed him as co-director. *SEESAW* (1973), his first show as solo director, was an uneven musical with a troubled run, but it was Bennett's from start to finish and was beloved by many. The same can be said for *A CHORUS LINE* (1975), a show that throughout its record-breaking run was always identified more with Bennett than any composer, writers or cast. *Ballroom* (1978) was a conventional musical that failed to have a wide appeal, but again, it was a show with a single vision. Bennett's last musical, *DREAMGIRLS* (1981), revealed the director-choreographer at his peak, recreating the high-powered world of the entertainment business. Regardless of who wrote the score or libretto or who produced or performed, the four Bennett-directed musicals were Michael Bennett productions. It was a distinction afforded to few, and none so young or quickly gone.

ROBERT RUSSELL BENNETT (1894–1981), the most prolific and influential orchestrator and MUSIC DIRECTOR in the American theatre, arranged, conducted and/or orchestrated the music for over 300 Broadway musicals. Bennett did most of the RODGERS and HAMMERSTEIN musicals, as well as *ROSE-MARIE* (1924), *OF THEE I SING* (1931), *ANYTHING GOES* (1934), *FINIAN'S RAINBOW* (1947), *KISS ME, KATE* (1948), *BELLS ARE RINGING* (1956), *MY FAIR LADY* (1956), *CAMELOT* (1960) and many others.

BUSBY BERKELEY (1895–1976) was a choreographer mostly known for the kaleidoscopic dance routines he created for a series of movies in the 1930s and 1940s but he also choreographed over twenty Broadway musicals in the 1920s before going to Hollywood. His musical theatre credits include *The Wild Rose* (1926), *A CONNECTICUT YANKEE* (1927), *Present Arms* (1928), *EARL CARROLL VANITIES* (1928) and *Sweet and Low* (1930). After a forty-year absence, Berkeley returned to Broadway to supervise the 1971 revival of *NO, NO, NANETTE*.

MILTON BERLE (1908–), the veteran comic of vaudeville, films and the early years of television, appeared in a handful of Broadway musicals, most memorably *EARL CARROLL VANITIES* (1932), *LIFE BEGINS AT 8:40* (1935) and the 1943 *ZIEGFELD FOLLIES*.

IRVING BERLIN (1888–1989), America's most popular songwriter, only spent a third of his time and talents in the musical theatre, but he provided songs for many memorable revues and book musicals and he helped merge theatre music and popular music. Berlin was born in rural Russia and emigrated as a child to New York's Lower East Side. He worked as a singing waiter and song plugger, eventually writing lyrics for other composers. Berlin plucked out his own melody for the song "Alexander's Ragtime Band" in 1911, and when it became a nationwide hit, he proceeded to write both music and lyrics from then on. Berlin's songs were heard in Broadway shows as early as 1910 but his first full score was *WATCH YOUR STEP* (1914), a "syncopated" musical starring VERNON and IRENE CASTLE. Throughout the 1910s and 1920s Berlin scored various shows, from the *ZIEGFELD FOLLIES* to his own revue series, the *MUSIC BOX REVUES*, as well as the Army revue *YIP, YIP, YAPHANK* (1918) and the MARX BROTHERS vehicle *THE COCOANUTS* (1925). In the 1930s he wrote the scores for two outstanding musicals, *FACE THE MUSIC* (1932) and *AS THOUSANDS CHEER* (1933). During all this time much of Berlin's energy had gone into writing individual songs for Tin Pan Alley and in the 1930s he added Hollywood to his domain, scoring several notable film musicals. Berlin returned to Broadway in 1940 with the book musical *LOUISIANA PURCHASE* and had his greatest hit in 1946 with *ANNIE GET YOUR GUN*. *MISS LIBERTY* (1949) failed to run but *CALL ME MADAM* (1950) was a success. When Berlin's last musical, *MR. PRESIDENT* (1962), flopped, he decided to retire and lived as recluse for the last twenty years of his life. Berlin was adept at capturing the moods and sentiments of the American public, from the dance-crazy 1910s, the sizzling 1920s, the heartfelt Depression years, the patriotic 1940s to the swinging post-war years. Few of Berlin's book musicals are revived today but his songs have become an irreplaceable part of American culture.

HERSCHEL BERNARDI (1923–1986), a versatile character actor on stage, television and film, played Teyve in *FIDDLER ON THE ROOF* (1964) for 702 of its Broadway performances and reprised the role in the 1981 revival. Bernardi also gave memorable performances as the gypsy king Johnny Dembo in *Bajour* (1964) and in the title role of *ZORBA* (1968).

LEONARD BERNSTEIN (1918–1990), the world-renowned classical conductor, composer and lecturer, was only involved with a half-dozen Broadway shows, but he brought a musical intelligence to the stage that has rarely been equaled. Bernstein was born in Lawrence, Massachusetts, and showed remarkable musical talent at an early age. After studying music at Harvard University, he worked with the Curtis Institute of Music in Philadelphia and the Tanglewood Summer Music Festival. Bernstein's conducting career took off in 1943 when, as a last-minute replacement, the twenty-five-year-old conducted a concert by the New York Philharmonic. His first Broadway musical was *ON THE TOWN* (1944), in which he composed the score based on his earlier "Fancy Free" ballet music. *WONDERFUL TOWN* (1953), another delightful musical that focused on New York City, was less ballet and more musical comedy. *CANDIDE* (1956) gave Bernstein the chance to use his vast classical music knowledge and compose a musical in the comic opera mode. *WEST SIDE STORY* (1957) was an even bolder project as he utilized ballet music, opera, modern dance sounds, Spanish themes and musical comedy in a daring and enthralling way. Bernstein left the theatre in 1957 to become the music director of the Philharmonic and to pursue his worldwide tours and recording engagements. He returned to Broadway in 1976 for the ill-fated *1600 PENNSYLVANIA AVENUE*. Bernstein also wrote some individual lyrics for each of these musicals but was rarely credited for them. In addition to the musical vitality that he brought to Broadway, Bernstein is also responsible for bringing an integrity to musical theatre composing that was rarely seen before. His Broadway scores were created with the same inventiveness that he brought to the opera and concert hall.

BEST FOOT FORWARD (1941) is that rare thing: a campus musical not about the big football game. It is prom time at Winsocki Prep School, where a movie star has received an invitation from a male student and, as a publicity stunt, she accepts. Complications arise with the student's girlfriend and the celebrity-hungry promgoers so the star quietly slips back to Hollywood. John Cecil Holm wrote the amusing libretto and movie songwriters HUGH MARTIN and RALPH BLANE provided the songs, most memorably "Buckle Down, Winsocki." The show ran for 326 performances and brought attention to the up-and-coming performers NANCY WALKER and June Allyson, just as the 1963 Off-Broadway revival introduced LIZA MINNELLI and Christopher Walken.

THE BEST LITTLE WHOREHOUSE IN TEXAS (1978) was one of the handful of musicals in the 1970s that was developed and showcased Off Off Broadway, played Off Broadway successfully, then moved to the Great White Way for a long run. This pleasant if uneven musical was put together by four former Texans: composer-lyricist Carol Hall, directors TOMMY TUNE and Peter Masterson and co-librettist Larry L. King. The book, by King and Masterson, was based on an actual Texas establishment that had operated from the 1840s until it was closed in 1973 by a righteous Houston media preacher. The musical version fluctuated between raunchy humor and touching character songs, but there was no question about Tune's inventive choreography and Hall's commendable score. "Bus from Amarillo," "Good Old Girl," "Hard Candy Christmas" and "Girl, You're a Woman" had a depth that was not evident in the story and it was the more rousing songs—"The Sidestep," "Twenty-Four Hours of Lovin'," "20 Fans"—that most pleased audiences for 1,703 performances. A similar plot, also based on fact, was musicalized in *TENDERLOIN* (1960).

BETWEEN THE DEVIL (1937) was a musical farce more in the style of the 1910s than the 1930s but it had a commendable score by HOWARD DIETZ and ARTHUR SCHWARTZ. The libretto, by Dietz, dealt with a widower who remarries only to have his first wife show up. This time-worn premise was kept lively by JACK BUCHANAN as the unintentional bigamist and Eyelyn Lane and Adele Dixon as his wives. Three wonderful songs came from the score: "By Myself," "Triplets" and "I See Your Face Before Me." (93 performances)

BIBLICAL MUSICALS have shown up on Broadway from time to time but, for some reason, there was an outpouring of them in the 1970s. The gospels were musicalized on Broadway with *JESUS CHRIST SUPERSTAR* (1971) and *Your Arms Too Short to Box with God* (1976) and Off Broadway with *GODSPELL* (1971). The Old Testament was also represented when Genesis' Noah was featured in *TWO BY TWO* (1970) and biblical Joseph was brought to life in *JOSEPH AND THE AMAZING TECHNICOLOR DREAMCOAT* (Off Broadway in 1976, on Broadway in 1981). The only other notable biblical musical not part of this onrush was *THE APPLE TREE* (1966) in which Mark Twain's version of Adam and Eve was musicalized.

BIG RIVER (1985) was a faithful adaptation by William Hauptman of Mark Twain's *The Adventures of Huckleberry Finn* with a score by country music songwriter-performer Roger Miller. Most of the major events of the novel were recreated, from Huck's running away from his drunken father in Hannibal to his adventures on the Mississippi with fugitive slave Jim to the happy conclusion down in Arkansas. Daniel H. Jenkins and Ron Richardson as Huck and Jim headed the cast that also included RENE AUBERJONAIS, BOB GUNTON, Susan Browning and PATTI COHENOUR. The Miller score was appropriately folksy with some praiseworthy lyric moments in "River in the Rain," "Leaving's Not the Only Way to Go" and "Worlds Apart." (1,005 performances)

KEN BILLINGTON (1946–   ), a lighting designer of Broadway plays and musicals as well as opera, lit the musicals *ON THE TWENTIETH CENTURY* (1978), *WORKING* (1978), *SWEENEY TODD* (1979), *Copperfield* (1981), *A Doll's Life* (1982), *Grind* (1985), *Roza* (1987), the Broadway version of *Meet Me in St. Louis* (1989) and others.

BIOGRAPHICAL MUSICALS have generally been inaccurate and romanticized versions of the truth but often made for solid entertainment. Show business biographies, in particular, have been able to get a lot of milage out of the charisma of the songwriter or entertainer. *GEORGE M!* (1968), for example, told us little about GEORGE M. COHAN but it captured the spirit of the man by presenting so many of his songs in a high-style fashion. Similarly unreliable but entertaining show business biographies include *FUNNY GIRL* (1964), about FANNY BRICE; *MACK AND MABEL* (1974), about Mack Sennett and Mabel Normand; *BARNUM* (1980), about P. T. Barnum; *THE WILL ROGERS FOLLIES* (1991); and *JELLY'S LAST JAM* (1992), about Jelly Roll Morton. Less enjoyable were musical biographies on Sophie Tucker called *Sophie* (1963), the MARX BROTHERS as *Minnie's Boys* (1970), Molly Goldberg in *Molly* (1973), *Harrigan 'n Hart* (1985) and actors Edmund Kean and Laurette Taylor in *Kean* (1961) and *Jennie* (1963). Edvard Grieg's life was supposedly told in *SONG OF NORWAY* (1944), Franz Schubert's romantic troubles were set to his own music in *BLOSSOM TIME* (1921) and various Strauss family members were the subject of *The Great Waltz* (1934). Sharpshooter Annie Oakley seemed unlikely musical biography material but *ANNIE GET YOUR GUN* (1946) was the most popular of them all. And *GYPSY* (1959), the best show business musical biography, was, ironically, not so much about GYPSY ROSE LEE as about her mother. Outside the world of show business, political biographies have been the most abundant. *FIORELLO!* (1959) brought New York Mayor LaGuardia to the musical stage successfully but Mayor Jimmy Walker proved less interesting in *Jimmy* (1969). Eva and Juan Peron fascinated audiences in *EVITA* (1979) but there was less interest in King Henry VIII in *Rex* (1976), Joan of Arc and King Charles VI of France in *Goodtime Charley* (1975), Theodore Roosevelt in *Teddy and Alice* (1987) and a dozen or so presidents and first ladies in *1600 PENNSYLVANIA AVENUE* (1976). Only KATHARINE HEPBURN kept Gabrielle Chanel lively in *COCO* (1969) but similar luck did not befall *Legs Diamond* (1988), *Mata Hari* (closed out of town in 1967) and baseballer Jack Robinson in *The First* (1981). The Von Trapp family became Broadway favorites in *THE SOUND OF MUSIC* (1959) but *THE ROTHSCHILDS* never quite caught on. There are several musical biographies that copied reality somewhat but changed the names to avoid legal trouble. For example, everyone knew that Sally Adams in *CALL ME MADAM* (1950) was really Pearl Mesta and that it was the Supremes that became the *DREAMGIRLS* (1981). Also, some mention must be made of the infamous subjects of *ASSASSINS* (1990), an original musical that viewed biography as tragicomic nightmare.

PATRICIA BIRCH (1934–) is a respected Broadway choreographer whose musicals, although not always successful, held interesting challenges for traditional dancing. Her most famous shows were *GREASE* (1972), *OVER*

THERE (1974) and *THEY'RE PLAYING OUR SONG* (1979), but Birch's more ingenious choreography was seen in such non-dancing musicals as *YOU'RE A GOOD MAN, CHARLIE BROWN* (1967), *THE ME NOBODY KNOWS* (1970), *A LITTLE NIGHT MUSIC* (1973), the environmental revival of *CANDIDE* (1974), *PACIFIC OVERTURES* (1976), *Roza* (1987), *Anna Karenina* (1992) and others. Birch has also served as director on occasion.

BLACK AND BLUE (1989) was a glittering musical revue that offered little originality in concept or staging but featured such wonderful old songs and top-notch performers that it had audiences cheering for 824 performances. The show was conceived, directed and designed by Claudio Segovia and Hector Orezzeli with vibrant choreography by Cholly Atkins, Henry Letang, Frankie Manning and Fayard Nicholas. Among the skilled singers and dancers were Ruth Brown, Bunny Briggs, LINDA HOPKINS and SAVION GLOVER.

THE BLACK CROOK (1866) was an extravagant music–dance–drama that, for all practical purposes, signified the birth of the American musical theatre. *The Black Crook* was not an innovative stroke of genius as much as a lucky accident but there is no question of its impact: The Broadway musical begins here. The circumstances of the show's origin give *The Black Crook* legendary status. Impressarios Henry C. Jarrett and Harry Palmer had imported a French ballet troupe to perform at the Academy of Music but the building burnt down in the spring of 1866. William Wheatley, the manager of a large theatre called Niblo's Garden, had contracted to present a problematic piece of German romanticism called *The Black Crook* by the American melodramatist Charles M. Barras, but he saw little chance for success when he read the completed script. When Jarrett and Palmer suggested they add the troupe of ballet dancers to his melodrama, Wheatley agreed. Songs from local music shops were added, the ballarinas became spirits and water sprites and the whole five-and-a-half-hour spectacular opened to a bewildered but enthralled audience. The plot of *The Black Crook* was a clumsy reworking of the *Faust* legend as the crook-backed magician Herzog tries to sell the soul of the painter Rudolf to the devil. But a fairy queen warns the young artist and takes him off to a magical land where he weds her beautiful daughter. The combination of dance, spectacle, story and song was irresistible and the show ran for 475 performances. Nothing in the score was very memorable and the songs changed throughout the long run, as did the performers and some of the scenes. The most talked-about feature of *The Black Crook* was the scantily clad chorines who showed more leg than previously seen outside of ballet. Clergymen and civic leaders who castigated the production from pulpits and newspaper editorials only heightened the public's interest. The show toured extensively and was revived in New York fifteen times. The 1954 musical *The Girl in Pink Tights* was a less than accurate version of the circumstances surrounding the original *The Black Crook*.

BLACK MUSICALS, in the many meanings of the term, go back to the earliest musical entertainments in America. Minstrel shows were originally composed and performed by black singers and musicians and were extremely popular with all kinds of audiences. But during the nineteenth century, white artists started performing their version of the minstrel show and the derogatory exaggerations that we associate with the term were developed. Black musicals on Broadway can be divided into several different categories. Most musicals and revues with black characters and settings were written by white songwriters, such as *BLACKBIRDS OF 1928*, *PORGY AND BESS* (1935), *CABIN IN THE SKY* (1940), *LOST IN THE STARS* (1949), *HALLELUJAH, BABY!* (1967), *PURLIE* (1970) and others. There were the exceptions when black creators got to write, direct and produce their own Broadway shows, such as *IN DAHOMEY* (1903) and *SHUFFLE ALONG* (1921), but for the most part black artists of the past were accepted as performers only. Another category of black musical was the exotic Caribbean shows, which placed black characters in quaint, sometimes tribal surroundings that were palatable to white audiences. *HOUSE OF FLOWERS* (1954), *JAMAICA* (1957) and *ONCE ON THIS ISLAND* (1990) were among the best of this type. *FINIAN'S RAINBOW* (1947) was the first Broadway musical to use black and white characters together in its plot and it boasted the first integrated chorus as well. Interracial romances were used in *KWAMINA* (1961) and *NO STRINGS* (1962), showing that fully developed black characters could exist outside the "all-Negro" musicals of the past. Another category put black characters and idioms into white vehicles, such as *CARMEN JONES* (1943), *THE WIZ* (1975), *Timbuktu* (1978) and the all-black versions of *HELLO, DOLLY!* in 1967, *GUYS AND DOLLS* in 1976, and *OH, KAY!* in 1990. The most popular form of black musical is the revue celebrating black artists of the past. *AIN'T MISBEHAVIN'* (1978), *Eubie* (1978), *SOPHISTICATED LADIES* (1981) and *BLACK AND BLUE* (1989) were among the best of the many shows of this type. Finally, there is the true black musical, a revue or book show that seeks to explore the black experience in America today. *GOLDEN BOY* (1964), *Ain't Supposed to Die a Natural Death* (1971), *DON'T BOTHER ME, I CAN'T COPE* (1972), *RAISIN* (1973), *DREAMGIRLS* (1981), *THE TAP DANCE KID* (1983) and *JELLY'S LAST JAM* (1992) were not all written by black artists but they were laudable shows that sought to reveal the complexity of black life in musical terms.

BLACKBIRDS OF 1928 (1928) was the longest-running musical revue of the decade (518 performances) and a sensational debut for the team of JIMMY McHUGH (composer) and DOROTHY FIELDS (lyricist). The all-black cast included ADELAIDE HALL and BILL "Bojangles" ROBINSON who sang such period favorites as "Diga, Diga Doo," "Doin' the New Low-Down" and "I Can't Give You Anything But Love." There was even a short musicalized version of the play *Porgy*, six years before the GERSHWINS' folk opera appeared. *Blackbirds of 1928* was so successful that subsequent versions were produced in 1930, 1933 and 1939, but none matched the original's quality or popularity.

VIVIAN BLAINE (1921–), the bright and funny actress who appeared in vaudeville, on Broadway and in films, created the role of Miss Adelaide in *GUYS AND DOLLS* (1950) and repeated the performance in London and on film. Blaine's other musical credits are *Say, Darling* (1958) and *COMPANY* (1971), in which she played the cynical Joanne later in the run.

EUBIE BLAKE (1883–1983), the black singer and pianist who made many recordings during his long career, composed the music for the acclaimed black musical *SHUFFLE ALONG* (1921) with lyrics by his partner NOBLE SISSLE. The team also provided the score for *Elsie* (1923), *Chocolate Dandies* (1924) and later editions of *Shuffle Along* in 1932 and 1952. *Eubie* (1978), a musical revue celebrating Blake's work, ran on Broadway for 439 performances.

RALPH BLANE (1914–), a composer-lyricist who usually worked with HUGH MARTIN, spent most of his career in Hollywood but the team did provide the score for the popular Broadway musical *BEST FOOT FORWARD* (1941). Blane started out as a vocal arranger and singer and appeared in *New Faces of 1936*, *HOORAY FOR WHAT!* (1937) and *LOUISIANA PURCHASE* (1940). Blane and Martin's most famous movie, *Meet Me in St. Louis*, was adapted into a Broadway musical using their songs in 1989.

MARC BLITZSTEIN (1905–1964) was a classically trained composer whose work in the theatre usually utilized the elements of opera. Blitzstein made a bold and electrifying debut with his book, music and lyrics for *THE CRADLE WILL ROCK* (1937). *REGINA* (1949), his musicalization of Lillian Hellman's drama *The Little Foxes*, and *JUNO* (1959), his musical based on Sean O'Casey's *Juno and the Paycock*, were both vigorous and challenging works but neither was a box office success. Blitzstein is perhaps best remembered for his 1954 adaptation-translation of Bertolt Brecht and KURT WEILL's *THE THREEPENNY OPERA*, the first successful American production of the unique musical.

BLOOMER GIRL (1944) was a popular wartime piece of musical Americana that addressed some very serious issues under its romantic plot. The libretto, by Sig Herzig and FRED SAIDY, was about a headstrong girl, Eveline, in 1861 Cicero Falls, New York, who rebels against her manufacturer father and joins her radical aunt Dolly Bloomer, who is an abolitionist and an advocate of bloomers rather than hoop skirts. Aside from the obvious women's rights issues, *Bloomer Girl* also dealt with racial equality (Eveline falls in love with a Southern slave owner) and the plight of women who await the men to return from the war. The score by HAROLD ARLEN (music) and E. Y. HARBURG (lyrics) was another step in their quest for sociologically potent musicals. "Right as the Rain" was the pleasant duet for the lovers but the issues of the show were more evident in songs such as "When the Boys Come Home," "Sunday in Cicero Falls," "It Was Good Enough for Grandma" and "The Eagle and Me," the last a plea for freedom sung by DOOLEY WILSON. CELESTE HOLM played Eveline and David Brooks was her love interest. Harburg and William Schorr directed and AGNES DE MILLE did the choreography, which included a lyrical "Civil War Ballet." (654 performances)

BLOSSOM TIME (1921) was the first of several Broadway musicals over the years to use CLASSICAL MUSIC for its score. SIGMUND ROMBERG adapted Franz Schubert's music into songs and DOROTHY DONNELLY wrote lyrics for them as well as providing a biographical libretto about the great composer's life. The result was the biggest hit of the 1921–1922 season; it ran 516 performances, inspired four road companies and was revived in New York five times during the next twenty-two years. "Song of Love," taken from the first movement of Schubert's *Unfinished Symphony*, and his "Serenade" were the standout hits in the famous score.

LARRY BLYDEN (1925–1975), an affable character actor in Broadway plays and musicals, played nightclub owner Sammy Fong in *FLOWER DRUM SONG* (1958), the Snake and other roles in *THE APPLE TREE* (1966) and Hysterium in the 1972 revival of *A FUNNY THING HAPPENED ON THE WAY TO THE FORUM*. Blyden's other musical credits included *WISH YOU WERE HERE* (1952) and *Foxy* (1972).

JERRY BOCK (1928–   ), the composer who worked with lyricist SHELDON HARNICK from 1958 to 1970, has captured a variety of different subjects and places in his highly evocative music. Bock was born in New Haven, Connecticut, and raised in Flushing, New York. As a high school student and while studying at the University of Wisconsin, he wrote songs that eventually got him jobs composing for television and adult summer camps. Bock collaborated with lyricist Larry Holofcener for awhile, contributing songs for the Broadway revue *Catch a Star* (1955) and doing a complete score for the SAMMY DAVIS, JR., vehicle *Mr. Wonderful* (1956). He met Harnick in 1956 and their first musical, *The Body Beautiful* (1958), was promising but failed to run. The team's *FIORELLO!* (1959) was a warm biography of LaGuardia and, at the same time, a sly satire on New York politics. The show won the PULITZER PRIZE and enjoyed a successful run. *TENDERLOIN* (1960) was also about "little Old New York" and its score was just as accomplished but the show only had a moderate run. *SHE LOVES ME* (1963), a charming musical with a very European flavor, boasted Bock and Harnick's most enchanting score yet. Their biggest hit, *FIDDLER ON THE ROOF* (1964), combined all the warmth, comedy and lyric power that their previous shows had foreshadowed and became one of Broadway's perennial favorites. *THE APPLE TREE* (1966) pushed the team into the area of parody and little of it was memorable. Bock and Harnick's last musical together, *THE ROTHSCHILDS* (1970), suffered from book and preparation problems and had a modest run. The two men ended their collaboration in 1970. Bock has a gift for recreating the musical sounds of past eras and diverse places and his work has a subtlety and charm not usually found in big Broadway musicals.

MARY BOLAND (1880–1965), the comic actress who was on the stage from 1905 and appeared in dozens of films, was featured in two memorable Broadway musicals, *FACE THE MUSIC* (1932) and *JULIBEE* (1935).

RAY BOLGER (1904–1987), the agile comedian-dancer who will always be remembered as the Scarecrow in the film musical *The Wizard of Oz* (1939), was a popular musical star with a long career on Broadway. Bolger's two most memorable stage roles were the nimble music teacher-turned-dancer Junior Dolan in *ON YOUR TOES* (1936) and the cross-dressing Charley in *WHERE'S CHARLEY?* (1948). His other Broadway credits included *The Merry World* (1926), *Heads Up!* (1929), *LIFE BEGINS AT 8:40* (1934), *BY JUPITER* (1942), *ALL AMERICAN* (1962) and *Come Summer* (1969).

GUY BOLTON (1884–1979) was one of Broadway's most prolific librettists, writing the books for over fifty musicals in New York and London during a fifty-year career. Bolton was born in England to American parents and went to schools in New York and Paris studying to become an architect. He made his playwriting debut in London in 1912 and his Broadway musical debut with *90 in the Shade* (1915). That same year he collaborated with composer JEROME KERN on *Nobody Home* and *VERY GOOD EDDIE*, the first two PRINCESS THEATRE MUSICALS. P. G. WODEHOUSE joined them as lyricist for *Have a Heart* (1917) and the trio of Bolton, Wodehouse and Kern became the most influential collaborative team of the era. Other Princess musicals include *OH, BOY!* (1917), *LEAVE IT TO JANE* (1917) and *OH, LADY, LADY!* (1918). The trio broke up in 1919 but Bolton and Wodehouse would collaborate on a half dozen other musicals, most notably *SALLY* (1920), *OH, KAY!* (1926) and *ANYTHING GOES* (1934). The threesome would be reunited for *Sitting Pretty* (1924) but the Princess series had ended. After Wodehouse left the musical theatre in 1934, Bolton collaborated with various composers and lyricists as he had been doing since 1916. Some of the most famous Bolton-scripted musicals include *TIP-TOES* (1925), *RIO RITA* (1927), *The Five O'Clock Girl* (1927)—all three with co-librettist Fred Thompson—as well as *ROSALIE* (1928), *GIRL CRAZY* (1930), *FOLLOW THE GIRLS* (1944), *Ankles Aweigh* (1955) and *Anya* (1965), the last based on his play *Anastasia*. Bolton also scripted fifteen London musicals during the 1930s. The librettos Bolton wrote for the Princess Theatre shows brought a sassy, youthful tone to musicals that contrasted sharply with the heavy-handed treatments found in European-like operettas. Bolton retained much of this exuberance throughout his career but by the 1920s a new generation of musical playwrights outshone the man who had invented their model.

BOMBO (1921) was an extravagant musical vehicle for AL JOLSON who played the black-faced servant Bombo who attends on, of all people, Christopher Columbus. The silly show had a score by SIGMUND ROMBERG but it was the three interpolated songs that became some of Jolson's greatest hits: "California, Here I Come," "Toot, Toot, Tootsie!" and "April Showers." (219 performances)

SHIRLEY BOOTH (1898?–1992) had acclaimed careers in plays, film and television but she also starred in Broadway musicals, usually playing crusty, comic roles. Booth was born in New York and made her stage debut in 1925. Her first musical was the Gilbert and Sullivan spoof *Hollywood Pinafore* (1945) in which she played columnist Louhedda Hopsons. Her loveable Aunt Cissy in *A TREE GROWS IN BROOKLYN* (1951) and her delightful Lottie Gibson in *By the Beautiful Sea* (1954) were notable comic performances yet her perceptive Juno Boyle in the tragic musical *JUNO* (1959) was just as skillful. Booth's last Broadway musical was the short-lived *Look to the Lilies* (1970).

IRENE BORDONI (1895–1953) was an exotic, coquettish leading lady who specialized in French mademoiselle roles in Broadway musicals. The Corsica-born actress was on the French stage before coming to America in 1912. Her two most memorable roles were in COLE PORTER's *Paris* (1928), where she introduced "Let's Do It," and as Mme. Bordelaise in IRVING BERLIN's *LOUISIANA PURCHASE* (1940). Bordoni's other Broadway credits included *Broadway to Paris* (1912), *Hitchy-Koo* (1917), *The French Doll* (1922) and *Great Lady* (1938).

BARRY BOSTWICK (1945–   ), a leading man in plays, musicals and on television, played Danny Zuko in the original cast of *GREASE* (1972), the bandit Jamie Lockhart in *THE ROBBER BRIDEGROOM* (1976) and the sleuth Nick Charles in *Nick and Nora* (1991).

THE BOY FRIEND (1954), a BRITISH IMPORT with book, music and lyrics by Sandy Wilson, was a PASTICHE MUSICAL that managed to spoof 1920s musicals and still be entertaining in its own right. The plot is a collection of familiar cliches: rich girl at a boarding school for young ladies on the French Riviera falls for a delivery boy who is really an heir in disguise and so on and so on. JULIE ANDREWS attracted a good deal of attention with her Broadway debut as the heroine. Wilson's songs were too accurately period to become popular in the 1950s but in the context of the show they were enjoyable: "Won't

You Charleston with Me?" "I Could Be Happy with You," "It's Never Too Late to Fall in Love," "Poor Little Pierrette" and the delightfully naive title song. *The Boy Friend* was a major hit in London, running 2,048 performances, but it only ran a modest 485 performances on Broadway. The musical was revived Off Broadway in 1958, again on Broadway in 1970 and remains a favorite with all kinds of producing groups.

THE BOYS FROM SYRACUSE (1938), with its tight libretto based on Shakespeare's *A Comedy of Errors* and its scintillating RODGERS and HART score, is one of the most easily revived of 1930s musicals. GEORGE ABBOTT produced, wrote and directed this agreeable musical farce about two sets of twins confusing everyone in ancient times. JIMMY SAVO, Teddy Hart, EDDIE ALBERT and Ronald Graham played the twins and GEORGE BALANCHINE choreographed the silly but loveable show. The Rodgers and Hart score included "Falling in Love with Love," "Sing for Your Supper," "This Can't Be Love," "The Shortest Day of the Year" and "What Can You Do with a Man?" The musical ran for 235 performances and a 1963 Off-Broadway revival ran for 469 performances.

EDDIE BRACKEN (1920–), a character actor known for his many film appearances, was featured in the Broadway musicals *TOO MANY GIRLS* (1939) and *Shinbone Alley* (1957) and played Horace Vandergelder in the 1978 revival of *HELLO, DOLLY!*

DONALD BRIAN (1877–1948), a personable leading man of many Broadway musicals between 1901 and 1939, was featured in such renowned hits as *LITTLE JOHNNY JONES* (1904), *FORTY-FIVE MINUTES FROM BROADWAY* (1906), *The Merry Widow* (1907) and *THE GIRL FROM UTAH* (1914). Brian's final Broadway musical was *VERY WARM FOR MAY* (1939).

FANNY BRICE (1891–1951) was a singer-comedienne who developed very distinct characters on stage even though most of her Broadway shows were revues. Brice was born in New York and appeared in burlesque and vaudeville before her Broadway musical debut in the *Follies of 1910*. She became one of the *Follies'* most beloved performers and producer FLORENZ ZIEGFELD starred her in six more editions between 1911 and 1923. Brice also appeared in the 1924 *MUSIC BOX REVUE*, *Sweet and Low* (1930) and *Crazy Quilt* (1931), as well as two more editions of the *Follies* produced by the SHUBERT BROTHERS. Her few book musicals included *The Honeymoon Express* (1913) and *Fioretta* (1929). Among Brice's most memorable characterizations were the broadly-accented Jewish lady, the tough but sympathetic torch singer of the streets and the hysterical brat Baby Snooks, the last making her a radio favorite in the 1930s and 1940s. BARBRA STREISAND portrayed Brice in the highly romanticized musical biography *FUNNY GIRL* (1964).

BRIGADOON (1947) is one of the American theatre's most romantic musical fantasies and one that has retained its charm over the decades. It was also the show that secured the reputation of ALAN JAY LERNER and FREDERICK LOEWE, the team that would bring post-war Broadway to its most lyrical heights. Lerner wrote the original libretto about a Scottish village called Brigadoon that appears only one day every one hundred years. When Tommy and Jeff, two New Yorkers on holiday, stumble onto Brigadoon, they are caught up in the mysticism as well as the romance of the town. Much of the magic of *Brigadoon* came from the enchanting Lerner and Loewe score that featured "The Heather on the Hill," "There But for You Go I," "I'll Go Home with Bonnie Jean," "My Mother's Wedding Day" and "Almost Like Being in Love." AGNES DE MILLE provided the stunning choreography that included the lovely "Come to Me, Bend to Me" ballet and the powerful "Sword Dance" and OLIVER SMITH's evocative settings expertly recreated the misty Scottish Highlands on stage. *Brigadoon* was unusually gentle and atmospheric for a big Broadway hit but it charmed audiences for 581 performances and is still widely produced today.

BRITISH IMPORTS have always been part of the Broadway musical scene, for European theatre and dance companies have toured America since pre-Revolutionary War days. The Gilbert and Sullivan comic operettas were the most famous of the London musical imports in the late nineteenth century, but they were not the only popular transfers. In the year 1900 the most talked about musical on Broadway was *Floradora*, a British product. Americans got their first taste of West End favorites BEATRICE LILLIE, GERTRUDE LAWRENCE, Jessie Matthews and JACK BUCHANAN in the imported *Andre Charlot's Revue of 1924* and Noel Coward's *Bitter Sweet* came to these shores in 1929. But the imports dwindled during the Depression and did not return in full force for another forty years. There were the occasional British successes after World War II, such as *THE BOY FRIEND* (1954), *STOP THE WORLD—I WANT TO GET OFF* (1962) and *OLIVER!* (1963), but for the most part it was Broadway that was sending the hits to London. All that started to change in the early 1970s when the ANDREW LLOYD WEBBER–TIM RICE musicals arrived and attracted a wider (and younger) audience than had been seen on Broadway in years. *JESUS CHRIST SUPERSTAR* (1971) began the assault but it was most felt with the team's *EVITA* (1979) and Webber's *CATS* (1982) and *THE PHANTOM OF THE OPERA* (1988). Even *ME AND MY GIRL*, a 1937 London hit that did not even try to cross the Atlantic back then, came to Broadway in 1986 and charmed everyone. Not only were native British products succeeding but foreign musicals developed and produced in London came over with a vengeance, as in the case of *LES MISÉRABLES* (1987) and *MISS SAIGON* (1991). The British invasion seemed to have quieted down by

1991, but as long as there is Broadway there will be West End musicals playing there.

HELEN BRODERICK (1891–1959) played a series of droll, wise-cracking comic characters in Broadway musicals before going to Hollywood to play the same kind of role in movie musicals. Broderick started in vaudeville where she performed with her husband Lester Crawford. She appeared in the chorus of the *Follies of 1907*, *The Honeymoon Express* (1913) and other shows before making a name for herself in COLE PORTER's *FIFTY MILLION FRENCH-MEN* (1929). Broderick's stage career culminated in the delightful characterizations she created for the revues *THE BAND WAGON* (1931), *EARL CARROLL VANITIES* (1932) and *AS THOUSANDS CHEER* (1933).

GEORGIA BROWN (1933–   ), a British actress-singer who made several impressive appearances on Broadway, is most remembered for playing Nancy in *OLIVER!* (1963). Brown made her New York debut joining the Off-Broadway *THE THREEPENNY OPERA* in 1957. She played the title roles in the short-lived musicals *CARMELINA* (1979) and *Roza* (1987), as well as Mrs. Peachum in the 1989 Broadway revival of *The Threepenny Opera*.

LEW BROWN (1893–1958) is mostly remembered as the colyricist for the celebrated team of DeSYLVA, BROWN and HENDERSON that wrote a series of revues and musicals in the roaring twenties. Brown was born in Odessa, Russia, and emigrated as a boy to America. He left school to pursue a career on Tin Pan Alley, where he met and collaborated with Albert von Tilzer on a handful of popular songs. GEORGE WHITE formed the team of DeSylva, Brown and Henderson in 1925 to write songs for his annual *SCANDALS* revues. B. G. DeSylva coordinated the team and wrote lyrics with Brown while Ray Henderson provided the music. Their first *Scandals* edition in 1925 got little attention but their 1926 edition was the longest-running show of the whole series, with a remarkable score and sketches by the new team. DeSylva, Brown and Henderson scored other *Scandals* as well as book musicals, the most successful being *GOOD NEWS!* (1927), *Manhattan Mary* (1927), *HOLD EVERYTHING!* (1928), *FOLLOW THRU* (1929) and *FLYING HIGH* (1930). The team disbanded in 1930 when DeSylva went to Hollywood but Brown and Henderson worked on one more *Scandals* in 1931 and separately they contributed to other shows in the 1930s. The team of DeSylva, Brown and Henderson only existed for five years but in that short time they captured all the carefree vivacity of the Jazz Age in their shows.

CAROL BRUCE (1919–   ), a singer-actress with a unique voice quality, appeared in a handful of Broadway musicals beginning with *LOUISIANA PURCHASE* (1940). Bruce's other credits include Julie in the 1946 revival of *SHOW BOAT*, the pensione owner Signora Fioria in *DO I HEAR A WALTZ?* (1965) and Mrs. Boyd in *Henry, Sweet Henry* (1967).

YUL BRYNNER (1915–1985) will always be most remembered for his portrayal of the King of Siam in *THE KING AND I* (1951), a character he originated on Broadway, recreated on film and revived on numerous occasions. The Russian-born Brynner made his Broadway musical debut in *Lute Song* (1946) and much later played Odysseus in the short-lived musical *Home Sweet Homer* (1975). The rest of his time was devoted to films and playing the King, a role he performed 4,631 times before his death.

JACK BUCHANAN (1891–1957), one of the British theatre's most affable leading men in musicals, only appeared in a handful of Broadway shows but in each he was memorable: *Andre Charlot's Revue of 1924*, *Charlot's Revue of 1926* and *BETWEEN THE DEVIL* (1937). The Scottish-born Buchanan was also a successful producer, director and choreographer in London.

BETTY BUCKLEY (1947–), a leading lady in musicals on and off Broadway since 1969, played Martha Jefferson in *1776* (1969), Grizabella, the faded glamour cat who sings "Memory" in the New York production of *CATS* (1982), the title role in *THE MYSTERY OF EDWIN DROOD* (1985) and the less-than-understanding mother in *Carrie* (1988).

CAROL BURNETT (1933–), one of television's most successful comediennes, starred in two Broadway musicals that were perfectly suited to her versatile comic talents: *ONCE UPON A MATTRESS* (1959), in which she played the gawky Princess ("Fred") Winnifred, and *FADE IN–FADE OUT* (1964), where she played Hollywood hopeful Hope Springfield and got to do a smashing Shirley Temple impersonation.

DAVID BURNS (1902–1971) was an accomplished character actor whose comic roles brightened many musicals in London and on Broadway. Burns is most remembered for his snarling Mayor Shinn in *THE MUSIC MAN* (1957), the lecherous husband Senex in *A FUNNY THING HAPPENED ON THE WAY TO THE FORUM* (1962) and the growly Horace Vandergelder in *HELLO, DOLLY!* (1964). He made his Broadway musical debut in *FACE THE MUSIC* in 1932 and his London debut in *Nymph Errant* in 1933. Among his other Broadway credits were *Billion Dollar Baby* (1945), *MAKE MINE MANHATTAN* (1948), *Heaven on Earth* (1948), *Out of This World* (1950), *Two's Company* (1952), *DO RE MI* (1960) and *Lovely Ladies, Kind Gentlemen* (1970). Burns died during the out-of-town tryouts for *70, GIRLS, 70* (1971).

ABE BURROWS (1910–1985) was the ingenious librettist and director who helped create two of composer FRANK LOESSER's greatest successes, *GUYS AND DOLLS* (1950) and *HOW TO SUCCEED IN BUSINESS WITHOUT REALLY TRYING* (1961). His other libretto credits include *CAN-CAN* (1953), *SILK STOCKINGS* (1955) and *First Impressions* (1959). Burrows was also an accomplished director of musicals and Broadway comedies.

RICHARD BURTON (1925–1984), the renowned Welsh actor who captivated audiences in classical pieces, modern plays and films, appeared in only one Broadway musical, but he was unforgettable as King Arthur in *CAMELOT* (1960).

BUSINESS AND LABOR are recurring subjects for musicals; the former usually as a topic for satire or nonsense, the latter often more fervent. From the Fordyce Drop Forge and Tool Factory in *FINE AND DANDY* (1930) to the Louisiana Purchasing Company in *LOUISIANA PURCHASE* (1940) to the toymakers B. G. Bigelow, Inc. in *FLAHOOLEY* (1951) to the World Wide Wickets Company of *HOW TO SUCCEED IN BUSINESS WITHOUT REALLY TRYING* (1961), big business has proved to be an ideal milieu for light-hearted musical comedy. A less frolicsome approach was taken in *I CAN GET IT FOR YOU WHOLESALE* (1962), which explored greed and ambition in the garment industry, and *WHAT MAKES SAMMY RUN?* (1964), which dealt with the ruthless politics of the movie business. But they were the exception. Other musicals set in the world of big business include *DO RE MI* (1960), *HOW NOW DOW JONES* (1967), *PROMISES, PROMISES* (1968) and *THE ROTHS-CHILDS* (1970). Plays dealing with labor and labor relations became prevalent in the 1930s and musicals sometimes tackled the touchy subject. *PINS AND NEEDLES* (1937), produced by a labor union, was good-humored about the topic and the musical revue humanized sociopolitical ideas in a clever way. *THE CRADLE WILL ROCK* (1938), on the other hand, was a rather grim and strident musical that pitted the common laborer against the powerful boss Mr. Mister. The most successful musical dealing with labor relations was *THE PAJAMA GAME* (1954) but the conflicts at the Sleep-Tite Pajama factory were more romantic than political. Perhaps the most revealing musical about the laborer was *WORKING* (1978), which musicalized the actual words and feelings of those in different occupations.

BY JUPITER (1942), a RODGERS and HART musical mostly forgotten today, was actually the team's longest-running show (427 performances) and, sadly, their last new musical together. The two songwriters wrote their own libretto based on a 1932 play *The Warrior's Husband* about a romantic battle of the sexes between Greek warriors and the independent Amazons. The score featured "Wait Till You See Her," "Nobody's Heart" and "Ev'rything I've Got," but it was RAY BOLGER's wonderful performance that made the show so popular. JOSHUA LOGAN directed *By Jupiter* and ROBERT ALTON did the fanciful choreography.

BYE BYE BIRDIE (1960) was an entertaining, unpretentious musical that took rock and roll, teenagers, parents and itself rather lightly. MICHAEL STEWART wrote the amusing libretto about Conrad Birdie, an Elvis Presley-like idol who is drafted, and his manager's efforts to capitalize on the situation by staging a farewell TV appearance in an all-American town. The parallel romances in the musical were not about the rock and roll star, but concerned the manager and his secretary and the teenage girl whose devotion to Birdie is upsetting her boyfriend. The agreeable cast included Dick Van Dyke, CHITA RIVERA, Dick Gautier, KAY MEDFORD, PAUL LYNDE, SUSAN WATSON and Michael J. Pollard under the sparkling direction of GOWER CHAMPION. CHARLES STROUSE and LEE ADAMS wrote the engaging score that included "Put on a Happy Face," "A Lot of Livin' to Do," "How Lovely to Be a Woman," "Kids," "Baby, Talk to Me" and "The Telephone Hour." *Bye Bye Birdie* was the first Broadway book musical for Champion, Stewart, Strouse and Adams, and the newcomers came up with a surprise hit that ran 607 performances.

C

CABARET (1966) was a remarkable musical theatre achievement; it was daring, cynical and uncompromising but, at the same time, it was also very traditional and satisfying. Joe Masteroff based his libretto on John Van Druten's 1951 play *I Am a Camera* and the Christopher Isherwood stories about Berlin in the 1920s. A sleezy cabaret, the Kit Kat Klub, acts as a metaphor for the rise of Nazi Germany as the story follows two couples who try to find happiness even as time is running out. The American writer Cliff (BERT CONVY) meets the British cabaret singer Sally Bowles (Jill Haworth), and they decide to live together but eventually the romance fades as each realizes that in the real world they are incompatible. Running parallel is a subplot about the Jewish fruit merchant Herr Schultz (JACK GILFORD), who hopes to wed the landlady Fraulein Schneider (LOTTA LENYA), but the growing anti-Semitism in Berlin convinces her to break off the engagement. These rather conventional stories were interrupted and commented on by the cabaret's Master of Ceremonies (JOEL GREY) and the tawdry acts at the Kit Kat Klub. The songs by JOHN KANDER and FRED EBB had a KURT WEILL–Bertolt Brecht quality to them but were also uniquely their own with a skillful sense of period and an ear for the expected Broadway sound. "Don't Tell Mama," "Two Ladies," "If You Could See Her" and the title number were very entertaining but also had a hard edge to them. More traditional but just as accomplished were "Married," "It Couldn't Please Me More" and "Why Should I Wake Up?" HAROLD PRINCE directed the talented cast (in which Grey was unforgettable), RON FIELD did the anti-romantic choreography and BORIS ARONSON designed the harsh settings that suggested German expressionistic painting. *Cabaret* managed to be brilliantly innovative and, at the same time, very popular. (1,165 performances)

CABIN IN THE SKY (1940), a musical fantasy about Negro life in the South, boasted a strong cast and a wonderful score by composer VERNON DUKE and lyricist JOHN LATOUCHE. The libretto, by Lynn Root, told of the recently deceased Little Joe Jackson who is given a chance to return to life to correct his past mistakes. The Lawd's General guides him while Lucifer, Jr., throws temptation his way but, with the help of his wife Petunia, Joe succeeds. DOOLEY WILSON played Joe but it was ETHEL WATERS as Petunia singing "Taking a Chance on Love" that made the production so memorable. TODD DUNCAN and REX INGRAM played the good and evil forces with Katherine Dunham as the temptress Georgia Brown. Also in the score was "Honey in the Honeycomb," "Do What You Wanna Do," "Love Turned the Light Out" and the title song. GEORGE BALANCHINE not only choreographed, with the assistance of Dunham, but also co-directed with Albert Lewis. *Cabin in the Sky* was simplistic folklore but it had a sensitivity and integrity rare for musicals about black Americans. (156 performances)

IRVING CAESAR (1895–) contributed lyrics to some two dozen Broadway musicals between 1918 and 1943, including *HIT THE DECK* (1927) and several editions of the *GREENWICH VILLAGE FOLLIES* and *GEORGE WHITE'S SCANDALS*. He wrote the two most popular songs to come from *NO, NO, NANETTE* (1925)—"Tea for Two" and "I Want to Be Happy"—as well as the lyrics for "Swanee," GEORGE GERSHWIN's single biggest hit.

SID CAESAR (1922–), the seemingly multilingual comic famed for his television shows, appeared in *MAKE MINE MANHATTAN* (1948) and played several diverse roles in *LITTLE ME* (1962).

SAMMY CAHN (1913–1993), one of Hollywood's most successful lyricists, only scored one hit on Broadway: *HIGH BUTTON SHOES* (1947) with music by JULE STYNE. His other Broadway credits include *Skyscraper* (1965), *Walking Happy* (1966) and *Look to the Lilies* (1970). Cahn appeared on Broadway in *Words and Music* (1974), a revue of his songs for the theatre and the movies.

ANNE CALDWELL (1867–1936) wrote librettos and lyrics for composers JEROME KERN, Ivan Caryll, VINCENT YOUMANS and others. Her two dozen Broadway productions include *Chin-Chin* (1914), *Tip Top* (1920), *Hitchy-Koo* (1920), *Criss-Cross* (1926) and *Oh, Please!* (1926).

CALL ME MADAM (1950) reunited IRVING BERLIN and ETHEL MERMAN four years after their smash collaboration in *ANNIE GET YOUR GUN* (1946) and the result was another delightful musical comedy. The book by

HOWARD LINDSAY and RUSSEL CROUSE, inspired by real-life Washington hostess Pearl Mesta, was a light and comic tale of a gauche American who is appointed ambassador to a small European country. The Berlin score had more than its fair share of hits: "It's a Lovely Day Today," "You're Just in Love," "The Hostess with the Mostes' on the Ball" and "They Like Ike," the last becoming Eisenhower's official campaign song in 1952. (644 performances)

CALL ME MISTER (1946) was a timely musical revue about ex-GIs adjusting to civilian life after World War II. Much of the satire on military life was good-natured and the talented cast kept the revue breezy and light. BETTY GARRETT, singing the show's musical high point, "South America, Take It Away," got most of the plaudits but also enjoyable were Jules Munshin, Bill Callahan, MARIA KARNILOVA, Lawrence Winters, Paula Barre and GEORGE S. IRVING. HAROLD ROME's songs were not as accomplished as those in his earlier revue *PINS AND NEEDLES* (1937) but the sketches by Arnold Auerbach and Arnold B. Horwitt were on target. The show had two serious moments: a respectful salute to the late FDR called "Face on a Dime" and "The Red Ball Express," a song about post-war discrimination against blacks who had served faithfully in the military. (734 performances)

CAMELOT (1960) has become a perennial favorite of musical theatre patrons but it is often forgotten how difficult a time its creators had in presenting it and how disappointed both audiences and critics were when it first opened. ALAN JAY LERNER adapted T. H. White's epic chronicle *The Once and Future King* into musical terms by concentrating on the romance of King Arthur and Guenevere, the ideas behind the Knights of the Round Table and the eventual destruction of those ideas because of Guenevere's infidelity with Sir Lancelot. It was amitious storytelling for a musical and Lerner never quite succeeded in blending the charm and whimsy of Act I with the tragic themes of Act II. But there were many wonderful things in *Camelot* and audiences have made it a beloved show despite its flaws. RICHARD BURTON was a splendid Arthur and JULIE ANDREWS shone as Guenevere. Also in the strong cast were ROBERT GOULET as Lancelot, Robert Coote and Roddy McDowell. MOSS HART directed and OLIVER SMITH created the fanciful sets. The score by FREDERICK LOEWE and Lerner was an imaginative mix of the royal and the conversational: "The Simple Joys of Maidenhood," "How to Handle a Woman," "I Loved You Once in Silence," "What Do the Simple Folk Do?" "C'est Moi," "Before I Gaze at You Again," the title song and "If Ever I Would Leave You," the biggest hit from the show. (873 performances)

CAN-CAN (1953), with its two parallel plots and predictable story, was a bit old-fashioned even in its day but a sparkling COLE PORTER score and the vibrant debut of GWEN VERDON made the show seem special. ABE

BURROW's libretto is set in 1893 Paris where a young judge is sent to investigate reports of the lewd can-can being performed at Madame Pistache's dance-café. Of course he falls in love with both the dance and the proprietor and even successfully defends both in court. A secondary story about the dancer Claudine (Verdon) and her two rival suitors, a sculptor and an art critic, provided the musical's comic subplot. The French actress Lilo played Pistache but the audiences fell for Verdon, particularly in MICHAEL KIDD's showstopping "Garden of Eden" ballet. Also in the cast were Peter Cookson, Hans Conreid and Erik Rhodes. Although unappreciated at the time, several of Porter's songs went on to become standards: "C'est Magnifique," "It's All Right with Me," "I Love Paris" and the rousing title song. *Can-Can* played for 892 performances and showed that Cole Porter, after three decades of scoring Broadway musicals, was still in top form.

CANDIDE (1956) contains one of the musical theatre's greatest scores but book problems kept this comic operetta from success for nearly twenty years. The eminent playwright Lillian Hellman adapted Voltaire's satiric novel for the musical stage, retaining much of the book's cynicism but little of its charm. The naive hero Candide travels the world pursuing his stolen love Cunegonde but meets with disasters, greed, war and treachery at every turn. Finally he rejects the philosophy of his old tutor Dr. Pangloss ("all's for the best in this best of all possible worlds") and settles down to a simple life with Cunegonde. LEONARD BERNSTEIN's music captured the eighteenth century technically and temperamentally and the lyrics by poet Richard Wilbur, JOHN LATOUCHE, Dorothy Parker, Hellman and Bernstein as well were audacious and brilliant. Tyrone Guthrie directed the superb cast: ROBERT ROUNSE-VILLE as Candide, BARBARA COOK as Cunegonde, MAX ADRIAN as Pangloss and IRRA PETINA as the bizarre Old Lady who keeps popping up. The production also boasted sumptuous scenery by OLIVER SMITH, but audiences could not warm up to the heavy-handed libretto and *Candide* closed after only seventy-three performances. The original cast recording became a favorite nonetheless with "The Best of All Possible Worlds," "I Am Easily Assimilated," "Glitter and Be Gay" and "Make Our Garden Grow" continuing to delight listeners. The biggest hit from the show was the overture itself, which was widely performed in concert halls around the world. But true success did not come to *Candide* until the Chelsea Theatre Center of Brooklyn revived the musical in 1973 with a totally new libretto by HUGH WHEELER, some new songs with lyrics by STEPHEN SONDHEIM and a sensational environmental staging by HAROLD PRINCE. The new version finally found the fun and the eccentric humor of Voltaire's original but musically it was not as potent as the 1956 production's vibrant voices and lush orchestrations. Regardless, the Chelsea's revival moved to Broadway, where it ran a raucous 740 performances. Since then, *Candide* has entered the repertory of opera companies and has seen many successful regional theatre productions.

EDDIE CANTOR (1892–1964) was a popular comic actor and singer who played the same diminutive but ambitious clown character in vaudeville, on Broadway, in films and on the radio. Cantor made his Broadway musical debut in the 1917 *ZIEGFELD FOLLIES* and appeared in four subsequent editions. His other shows included *Broadway Brevities* (1920), *Make It Snappy* (1922), *Kid Boots* (1923) and *Banjo Eyes* (1941). His most memorable stage performance was as the hypochondriac Henry Williams in *WHOOPEE* (1928). Cantor's distinctive comic characteristics included his rolling eyes, his energetic bouncing up and down as he gleefully clapped his hands and his signature exit waving a handkerchief as he danced off stage.

LEN CARIOU (1939–), a versatile leading man in plays and musicals, made his Broadway musical debut as LAUREN BACALL's love interest, director Bill Sampson, in *APPLAUSE* (1970). The Canadian-born Cariou also played the lawyer Fredrik in *A LITTLE NIGHT MUSIC* (1973), the title role in *SWEENEY TODD* (1979), the nightclub performer Harry Aikens in *DANCE A LITTLE CLOSER* (1983) and the "bully" Roosevelt in *Teddy and Alice* (1987).

CARMELINA (1979) was a problematic musical that never found an audience even though it did have an agreeably old-fashioned score by ALAN JAY LERNER (lyrics) and BURTON LANE (music). Lerner and JOSEPH STEIN adapted the 1969 film *Bueno Sera, Mrs. Campbell* about an Italian mother who claims to be the widow of an American soldier from World War II but is really getting financial support from three ex-GIs, each thinking he fathered her daughter. The story was oddly uninvolving, but GEORGIA BROWN was more than competent in the leading role. The score was highly romantic and sometimes rather witty: "It's Time for a Love Song," "Why Him?" "Someone in April" and "One More Walk around the Garden." Despite some favorable reviews, *Carmelina* only lasted seventeen performances.

CARMEN JONES (1943) was much more than a new translation of Bizet's opera *Carmen*. Librettist-lyricist OSCAR HAMMERSTEIN moved the opera's locales from a cigarette factory and a bullfighting arena in Seville, Spain, to a parachute factory in the American South during World War II with boxing replacing bullfighting. All the characters were southern blacks and Hammerstein let the soaring music take on a new relevance when put in an African-American idiom. *Carmen Jones* ran a surprising 502 performances and returned to New York twice more in the 1940s.

CRAIG CARNELIA (1949–), a very promising composer-lyricist whose work throughout the 1980s has been exceptionally engaging, has yet to have a major hit but is greatly admired in the business. Carnelia provided songs for the Off-Broadway revues *Notes: Songs* (1978), *Diamonds* (1984) and *No Frills Revue* (1987), as well as the Broadway musical *WORKING* (1978). His complete scores for *Is There Life after High School?* (1982) on Broadway and *Three Postcards* (1987) Off Broadway had short runs but revealed a new theatre creator with a superior sense of character, pathos and drama.

CARNIVAL (1961) was an enchanting musical set in the make-believe world of carnival entertainers. MICHAEL STEWART's libretto and BOB MERRILL's songs had an innocent and faraway quality that made the show gently mesmerizing. Stewart adapted his story from the 1953 film *Lili* in which an orphan (Anna Maria Alberghetti) joins a seedy traveling carnival, falls for the magician Marco the Magnificent (James Mitchell) but ends up in love with the crippled puppeteer (JERRY ORBACH). The tale was hardly riveting material but the characters were perceptively portrayed and GOWER CHAMPION directed the show with superb inventiveness. The film's song "Hi Lili, Hi Lo" had been a hit but Merrill came up with the equally simple and charming "Theme from *Carnival*," better known as "Love Makes the World Go Round." Also in the fine score were "Mira," "Always Always You," "Sword, Rose and Cape" and "Grand Imperial Cirque de Paris." (719 performances)

CAROUSEL (1945) was RODGERS and HAMMERSTEIN's second collaboration together and, in the opinion of many, it had the finest of their many outstanding scores. Hammerstein adapted Ferenc Molnar's 1921 play *Liliom* from its Hungarian setting to a New England factory town in 1888. The boastful carousel barker Billy Bigelow (JOHN RAITT) falls in love with a local girl, Julie (JAN CLAYTON). Despite their different temperaments they wed, but love is not enough in hard times and Billy turns to crime and is killed during an attempted robbery. The story then turns fantastical as Billy is given a chance to return to earth to see his grown daughter and give her what little bit of wisdom he has learned. In a less tragic subplot, Julie's friend Carrie (Jean Darling) is romanced and won by the fish salesman Mr. Snow (Eric Mattson). *Carousel* had more music than most musicals, including an intoxicating "Carousel Waltz" and an eight-minute musical "Soliloquy." Other highlights of the splendid score included "If I Loved You," "June Is Bustin' Out All Over," "What's the Use of Wond'rin'?" and "You'll Never Walk Alone." ROUBEN MAMOULIAN directed, the THEATRE GUILD produced and AGNES DE MILLE did the dances, including an imaginative carousel ballet-pantomime that took the place of an overture. (890 performances)

DAVID CARROLL (1950–1992), an actor-singer who was proving to be one of the most impressive leading men in musicals, died of AIDS at the peak of his career. Carroll appeared in some Off-Broadway musicals in the 1970s and made his Broadway debut in the revue *Rodgers and Hart* (1975). He played roles in the short-lived musicals *Oh, Brother!* (1981), *Seven Brides for Seven*

Brothers (1982) and *The Wind in the Willows* (1985), but gained attention as Rodolfo opposite Linda Rondstadt in the Public Theatre's reworking of *La Bohème* (1984). Carroll played the Russian chess champion Anatoly in the Broadway version of *Chess* (1988) and originated the role of the Baron in *GRAND HOTEL* (1989). He died in 1992 while recording the cast album of *Grand Hotel*.

DIAHANN CARROLL (1935–   ), the classy black singer-actress whose career includes nightclubs, films and television, gave stylish performances in both of her Broadway musical efforts: the innocent Ottilie in *HOUSE OF FLOWERS* (1954) and the fashion model Barbara Woodruff in *NO STRINGS* (1962).

EARL CARROLL (1893–1948), the producer-director who also wrote songs, presented a series of elaborate Broadway revues that bore his name. The *EARL CARROLL VANITIES* (editions between 1924 and 1940) and the *Earl Carroll Sketchbook* (1929 and 1935) featured beautiful girls, risqué humor and spectacular scenery much in the style of the *ZIEGFELD FOLLIES* and *GEORGE WHITE'S SCANDALS*. Carroll also wrote the scores for a few mostly forgotten Broadway musicals in the 1910s.

JACK CASSIDY (1925–1976) was a skillful and durable leading man who brightened up many musicals but appeared in too few hits to become a major star. Cassidy made his Broadway musical debut in the chorus of *SOMETHING FOR THE BOYS* (1943) and was in the ensembles of several shows in the 1940s before gaining attention as the summer camp waiter-dancer Chick Miller in *WISH YOU WERE HERE* (1952). He had featured roles in the unsuccessful musicals *Sandhog* (1954), *Shangri-La* (1956), *SHE LOVES ME* (1963) and *FADE IN–FADE OUT* (1964). His villainous Max Mencken in *IT'S A BIRD, IT'S A PLANE, IT'S SUPERMAN* (1966) was witty and memorable but that show also failed to run. Cassidy's last Broadway effort was the short-lived *Maggie Flynn* (1968).

VERNON and IRENE CASTLE (1887–1918; 1893–1969) were the most famous ballroom dance team during the early years of the century and not only influenced other professional dancers but popularized the Castle Walk, tango, polka and other dances with people in both America and Europe. The Arkansas-born Irene and British-born Vernon first gained attention as a team in Paris in 1912 and went on to appear in a handful of Broadway shows, most memorably *WATCH YOUR STEP* (1914). The team's career came to a sudden end in 1918 when Vernon Castle died in a plane crash.

THE CAT AND THE FIDDLE (1931) was an ambitious attempt by JEROME KERN and OTTO HARBACH to create a modern operetta. Harbach wrote the book and lyrics, setting the story of two lovers who are musicians in contemporary Brussels. He writes serious music, she writes American jazz. After several complications, the two end up singing together in harmony. The musical's approach was unusual: no chorus, comic bits or unneccesary filler were used. Kern's score was almost continuous with much underscoring, recitatives and extended musical lead-ins for songs. "I Watch the Love Parade," "Try to Forget," "One Moment Alone," "She Didn't Say 'Yes' " and "The Night Was Made for Love" were standouts in an exceptional score. *The Cat and the Fiddle* did not inspire any trend toward modern operetta but it did run 395 performances.

CATS (1982), the international sensation from London, is more revue than musical comedy for it has no formal libretto and only the thinnest excuse for a story. But like the best revues, it maintains its unity through imagination, variety and its score. Composer ANDREW LLOYD WEBBER set T. S. Eliot's poems from *Old Possum's Book of Practical Cats* to music and tied the whole thing together with a "Jellicle Ball" and a stirring finale in which the aged cat Grizabella ascends to a heavenly "Heaviside Layer." There is no dialogue and few of the many characters ever reappear after their initial introductory musical number. For the Broadway production, designer JOHN NAPIER converted the Winter Garden Theatre into a junkyard with a cat's-eye view and director TREVOR NUNN and choreographer Gillian Lynne placed the action all over the theatre. The New York cast featured BETTY BUCKLEY, KEN PAGE, HARRY GROENER, TERRENCE MANN and Timothy Scott. "Memory," the only song in the show not taken directly from an Eliot poem, became one of the few Broadway songs from the 1980s to become a nationwide hit. (still running as of 3/1/93)

CELEBRATION (1969) was a daring experiment in which librettist-lyricist TOM JONES and composer HARVEY SCHMIDT attempted to create a musical that was primitive, bare bones theatre. The original libretto was an allegorical tale enacted on a wooden platform on a dateless New Year's Eve. The show broke most conventions by going back to theatre's first convention: simple storytelling around a fire. The musical was about the battle between winter and summer, youth versus old age, idealism against reality. The innocent Orphan is befriended by the confidence man Potemkin who shows him the world of Mr. Rich. The boy hopes to bring his garden back to life and uses an eager singer named Angel to conquer the world of artificiality. *Celebration* was actually much more engaging than it sounds, if a bit cold at times. But this darker version of *THE FANTASTICKS* was too much for Broadway audiences, and despite Jones' admirable staging and generally favorable reviews, the musical only managed to run 110 performances. The score was very imaginative and had several top-notch songs, including "Survive," "Where Did It Go?" "Somebody," "My Garden" and "It's You Who Makes Me Young." *Celebration* was not for all tastes but it did show Jones and Schmidt at their most potent.

GOWER CHAMPION (1920–1980) was the director-choreographer most associated with post-war Broadway's biggest and brightest entertainments. Champion started as a dancer on stage and screen but moved into directing with the Broadway revue *LEND AN EAR* (1948). In the 1960s he staged some of the musical theatre's happiest shows: *BYE BYE BIRDIE* (1960), *CARNIVAL* (1961) and *HELLO, DOLLY!* (1964). Champion was equally successful with the two-character *I DO! I DO!* (1966), the slight but enjoyable *SUGAR* (1972), the polished revival *IRENE* (1973) and the LIZA MINNELLI vehicle *THE ACT* (1977). But he also had a series of short-lived musicals, such as *THE HAPPY TIME* (1968), *MACK AND MABEL* (1974), *Rockabye Hamlet* (1976) and *A Broadway Musical* (1978). Champion's career ended with the hit *42ND STREET* (1980), which opened on the day he died. More in an old-fashioned vein than his contemporary director-choreographers such as BOB FOSSE or MICHAEL BENNETT, Champion was nonetheless very original in his staging ideas and one of the few creators on Broadway that could come up with a sparkling, optimistic sense of glamour.

CAROL CHANNING (1921–) has appeared in only a few Broadway musicals yet she remains one of the legends of the American musical theatre. The Seattle-born Channing's first featured role on Broadway was in the revue *LEND AN EAR* (1948), where her unique voice and wide-eyed comic naïvete first gained notice. She utilized these talents superbly in *GENTLEMEN PRE-FER BLONDES* (1949) with the role of golddigger-with-a-heart-of-gold Lorelei Lee. After the unsuccessful *The Vamp* (1955) and *Show Girl* (1961), Channing scored another triumph as Dolly Levi in *HELLO, DOLLY!* (1964). She reprised Lorelei Lee in the 1974 *Lorelei* and brought her Dolly Levi back to Broadway in 1978.

SYDNEY CHAPLIN (1926–), an affable leading man with a pleasing voice, played the romantic interest for the vivacious stars in three Broadway musicals: the playwright beloved by JUDY HOLLIDAY in *BELLS ARE RINGING* (1956), the unemployed Tom Bailey who attracts CAROL LAWRENCE in *SUBWAYS ARE FOR SLEEPING* (1961) and the gambler Nick Arnstein who dazzles FANNY BRICE (BARBRA STREISAND) in *FUNNY GIRL* (1964). Chaplin is the son of filmmaker Charlie Chaplin.

MARTIN CHARNIN (1934–) is a Broadway lyricist, director, television producer and actor who is most known for the 1977 hit *ANNIE*. Charnin started as an actor and played one of the Jets in *WEST SIDE STORY* (1957). He began his writing career by contributing lyrics to a handful of revues on and off Broadway in the late 1950s and 1960s. He collaborated with RICHARD RODGERS on *TWO BY TWO* (1970) and *I Remember Mama* (1979) on Broadway, as well as *The First* (1981), a short-lived musical about baseballer Jackie Robinson. Charnin wrote the lyrics and directed the megahit *Annie*

(1977) and repeated the same chores for its unsuccessful sequel *Annie II: Miss Hannigan's Revenge* that closed in 1990 prior to its Broadway opening.

CHICAGO (1975) was a vibrant CONCEPT MUSICAL that used the techniques of vaudeville to tell a wildly improbable tale of sin and sincerity in 1920s Chicago. Director BOB FOSSE and lyricist FRED EBB adapted Maurine Dallas Watkins' 1926 play of the same name about a murderess who uses the press, her gullible husband and a shyster lawyer to beat the rap. The score by JOHN KANDER and Ebb captured the jazzy 1920s beautifully and sometimes parodied classic vaudeville numbers. But what made *Chicago* a hit was the razzle-dazzle direction and choreography by Fosse and the star turns by GWEN VERDON, CHITA RIVERA and JERRY ORBACH. TONY WALTON's sleek art deco setting put the orchestra onstage and each song and new section of the story was introduced by a Master of Ceremonies as if they were variety acts. Highlights of the score included "All That Jazz," "Nowadays," "Mr. Cellophane," "All I Care About" and "The Cell Block Tango." *Chicago* was cold-hearted, cynical and lacked the complexity of the team's earlier *CABARET* (1966) but it was theatrically high-powered enough to please audiences for 898 performances.

A CHORUS LINE (1975) was a phenomenon that few could forsee being so successful but the musical appealed to audiences in such a personal way that its effect was not hard to understand. Starting out as a discussion about dancers, then a workshop and then a full production at the Public Theatre for 101 performances, *A CHORUS LINE* moved to Broadway where it stayed for over fourteen years, holding the new record for the longest run (6,137 performances). The show was the brainchild of director-choreographer MICHAEL BENNETT, who staged the musical with affection and skill. The non-linear libretto, by James Kirkwood, Nicholas Dante and some help by NEIL SIMON, explored the dreams, fears and painful memories of eighteen dancers who are auditioning for the chorus line of a Broadway musical. Many of the songs, by MARVIN HAMLISCH (music) and Edward Kleban (lyrics), were character numbers reminiscing about the past while others were straightforward ballads or comic turns. "At the Ballet," "Nothing," "I Hope I Get It," "The Music and the Mirror" and "What I Did for Love" were memorable but *A Chorus Line* really came to life when it danced. Included in the original cast were DONNA McKECHNIE, Kelly Bishop, Wayne Cilento, Robert LuPone, PRISCILLA LOPEZ, Pamela Blair, Thommie Walsh and Sammy Williams. Bob Avian helped with the choreography and ROBIN WAGNER did the simple but evocative set. Although *A Chorus Line* was about a small group of unique individuals, it struck a nerve in everyone who had ever had to present themselves before strangers to get a job or pursue the dream that they longed for. With such a universal appeal and its unabashed love for the musical theatre itself, it is appropriate that *A Chorus Line* is Broadway's greatest success story.

CITY OF ANGELS (1989) was a popular musical comedy takeoff on Hollywood and the detective novel that boasted a clever libretto by LARRY GELBART and a tuneful score by CY COLEMAN (music) and David Zippel (lyrics). The double-plotted story tells of a novelist named Stine whose detective book is being filmed by Hollywood producer Buddy Fidler. Running parallel to this, and commenting on each other, is the tale of the novel/movie itself, which features a hard-boiled private eye named Stone. The crosscutting back and forth between the two plots was more entertaining than confusing and ROBIN WAGNER's sets helped by keeping fiction in black and white and reality in color. JAMES NAUGHTON as Stone and Gregg Edelman as Stine were delightful foils for each other, and they were nicely supported by RENE AUBERJONOIS, RANDY GRAFF and Dee Hoty. The songs seemed to take a backseat to the libretto in *City of Angels* but there were fun moments with "What You Don't Know about Women," "The Buddy System," "Lost and Found" and "You're Nothing without Me." (878 peformances)

BOBBY CLARK (1888–1960), the daffy comic actor who lit up the stage in several Broadway musicals, started in vaudeville where, with his partner Paul McCullough, he had a twenty-seven-year career headlining on various circuits. Clark's Broadway musical debut was in 1922's edition of the *MUSIC BOX REVUE*, followed by roles in *The Ramblers* (1926), *Here Goes the Bride* (1931), *Walk a Little Faster* (1932), *Thumbs Up!* (1934), *Star and Garter* (1942), *MEXICAN HAYRIDE* (1944), the 1947 revival of *SWEETHEARTS* and others. His two most memorable roles were the White House advisor Colonel Holmes in *STRIKE UP THE BAND* (1930) and Waldo Wellington, the husband of the first female to become U. S. president, in *AS THE GIRLS GO* (1948). Clark's comic trademarks included painted-on glasses, a cigar and a too-short cane.

CLASSICAL MUSIC in musicals occurs more often than is generally known but only a few of the attempts have been very successful. *KISMET* (1953), based on themes by Borodin, is perhaps the most effective use of classical music in a Broadway score. That show's lyrics and musical adaptation were by GEORGE FORREST and ROBERT WRIGHT who, during their long career together, wrote a handful of musicals utilizing classical composers: *THE SONG OF NORWAY* (1944) used Grieg's music, *Magdalena* (1948) featured Brazilian composer Villa-Lobos, and *Anya* (1965) relied on Rachmaninoff. OSCAR HAMMERSTEIN II kept the original story of *Carmen* but radically changed the opera's characters and locale and put new lyrics to Bizet's music in *CARMEN JONES* (1943). Offenbach showed up on Broadway in *The Love Song* (1925) and *The Happiest Girl in the World* (1961). Various Strausses could be heard in *The Great Waltz* (1934), *Three Waltzes* (1937) and *Mr. Strauss Goes to Boston* (1945), and Chopin pieces were used in *White Lilacs* (1928) and *Polonaise* (1945). *Rhapsody* (1944) had music originally by Fritz Kreisler and even Tchaikovsky tread the boards of Broadway in *Nadja* (1925) and *Music in My Heart* (1947). SIGMUND ROMBERG used themes by Schubert for his very popular *BLOSSOM TIME* (1921). And, depending on your definition of classical, there was the short-lived musical *Teddy and Alice* (1987) in which all the music was by John Philip Sousa.

JAN CLAYTON (1917–), an actress-singer who appeared in a few Broadway musicals, is most remembered for her debut performance as Julie Jordan in *CAROUSEL* (1945).

CLOSER THAN EVER (1989) was one of the best musical revues of the 1980s, an intimate Off-Broadway show with a bright cast and a superb score. RICHARD MALTBY, JR., and DAVID SHIRE came up with the perceptive repertoire of songs that complimented their 1977 revue *STARTING HERE, STARTING NOW*. That show celebrated life and love for a generation on the brink of discovery. *Closer Than Ever*'s songs had a more mature viewpoint and explored the various decisions and compromises that people make later in life. "You Want to Be My Friend?" "One of the Good Guys," "What Am I Doin'?" "If I Sing," "Miss Byrd" and "Life Story" were outstanding numbers in a never-disappointing score. (288 performances)

IMOGENE COCA (1908–), one of television's favorite comediennes, appeared in featured roles in several musicals in the 1930s. The elf-like Coca made her Broadway debut as a dancer in *When You Smile* (1925) then appeared in *THE GARRICK GAIETIES* (1930), *Shoot the Works!* (1931) and *FLYING COLORS* (1932) before gaining recognition for her performance in *New Faces* (1934). Her other shows include *Fools Rush In* (1934), *New Faces of 1936* and *The Straw Hat Revue* (1939) before her television career began. Coca returned to Broadway after a thirty-eight-year absence to play the religious nut Letitia Primrose in *ON THE TWENTIETH CENTURY* (1978).

COCO (1969) marked KATHARINE HEPBURN's only venture into musical comedy, and although her vehicle was less than satisfactory, she managed to make something special out of the occasion. ALAN JAY LERNER wrote the biographical libretto about dress designer Gabrielle "Coco" Chanel and her attempted comeback in the fashion world after World War II. André Previn provided the forgettable music and Lerner wrote the lyrics, some of which were quite witty. CECIL BEATON devised a stunning set but, ironically, his costumes did not impress. Because of Hepburn's appeal, *Coco* managed to run 332 performances.

THE COCOANUTS (1925) featured the MARX BROTHERS in a daffy musical by GEORGE S. KAUFMAN and MORRIE RYSKIND with a score by IRVING BERLIN. The script took off from the recent land development boom in Florida as Groucho played a hotel owner with an unethical real estate business on the side. The plot, such as it was, concerned a rich dowager's stolen necklace but the zany antics of the clowning brothers was all that mattered. Even Berlin's songs, as light-hearted and appealing as they were, got little attention. (276 performances)

GEORGE M. COHAN (1878–1942), the theatre dynamo who wrote music, lyrics and librettos for two dozen Broadway musicals and often acted in, directed and produced them as well, did more than any other individual to create the fast-paced American musical comedy. Cohan was born into a vaudeville family and was performing at an early age. Before he was twenty he had his first songs published, was writing sketches for vaudeville and managing the family act, The Four Cohans. His dream was to conquer Broadway and after two unsuccessful musicals, Cohan had a hit with *LITTLE JOHNNY JONES* (1904). Not only did he write the libretto and score but he also directed and co-produced it with SAM HARRIS and played the title role. He repeated the writing-directing chores for *FORTY-FIVE MINUTES FROM BROADWAY* (1904) and it was an even greater success. Cohan had his formula perfected with *GEORGE WASHINGTON, JR.* (1906) and played the title role again. With these three hits Cohan developed a brash, vivid kind of musical in which the plot was solid and the songs were hummable with lyrics that were conversational rather than operatic. Cohan would follow this same formula and present musicals until 1928. Among the more notable were *The Honeymooners* (1907), *The Talk of New York* (1907), *The Yankee Prince* (1908), *The Man Who Owns Broadway* (1909), *The Little Millionaire* (1911), *Hello, Broadway!* (1914), *The Cohan Revue* (1916 and 1917), *Little Nellie Kelly* (1922), *The Merry Malones* (1928) and *Billie* (1928). In 1937 Cohan played FDR in RODGERS and HART's *I'D RATHER BE RIGHT* but his own shows seemed old-fashioned by the late 1920s. His talent was not an adaptable one and the musical theatre left Cohan behind as it built on his original ideas. The popular 1968 musical *GEORGE M!* was loosely based on Cohan's life and used many of his songs. Cohan's legacy can still be seen in *HELLO, DOLLY!* (1964), *ANNIE GET YOUR GUN* (1946), *THE MUSIC MAN* (1957), *ANNIE* (1977) and other vivacious, high-spirited, tuneful musicals that celebrate the American spirit.

PATTI COHENOUR (1952–   ), an actress-singer with an operatic voice, appeared in the Broadway productions of *A Doll's Life* (1982) and the 1981 revival of *The Pirates of Penzance* before attracting attention for her Mimi in *La Bohème* at the Public Theatre in 1984. Cohenour also played Mary Jane Wilkes in *BIG RIVER* (1985), the seemingly innocent Rosa Bud in *THE MYSTERY OF EDWIN DROOD* (1985) and alternated the role of Christine Daae with Sarah Brightman in *THE PHANTOM OF THE OPERA* (1988).

JACK COLE (1914–1974) was an ingenious choreographer who brought the dance and rhythms of foreign cultures to his Broadway shows. Cole choreographed such notable musicals as *KISMET* (1953), *JAMAICA* (1957), *A FUNNY THING HAPPENED ON THE WAY TO THE FORUM* (1962) and *MAN OF LA MANCHA* (1965). His protégées were dancer GWEN VERDON and dancer-choreographer CAROL HANEY, who would develop Cole's ideas in their subsequent work.

CY COLEMAN (1929–   ), one of the most tuneful of Broadway composers, has used jazz, big band and traditional musical comedy themes in his exciting scores. Born in the Bronx, Coleman started playing piano at four and continued on to study classical music at the New York College of Music. After graduating, he played at supper clubs while he wrote his own compositions. With lyricist Joe McCarthy, Jr., he wrote some songs but his career gained momentum when he and lyricist CAROLYN LEIGH decided to work together and soon had several hit singles on the charts. Their first Broadway musical together was *WILDCAT* (1960), a vehicle for LUCILLE BALL, but the Coleman–Leigh score was vivacious and engaging. Their songs for the NEIL SIMON-scripted *LITTLE ME* (1962) were even better. Coleman next worked with veteran lyricist DOROTHY FIELDS on her last two shows: *SWEET CHARITY* (1966) and *SEESAW* (1973). Librettist-lyricist MICHAEL STEWART collaborated with Coleman on *I LOVE MY WIFE* (1977) and the team of BETTY COMDEN and ADOLPH GREEN joined him for the high-spirited *ON THE TWENTIETH CENTURY* (1978). *BARNUM* (1980), again with Stewart, was a popular success with its circus-like presentation and tuneful score but *Welcome to the Club* (1989), with lyrics by Coleman and A. E. Hotchner, was a quick failure. Coleman had two hits in a row with *CITY OF ANGELS* (1989), lyrics by David Zippel, and *THE WILL ROGERS FOLLIES* (1991), lyrics by Comden and Green. The music in Coleman's shows is melodic, brash and optimistic. He is perhaps the most visible descendant of the GEORGE M. COHAN style of musical theatre.

ALVIN COLT (1915–   ), a costume designer on Broadway since *ON THE TOWN* (1944), has provided the costumes for many musicals, including *GUYS AND DOLLS* (1950), *FANNY* (1954), *LI'L ABNER* (1956), *GREENWILLOW* (1960), *HERE'S LOVE* (1963) and *SUGAR* (1972).

BETTY COMDEN (1915–   ) and ADOLPH GREEN are the lyricist–librettist team with the longest collaboration in the history of the American theatre. They have written the book and/or lyrics for fifteen Broadway musicals since 1944, as well as film scripts in Hollywood. Comden and Green have worked with many different composers, from JULE STYNE to LEONARD BERNSTEIN to CY COLEMAN, but the two have always worked together. Comden was born in New York City and attended New York University where she met Green. They joined the Washington Square Players and started writing sketches and songs to perform themselves in cabarets and nightclubs. Their first Broadway musical was the highly inventive *ON THE TOWN* (1944) in which they performed and wrote lyrics for Bernstein's music. The success of the show encouraged them to concentrate on writing full time. *Billion Dollar Baby* (1945), with music by Morton Gould, failed but the team was invited out to Hollywood where they wrote film scripts off and on for the next two decades. Back on Broadway, Comden and Green wrote sketches and lyrics for the musical revue *TWO ON THE AISLE* (1951) with composer Styne and then reunited with Bernstein for *WONDERFUL TOWN* (1953). They collaborated with Styne on some of the score for *PETER PAN* (1954) and worked with him again on *BELLS ARE RINGING* (1956), *Say, Darling* (1958), *DO RE MI* (1960), *SUBWAYS ARE FOR SLEEPING* (1961), *FADE IN–FADE OUT* (1964) and *HALLELUJAH, BABY!* (1967). The team wrote the libretto for the popular *APPLAUSE* (1970) and supplied some lyrics for the slightly altered revival of *GENTLEMEN PREFER BLONDES* called *Lorelei* (1974). With composer Coleman they created the wonderfully animated *ON THE TWENTIETH CENTURY* (1978), but it failed to run, as did their *A Doll's Life* (1982). The team again had a hit with *THE WILL ROGERS FOLLIES* (1991) in which they wrote lyrics for Coleman's music. The librettos and lyrics by Comden and Green are usually in the conventional musical comedy tradition but they have an energy and playfulness that keeps them from being dated.

COMIC STRIP MUSICALS go back to the turn of the century with the popular *Buster Brown* in 1905 and VICTOR HERBERT's *Little Nemo* in 1908. The three most successful musicals to be inspired by the comics were *LI'L ABNER* (1956), the Off-Broadway *YOU'RE A GOOD MAN, CHARLIE BROWN* (1967), based on "Peanuts," and *ANNIE* (1977), based on "Little Orphan Annie." Other not-so-profitable "funnies" include *Bringing Up Father* (1925), *IT'S A BIRD, IT'S A PLANE, IT'S SUPERMAN* (1966), the Off-Broadway *Snoopy* (1982) and *Doonesbury* (1983). Fictional cartoonists were leading characters in the musicals *Rumple* (1957) and *WOMAN OF THE YEAR* (1981).

COMPANY (1970) was a CONCEPT MUSICAL, perhaps the first totally satisfying one, that opened up the theatrical possibilities of the American musical in the 1970s. *Company* showed audiences that linear plotlines were not as necessary as character, theme and manner of presentation. It was this show that led the way for the adventurous concept musicals to follow, most notably *A CHORUS LINE* (1975). George Furth wrote the libretto about a Manhattan bachelor and the way he affects and is effected by his married friends. Episodic in structure and at times expressionistic, *Company* explored relationships in the modern world in a funny, frantic and ultimately perceptive way. The score by STEPHEN SONDHEIM was his finest yet as his songs revealed subtext, told stories and commented on the action in ways rarely seen before. Few of the songs would survive outside of the show's context but they were superior nonetheless: "Someone Is Waiting," "Sorry-Grateful," "The

Ladies Who Lunch," "The Little Things You Do Together," "Another Hundred People," "Getting Married Today," "Being Alive" and the extraordinary title song. Dean Jones played the bachelor Bobby (and was soon replaced by LARRY KERT) and Barbara Barrie, ELAINE STRITCH, Charles Braswell, Steve Elmore and Beth Howland were among his friends. HAROLD PRINCE directed with a bold and terrific style and MICHAEL BENNETT provided the unconventional choreography. Also memorable was BORIS ARONSON's skeletal set that depicted New York City thematically rather than realistically. (706 performances)

CONCEPT MUSICALS are difficult to define and, consequently, even harder to trace historically. To some, any musical that is bold and original in some aspect is labeled a concept musical, but a less vague description might be that of a musical that puts as much importance on the unique manner of its presentation as on its content. Concept musicals tend to be less linear and more thematic than the usual fare, which suggests that the plays and musicals by Bertolt Brecht might be the source of the genre. Looking specifically at Broadway, though, many point to *LADY IN THE DARK* (1941) as the granddad of the concept musical. The show was highly expressionistic and took a psychological approach to character, the plot being secondary in importance. *ALLEGRO* (1947) was a less successful musical but one that also used a bold method of telling a rather conventional story. *LOVE LIFE* (1948), another box office disappointment, may be the best candidate for the first concept musical; it disregarded the traditional use of time, interrupted its action with jolting vaudeville numbers that commented on the story and even tried to illustrate sociopolitical ideas through a long-term personal relationship. *WEST SIDE STORY* (1957) has been called a concept musical because of its unique use of dance but few musicals are more traditional when it comes to plotting and characters. *ANYONE CAN WHISTLE* (1964) was so disarming in its presentation and *HALLELUJAH, BABY!* (1967) was so all-encompassing in its scope that they have also been pointed out as fledgling concept shows. The allegorical *CELEBRATION* (1969) was similarly offbeat and unconventional; the fact that all three shows failed at the box office was also indicative of something conceptual. Wherever it may have come from, the concept musical truly arrived with *COMPANY* (1970), a show that managed to be palatable even as it broke just about every rule of musical comedy. *Company* was expressionistic and psychological, it played around with time and place and it was unabashedly contemporary. The musical was successful in its own right but, more importantly, it opened the doors for similarly adventurous shows: *GODSPELL* (1971), *FOLLIES* (1971), *A CHORUS LINE* (1975), *CHICAGO* (1975), *PACIFIC OVERTURES* (1976), *EVITA* (1979), *NINE* (1982), *GRAND HOTEL* (1989), *ASSASSINS* (1990), *JELLY'S LAST JAM* (1992) and others. Some of the techniques of the concept musical would even work their way into traditional, escapist Broadway musicals, *BARNUM* (1980) and *THE WILL ROGERS FOLLIES* (1991) being the most notable examples. Where the concept musical is headed is anybody's guess; its unpredictability and tendency to surprise are among its strongest elements.

A CONNECTICUT YANKEE (1927) had a better book than the other RODGERS and HART musicals of the 1920s because HERBERT FIELDS rewrote the famous Mark Twain story in musical theatre terms. On the eve of his wedding, Martin (WILLIAM GAXTON) gets knocked unconscious and dreams he's back in King Arthur's Camelot. After winning over the court, Martin proceeds to modernize Camelot and falls for the lovely Dame Alisande. When he awakes, Martin realizes he is engaged to the wrong woman and seeks the hand of Alisande's modern counterpart. In addition to the charming score that included the hit songs "Thou Swell" and "My Heart Stood Still," the choreography by BUSBY BERKELEY was much praised and the show ran 418 performances. A 1943 revival of *A Connecticut Yankee* featured some new Rodgers and Hart songs, including the hilarious "To Keep My Love Alive" sung by VIVIENNE SEGAL as Morgan Le Fay.

JANE CONNELL (1925–), one of Broadway's favorite character actresses, played comic supporting roles in several plays and musicals. Connell appeared in the Broadway musicals *New Faces of 1956* and *Drat! The Cat!* (1965) before gaining recognition for her performance as ugly duckling Agnes Gooch in *MAME* (1966), a role she reprised in the 1983 revival. Her other musical credits include the madwoman Gabrielle in *DEAR WORLD* (1969), the dotty Duchess of Dene in *ME AND MY GIRL* (1986) and Mother in *CRAZY FOR YOU* (1992).

BERT CONVY (1935–1991), a stage and television actor intermittently on Broadway, created two memorable musical roles: the radical student Perchick in *FIDDLER ON THE ROOF* (1964) and the American writer Cliff Bradshaw in *CABARET* (1966).

BARBARA COOK (1927–), a superior leading lady and singer with a crystal-clear soprano voice, appeared in a series of beloved but unsuccessful Broadway musicals that made her a favorite of many but kept her from attaining widespread stardom. Cook made her Broadway musical debut as the ingenue Sandy in *FLAHOOLEY* (1951), toured as Ado Annie in *OKLAHOMA!* in 1953 and played the Amish Hilda Miller in *PLAIN AND FANCY* (1955). Her sparkling portrayal of Cunegonde in *CANDIDE* (1956) revealed her to be one of Broadway's most exceptional performers but that musical failed to run. Cook's only hit show was *THE MUSIC MAN* (1957) in which she originated the role of librarian Marian Paroo. The lovestruck Liesl in *THE GAY LIFE* (1961) and the dreamy Amalia Balash in *SHE LOVES ME* (1963) were also expert performances but neither show lasted long. Cook then appeared in *Something More!* (1964), the 1966 revival of *SHOW BOAT* and in the offbeat musical *THE GRASS HARP* (1971) before leaving the musical theatre to concentrate on her singing career. No one has starred in as many cult musical favorites as she has, and ironically, Cook finally achieved stardom in concert and in nightclubs performing songs from the many failures she had appeared in.

JOE COOK (1890–1959), a unique clown who starred in vaudeville with his famous juggling routines and Rube Goldberg inventions, appeared in three editions of the *EARL CARROLL VANITIES* in the 1920s. Cook's other musical credits included *Hitchy-Koo* (1919), *Rain or Shine* (1928), *FINE AND DANDY* (1930) and *Hold Your Horses* (1933).

MARILYN COOPER (1936–   ), a veteran character actress who has appeared in several Broadway comedies and musicals, is most remembered for her frumpy housewife Jan Donovan in *WOMAN OF THE YEAR* (1981). Cooper's other musical credits include *Mr. Wonderful* (1956), Rosalia in *WEST SIDE STORY* (1957), Agnes in *GYPSY* (1959), *I CAN GET IT FOR YOU WHOLE-SALE* (1962), *HALLELUJAH, BABY!* (1967), *TWO BY TWO* (1970) and *Ballroom* (1978).

NOEL COWARD (1899–1973), the international celebrity who wrote plays, screenplays, music, lyrics and librettos, as well as acting and directing in every media, was the author of several London musicals but only a few were seen on Broadway, most notably *Bitter Sweet* (1929) and *High Spirits* (1964).

THE CRADLE WILL ROCK (1938), with book, music and lyrics by MARC BLITZSTEIN, was called "a play in music" and many had trouble figuring out exactly how to categorize the show. In Steeltown, USA, a battle arises between Mr. Mister, who owns everything and just about everyone, and the idealistic union organizer Larry Foreman who opposes him. Before the play is finished issues ranging from labor to prostitution to religion to the freedom of the press are addressed. *The Cradle Will Rock* was more grim than powerful, more daring than enlightening, but it was a unique theatre piece that has been revived on occasion. Actually, the history of the original production is of more importance than the play itself. With John Houseman as producer and Orson Welles as director, *The Cradle Will Rock* was scheduled as a Federal Theatre Project production in a Broadway house in 1937. When the project got nervous about the controversial piece and canceled it on opening day, Welles led the cast and audience to a small theatre twenty blocks uptown. There it was performed nineteen times with Blitzstein at the piano on the bare stage and the actors delivering their lines and songs from seats in the audience because of the union's refusal to permit the performers on stage. The show later moved to a small Broadway theatre where it continued for 108 performances presented in a more conventional fashion. HOWARD DA SILVA and Will Gere played the two rival characters and Hiram Sherman, Olive Stanton and Blitzstein were also in the cast. In 1938 a small record company called Musicraft recorded the full score on seven 78s, making it the first original cast album in the history of the musical theatre.

CHERYL CRAWFORD (1902–1986), the distinguished theatre producer who always sought challenging projects, presented such unique musical productions as *ONE TOUCH OF VENUS* (1943), *BRIGADOON* (1947), *LOVE LIFE* (1948), *REGINA* (1949), *FLAHOOLEY* (1951), *PAINT YOUR WAGON* (1951), *Jennie* (1963) and *CELEBRATION* (1969).

CRAZY FOR YOU (1992), a substantially rewritten version of the GERSHWINS' *GIRL CRAZY* (1930), retained five of the song standards from the popular Depression musical and interpolated five others from George and Ira Gershwin's movie career. In the new libretto by Ken Ludwig, the hero goes out West to foreclose on a vaudeville theatre and a case of mistaken identity with a zealous impresario keeps things lively until the obligatory happy ending. HARRY GROENER and Jodi Benson headed the spirited cast under the direction of Mike Ockrent, and Susan Stroman provided the clever choreography. But, as usual, it was the Gershwin score that mattered most. "Slap That Bass," "Things Are Looking Up," "Nice Work If You Can Get It," "Shall We Dance?" and "They Can't Take That Away from Me" were the Hollywood additions. (still running as of 12/1/92)

RUSSEL CROUSE (1893–1966), a former journalist and publicist, teamed up with HOWARD LINDSAY in 1934 and together they wrote a series of successful Broadway plays and musicals over the next thirty years. The team's most remembered librettos include *ANYTHING GOES* (1934), *RED, HOT AND BLUE!* (1936), *CALL ME MADAM* (1950) and *THE SOUND OF MUSIC* (1959).

GRETCHEN CRYER (1935–   ), a lyricist-librettist and actor-singer, and her collaborator-composer NANCY FORD are the first and most successful female songwriting team in the American musical theatre. Cryer was born in rural Indiana and went to college at De Pauw University where she met fellow student Ford. While Ford worked in New York as a pit pianist for shows, Cryer appeared in the cast of *SILK STOCKINGS* (1955), *LITTLE ME* (1962) and *110 IN THE SHADE* (1963) on Broadway. All the time the two kept writing together and their ANTI-WAR MUSICAL *Now Is the Time for All Good Men* had a brief run Off Broadway in 1967. Cryer and Ford's next project, *THE LAST SWEET DAYS OF ISAAC* (1970), was an Off Broadway sensation and established the team as one of the best to come from the 1960s rock movement. Their only Broadway production to date was *Shelter* (1973), a piece about technology and its effect on interpersonal communication, that lasted only a month. Back off Broadway, *I'M GETTING MY ACT TOGETHER AND TAKING IT ON THE ROAD* (1978) became their biggest hit and arguably their finest musical.

Cryer's lyrics and libretto cannot be simply categorized as feminist or anti-war; her emphasis is on character relationships in modern society and her work is never preachy or simplistic.

JOHN CULLUM (1930–   ), the versatile actor equally at home in musicals and dramas, has played strong-willed characters in various types of Broadway shows. Cullum made his musical debut as Sir Dinadan in *CAMELOT* (1960) and had his first major role as the psychiatrist Dr. Mark Bruchner who discovers Daisy's former life in *ON A CLEAR DAY YOU CAN SEE FOREVER* (1966). His most acclaimed role was the family patriarch Charlie Anderson in *SHEN-ANDOAH* (1975), which he revived on Broadway in 1989. Cullum also played the madcap theatrical producer Oscar Jaffe in *ON THE TWENTIETH CEN-TURY* (1978).

D

DAMES AT SEA (1968) was an Off-Broadway PASTICHE MUSICAL that captured the silly innocence of the early Ruby Keeler–Dick Powell movies. Its libretto, by George Haimsohn and Robin Miller, was very similar to that of the film and later Broadway musical *42ND STREET* (1980) but *Dames at Sea* was an intimate six-character piece that was more cheerful and on target than it was grandiose. BERNADETTE PETERS shone in the Ruby Keeler role and the skillfully accurate songs by Jim Wise (music) and Haimsohn and Miller (lyrics) were amusing enough for the musical to run 575 performances.

DAMN YANKEES (1955) was a popular musical comedy that proved that SPORTS MUSICALS could be profitable, even with the much-jinxed subject of baseball. GEORGE ABBOTT and Douglas Wallop wrote the libretto, based on a Wallop novel, about a middle-aged fan of the Washington Senators who sells his soul to the devil in order to be a young baseballer who can lead his team to the World Series. This yet-another variation on the Faust legend was kept lively by a seductive devil's assistant named Lola, a score that was filled with tuneful songs and choreography by the ever-inventive BOB FOSSE. GWEN VERDON was triumphant as Lola and there was fine work by RAY WALSTON as the devil and Stephen Douglass as the hero. RICHARD ADLER and JERRY ROSS wrote their second (and last) score, which included such favorites as "Heart," "Whatever Lola Wants," "Two Lost Souls," "A Little Brains—A Little Talent," "Shoeless Joe from Hannibal, Mo" and "Those Were the Good Old Days." Abbott directed and the fast-paced show ran 1,019 performances.

DANCE A LITTLE CLOSER (1983), a one-performance flop based on Robert Sherwood's PULITZER PRIZE play *Idiot's Delight* (1939), is notable for its admirable score and for being the last Broadway musical by ALAN JAY LERNER. The updating of the story to the eve of World War III destroyed the charm of the original but some of the offbeat characters remained and they had some splendid songs by Lerner (lyrics) and CHARLES STROUSE (music) to sing: "Another Life," "There's Always One You Can't Forget," "He Always Comes Home to Me" and the lovely title song. Subsequent interest in this short-lived show may mean we have not heard the last of this wonderful score.

DANCE IN MUSICALS goes back to *THE BLACK CROOK* (1866), the first musical and one that owed its uniqueness to the fact that ballet dancers were worked into the show. In the early musicals, the existence of a chorus line defined the Broadway musical. Dance was such a vital element that a musical without dances and psuedo-ballet sequences was unheard of. By the turn of the century, ballet was replaced by more up-to-date dances, including cakewalks, the tango, ballroom dancing and even ragtime hoofing. *WATCH YOUR STEP* (1914) was the first "syncopated musical" with VERNON and IRENE CASTLE redefining theatre dance rhythms. But the idea of dance truly incorporated into the action did not exist. GEORGE BALANCHINE and others provided stunning dance and ballet sequences in 1930s musicals (most memorably the "Slaughter on Tenth Avenue" from 1936's *ON YOUR TOES*), but the dances were set pieces that existed on their own. It was AGNES DE MILLE who took dance and ballet and used it to not only tell the story but to explore characterization. In *OKLAHOMA!* (1943), *BRIGADOON* (1947) and other shows, De Mille presented a form of theatre dance that shaped the way we still view Broadway dancing. JEROME ROBBINS developed the form further by applying modern dance in musicals like *ON THE TOWN* (1944), and in *WEST SIDE STORY* (1957) he used dance to illustrate tension as well as story, character and mood. The emergence of the director-choreographer in the 1960s illustrated the new role dance played in the creation of musicals; now the whole show was choreographed and formal separate dance numbers were somewhat passe. Musicals like *FIDDLER ON THE ROOF* (1964), *MAN OF LA MANCHA* (1965), *COMPANY* (1970) and other seemingly non-dance shows were, in fact, one uninterrupted set piece. More recently this has been seen in musicals such as *NINE* (1982), *CATS* (1982), *GRAND HOTEL* (1989) and *ONCE ON THIS ISLAND* (1990). Finally, there are two unique shows to be included in any discussion of dance in musicals: *DANCIN'* (1978), which had nothing but dance, and *A CHORUS LINE* (1975), which was all about dancing in Broadway musicals.

DANCIN' (1978) was choreographer-director BOB FOSSE's final solution to the problems of libretto, writers, characters and original songs: do a show without them. *Dancin'* was pure dance with no attempt to unify the program thematically or even conceptually. A company of precise, talented dancers performed twenty-three numbers to old songs, few of them from the Broadway repertory. Fosse's originality and the evening's wide variety made *Dancin'* an audience favorite for 1,774 performances.

GRACIELA DANIELE (1939–   ) is a choreographer-turned-director who first established her career with several musicals at JOE PAPP's Public Theatre. Daniele choreographed the popular revivals of *The Pirates of Penzance* (1981) and *ZORBA* (1983), *THE RINK* (1984), *THE MYSTERY OF EDWIN DROOD* (1985) and others. She directed and choreographed *Dangerous Games* (1989) and *ONCE ON THIS ISLAND* (1990). The Argentine-born Daniele started as a dancer, making her Broadway debut in *WHAT MAKES SAMMY RUN?* (1964), also appearing in *Here's Where I Belong* (1968), *PROMISES, PROMISES* (1968) and *CHICAGO* (1975).

DANNY DANIELS (1924–   ) is a choreographer whose dance numbers displayed vitality and originality but success has eluded him as most of his musicals failed to run. His Broadway credits include *High Spirits* (1964), *Walking Happy* (1966), *I Remember Mama* (1979) and *THE TAP DANCE KID* (1983), as well as several Broadway-bound musicals that closed out of town. Daniels started as a performer and had featured roles in *BEST FOOT FORWARD* (1941), *STREET SCENE* (1947), *MAKE MINE MANHATTAN* (1948) and other musicals.

WILLIAM DANIELS (1927–   ), a character actor in many plays, films and on television, played Daisy's practical fiance Warren in *ON A CLEAR DAY YOU CAN SEE FOREVER* (1965) and the "obnoxious and disliked" patriot John Adams in *1776* (1969).

HOWARD DA SILVA (1909–1986), one of Broadway's most durable and accomplished character actors, created some very unique roles in Broadway musicals: the union man Larry Foreman in *THE CRADLE WILL ROCK* (1937), the villainous Jud Fry in *OKLAHOMA!* (1943), the crooked politician Ben Marino in *FIORELLO!* (1959) and Ben Franklin in *1776* (1969).

BRIAN DAVIES (1939–   ), a juvenile actor on Broadway in the 1960s, originated the role of the young Nazi Rolf in *THE SOUND OF MUSIC* (1959) and the naive Hero in *A FUNNY THING HAPPENED ON THE WAY TO THE FORUM* (1962).

SAMMY DAVIS, JR. (1925–1990), the celebrated black entertainer who was widely known from films, nightclubs, television and recordings, starred in three Broadway musicals: *Mr. Wonderful* (1956), *GOLDEN BOY* (1964) and the 1978 revival of *STOP THE WORLD—I WANT TO GET OFF*.

EDITH DAY (1896–1971), the irresistible leading lady of Broadway and West End musicals, is most notable for originating the role of Irene O'Dare in *IRENE* (1919). The Minneapolis-born Day made her Broadway debut in *Pom-Pom* (1916) and appeared in *Follow Me* (1916) and *Going Up!* (1917) before achieving stardom with *Irene*. After starring in *Jenny* (1922), *Orange Blossoms* (1922) and *Wildflower* (1923), Day settled in London where she became known as the Queen of Drury Lane for her many starring roles in American operettas.

DEAR WORLD (1969) was an ambitious attempt to musicalize Jean Giraudoux's whimsical fantasy *The Madwoman of Chaillot*. Jerome Lawrence and Robert E. Lee's libretto stuck to the original for the most part and JERRY HERMAN's score tried to be less Broadway and more European sounding but the project never quite came together. The gentleness of the French comedy, about an insane Countess who cures the world's ills in one afternoon, was too often lost when brassy musical numbers like the title song intervened. Other numbers, such as "Each Tomorrow Morning" and "Kiss Her Now," were worthy of Giraudoux and were quite effective. ANGELA LANSBURY, as the withered but ever-hopeful madwoman, was luminous but audiences stayed away and *Dear World* closed after 132 performances.

DEAREST ENEMY (1925), the first collaboration of librettist HERBERT FIELDS with RODGERS and HART, was an inventive musical comedy set during the Revolutionary War. The story concerns the factual patriot Mrs. Robert Murray and how she detained British General Howe from destroying the American army by wining and dining him in her New York mansion. "Here in My Arms" and "Bye and Bye" were the tuneful hits from the Gilbert and Sullivan-like score. (286 performances)

REGINALD DE KOVEN (1859–1920) was the composer of twenty-four Broadway operettas, most of them in collaboration with librettist-lyricist HARRY B. SMITH. Although many of these shows were foreign in subject and setting, De Koven created an American, almost contemporary sound for his operettas. His most successful and best-remembered work was *ROBIN HOOD* (1891).

AGNES DE MILLE (1905–   ), the renowned choreographer and sometime director, is most responsible for making narrative dance become an accepted part of the book musical. De Mille was born in New York City to a famous theatrical family. Her uncle Henry De Mille was an accomplished nineteenth-century playwright and her other uncle was pioneer film director Cecil B. De Mille. She was educated at UCLA then started her dance career in ballet and later appeared on Broadway in *Grand Street Follies* (1928). De Mille's first assignments as choreographer were in London, after which she co-choreographed *HOORAY FOR WHAT!* (1937) and *Swingin' the Dream* (1939) on Broadway. Her first New York solo credit, *OKLAHOMA!* (1943), would change the way audiences thought about ballet in musicals. The justly famous dream ballet in *Oklahoma!* would foreshadow other extended dance sequences in her choreography for *ONE TOUCH OF VENUS* (1943), *BLOOMER GIRL* (1944), *CAROUSEL* (1945) and *BRIGADOON* (1947). De Mille's other choreography credits include *GENTLEMEN PREFER BLONDES* (1949), *PAINT YOUR WAGON* (1951), *The Girl in Pink Tights* (1954), *Goldilocks* (1958), *JUNO* (1959), *KWAMINA* (1961) and *110 IN THE SHADE* (1963). She also directed the Broadway productions of *ALLEGRO* (1947), *Out of This World* (1950) and *Come Summer* (1969). Among De Mille's dance innovations are her emphasis on characterization and her use of psychology in motivating movement.

THE DESERT SONG (1926) holds up better today than most operettas, and audiences still thrill to its exotic locale and melodic score. Librettist-lyricists OTTO HARBACH and OSCAR HAMMERSTEIN II teamed with composer SIGMUND ROMBERG for the first time and came up with a story that was taken from recent headlines: a Riff revolt in French Morocco, the dashing exploits of Lawrence of Arabia and America's fascination with Rudolph Valentino in *The Sheik*. The libretto concerns the love affair of a French lady who is stolen away to the desert by the mysterious "Red Shadow" of the Riffs. They fall in love but when the bandit is discovered to be the son of the French governor, quick thinking and a robust climax are needed to secure the lovers' happiness. Romberg's score contains such enduring operetta standards as "One Alone," "The Riff Song" and the title song. There was even a musical comedy number called "It" that referred to heartthrob Clara Bow. The show ran for 471 performances and inspired three movie versions.

ANDRE DE SHIELDS (1946–), a vibrant black singer-dancer-actor who has been featured in musicals on and off Broadway, is best remembered for his performance in the title role of *THE WIZ* (1975) and as one of the agile quintet in *AIN'T MISBEHAVIN'* (1978).

DESTRY RIDES AGAIN (1959) was a competent but unexceptional musical version of the oft-filmed story of gentle lawman Thomas Jefferson Destry, Jr., who brings peace to the boisterous frontier town of Bottleneck in the days of the Wild West. Andy Griffith was an affable Destry and DOLORES GRAY delighted audiences as the spicy saloon gal Frenchy but their songs, by HAROLD ROME, were mostly forgettable. MICHAEL KIDD directed and choreographed with great verve and the show's rousing dances were among the best of the season. (473 performances)

B. G. ("Buddy") DESYLVA (1895–1950), the lyricist-librettist mostly known for his collaboration with LEW BROWN and RAY HENDERSON, made important contributions to Broadway before the famous team was formed and was active long after they disbanded. DeSylva was born in New York but was raised in California, where he wrote songs while attending the University of Southern California. One of his lyrics, "Chloe," caught the attention of AL JOLSON who provided music and put it in his Broadway musical *SINBAD* (1918). DeSylva moved to New York where he and co-lyricist Arthur Jackson collaborated with the young GEORGE GERSHWIN on their first Broadway musical, *La La Lucille* (1919). DeSylva worked with Gershwin again on editions of *GEORGE WHITE'S SCANDALS* in 1923 and 1924 until producer White formed the team of DeSylva, Brown and Henderson to write for his annual shows. DeSylva coordinated the trio and wrote lyrics with Brown for Henderson's music. The 1925 edition of the *Scandals* was the new team's first effort and drew little attention but their 1926 edition was a sensation with one of the best scores ever written for an annual revue. The trio moved on to book musicals and had success with *GOOD NEWS!* (1927), *HOLD EVERYTHING!* (1928), *FOLLOW THRU* (1929), *FLYING HIGH* (1930) and others. The team separated in 1930 when DeSylva went to Hollywood to write for films. When he returned to Broadway, it was as producer of COLE PORTER's *DuBARRY WAS A LADY* (1939), *PANAMA HATTIE* (1940) and IRVING BERLIN's *LOUISIANA PURCHASE* (1940). DeSylva's talent was for care-free, exuberant lyrics and breezy librettos that reflected the spirit of the Jazz Age.

JOAN DIENER (1934–   ), an adept singer-actress, is most remembered for creating the roles of the sensuous Lalume in *KISMET* (1953) and the sluttish Aldonza in *MAN OF LA MANCHA* (1965), both of which she reprised in London. Diener's other Broadway credits include the short-lived musicals *Cry for Us All* (1970) and *Home Sweet Homer* (1975). In 1992 she reprised her Aldonza during the Broadway revival of *Man of La Mancha*.

HOWARD DIETZ (1896–1983), the lyricist-librettist who was also an MGM executive in charge of publicity for over thirty years, wrote musicals and revues with several composers but is mostly known for the shows he and ARTHUR SCHWARTZ scored together. Dietz was born in New York City and attended Columbia where he wrote light verse for popular magazines. His publicity career started when he won an advertisement contest and later worked his way up to head of MGM's promotion department. Dietz's songwriting career also began in college and some of his songs were interpolated into Broadway shows. He collaborated with JEROME KERN on *Dear Sir* (1924) but fame did not come until the successful revue *THE LITTLE SHOW* (1929) in which he worked with Schwartz for the first time. They followed this with *THREE'S A CROWD* (1930), *THE BAND WAGON* (1931), *FLYING COLORS* (1932) and *AT HOME ABROAD* (1935), considered four of the finest revues during this golden age for the genre. Dietz and Schwartz also attempted the book musical but their two efforts at this time, *REVENGE WITH MUSIC* (1934) and *BETWEEN THE DEVIL* (1937), suffered from libretto problems and were not successful. During the 1940s Dietz collaborated with composer VERNON

DUKE on a few shows that failed to run but he had a hit again in 1948 with the revue *INSIDE U.S.A.* written with Schwartz. Film projects kept Dietz away from Broadway for over a decade but he and Schwartz once again attempted the book musical with *THE GAY LIFE* (1961) and *JENNIE* (1963), both flops with some exceptional songs. Because Dietz's finest work was written for musical revues, few of his shows are produced today. But he has left behind a repertoire of song standards filled with wit, intelligence and romance.

CHARLES DILLINGHAM (1868–1934), the prolific producer of over sixty musicals between 1903 and his death in 1934, presented several works by composers VICTOR HERBERT and JEROME KERN. Among Dillingham's many hits were *MLLE. MODISTE* (1905), *THE RED MILL* (1906), *WATCH YOUR STEP* (1914), *Stop! Look! Listen!* (1915), *The Century Girl* (1916) and *SUNNY* (1925). He also produced a series of lavish stage spectaculars for the colossal Hippodrome Theatre.

DO I HEAR A WALTZ? (1965) was a surprisingly leaden musical despite the efforts of its talented composer RICHARD RODGERS, lyricist STEPHEN SONDHEIM and librettist ARTHUR LAURENTS, who adapted his play *The Time of the Cuckoo* for the musical stage. The tale of an American spinster on vacation in Venice and her ill-fated romance with a married Italian shopkeeper was oddly uninvolving in the musical version. ELIZABETH ALLEN and Sergio Franchi were competent as the lovers and CAROL BRUCE as a pensione keeper was quite skillful but the score was strained and distant. The title song, a lovely waltz, was the exception and it enjoyed some popularity. (220 performances)

DO RE MI (1960) was an agreeable musical comedy that featured two beloved clowns, PHIL SILVERS and NANCY WALKER, and a pleasing score by JULE STYNE (music) and BETTY COMDEN and ADOLPH GREEN (lyrics). The Garson Kanin libretto, based on his own novel, was a silly affair about Hubie Cram, a nobody with big-shot ideas, and his put-upon wife. Hubie decides to invade the music business and gets involved with racketeers and jukeboxes, creating along the way a singing star out of a waitress. Silvers and Walker made the tired material seem fresh and they were helped by NANCY DUSSAULT, DAVID BURNS and John Reardon. The score contained the hit single "Make Someone Happy" but the highlight of the musical was Walker's hilarious rendition of "Adventure." Also of interest in *Do Re Mi* were BORIS ARONSON's vivid, expressionistic sets that suggested a colorful jukebox. (400 performances)

JACK DONAHUE (1892–1930), an agile dancer and leading man, appeared in a handful of Broadway musicals but is best remembered as MARILYN MILLER's co-star in *SUNNY* (1925) and *ROSALIE* (1928).

DOROTHY DONNELLY (1880–1928), the lyricist-librettist for a handful of musicals in the 1920s, is most remembered for her four collaborations with composer SIGMUND ROMBERG: *BLOSSOM TIME* (1921), *THE STUDENT PRINCE* (1924), *My Maryland* (1927) and *My Princess* (1927).

DON'T BOTHER ME, I CAN'T COPE (1972) was a top-flight musical revue that explored various aspects of contemporary life, with emphasis on black pride and dignity. Yet much of the show was gloriously fun and very satiric at times. Vinnette Carroll put together the musical at a workshop at her Urban Arts Corp Theatre. After touring several cities, the revue opened on Broadway and stayed for 1,065 performances. MICKI GRANT wrote the songs that utilized gospel, folk, rock and calypso rhythms, Carroll directed and George Faison did the choreography. "Fighting for Pharoh," "Good Vibrations," "Questions" and the witty title song were highlights in the all-sung musical.

STEPHEN DOUGLASS (1921–   ), a leading man in Broadway plays and musicals in the 1950s and 1960s, played the steadfast Ulysses in *THE GOLDEN APPLE*, the young "shoeless Joe" Hardy in *DAMN YANKEES* (1955) and the devoted Sheriff File in *110 IN THE SHADE* (1963). Douglass also played Ravenal in the 1966 revival of *SHOW BOAT*.

ALFRED DRAKE (1914–1992), one of Broadway's most dashing and full-voiced leading men, got to introduce three of the American theatre's outstanding musical roles: Curly in *OKLAHOMA!* (1943), Fred Graham/Petrucio in *KISS ME, KATE* (1948) and the poet-beggar Hajj in *KISMET* (1953). Drake made his Broadway musical debut in 1936 in the chorus of *White Horse Inn* and then played one of the youngsters in *BABES IN ARMS* (1937). He appeared in *The Two Bouquets* (1938), *One for the Money* (1939), *The Straw Hat Revue* (1939) and *Two for the Show* (1940) before achieving fame in *Oklahoma!* Drake's other musical credits included Barnaby Goodchild in *Sing Out, Sweet Land* (1944), the outlaw MacHeath in *The Beggar's Holiday* (1946), the union man Larry Foreman in the 1947 revival of *THE CRADLE WILL ROCK*, the renowned actor Edmund Kean in the short-lived *Kean* (1961) and the Maurice Chevalier role of Honoré in the Broadway version of *Gigi* (1973). Drake was not only a superb singer but also an accomplished actor as well who played classical roles on occasion.

DREAMGIRLS (1981), one of the most sensational Broadway productions of the decade, was director MICHAEL BENNETT's high-powered vision of the entertainment world as seen through a sixties pop group. Tom Eyen wrote the tough-as-nails libretto that followed the fortunes and compromises of a Supremes-like trio over a ten-year period and his lyrics, along with Henry Krieger's Motown-sounding music, captured the era vividly. Outstanding numbers from the score included "I Am Changing," "Cadillac Car," "And I Am Telling You I'm Not Going" and "When I First Saw You." Jennifer

Holliday, Cleavant Derricks, Loretta Devine, Sheryl Lee Ralph and Ben Harney headed a strong cast but it was Bennett's dazzling use of song, story, character and design together that made *Dreamgirls* so memorable. (1,522 performances)

DUBARRY WAS A LADY (1939) did not introduce a notable COLE PORTER ballad, as his shows usually did, but his comic songs in this musical were top-notch and stars BERT LAHR and ETHEL MERMAN made the most of them and the silly plot. The libretto by B. G. DeSYLVA and HERBERT FIELDS is a variation on the old dream device: Louis Blore, a washroom attendant at New York's ritzy Club Petite, accidentally drinks a Mickey Finn and dreams he is the French King Louis XV and that his heart's desire, singer May Daly, is Madame DuBarry. The gimmick allowed Lahr and Merman to engage in anachronistic comic bits and fun duets such as "Friendship" and "But in the Morning, No." Also in the score were "Katie Went to Haiti," "Do I Love You?" and "Well, Did You Evah?" the last introduced smashingly by Betty Grable. *DuBarry Was a Lady* had stunning sets and costumes by RAOUL PENE DU BOIS, which recreated sleek 1930s New York City and eighteenth-century Paris. (408 performances)

RAOUL PENE DU BOIS (c.1913–1985) was a costume and scenic designer for films, ballet, nightclubs, the Rockettes and theatre in New York, London and Paris. His most memorable Broadway musical designs included *DUBARRY WAS A LADY* (1939), *PANAMA HATTIE* (1940), *LEND AN EAR* (1948), *CALL ME MADAM* (1950), *WONDERFUL TOWN* (1953), *BELLS ARE RINGING* (1956), *GYPSY* (1959) and the popular revivals of *NO, NO, NANETTE* in 1971 and *IRENE* in 1973.

VERNON DUKE (1903–1969) was one of Broadway's most gifted composers but he never enjoyed the kind of success that he deserved. Duke was born in Russia and as a teenager studied at the Kiev Conservatory of Music before his family fled the revolution. His talent for classical composition attracted the attention of Diaghilev and Duke composed some pieces for the Ballet Russe. Throughout his life, he continued to write ballet and symphonic music under his real name, Vladimir Dukelsky. His theatre career started in London in 1926 where he wrote the music for three West End musicals. By 1929 he settled in America and made his Broadway debut with the musical *Walk a Little Faster* (1932). Duke contributed music to some editions of the *ZIEGFELD FOLLIES* and other revues before writing his finest score, *CABIN IN THE SKY* (1940) with lyricist JOHN LATOUCHE. A series of promising but unsuccessful shows followed: *Banjo Eyes* (1941), *The Lady Comes Across* (1942), *Sadie Thompson* (1944), *Two's Company* (1952) and *The Littlest Revue* (1956). Duke had a better musical background than most Broadway composers and he was greatly respected by his colleagues. But the commercial theatre never used him effectively and Broadway failed to recognize one of its most imaginative artists.

SANDY DUNCAN (1946–), a perky actress-singer intermittently in Broadway musicals, made her debut in *Canterbury Tales* (1969) and gained attention playing Maisie in the 1970 revival of *THE BOY FRIEND*. Duncan is most remembered for her performance as *PETER PAN* in the 1979 Broadway revival.

TODD DUNCAN (1900–), the full-voiced black singer and actor, provided some unforgettable moments on Broadway. Duncan originated the role of the cripple Porgy in *PORGY AND BESS* (1935) and repeated his performance in the 1942 Broadway revival. He also played the Lawd's General in *CABIN IN THE SKY* (1940) and the troubled minister Stephen Kumalo in *LOST IN THE STARS* (1949).

JIMMY DURANTE (1893–1980), one of America's most distinctive and beloved clowns, appeared in a handful of Broadway musicals playing uncouth characters with big hearts. Durante started as a member of the vaudeville team of Clayton, Jackson and Durante, which was featured in the Broadway musicals *Show Girl* (1929) and *THE NEW YORKERS* (1930). His two most memorable roles were the circus publicist Claudius Bowers in *JUMBO* (1935) and the jailbird Policy Pinkle in *RED, HOT and BLUE!* (1936). His other shows included *Strike Me Pink* (1933), *Stars in Your Eyes* (1939) and *Keep Off the Grass* (1940). With his famous "schnozzola," his gravel voice and bright smile, Durante was one of show business's most recognized comics with careers in film, television, stage and nightclubs.

NANCY DUSSAULT (1936–), a vivacious leading lady in musicals and opera, made a notable Broadway debut as Tilda in *DO RE MI* (1960). Dussault's other musical credits include the inquiring Emily in *Bajour* (1964) and *Whispers on the Wind* (1970).

E

EARL CARROLL VANITIES (1923–1940), a series of musical revues that hoped to rival the *ZIEGFELD FOLLIES* and *GEORGE WHITE'S SCANDALS*, was the most risqué and comedy-oriented of the various Broadway revue series. EARL CARROLL provided music, lyrics, sketches and directed many of the eleven editions of the *Vanities*. Like the *Ziegfeld Follies*, the emphasis of the *Vanities* was on beautiful girls, but Carroll's beauties were presented in sexy and sometimes lewd exhibitions, which kept the producer at odds with the law and secured the series' popularity. Many fine comics appeared in editions of the *Vanities*, including JIMMY SAVO, PATSY KELLY, W. C. FIELDS, JOE COOK, HELEN BRODERICK, LILLIAN ROTH, Jack Benny, SOPHIE TUCKER and MILTON BERLE.

FRED EBB (1932–   ), the lyricist and sometime librettist who works exclusively with composer JOHN KANDER, is one of the most intelligent and challenging lyricwriters to come out of the 1960s. Ebb was born in New York City and attended New York University and Columbia. His first collaborator was composer Paul Klein, with whom he wrote individual songs and contributed to a handful of Off-Broadway revues in the late 1950s. Ebb also wrote sketches for the television show "That Was the Week That Was." He met Kander in 1962 and they came up with some song singles that became hits on the charts. The team's first Broadway musical was *FLORA, THE RED MENACE* (1965), which is remembered more as LIZA MINNELLI's first major role than for Kander and Ebb's debut. Their next production was their most famous: *CABARET* (1966). The score was a mixture of romantic book songs in the traditional mode and cynical, sly songs for the cabaret scenes. It all came together in one of the most innovative shows of the decade. Kander and Ebb provided a gentle, engaging score for *THE HAPPY TIME* (1968), an ethnic-sounding one for *ZORBA* (1968) and a raucous one for *70, GIRLS, 70* (1971). The team's *CHICAGO* (1975) utilized vaudeville and 1920s jazz themes in a highly stylized production with a very dark subtext. Their next two shows were star vehicles, *THE ACT* (1977) with Minnelli and *WOMAN OF THE YEAR* (1981) with LAUREN BACALL, and their musical *THE RINK* (1984) had a rich score but a book that kept it from running. The 1991 Off-Broadway musical revue *And the World Goes 'Round* celebrated the team's theatre, film and television work. Kander and Ebb's most recent effort, *The Kiss of the Spider Woman*, has been produced in various places but has yet to arrive on Broadway. Ebb is a lyricist who can write bright musical comedy songs as effectively as he can create terse, unromantic ones and his craftsmanship is always superior.

BUDDY EBSEN (1908–), the tall, leggy dancer-actor who is most known for his television roles, danced with his sister Vilma in a handful of Broadway musicals, most notably *WHOOPEE* (1928), *FLYING COLORS* (1932) and the 1934 *ZIEGFELD FOLLIES*.

WILLIAM and JEAN ECKART (1920– ; 1921–) are a husband and wife team of scenic and lighting designers who have collaborated together on theatre, film and television productions since 1951. Their most memorable Broadway musicals include *THE GOLDEN APPLE* (1954), *DAMN YANKEES* (1955), *LI'L ABNER* (1956), *FIORELLO!* (1959), *SHE LOVES ME* (1963), *ANYONE CAN WHISTLE* (1964), *FLORA, THE RED MENACE* (1965), *MAME* (1966) and *HALLELUJAH, BABY!* (1967).

EL CAPITAN (1896) was a dashing musical set in South America with music by the renowned John Philip Sousa. Charles Klein wrote the action-packed libretto about a band of rebels who seek to overthrow Don Medigua, the viceroy of Peru. Medigua captures and executes the rebels' leader, El Capitan, and disguises himself as the outlaw to infiltrate the enemy's ranks. Sousa and Tom Frost provided the lyrics for the stirring music, much of which was from previous Sousa works. The show's highlight was the rousing march "El Capitan." (112 performances)

LEHRMAN ENGEL (1910–1982), one of the American theatre's most prolific and accomplished conductors and MUSIC DIRECTORS, conducted over one hundred Broadway musicals, including *THE CRADLE WILL ROCK* (1937), *CAROUSEL* (1945), *ANNIE GET YOUR GUN* (1946), *BRIGADOON* (1947), *GUYS AND DOLLS* (1950), *WONDERFUL TOWN* (1953) and *FANNY* (1954). Engel was also an author, teacher and a composer of incidental music for many plays.

A. L. ERLANGER (1860–1930), one of the American theatre's most ruthless and powerful producers, controlled over 650 theatres across the country with his partner Marc Klaw. On Broadway Erlanger aggressively presented over fifty musicals in order to compete with the SHUBERT BROTHERS and other producers but few of his products were of the quality of his competitors. The most notable Erlanger musicals were *The Ham Tree* (1905), *FORTY-FIVE MINUTES FROM BROADWAY* (1906), *THE PINK LADY* (1911), *Two Little Girls in Blue* (1921), *The Perfect Fool* (1921), *Honeymoon Lane* (1926) and the 1927 edition of the *ZIEGFELD FOLLIES*.

ERTÉ (1892–1990), the world-famous Russian-born fashion designer and illustrator, came to America in the early 1920s and designed costumes for FLORENZ ZIEGFELD's productions on Broadway as well as seven editions of *GEORGE WHITE'S SCANDALS*.

RUTH ETTING (1907–1978), the renowned nightclub torch singer, appeared in a few Broadway shows, most memorably *WHOOPEE* (1928) where she sang her signature song "Love Me or Leave Me." Etting's other musicals included the 1927 and 1931 editions of the *ZIEGFELD FOLLIES* and *Simple Simon* (1930) in which she introduced "Ten Cents a Dance."

EVANGELINE (1874) was billed as an "American Opera-Bouffe Extravaganza" but it was really a burlesque of the Longfellow poem. Evangeline, the "belle of Acadia," loves Gabriel but must endure a series of adventures and travel from New England to Africa to the Wild West before the lovers are united. The heroine's hardships were more comic than arduous and a sequence with a dancing cow became an audience favorite. *Evangeline* was one of the earliest musicals in which all of the songs were written by the same team: Edward E. Rice wrote the music and J. Cheever Goodwin provided the lyrics as well as the libretto. The show originated in Boston and only played for sixteen performances during its initial New York engagement but it soon became one of the most popular musicals of the century. *Evangeline* toured everywhere and in 1885 it returned to New York for an astounding run of 251 performances.

MAURICE EVANS (1901–1989), the distinguished Shakespearean actor who performed in New York and London, appeared in one Broadway musical, as the muckraking Dr. Brock in *TENDERLOIN* (1960).

EVITA (1979) was a well-established London hit when it arrived on Broadway with an American cast and HAROLD PRINCE's dynamic staging. ANDREW LLOYD WEBBER (music) and TIM RICE (lyrics) told the story of Argentina's Eva Peron from an ambitious girl of fifteen to a popular actress to first lady of the nation to international celebrity to her death at thirty-three from cancer. Commenting on the saga throughout was the young radical Che Guevera, who gave a sociopolitical point of view to the proceedings. The all-sung musical boasted the hit song "Don't Cry for Me, Argentina," as well as other potent numbers such as "On This Night of a Thousand Stars," "High Flying Adored," "I'd Be Surprisingly Good for You" and "Another Suitcase in Another Hall." PATTI LUPONE became a Broadway star playing Eva and she was ably supported by MANDY PATINKIN as Che and BOB GUNTON as Juan Peron. But the production's crowning achievement was Prince's masterly direction that utilized multimedia, Brechtian techniques and even Russian biomechanics to raise the gossipy subject matter to high art. (1,567 performances)

F

NANETTE FABRAY (1922–), a superbly gifted singer-actress-comedienne, gave many memorable stage, film and television performances but always seemed to fall short of widespread musical stardom. Fabray was noticed with her Broadway debut in *Meet the People* (1940) and was featured in *LET'S FACE IT!* (1941), *My Dear Public* (1943) and *Jackpot* (1944). The roles of the family matriarch Sarah Longstreet in *HIGH BUTTON SHOES* (1947) and the never-aging wife Susan Cooper in *LOVE LIFE* (1948) proved her to be one of the finest musical performers on Broadway. Fabray later appeared in three unsuccessful shows: *Arms and the Girl* (1950), *Make a Wish* (1951) and *MR. PRESIDENT* (1962).

FACE THE MUSIC (1932) was a high-spirited musical satire, IRVING BERLIN's only major attempt at the genre. MOSS HART provided the clever libretto about a Broadway producer during the Depression who gets involved in a police corruption scandal in New York City. Berlin's score was appropriately sly with the former Manhattan elite reduced to eating at the Automat and singing "Let's Have Another Cup o' Coffee." Other songs from the show included "On a Roof in Manhattan," "I Say It's Spinach" and the haunting "Soft Lights and Sweet Music." *Face the Music* was expert musical satire but it suffered from comparisons with the recently opened *OF THEE I SING* (1931) and only ran 165 performances.

FADE IN–FADE OUT (1964) was a musical vehicle for CAROL BURNETT but there were so many mutual bad feelings between the star and the production's management that she never returned to Broadway again. BETTY COMDEN and ADOLPH GREEN wrote an original libretto spoofing Hollywood in the 1930s and allowing Burnett to use her many comic talents. The score by JULE STYNE (music) and Comden and Green (lyrics) was far from their best but it did contain the dreamy "The Usher from the Mezzanine" and the silly "You Mustn't Be Discouraged" in which Burnett impersonated Shirley Temple and TIGER HAYNES played BILL "Bojangles" ROBINSON. JACK CASSIDY, Lou Jacobi and Tina Louise were also featured and the show was directed by GEORGE ABBOTT. *Fade In–Fade Out* opened to less than enthusiastic reviews and soon closed temporarily due to Burnett's back injuries. During a three-month hiatus the show was revised somewhat while the lawyers argued the legal implications. When the production reopened, business was weak and after 271 performances it closed for good.

SAMMY FAIN (1902–1989), a Hollywood composer seen intermittently on Broadway, provided the music for *HELLZAPOPPIN* (1938), *GEORGE WHITE'S SCANDALS* (1939), *Boys and Girls Together* (1940), *Ankles Aweigh* (1955), *Something More!* (1964) and others. His most remembered theatre credit is the score for the offbeat musical *FLAHOOLEY* (1951) with lyrics by E. Y. HARBURG.

FALSETTOS (1992) took thirteen years and three Off-Broadway musicals to finally arrive on Broadway. Composer-lyricist-librettist WILLIAM FINN's small musical *In Trousers* was produced Off Broadway in 1979 and in it he introduced the character of Marvin, a neurotic but indomitable bisexual searching for true love in an age of sexual confusion. Finn expanded and continued his hero's story in *March of the Falsettos* (1981) in which Marvin divorces his wife to live with his male lover but gets jealous when his ex-wife falls in love with his own psychiatrist. Nine years later the saga continued in *Falsettoland* (1990), co-written with JAMES LAPINE, with Marvin's son going through the pains of adolescence and Marvin's lover dying from AIDS. The whole story was put together and, titled *Falsettos*, opened on Broadway in 1992. All three of the shows were completely sung with Finn using everything from softshoe melodies to operatic recitative to musicalize the offbeat, witty and ultimately moving events. MICHAEL RUPERT, Stephen Bogardus and CHIP ZIEN played Marvin, his lover and his psychiatrist in the final three versions of the story and each production was directed by Lapine. The brittle, inventive score offered few conventional songs as such, but among the standout musical sequences were "The Thrill of First Love," "The Chess Game," "I Never Wanted to Love You," "The Games I Play," "Year of the Child," "The Baseball Game," "Holding to the Ground," "Unlikely Lovers" and "What Would I Do?"

FANNY (1954) was a highly romantic and sentimental musical that was based on French filmmaker Marcel Pagnol's trilogy *Marius, Fanny* and *Cesar*.

JOSHUA LOGAN and the playwright S. N. Behrman condensed all three films into one musical play retaining much of the plot but little of the story's intimacy or subtlety. In the port of Marseilles, the lovers Marius and Fanny separate when the young man goes off to sea. When Fanny realizes she is pregnant, she weds the old man Panisse. Years later, after Panisse's death, she is reunited with Marius and they plan to raise their son together. The charming cast was led by ENZIO PINZA, FLORENCE HENDERSON, WALTER SLEZAK and WIL-LIAM TABBERT, directed by Logan and choreographed by HELEN TAMIRIS. HAROLD ROME wrote the score, which included the popular title song, "Never Too Late for Love," "Why Be Afraid to Dance?" "Love Is a Very Light Thing" and "Be Kind to Your Parents." *Fanny* was producer DAVID MERRICK's first Broadway venture and it ran a profitable 888 performances.

THE FANTASTICKS (1960), the longest-running musical of the American theatre, is also one of its most ageless works. Librettist-lyricist TOM JONES and composer HARVEY SCHMIDT created a whimsical but truthful situation and told it in such universal terms that it is not difficult to understand why the Off-Broadway *The Fantasticks* has been popular with all sorts of performing groups all over the world. The plot is based on Edmond Rostand's *Les Romanesques* and tells of two young lovers separated by feuding fathers. When the boy rescues the girl from the outlaw El Gallo, the families are reconciled and a happy ending seems evident. But the lovers learn that the whole feud and the rescue was set up by the fathers as a way of guaranteeing a pre-arranged marriage. Disillusioned and bitter, the boy and girl separate and are only reunited after they have suffered the anti-romantic cruelties the outside world has to offer. El Gallo acts as the musical's narrator and JERRY ORBACH gave the character an enchanted mixture of wry humor and somber reflection. Kenneth Nelson and Rita Gardner were the original set of lovers and Word Baker directed with imaginative simplicity. *The Fantasticks* started as a one-act musical for a summer season at Barnard College where producer Lore Noto saw it and raised the necessary $16,500 to open a full-length version Off Broadway. The musical received less-than-enthusiastic reviews when it premiered in 1960 but a Vernon Rice Award, word of mouth and the popularity of the song "Try to Remember" helped it along. Once *The Fantasticks* did catch on, it never let go; it is still running, as of this writing, thirty-two years later.

A. H. FEDER (1909–), the innovative lighting designer for theatre, ballet and opera, did the lighting for the Broadway musicals *THE CRADLE WILL ROCK* (1938), *THE BOY FRIEND* (1954), *MY FAIR LADY* (1956), *CAMELOT* (1960), *ON A CLEAR DAY YOU CAN SEE FOREVER* (1965), *Goodtime Charley* (1975), *CARMELINA* (1979) and others.

CY FEUER (1911–), a producer-turned-director, co-produced exclusively with ERNEST MARTIN after their initial production of *WHERE'S CHAR-*

LEY? (1948). Other Feuer and Martin Broadway musicals included *GUYS AND DOLLS* (1950), *CAN-CAN* (1953), *THE BOY FRIEND* (1954), *HOW TO SUCCEED* (1961) and *THE ACT* (1977). Feuer turned to directing in 1955 and staged the Feuer–Martin productions of *SILK STOCKINGS* (1955), *Whoop-Up!* (1958), *LITTLE ME* (1962), *Skyscraper* (1965) and *Walking Happy* (1966). Feuer also directed RICHARD RODGERS' last musical, *I Remember Mama* (1979).

FIDDLER ON THE ROOF (1964) remains one of the masterworks of the American theatre because of its timeless, universal appeal and the superb craftsmanship of its libretto and score. Yet the musical was very daring for its day because it shunned all the necessary ingredients for success; instead it was anti-romantic in its approach, uncommercial in its development and modest in its scope. No one was more surprised than its creators when *Fiddler on the Roof* became an international phenomenon. JOSEPH STEIN wrote the libretto that took Sholom Aleichem's stories and created a unified whole by using the little Russian village of Anatevka as the musical's focal point. The tale of dairyman Tevye and his family adjusting to a changing world while trying to hold on to tradition was conventional and warmly sentimental. But JEROME ROBBINS' staging of the piece and the way JERRY BOCK and SHELDON HARNICK's songs were integrated into the action was innovative and exciting. Musical sequences such as the opening "Tradition," "Tevye's Dream" and the wedding scene were extraordinary examples of libretto, music, lyrics and dance blending together powerfully. The celebrated score also included "Matchmaker, Matchmaker," "To Life," "Far from the Home I Love," "Sunrise, Sunset" and "If I Were a Rich Man." ZERO MOSTEL was a jubilant Teyve but the years since have produced several memorable interpretations of the role by HERSHEL BERNARDI, Luther Adler, Jan Peerce, Paul Lipson, Topol and others. Also in the original cast were MARIA KARNILOVA as Teyve's long-suffering wife, BEATRICE ARTHUR, Johanna Merlin, BERT CONVY, AUSTIN PENDLETON and Julia Migenes. BORIS ARONSON designed the Marc Chagall-like sets and Robbins did the singular choreography. *Fiddler on the Roof* ran 3,242 performances, making it the longest-running musical on record for the next twelve years. The show has been revived a number of times on Broadway and everywhere else.

RON FIELD (1934–1989), a dancer-turned-choreographer-turned director, appeared in the dancing chorus of the Broadway musicals *LADY IN THE DARK* (1941), *GENTLEMEN PREFER BLONDES* (1949), *KISMET* (1954) and others. He started to choreograph on Broadway in 1962 and did the dances for *CABARET* (1966), *ZORBA* (1968), *RAGS* (1986) and other shows. Field also directed and choreographed *APPLAUSE* (1970), the 1971 revival of *ON THE TOWN* and *King of Hearts* (1978).

DOROTHY FIELDS (1904–1974), the lyricist-librettist who contributed to several Broadway musicals, revues and Hollywood films, had one of the longest careers in musical theatre history (from 1928 to 1973) and also one of the most varied. Fields was born into a famous show business family: Her father LEW FIELDS was a popular actor and producer and her brothers HERBERT and JOSEPH were successful librettists. She began writing light verse as a schoolgirl and later collaborated with composer JIMMY McHUGH on songs for the Cotton Club revues. Fields' Broadway debut was the hit revue *BLACK-BIRDS OF 1928* written with McHugh. The team wrote a few more shows together but when none of them succeeded Fields went to Hollywood where she scored movie musicals with JEROME KERN, McHugh and others. When she returned to Broadway in 1939, Fields worked with composer ARTHUR SCHWARTZ on *Stars in Your Eyes*. With her brother Herbert she wrote the librettos for three successful COLE PORTER musicals—*LET'S FACE IT!* (1941), *SOMETHING FOR THE BOYS* (1943), *MEXICAN HAYRIDE* (1944)—and the book for IRVING BERLIN's biggest hit, *ANNIE GET YOUR GUN* (1946). Fields collaborated with SIGMUND ROMBERG on *UP IN CENTRAL PARK* (1945), with Morton Gould on *Arms and the Girl* (1950) and with Albert Hague on *REDHEAD* (1959). But her finest book scores in the 1950s were *A TREE GROWS IN BROOKLYN* (1951) and *By the Beautiful Sea* (1954), both with Schwartz. Fields' career took on new life with her two collaborations with composer CY COLEMAN: *SWEET CHARITY* (1966) and *SEESAW* (1973), musicals with scores as young and fresh as her first effort forty years earlier. Fields was a prodigious talent who was equally at home with character lyrics, romantic film songs and dazzling revue numbers. Few have made the crossover from one medium to another and from one decade to another so effortlessly.

HERBERT FIELDS (1897–1958), one of the prolific Fields show business family, wrote the librettos for a series of musical comedies for RODGERS and HART, including *DEAREST ENEMY* (1925), *PEGGY-ANN* (1926), *A CON-NECTICUT YANKEE* (1927), and for COLE PORTER, including *FIFTY MILLION FRENCHMEN* (1929), *DUBARRY WAS A LADY* (1939), *PANAMA HATTIE* (1940) and *MEXICAN HAYRIDE* (1944). With his sister DOROTHY FIELDS he wrote the books for *UP IN CENTRAL PARK* (1945), *ANNIE GET YOUR GUN* (1946), *By the Beautiful Sea* (1954), *REDHEAD* (1959) and others.

JOSEPH FIELDS (1895–1966), a playwright as well as a librettist, collaborated on the librettos for *GENTLEMEN PREFER BLONDES* (1949), *WONDERFUL TOWN* (1953), *The Girl in Pink Tights* (1954) and *FLOWER DRUM SONG* (1958). He is the brother of librettist HERBERT FIELDS and lyricist-librettist DOROTHY FIELDS and the son of actor-producer LEW FIELDS.

LEW FIELDS (1867–1941) made three major contributions to the American musical theatre: As a member of the comedy team of Weber and Fields, he produced a series of popular musical burlesques; as an independent producer, he presented the early RODGERS and HART musicals; and as the patriarch of an illustrious theatre family, he promoted the careers of DOROTHY, HERBERT and JOSEPH FIELDS. Lew Fields teamed up with actor JOE WEBER in the 1880s and they became famous as the "Dutch comics," broadly played immigrant characters who appeared in musicals that parodied the plays of the day. The team was so successful that they bought their own theatre in 1896 and for eight years produced these musical burlesques on Broadway. Weber and Fields broke up in 1904 and each became independent producers but after 1912 they would occasionally be reunited on stage. As a solo producer, Fields was most noted for presenting six musicals scored by the young Rodgers and Hart, often with librettos by his son Herbert, including *PEGGY-ANN* (1926), *A CONNECTICUT YANKEE* (1927) and *Present Arms* (1928).

W. C. FIELDS (1879–1946), the unsentimental comedian who reached worldwide recognition through the movies, was a vaudeville headliner and a Broadway star before starting his screen career in 1925. Fields began as a juggler at the turn of the century and by 1915 was featured in that season's *ZIEGFELD FOLLIES*. He was one of the series' favorite attractions and starred in six further editions as well as in *GEORGE WHITE'S SCANDALS* and *EARL CARROLL VANITIES*. Fields' most famous stage performance was that of con man Professor Eustace McGargle in the musical *POPPY* (1923).

FIFTY MILLION FRENCHMEN (1929) was not COLE PORTER's first Broadway show but it was his first hit and one that propelled him to fame. HERBERT FIELDS wrote a comic-romantic tale about a millionaire in Paris who has to disguise himself as a tour guide to win his sweetheart. WILLIAM GAXTON played the hero and got to sing the unforgettable Porter song "You Do Something to Me." Also in the cast were Genevieve Tobin, HELEN BRODERICK, Betty Compton and Evelyn Hoey, who introduced "Find Me a Primitive Man." The score also included "You've Got That Thing," "Paree, What Did You Do to Me?" and "The Tale of the Oyster." Also noteworthy in the production were NORMAN BEL GEDDES' sets that recreated many of the Paris landmarks on stage. (254 performances)

FINE AND DANDY (1930) is worth remembering today for the superb songs by composer Kay Swift (her only Broadway score) but at the time it was popular as a vehicle for comic JOE COOK. The silly plot, by Donald Ogden Stewart and Cook himself, was about labor–management problems at the Fordyce Drop Forge and Tool Factory. The story allowed Cook plenty of time to juggle, do acrobatics and tell his hilarious nonsequitur stories. Also featured in the show was the energetic tapping of ELEANOR POWELL. The Swift songs, with lyrics by Paul James, included "Can This Be Love?" the optimistic title number and a ditty actually called "Let's Go Eat Worms in the Garden." (255 performances)

FINIAN'S RAINBOW (1947) is one of Broadway's most beguiling musical masterworks and, along with *BRIGADOON* (1947), the finest example of musical fantasy. The libretto, by E. Y. HARBURG and FRED SAIDY, is set in Rainbow Valley in "Missitucky, USA" where the Irish immigrant Finian has arrived to bury a crock of gold he's stolen from the leprechaun Og back in Glocca Morra. Finian's daughter falls in love with the local labor organizer and Og, searching for his gold, realizes he is turning into a human and falling in love with two women at once. Before all is resolved, a bigoted senator is turned black and then white again and a mute beauty is given the gift of speech by Og. The satirical, leftist plot was tempered by one of the American theatre's greatest musical scores, written by BURTON LANE (music) and Harburg (lyrics). "How Are Things in Glocca Morra?" "Old Devil Moon" and "If This Isn't Love" became hits but just as accomplished were "Look to the Rainbow," "Necessity," "The Great Come-and-Get-It Day," "When the Idle Poor Become the Idle Rich," "The Begat" and two delightful numbers for DAVID WAYNE as Og: "Something Sort of Grandish" and "When I'm Not Near the Girl I Love." Also in the cast were Ella Logan, Albert Sharpe and Donald Richards. *Finian's Rainbow* was a bold and joyous experiment and it worked beautifully. The musical boasted the first fully integrated chorus in Broadway history and its ideas were as uncompromising as they were entertaining. (As late as the 1970s the musical and its film version were not allowed in South Africa.) For Harburg, Saidy and Lane, fantastical satire was the way to address life's less than amusing subjects. (725 performances)

WILLIAM FINN (1952–), one of the most promising composer-lyricists to come out of the 1980s, began writing offbeat musicals as an English major at Williams College. To support himself after graduation Finn wrote history plays for junior high school level. His small musical *In Trousers* was first produced Off Broadway in 1978 but it was its sequel, *March of the Falsettos* (1981), that prompted raves from critics and audiences alike. Finn provided the lyrics for *Dangerous Games* (1989) and the full score for *Romance in Hard Times* (1989); both were short-lived failures. But his second sequel *Falsettoland* (1990) was a success Off Broadway and revealed a deeper and even richer talent than previously seen. The two *Falsetto* musicals, with selections from *In Trousers*, were revived on Broadway together under the title *FALSETTOS* in 1992. Finn's musicals are sung through but are much sharper and contemporary than similarly sung shows. His success has revolved around the same characters introduced in *In Trousers* but Finn is versatile in his approach and very inventive in developing character.

FIORELLO! (1959) was a musical biography that was also a satirical look at American politics. Jerome Weidman and GEORGE ABBOTT's libretto presented a very warm and human portrait of Fiorello LaGuardia, New York City's favorite mayor, and concentrated on the ten years before he took office. The rise from small-time lawyer to surprise congressional victor to World War I hero to mayor was not handled solemnly and the shrewd view of city corruption kept the musical entertainingly honest. Tom Bosley was an admirable LaGuardia and the strong cast also included Ellen Hanley, Patricia Wilson, Nathaniel Frey and HOWARD DA SILVA who got to sing the show's two best numbers, "Politics and Poker" and "Little Tin Box." The score by JERRY BOCK and SHELDON HARNICK was topflight and also included "When Did I Fall in Love?" "Till Tomorrow," "The Bum Won" and "Gentleman Jimmy." *Fiorello!* ran 795 performances, won the esteemed PULITZER PRIZE and established the careers of Bock and Harnick.

THE FIREFLY (1912) was composer RUDOLF FRIML's first Broadway assignment and it was a sensational debut, putting the young Czech immigrant in the same league with VICTOR HERBERT. Friml got the job when Herbert feuded with opera star EMMA TRENTINI and producer ARTHUR HAMMERSTEIN needed a new composer for *The Firefly*. OTTO HARBACH provided the lyrics and the libretto, a Cinderella tale of an Italian street singer who disguises herself as a boy to be near the man she loves. When a music teacher hears her sing he tutors the waif and she becomes a famous prima donna who also gets the man of her dreams. *The Firefly* remains an operetta favorite because of Friml's intoxicating score, which includes "Sympathy," "Giannina Mia" and "Love Is Like a Firefly." (120 performances)

JULES FISHER (1937–), one of Broadway's busiest and most respected lighting designers, has provided the lighting for several musicals since 1964. Among his most famous credits were the lights he did for *JESUS CHRIST SUPERSTAR* (1971), *PIPPIN* (1972), *CHICAGO* (1975), *DANCIN'* (1978), *LA CAGE AUX FOLLES* (1983), *GRAND HOTEL* (1989), *THE WILL ROGERS FOLLIES* (1991) and *JELLY'S LAST JAM* (1992). Fisher is also a Broadway producer whose credits include *Beatlemania* (1977), *Dancin'*, *Rock n' Roll! The First Five Thousand Years* (1983), *THE RINK* (1984), *Big Deal* (1986) and *Elvis—A Musical Celebration* (1989).

FLAHOOLEY (1951) was an offbeat musical that had an unsuccessful run of only forty performances on Broadway but the show lives on as a cult favorite because of its quirky plot and exhilarating score by SAMMY FAIN (music) and E. Y. HARBURG (lyrics). The wacky libretto by FRED SAIDY and Harburg was a broad satire on big business, the McCarthy witch hunts and modern consumerism. B. G. Bigelow, Inc. manufactures a laughing doll named Flahooley to compete with all the crying dolls on the market and soon all are involved with an Arabian princess, a magic lamp with a genie, and a reactionary group called the Capsul-anti. The cast featured BARBARA COOK, Jerome Courtland, Ernest Truex, Irwin Corey, the Bil Baird puppets and Yma Sumac who sang three songs that had no lyrics. With such a short run, none of the show's songs became popular but the whole score is sly and lyrical, including "Here's to Your Illusions," "He's Only Wonderful," "The Springtime Cometh" and "The World Is Your Balloon."

A FLOP MUSICAL, in the strictest sense, is a show that fails to turn a profit. In the 1920s a musical could run two or three months and be considered a hit. Today a show can run well over a year and still be classified a flop. But the true flop is the big, expensive musical put together by reputable people that closes in record time or closes before it even gets to Broadway. There are few celebrated writers, composers, producers or performers who have not had at least one major flop in their careers. How talented and important people manage to come up with so awful a show has never ceased to fascinate audiences and critics alike. Some of the more notable of these giant flops include *Around the World* (1946), *Shangri-La* (1956), *Breakfast at Tiffany's* (1966), *Prettybelle* (1971), *I Remember Mama* (1979), *Bring Back Birdie* (1981), *Carrie* (1988), *Annie II* (1990) and *Nick and Nora* (1991). The opposite side of the coin is the musical that failed to run and was classified as a flop even though time has shown that a truly remarkable work was overlooked. Among the most beloved flops of this sort are *THE THREEPENNY OPERA* (1933), *PORGY AND BESS* (1935), *LOVE LIFE* (1948), *FLAHOOLEY* (1951), *THE GOLDEN APPLE* (1954), *HOUSE OF FLOWERS* (1954), *CANDIDE* (1956), *TENDERLOIN* (1960), *THE GRASS HARP* (1971), *MACK AND MABEL* (1974), *THE ROBBER BRIDEGROOM* (1976), *MERRILY WE ROLL ALONG* (1981), *BABY* (1983) and *RAGS* (1986).

FLORA, THE RED MENACE (1965) is memorable for introducing the songwriting team of JOHN KANDER and FRED EBB to Broadway and for giving LIZA MINNELLI her first major role. The libretto by GEORGE ABBOTT and Robert Russell was based on Lester Atwell's novel *Love Is Just around the Corner* about American Communists during the Depression. Flora, an unemployed fashion designer right out of school, meets and falls for Harry who introduces her to the Party. The musical was rather soft-hearted and apolitical and the Communists were portrayed as merely silly or ineffectual so there wasn't much point to the story. But the Kander and Ebb score was thrilling and warm: "Dear Love," "All I Need," "Sing Happy," "Not Every Day of the Week" and "A Quiet Thing." Producer HAROLD PRINCE intended the show as a vehicle for BARBRA STREISAND, who had gained stardom with *FUNNY GIRL* the year before. When he couldn't get her, he cast nineteen-year-old Minnelli who gave an infectiously glowing performance. Despite its many fine points, *Flora, the Red Menace* only ran eighty-seven performances but it has been revived on occasion.

FLOWER DRUM SONG (1958) was a pleasant musical comedy by ROD-GERS and HAMMERSTEIN that, although not in the same league with their best work, had a lively score and entertaining characters. The libretto by JOSEPH FIELDS and Hammerstein, adapted from Chin Y. Lee's book of the same name, is set in San Francisco's Chinatown, where old ways in the community are challenged by young people with new ways in mind. Events center on the arrival of a contracted bride from China who is to wed nightclub owner Sammy Fong. But he prefers the Americanized Linda Low, so he instigates a series of deceptions and all ends happily with even the older generation satisfied. Miyoshi Umeki, LARRY BLYDEN, Pat Suzuki, Keye Luke and JUANITA HALL led the cast and the production was staged by GENE KELLY in his only Broadway directing credit. The Rodgers and Hammerstein score was lightweight but melodic with such songs as "I Enjoy Being a Girl," "Love, Look Away," "A Hundred Million Miracles," "You Are Beautiful" and "Don't Marry Me." (600 performances)

FLYING COLORS (1932) was a sparkling musical revue that opened at the low point of the Depression. HOWARD DIETZ and ARTHUR SCHWARTZ provided a vibrant score that included "Alone Together," "A Shine on Your Shoes" and "Louisiana Hayride" and Dietz wrote all of the sketches. The cast featured CLIFTON WEBB, TAMARA GEVA, PATSY KELLY, Larry Adler, IMOGENE COCA, Vilma and BUDDY EBSEN and Charles Butterworth, who performed a hilarious monologue about his plan to end the Depression. Another highlight of the revue was NORMAN BEL GEDDES' innovative scenery, which utilized a moving dance floor. *Flying Colors* managed to run 188 performances in a difficult season.

FLYING HIGH (1930) was the last Broadway musical by the illustrious team of DESYLVA, BROWN and HENDERSON and, like their previous *HOLD EVERYTHING!* (1928), it was the antics of BERT LAHR that got the most attention. The libretto, by B. G. DeSylva, Lew Brown and John McGowan, cashed in on the 1920s flying craze and centered on the romance between a mail pilot and his sweetheart. But Lahr, as the klutz mechanic Rusty Krause, and his mail-order fiancée, played by Kate Smith, were much more fun. The score was not the trio's best but "Thank Your Father" did stick around for years. (357 performances)

FOLLIES (1971) was not the lavish, escapist musical revue that its title suggested and what some of its audience expected. Instead it was an incisive musical play about the follies people have commited in their past and how their present is still haunted by them. James Goldman wrote the unique libretto about a reunion of old *Follies* performers held at a decaying theatre on the eve of its destruction. The four principle characters confront their past and try to justify their present as old musical routines are resurrected, ghosts of yesteryear look on and their own young counterparts appear. STEPHEN SONDHEIM's score embraced the old and the new and his songs were alternately entertaining and devastating. The pastiche numbers were unusually expert, with "Who's That Woman?" "Beautiful Girls," "Broadway Baby" and "Losing My Mind" as superb examples of past styles. The contemporary songs, such as "Could I Leave You?" "I'm Still Here" and "Too Many Mornings," were equally accomplished if sometimes difficult to warm up to. The large and talented cast included ALEXIS SMITH, GENE NELSON, JOHN McMARTIN, Dorothy Collins, Yvonne DeCarlo, Fifi D'Orsay, Ethel Shutta, Justine Johnson, Victoria Mallory and Kurt Peterson. HAROLD PRINCE and MICHAEL BENNETT co-directed and, with BORIS ARONSON's sets and FLORENCE KLOTZ's costumes, they created some stunning visual images that were unforgettable. *Follies* was an expensive production that could not make a profit even after 522 performances but it was a highly stylized masterpiece of sorts and has enjoyed subsequent success in concert and in revival.

FOLLOW THE GIRLS (1944) was a popular wartime entertainment that bordered on burlesque. The plot, such as there was one, concerned a burlesque queen, Bubbles LaMan, and her Long Island nightclub that catered to sailors. The score was forgettable but the antics of JACKIE GLEASON as Goofy Gale, Gertrude Niesen's star turn as Bubbles and a bevy of beautiful girls made this a favorite stop for enlisted men on leave in New York. *Follow the Girls* ran a not-so-surprising 882 performances.

FOLLOW THRU (1929), as the title implied, was a musical comedy about golf with a delightful score by DESYLVA, BROWN and HENDERSON and expert performances by JACK HALEY and ELEANOR POWELL. The Laurence Schwab–B. G. DeSylva libretto, subtitled "A Musical Slice of Country Club Life," concerned the rivalry of two women golfers over a club championship and over the same man. From the score came "Button Up Your Overcoat," "You Wouldn't Fool Me, Would You?" "I Want to Be Bad" and "My Lucky Star." (403 performances)

NANCY FORD (1935–) is the composer half of Cryer and Ford, the first successful female songwriting team in the American musical theatre. Ford was born in Kalamazoo, Michigan, and was educated at DePauw University, where she met GRETCHEN CRYER. In New York Cryer pursued an acting career while Ford played piano for *THE FANTASTICKS* and kept composing her own music. With Cryer providing lyrics and libretto, the team's *Now Is the Time for All Good Men* ran briefly Off Broadway in 1967. Their wise and sassy rock musical *THE LAST SWEET DAYS OF ISAAC* became the Off-Broadway hit of 1970. Cryer and Ford's only Broadway show, *Shelter* (1973), failed to find an audience so the team returned to Off Broadway for their finest work, *I'M GETTING MY ACT TOGETHER AND TAKING IT ON THE ROAD* (1978). Ford's music utilizes pop and rock but stays within the dramatic framework of the Broadway musical. Consequently, *The Last Sweet Days of Isaac* was the first rock musical to be seriously accepted by the traditional Broadway community.

GEORGE FORREST (1915–   ), a composer-lyricist who works exclusively with ROBERT WRIGHT, adapted classical music into Broadway scores with varying degrees of success. Wright and Forrest's most accomplished shows were *SONG OF NORWAY* (1944), which used the music of Edvard Grieg; *KISMET* (1953), utilizing themes by Alexander Borodin; and *GRAND HOTEL* (1989), in which their own compositions were used along with those of MAURY YESTON. Other musicals the team fashioned from the classics: *Gypsy Lady* (1946), using VICTOR HERBERT melodies; *Magdalena* (1948), based on the music of Heitor Villa-Lobos; and *Anya* (1965), in which Rachmaninoff variations were used. Wright and Forrest have powerful lyric talents and their scores were always done with care and intelligence.

THE FORTUNE TELLER (1898) was composer VICTOR HERBERT's sixth Broadway production but this was the show that firmly placed him as the premiere operetta composer in America. The lyrics and libretto were by the prolific HARRY B. SMITH and opera singer Alice Nielsen starred in the double leading role: the gypsy fortune teller and an heiress who is studying ballet. The story is one of mistaken identity as the two identical women get confused by their respective sweethearts. All works out in the end, helped by no less than the Hungarian military. Two popular songs from the score, "Romany Life" and "Gypsy Love Song," contain the most famous gypsy music heard in all of operetta. The original production of *The Fortune Teller* was a touring company so it only stayed in New York for forty performances.

FORTY-FIVE MINUTES FROM BROADWAY (1906) is arguably GEORGE M. COHAN's best musical. The tightly constructed melodrama had only five songs in its score and Act II of the three-act musical was all plot. The story is set in New Rochelle, New York—a community only forty-five minutes from Times Square at the time—and concerns a hidden will, a humble housekeeper who will inherit, and a secretary whose pride keeps him from marrying for money. The alluring FAY TEMPLETON played the housekeeper but VICTOR MOORE stole the show as the secretary. As usual, Cohan wrote the book, music and lyrics as well as directing the production, which introduced such delights as "Mary's a Grand Old Name," "I Want to Be a Popular Millionaire," "So Long, Mary" and the witty title song. (90 performances)

42ND STREET (1980) was not the first time the 1933 movie musical had hit the stage (the *ZIEGFELD FOLLIES OF 1936* and the 1968 Off-Broadway

DAMES AT SEA had spoofed the original) but this lavish DAVID MERRICK production celebrated the cliché-filled tale rather than burlesque it. MICHAEL STEWART and Mark Bramble provided the adaptation and a handful of Harry Warren–Al Dubin songs were added to the ones in the film score. The plot still told of the stage-struck chorus girl who lands the leading role in the big Broadway musical when the star breaks her ankle at the final hour. JERRY ORBACH, TAMMY GRIMES, Wanda Richert and LEE ROY REAMS led the large cast and GOWER CHAMPION directed and choreographed the production smashingly. *42nd Street* was Champion's last Broadway credit (he died on opening day) and the last major hit for Merrick. (3,485 performances)

BOB FOSSE (1927–1987), the dancer-turned-choreographer-turned-director, was one of the few Broadway directors who had a distinct and easily recognized style. Fosse was born in Chicago and was appearing on the stage as a professional dancer by the time he was a teenager. He performed on Broadway, on tour and, eventually, on film. His Broadway choreography debut was *THE PAJAMA GAME* (1954), which immediately secured his new career. Fosse provided similar dancing magic for *DAMN YANKEES* (1955), *BELLS ARE RINGING* (1955), *NEW GIRL IN TOWN* (1957) and *HOW TO SUCCEED IN BUSINESS WITHOUT REALLY TRYING* (1961). With *REDHEAD* (1959), he began his directing career, also choreographing each production as well: *LITTLE ME* (1962), *SWEET CHARITY* (1966), *PIPPIN* (1972) and *CHICAGO* (1975). Fosse was least interested in a musical's book and his shows sometimes suffered from weak librettos. With *DANCIN'* (1978), he eliminated the book altogether, and with *Big Deal* (1986), he avoided any collaborators by using old songs and did his own libretto. Fosse also had a successful career directing films and television specials and in 1973 he achieved the unheard-of feat of winning an Oscar, a Tony and an Emmy Award all in the same year. Although he was always more interested in style than content, Fosse had a definite vision for each musical he directed. This vision got rather dark and pessimistic in his later shows but the vitality of his work never waned.

BETH FOWLER (1940–) is a singer-actress who had featured roles in *Gantry* (1970), *A LITTLE NIGHT MUSIC* (1973), *1600 PENNSYLVANIA AVENUE* (1976), *BABY* (1983) and other musicals but is most remembered for her performance as Mrs. Lovett in the 1989 revival of *SWEENEY TODD*.

EDDIE FOY, JR. (1905–1983), was a sprightly comic who shone in featured roles in several Broadway musicals. Foy started as a member of his father's vaudeville act, Eddie Foy and the Seven Little Foys. He made his Broadway debut with *Show Girl* (1929) and subsequently appeared in *Smiles* (1930), *THE CAT AND THE FIDDLE* (1931), *AT HOME ABROAD* (1935) and the 1945 revival of *THE RED MILL*. His most memorable role was that of factory time-study expert Hines in *THE PAJAMA GAME* (1954). Foy later starred in the short-lived musicals *Rumple* (1957) and *Donnybrook* (1961).

ALISON FRASER (1955–), an actress-singer with a distinctly theatrical voice, played the role of the frustrated wife Trina in both *In Trousers* (1979) and *March of the Falsettos* (1981). Her other musical roles include the dual heroine Josephine/Monica in *ROMANCE, ROMANCE* (1988) and the York-shire maid Martha in *THE SECRET GARDEN* (1991).

VINTON FREEDLEY (1891–1969) was a successful producer of musicals who presented, with his partner ALEX AARONS, six of the GERSHWINS' shows and, on his own, four COLE PORTER musicals. Freedley started as an actor and, while appearing in *For Goodness Sake* (1922), met Aarons, the show's producer, and formed a partnership. Together they presented the Gershwins' *LADY, BE GOOD!* (1924), *TIP-TOES* (1925), *OH, KAY!* (1926), *FUNNY FACE* (1927), *Treasure Girl* (1928) and *GIRL CRAZY* (1930). After Aarons retired in 1933, Freedley produced Porter's *ANYTHING GOES* (1934), *RED, HOT AND BLUE!* (1936), *LEAVE IT TO ME!* (1938) and *LET'S FACE IT!* (1941), as well as musicals by others, most notably *CABIN IN THE SKY* (1940).

RUDOLF FRIML (1879–1972) was one of America's masters of romantic operetta and, along with SIGMUND ROMBERG, the chief inheritor of a tradition begun by VICTOR HERBERT. Friml was born in Prague and at an early age showed great musical promise. He was only ten years old when his first composition was published and he completed his studies under Antonin Dvorak at the Prague Conservatory in record time. As a concert pianist he toured Europe and eventually the United States, where he decided to stay in 1906. Disappointed at his lack of progress in the concert world, he gladly took over the composing duties for *THE FIREFLY* (1912) when Herbert feuded with the show's intended star EMMA TRENTINI. *THE FIREFLY* was Friml's Broadway debut and such a resounding hit that he devoted the rest of his career to operetta. Of the twenty shows that followed, the most notable were *High Jinks* (1913), *ROSE-MARIE* (1924), *THE VAGABOND KING* (1925) and *THE THREE MUSKETEERS* (1928), all of which are considered superlative exam-ples of the genre. His most frequent collaborator was OTTO HARBACH but he also worked with RIDA JOHNSON YOUNG, P. G. WODEHOUSE and OSCAR HAMMERSTEIN II. By 1934 Friml's career came to an end. The Depression signaled the end of the highly romantic operetta and Friml could not or would not adjust to the changing sound on Broadway.

ROBERT FRYER (1920–), usually in partnership with producer Lawrence Carr, has presented several musicals of diverse type and style on Broadway. His most notable productions include *A TREE GROWS IN BROOKLYN* (1951), *WONDERFUL TOWN* (1953), *SWEET CHARITY* (1966), *MAME* (1966),

CHICAGO (1975), *ON THE TWENTIETH CENTURY* (1978) and *SWEENEY TODD* (1979).

FUNNY FACE (1927) reunited the GERSHWINS and the ASTAIRES with a musical comedy hit that rivaled their earlier *LADY, BE GOOD!* (1924). The story of an aviator, a stolen bracelet, two comic crooks and a chase that leads to Atlantic City was an agreeable mess and VICTOR MOORE and Adele and Fred Astaire made the most of it. The song "High Hat," in particular, let Fred Astaire create a bouncy black tie dance routine that would become his trademark. The other George and Ira Gershwin songs included "He Loves and She Loves," "My One and Only," "The Babbitt and the Bromide," the title song and the irresistible "'S Wonderful." With a different libretto and several song interpolations, *Funny Face* became the 1983 hit *MY ONE AND ONLY*. (244 performances)

FUNNY GIRL (1964) was purportedly about FANNY BRICE, the *ZIEGFELD FOLLIES*, show business and a failed marriage, but what it came down to was BARBRA STREISAND, who turned the uneven vehicle into an electric tour de force. Isobel Lennart wrote the libretto, which traced Brice's career from an unknown in burlesque to star of the *Follies*, intermittently telling about her romance, marriage and separation from gambler Nick Arnstein (SYDNEY CHAPLIN). JULE STYNE (music) and BOB MERRILL (lyrics) provided songs typical of the period as well as conventional Broadway tunes. "People" was already popular before the show opened thanks to Streisand's recording of it. Also in the score were "Don't Rain on My Parade," "I Want to Be Seen with You Tonight," "Sadie, Sadie" and "The Music That Makes Me Dance." CAROL HANEY did the dances and among the directors who worked on the project were JEROME ROBBINS, BOB FOSSE and Garson Kanin. *Funny Girl* is often revived and is still a serviceable musical even without Streisand's performance that made it so special. (1,348 performances)

A FUNNY THING HAPPENED ON THE WAY TO THE FORUM (1962) was not only one of the funniest musicals in post-war Broadway history but it also marked the first full score, music and lyrics by STEPHEN SONDHEIM. Librettists LARRY GELBART and BURT SHEVELOVE based their farce on several plays by Plautus, utilizing the best of Roman comedy, burlesque and 1930s musical comedy. The plot concerns the clever slave Pseudolus (ZERO MOSTEL), who attempts to gain his freedom by procuring for his young master (BRIAN DAVIES) the beautiful but vapid Philia (Preshy Marker). Seasoned comics JACK GILFORD, John Carradine, Ruth Kobart and DAVID BURNS played various masters and servants who got involved in the chaos and RONALD HOLGATE was a braggart soldier named Miles Gloriosus. GEORGE ABBOTT directed with his customary talent for fast-paced musical comedy but it was JEROME ROBBINS, who was called in during out-of-town previews, that gave the show its winning touch. Because the script and the performers were so entertaining, few gave credit to Sondheim's score, which was witty, cheery and skillfully crafted. "Everybody Ought to Have a Maid" and the opening number "Comedy Tonight" eventually became well known but there was excellent work also in "Pretty Little Picture," "Impossible," "That'll Show Him" and "Lovely." The musical ran a sprightly 964 performances (still the longest run of Sondheim's career) and was successfully revived on Broadway in 1972 with PHIL SILVERS and LARRY BLYDEN.

G

HELEN GALLAGHER (1926–) is a multitalented performer who sang, danced and played character roles in several musicals but never quite achieved stardom. Gallagher appeared in the dancing chorus of *Seven Lively Arts* (1944), *BRIGADOON* (1947) and other musicals before getting a featured role in *HIGH BUTTON SHOES* (1947). Her other musical credits include *Touch and Go* (1949), *Make a Wish* (1951), the 1952 revival of *PAL JOEY*, the title role in *Hazel Flagg* (1953), the heroine's chum Nickie in *SWEET CHARITY* (1966), *Cry for Us All* (1970) and the eccentric actress Tallulah Bankhead in the Off-Broadway *Tallulah* (1983). Gallagher is most remembered for her sassy, dancing Lucille in the 1971 revival of *NO, NO, NANETTE*.

PAUL GALLO, a lighting designer who works on and off Broadway and in various regional theatres, has lit the musicals *THE MYSTERY OF EDWIN DROOD* (1985), *Smile* (1986), *CITY OF ANGELS* (1989), *CRAZY FOR YOU* (1992) and the 1992 Broadway revival of *GUYS AND DOLLS*.

VICTOR GARBER (1949–), a singer-actor who has given impressive performances in musicals, comedies and the classics, is best remembered for creating the roles of the sailor Anthony Hope in *SWEENEY TODD* (1979) and John Wilkes Booth in *ASSASSINS* (1990). Garber's other musical credits include *THEY'RE PLAYING OUR SONG* (1979) and the 1982 revival of *LITTLE ME*.

BETTY GARRETT (1919–), a character actress with many stage, film and television credits, was featured in the Broadway musicals *SOMETHING FOR*

THE BOYS (1943), *CALL ME MISTER* (1946) and *MEET ME IN ST. LOUIS* (1989).

THE GARRICK GAIETIES (1925), a small-scale musical revue that helped push the genre toward a more satirical, literate level, is best known for establishing the careers of RICHARD RODGERS and LORENZ HART. The THEATRE GUILD produced the revue for a few performances in order to raise money for furnishing their new theatre but the show was so popular that it ran 211 performances and inspired two sequels. Much of the humor in *The Garrick Gaieties* was at the expense of the Guild itself as the authors burlesqued the prestigious organization's heavy-hitting dramas. The revue opened with the witty "Guilding the Guild" production number and then went on to spoof everything from Calvin Coolidge to the New York subway to the Scopes "monkey trial." The Rodgers and Hart score included "Sentimental Me," "On with the Dance," "April Fool" and the indelible "Manhattan." The second *Garrick Gaieties* (1926) featured a delightful operetta lampoon called "Rose of Arizona" and the Rodgers and Hart standard "Mountain Greenery." The third and final edition in 1930 was less potent but it gave several up-and-coming songwriters a chance to contribute to a Broadway show: JOHNNY MERCER, E. Y. HARBURG, VERNON DUKE, MARC BLITZSTEIN and others.

WILLIAM GAXTON (1893–1963), one of Broadway's favorite leading men from the late 1920s through the 1940s, performed in many musicals, seven of them with his comic foil VICTOR MOORE. Gaxton made his Broadway debut in the 1922 edition of the *MUSIC BOX REVUE* and went on to create some of musical comedy's most amusing roles: the time-traveling Martin in *A CON-NECTICUT YANKEE* (1927), U. S. President John P. Wintergreen in *OF THEE I SING* (1931) and *LET 'EM EAT CAKE* (1933), the enterprising Billy Crocker in *ANYTHING GOES* (1934), the foreign correspondent Buckley in *LEAVE IT TO ME!* (1938) and the shady corporation president Jim Taylor in *LOUISIANA PURCHASE* (1940). Other Broadway musicals included *FIFTY MILLION FRENCHMEN* (1929), *Hollywood Pinafore* (1945) and *Nellie Bly* (1946). Gaxton usually played ambitious wheeler-dealers, which provided a comic contrast with Moore's more bumbling roles.

GAY DIVORCE (1932) is a noteworthy COLE PORTER musical that introduced the song "Night and Day" and concluded FRED ASTAIRE's Broadway career. It was Astaire's first show without his sister, Adele, and critics were skeptical, but Hollywood was not and Astaire went West to make movies and never returned. The plot of *Gay Divorce*, by Dwight Taylor, was little more than a French bedroom farce that concerned an unhappy wife, the paid correspondent needed for her divorce and the man who truely loved her. Besides Astaire, the cast featured Claire Luce, Erik Rhodes and Eric Blore, and the wonderful Porter score included "After You, Who?" "I've Got You on My

Mind," "I Still Love the Red, White and Blue" and the already mentioned "Night and Day," which quickly became the number-one hit across the country. (248 performances)

THE GAY LIFE (1961) was another attempt by songwriters HOWARD DIETZ and ARTHUR SCHWARTZ, masters of the revue format, to score a successful book musical. Fay and Michael Kanin adapted Arthur Schnitzler's episodic comedy of manners *The Affairs of Anatol* into a musical without capturing the European flavor or the subtilty of the original. In turn-of-the-century Vienna, the ladykiller Anatol (Walter Chiari) is finally brought to the altar by the youthful Liesl (BARBARA COOK), who has loved him for years, and her sly brother Mac (Jules Munchin). Chiari was problematic as the hero but Cook was luminous in a role that displayed her many talents. ELIZABETH ALLEN, as a gypsy who sings "Come A-Wandering with Me," was also marvelous. The Dietz–Schwartz score was one of their finest, though it never became very well known. "Magic Moment," "Why Go Anywhere at All?" "Who Can? You Can!" "Something You Never Had Before" and "For the First Time" are all extraordinary character songs. *The Gay Life* could not survive its mixed reviews and closed after 114 performances. The musical is occasionally revived but, not surprisingly, under its new title, *The High Life*.

LARRY GELBART (1926–   ), a screenwriter, playwright and television writer, wrote the librettos for two very successful musical comedies: *A FUNNY THING HAPPENED ON THE WAY TO THE FORUM* (with BURT SHEVELOVE) (1962) and *CITY OF ANGELS* (1989).

GARY GELD (1935–   ), the composer who collaborates exclusively with lyricist-librettist PETER UDELL, scored two popular Broadway musicals about life in the South: *PURLIE* and *SHENANDOAH*. Geld was educated at New York University and Juilliard and started writing pop songs with Udell in 1960. Their first Broadway musical was the long-running *Purlie* (1970), a contagious romp that joyfully captured the black idiom. The team's *Shenandoah* (1975) was much more solemn but its tale of Civil War Virginia pleased audiences for over 1,000 performances. Geld and Udell wrote a lovely score for the short-lived *Angel* (1978), a musical based on Thomas Wolfe's autobiographical *Look Homeward, Angel*. Their next two Broadway efforts, *Comin' Uptown* (1979) and *The Amen Corner* (1983), quickly closed. Geld's music mixes pop, rhythm and blues and folk in a way that is still very much Broadway. The team's best work is simplistic, conventional, even old-fashioned but contains moments of power and truth.

PAUL GEMIGNAMI, a respected MUSIC DIRECTOR and conductor of Broadway musicals, has been associated with many of the STEPHEN SONDHEIM musicals, as well as *ON THE TWENTIETH CENTURY* (1978), *EVITA* (1979), *DREAMGIRLS* (1981) and other shows.

PETER GENNARO (1924–) is a dancer and choreographer who has worked in ballet, television and the musical theatre. As a dancer, Gennaro appeared in *KISS ME, KATE* (1948), *GUYS AND DOLLS* (1950), *THE PAJAMA GAME* (1954) and as Carl in *BELLS ARE RINGING* (1956). He co-choreographed *WEST SIDE STORY* (1957) with JEROME ROBBINS and went on to choreograph several Broadway musicals on his own. Gennaro's most successful shows include *FIORELLO!* (1959), *THE UNSINKABLE MOLLY BROWN* (1960), the popular 1973 revival of *IRENE* and *ANNIE* (1977).

GENTLEMEN PREFER BLONDES (1949) boasted a spirited libretto, a tune-filled score and splashy production values but all that mattered was CAROL CHANNING who rose to stardom playing Lorelei Lee. The libretto was adapted from Anita Loos' 1926 comic novel of the same name by JOSEPH FIELDS who condensed several of gold digger Lorelei's misadventures to an ocean crossing on the *Île de France*. With her friend Dorothy (Yvonne Adair), Lorelei gets entangled with millionarires, British peers and a diamond tiara. JULE STYNE (music) and LEO ROBIN (lyrics) provided the delicious songs, most memorably "Bye, Bye, Baby," "A Little Girl from Little Rock" and "Diamonds Are a Girl's Best Friend." The last became Channing's signature song and the star's wide-eyed naïveté and sensual simplicity kept *Gentlemen Prefer Blondes* running for 740 performances. A slightly rewritten version of the musical, retitled *Lorelei* (1974), with five new songs by BETTY COMDEN, ADOLPH GREEN and Styne, ran for 320 performances with Channing again playing the indomitable heroine.

GEORGE M! (1968) was a mediocre musical biography of GEORGE M. COHAN that was grand musical entertainment because of its star, JOEL GREY; the incomparable Cohan songs; and the masterful direction and choreography by JOE LAYTON. MICHAEL STEWART and Fran and John Pascal wrote the libretto that followed Cohan's career and recreated numbers from his shows. Grey captured the spirit of the man more than his sound and likeness and he was supported by a personable cast that included Betty Ann Grove, BERNADETTE PETERS, Jerry Dodge, JILL O'HARA and Loni Ackerman. Dozens of Cohan songs were brought to life in *George M!* and for 427 performances audiences got a taste of what had made the Yankee Doodle Boy so popular.

GEORGE WASHINGTON, JR. (1906), was one of GEORGE M. COHAN's most unabashed flag-waving musicals. The plot was a ridiculous affair about an Anglophile father (Cohan's father, Jerry), a patriotic son (Cohan) and a satirical feud between two U.S. senators. Cohan wrote the libretto, music and lyrics and it was one of his strongest scores: "I Was Born in Virginia," "All Aboard for Broadway," "If Washington Should Come to Life" and "You're a Grand Old Flag." The last was originally titled "You're a Grand Old Rag"–but pressure from civic groups convinced Cohan to change the lyric. The song was the show's biggest hit and the first Broadway song to sell over a million copies of its sheet music. (81 performances)

GEORGE WHITE'S SCANDALS (1919–1939), a popular series of musical revues, was the closest rival to the *ZIEGFELD FOLLIES* and had several unique attributes of its own. GEORGE WHITE conceived the idea for the series when he was a dancer in the *Follies*. He wanted to create a kind of revue in which modern music and dance could be featured. White wrote sketches and lyrics for the first *George White's Scandals* (1919) as well as appearing in the show and it was a success. Over the next twenty years White would present thirteen editions of the *Scandals*. Unlike Ziegfeld, who put little emphasis on the songs in his revues, White sought out the newest and the best composers and lyricists for his shows. GEORGE GERSHWIN; the team of DESYLVA, BROWN and HENDERSON; Richard Whiting; and others got their first recognition through the *Scandals*, and several hit songs came from the series. Although no one could rival Ziegfeld's opulence and glamour, *George White's Scandals* made a valuable contribution to the American musical theatre that, in many ways, was more long-lasting than the *Follies*.

GEORGE GERSHWIN (1898–1937), one of America's greatest composers, excelled in writing musical comedy, musical satire, comic opera, folk opera, film scores and concert pieces. His work personifies the Jazz Age but his musical talents were so rich and varied that he cannot be easily classified. Gershwin was born in Brooklyn two years after his brother Ira and from a young age showed a proficiency for music. He pursued classical music even as he wrote popular songs and earned his living plugging sheet music on Tin Pan Alley. Gershwin's career took flight when the song "Swanee," lyric by IRVING CAESAR, was interpolated into AL JOLSON's *SINBAD* (1918) and it became popular across the country. His first full Broadway score was *La La Lucille* (1919) with B. G. DESYLVA and Arthur Jackson. The same team's songs became the highlights of the annual *GEORGE WHITE'S SCANDALS* from 1920 to 1924. Gershwin's first major book musical was *LADY, BE GOOD!* (1924) written with Ira and the brothers would go on to score a series of delightful 1920s musicals: *Tell Me More!* (1925), *TIP-TOES* (1925), *OH, KAY!* (1926), *FUNNY FACE* (1927), *ROSALIE* (1928), *Treasure Girl* (1928), *Show Girl* (1929) and *GIRL CRAZY* (1930). It was also in the 1920s that George Gershwin's famous concert works premiered: *Rhapsody in Blue* (1924), Concerto in F (1925) and *An American in Paris* (1928). The Gershwins turned to musical satire with *STRIKE UP THE BAND* (1930) and went as far as comic operetta with their landmark musical *OF THEE I SING* (1931). Their next two shows, *Pardon My English* (1933) and *LET'EM EAT CAKE* (1933), failed and the brothers spent the next two years completing *PORGY AND BESS* (1935), with DuBose Heyward contributing to the lyrics. This folk opera, today considered George Gershwin's masterwork, was greeted with respect but was not a commercial success. The brothers went out to Hollywood, where they scored three films with superb songs before George Gershwin's sudden death from a brain tumor in 1937. In addition to revivals of their shows, the Gershwins also had two posthumous Broadway hits: *MY ONE AND ONLY* (1983) and *CRAZY FOR YOU* (1992). George Gershwin was at the peak of his creative powers when he died at the age of thirty-nine. In a span of less than twenty years, he explored more areas of American music, opened up more new musical forms and created a repertoire of more varied song standards than any other composer.

IRA GERSHWIN (1896–1983), often thought of only as the man who wrote the words for his brother George's songs, was one of the American theatre's most accomplished lyricists who worked with several outstanding composers on innovative and landmark musicals. Ira Gershwin was born in Brooklyn two years before his brother. Because George showed a remarkable musical talent early on, Ira avoided any competition and started writing light verse and humorous pieces for newspapers and magazines. Using the pen name Arthur Francis, he wrote lyrics for VINCENT YOUMANS' music and their songs for *Two Little Girls in Blue* (1921) received some notice. With B. G. DESYLVA, Gershwin supplied the lyrics for "Stairway to Paradise" with his brother's music and the song became the hit of the 1922 edition of *GEORGE WHITE'S SCANDALS*. The two brothers collaborated on a full score for the first time in 1924 and the result was the delectable *LADY, BE GOOD!*. They also scored such light-hearted 1920s musicals as *Tell Me More!* (1925), *TIP-TOES* (1925), *OH, KAY!* (1926), *FUNNY FACE* (1927), *ROSALIE* (1928), *Treasure Girl* (1928) and *GIRL CRAZY* (1930). The brothers attempted satire with *STRIKE UP THE BAND* (1930) and comic operetta with the legendary *OF THEE I SING* (1931) and its acerbic sequel *LET 'EM EAT CAKE* (1933). Meanwhile, Ira Gershwin collaborated with other composers, such as HAROLD ARLEN in *LIFE BEGINS AT 8:40* (1934) and VERNON DUKE in the 1936 *ZIEGFELD FOLLIES*. The brothers moved in yet another direction with the folk opera *PORGY AND BESS* (1935), with DuBose Heyward writing many of the lyrics under Ira's tutelage. This masterful work only met with mild praise and the brothers went out to Hollywood where they scored three films before George's untimely death in 1937. The loss of his brother crippled Ira Gershwin and it was not until playwright MOSS HART convinced him to do the lyrics for the experimental *LADY IN THE DARK* (1941) did the surviving brother return to the theatre. The KURT WEILL–composed *Lady in the Dark* revealed that Gershwin's lyric powers were still acute and a second career, one without his brother, was launched. His next two Broadway musicals, *The Firebrand of Florence* (1945) with Weill and *Park Avenue* (1946) with ARTHUR SCHWARTZ, failed to run so Gershwin went back to Hollywood, where he scored films with JEROME KERN, Harry Warren, BURTON LANE and others. He never returned to Broadway but he had two hits there after his death: *MY ONE AND ONLY* (1983) and *CRAZY FOR YOU* (1992). Among Ira Gershwin's many talents were his unique use of slang in lyricwriting, an ingenious turn of phrase in his romantic songs and a satirical wit that was accurate and delightful.

TAMARA GEVA (1907–   ), an exotic dancer with a background in ballet, is most remembered for her performance as Vera Barnova in *ON YOUR TOES* (1936), in which she danced the "Slaughter on Tenth Avenue" ballet with RAY BOLGER. The Russian-born Geva was in GEORGE BALANCHINE's company as well as the Monte Carlo Ballet. Her other Broadway musicals were *WHOOPEE* (1928), *THREE'S A CROWD* (1930) and *FLYING COLORS* (1932).

JACK GILFORD (1913–1990), the sad-eyed actor equally adept at comedy, drama and musicals, played four memorable characters in Broadway book musicals: the mute King Sextimus in *ONCE UPON A MATTRESS* (1959), the nervous slave Hysterium in *A FUNNY THING HAPPENED ON THE WAY TO THE FORUM* (1962), the Jewish greengrocer Herr Schultz in *CABARET* (1966) and the philandering husband Jimmy in the 1971 revival of *NO, NO, NANETTE*. Gilford started in vaudeville in 1934 and appeared in *Meet the People* (1940), *Alive and Kicking* (1950) and *Once Over Lightly* (1955). His career has also included non-musical plays, films and television.

ANITA GILLETTE (1938–   ), a leading lady in plays and musicals, originated a few roles in Broadway musicals and was also a replacement for many others. Gillette made her debut in *CARNIVAL* (1961) and had feature roles in *ALL AMERICAN* (1962), *MR. PRESIDENT* (1962) and *Jimmy* (1969).

HERMIONE GINGOLD (1897–1987) was a popular comic performer on the London stage from 1908 but didn't appear on Broadway until 1953 in *John Murray Anderson's Almanac*. Her other New York credits included the meddling mother Mrs. Bennett in *First Impressions* (1959), the revue *From A to Z* (1960) and the grande dame Madame Armfeldt in *A LITTLE NIGHT MUSIC* (1973).

GIRL CRAZY (1930), with more hit songs than any other GERSHWIN show, is arguably the brothers' finest musical comedy score. GUY BOLTON and John McGowan concocted the story of a New York playboy sent to Custerville, Arizona, by his millionaire father to run a ranch and to keep him safely away from women and gambling. The son turns the place into a swinging nightclub where money and women abound and he even finds time to fall in love with one of the locals. ETHEL MERMAN, in her Broadway debut, caused a sensation with her rendition of "I Got Rhythm," which launched her remarkable musical theatre career. Also in the cast were WILLIE HOWARD, Allen Kearns and GINGER ROGERS singing the marvelous Gershwins' songs: "Embraceable You," "Bidin' My Time," "Could You Use Me?" "But Not for Me," "Sam and Delilah" and "Boy, What Love Has Done to Me." Under the title *CRAZY FOR YOU*, the musical was rewritten and produced successfully in 1992. (272 performances)

THE GIRL FROM UTAH (1914), an important show in the development of American musical comedy, was actually a British musical that played in London in 1913. For its Broadway version producer Charles Frohman hired JEROME KERN to compose seven new songs and for HARRY B. SMITH to revise the book and provide new lyrics. The story concerns a girl named Una who flees her native Utah and a bigamist Mormon who hopes to wed her. Una arrives in London and falls in love with an actor and all ends happily when the Mormon retreats. The Kern songs included "Why Don't They Dance the Polka Anymore?" "Some Sort of Girl," "You Never Can Tell," "We'll Take Care of You All" and the unforgettable "They Didn't Believe Me" (lyric by Herbert Reynolds). *The Girl from Utah* ran 120 performances and confirmed Kern's reputation as one of Broadway's most promising composers.

JACKIE GLEASON (1916–1987), the rotund comic actor beloved by television audiences, appeared in a few Broadway musicals in the 1940s, including *Artists and Models* (1943) and *FOLLOW THE GIRLS* (1944) where he gained attention as Goofy Gale. Gleason returned to Broadway as the jolly alcoholic Uncle Sid in the musical *TAKE ME ALONG* (1959).

JOANNA GLEASON (1950–), an actress-singer intermittently in Broadway musicals, played the mate-swapping Monica in *I LOVE MY WIFE* (1977), the Baker's Wife in *INTO THE WOODS* (1987) and the sleuth Nora Charles in the short-lived *Nick and Nora* (1991).

SAVION GLOVER (1973–), a tap-dancing actor who appeared in the Broadway musical *THE TAP DANCE KID* (1983) and was featured in the revue *BLACK AND BLUE* (1989), played the young Jelly Roll Morton in *JELLY'S LAST JAM* (1992).

GODSPELL (1971), an intimate but rousing musical version of St. Matthew's Gospel, was the surprise hit of its day. The show started as a student project at Carnegie-Mellon University, then workshopped Off Off Broadway and then moved to Off Broadway in 1971, where it played 2,124 performances. In 1976 *Godspell* ran on Broadway for another 527 performances as well as spurring seven national touring companies. The appeal of the little musical was as basic as theatre itself: stories enacted by a versatile company who used improvisation and mime to create what other musicals did with scenery and costumes. John-Michael Tebelak wrote the libretto and directed the show and STEPHEN

SCHWARTZ, in his musical theatre debut, provided the laudable score that encompassed rock, folk, hymns and even vaudeville-style songs. "Day by Day" was the musical's hit song but there were several other exceptional numbers as well, including "All for the Best," "Light of the World," "All Good Gifts" and "Turn Back, O Man."

THE GOLDEN APPLE (1954) is arguably the musical theatre's most beloved loser, a brilliant and charming show that failed to run but has gained enormous affection and respect over the years. Not quite like anything before or since, *The Golden Apple* was a satirical yet engaging musical comedy that retold events from Homer's *Iliad* and *Odyssey* reset in the turn-of-the-century American Northwest. The traveling salesman Paris arrives in Angel's Roost, Washington, in a balloon and soon steals Sheriff Menelaus' wife Helen off to Rhododendron. Duty-bound Ulysses pursues the couple, wins this wacky "Trojan War" in the boxing ring, then wanders for years trying to get home to his faithful wife Penelope. The musical was almost continually sung, although it retained a musical comedy feel rather than an operatic one. JOHN LATOUCHE (libretto and lyrics) and Jerome Moross (music) wrote a dazzling score that incorporated soft-shoe, romantic ballads, ragtime and spoofs of period songs. "Lazy Afternoon" enjoyed some popularity but all of the musical sequences were impeccable: "It's the Going Home Together," "Doomed, Doomed, Doomed," "My Love Is on the Way," "Windflowers" and "By Goona-Goona Lagoon." STEPHEN DOUGLASS as Ulysses and KAYE BALLARD as Helen led the amiable cast and HANYA HOLM came up with the inventive choreography. *The Golden Apple* opened Off Broadway, received rave reviews and did sellout business. The producers moved the musical to a Broadway house where it inexplicably ran only 125 performances and lost its investment.

GOLDEN BOY (1964) was a powerful musical play based on Clifford Odets' 1937 boxing drama of the same name. The story was modernized and shifted to Harlem in order to make the piece more relevant and Odets himself worked on the libretto before his death in 1963. Willian Gibson completed the script, and although uneven at best, it had some gripping sequences. CHARLES STROUSE and LEE ADAMS wrote their most atypical but potent score for *Golden Boy* and with SAMMY DAVIS, JR., as the eager then disillusioned young boxer, the production's fine qualities outweighed its drawbacks. Arthur Penn directed a cast that also included Paula Wayne, Billy Daniels, Kenneth Tobey and Louis Gossett. Donald McKayle provided the stunning dances that included a choreographed boxing match finale. "Night Song," "Lorna's Here," "This Is the Life," "I Want to Be with You" and "Don't Forget 127th Street" were highlights from the score that still seems fresh today. (569 performances)

GOOD NEWS! (1927) was the best book musical by the talented team of DESYLVA, BROWN and HENDERSON and one of the most popular shows of the 1920s. Laurence Schwab and B. G. DeSylva's libretto is set at Tait College, where everyone dances the Varsity Drag. As in most collegiate musicals, the plot revolves around football and whether or not the good-hearted hero can pass his astronomy exam and be allowed to play in the big game. *Good News!* was packed with zany characters, high-kicking dances and all around exuberance but it was the score that was most responsible for its 551 performance run. Five standards came from the show: "Just Imagine," "The Best Things in Life Are Free," "Lucky in Love," "The Varsity Drag" and the title song. *Good News!* is one of the few 1920s musical comedies that still holds up well today.

GOODSPEED OPERA HOUSE, an intimate, historical theatre in East Haddam, Connecticut, has been the source of a handful of Broadway musicals, most notably *MAN OF LA MANCHA* (1965), *SHENANDOAH* (1975) and *ANNIE* (1977). The Goodspeed has also revived many American musicals from the past, successful and not, and allowed them serious reconsideration.

MAX GORDON (1892–1978), the colorful producer of hit comedies and musicals in the 1930s, presented such fondly remembered Broadway revues as *THREE'S A CROWD* (1930), *THE BAND WAGON* (1931) and *FLYING COLORS* (1932). Other Gordon-produced musicals include *THE CAT AND THE FIDDLE* (1931), *ROBERTA* (1933), *The Great Waltz* (1934), *JUBILEE* (1935), *VERY WARM FOR MAY* (1939) and *Park Avenue* (1946).

ELLIOTT GOULD (1938–), the familiar film actor, started his career in Broadway musicals where he was featured in *Say, Darling* (1958), *IRMA LA DOUCE* (1960), *I CAN GET IT FOR YOU WHOLESALE* (1962) and *Drat! The Cat!* (1965).

ROBERT GOULET (1933–), the full-voiced singer who appears in nightclubs and makes many recordings, created two memorable roles on Broadway: Sir Lancelot in *CAMELOT* (1960) and the photographer Jacques Bonnard in *THE HAPPY TIME* (1968).

RANDY GRAFF (1955–), an actress-singer who made her Broadway debut in the short-lived *Savara* (1979), originated the role of Fantine in the New York production of *LES MISÉRABLES* (1987) and played the double role of Oolie/Donna in *CITY OF ANGELS* (1989).

GRAND HOTEL (1989) was much more than a musicalization of the familiar soap opera tale, for it eschewed a traditional, linear narrative for a bold, episodic approach to recreating the various levels of society in 1928 Berlin. Luther Davis wrote the libretto and ROBERT WRIGHT and GEORGE FORREST provided the songs, some of which came from a musical version of Vicki

Baum's novel that they had attempted back in 1958. In preparation for Broadway, *Grand Hotel* went through drastic changes and MAURY YESTON was brought in to write additional music and lyrics. But it was the artistic vision and creative staging of director-choreographer TOMMY TUNE that turned the old story into a dynamic theatrical tour de force. The plot still followed the fate of various characters who have checked into the plush Grand Hotel: a dashing thief known as the Baron, a famous prima ballerina in decline, a desperate business tycoon, an ambitious stenographer, a terminally ill clerk out on a last spree and so on. In TONY WALTON's impressionistic set, the hotel was suggested by decorative details and dozens of chairs that Tune arranged in various visual patterns to convey different locales. DAVID CARROLL and LILIANE MONTEVECCHI played the Baron and the ballerina in a love affair that was both passionate and distant. Other noteworthy players in the ensemble included Michael Jeeter, Jane Krakowski, KAREN AKERS and Timothy Jerome. The score contained several extended musical sequences but some individual songs that stood out were "Maybe My Baby Loves Me," "Who Couldn't Dance with You?" "Love Can't Happen," "Bonjour, Amour" and "We'll Take a Glass Together." (1,077 performances)

THE GRAND TOUR (1979) had an unlikely subject for a musical, Franz Werfel's comedy about anti-Semitism called *Jacobowsky and the Colonel*, but it did boast a fine score by JERRY HERMAN and strong performances by JOEL GREY and RONALD HOLGATE. MICHAEL STEWART and Mark Bramble wrote the libretto about a Jewish refugee who befriends a Polish colonel in 1940 France and much of it was very affecting. But *The Grand Tour* got mixed reviews in a theatre climate where only raves would do and the show closed after sixty-one performances.

MICKI GRANT, the black composer-lyricist who began her career performing, often appeared in her own works. Grant was born in Chicago and educated at the University of Illinois, Roosevelt University and De Paul University. She made her New York acting debut in 1962 and appeared in several Off-Broadway plays. In 1970 Grant formed a partnership with producer Vinnette Carroll and they presented a series of musical revues for the Urban Arts Corps. The most famous of these was *DON'T BOTHER ME, I CAN'T COPE* (1971), which moved to Broadway in 1972. Grant contributed to the scores of nine other musicals in the 1970s, most notably *Your Arms Too Short to Box with God* (1976), *WORKING* (1978), *Eubie* (1979) and *It's So Nice to Be Civilized* (1979). Grant's lyrics deal with the role of individuals, women in particular, within society at large and her music is often exultant and appealing.

THE GRASS HARP (1971) was an offbeat little musical that only lasted on Broadway for seven performances, but because of its delectable score, it keeps popping up from time to time. Based on Truman Capote's novella of the same name, the story tells of an eccentric spinster named Dolly who escapes from the real world and moves into a treehouse when her sister Verena attempts to sell Dolly's dropsy cure on the commercial market. Also involved in the tale is their lusty cousin Collin, their housekeeper Catherine and a traveling evangelist named Babylove. Kenward Elmsie adapted the book for the musical stage and provided the lyrics for Claibe Richardson's music. Although the libretto did not capture Capote's wry humor, the songs did and the score was filled with superb numbers: "Marry with Me," "Yellow Drum," "Floozies," "Chain of Love" and a jubilant song sequence called "The Babylove Miracle Show." BARBARA COOK was splendid in the role of Dolly, as were Ruth Ford as Verena, Karen Morrow as Babylove, CAROL BRICE as Catherine and RUSS THACKER as Collin. Despite its short run, *The Grass Harp* was later seen Off Broadway, in regional theatre and in a condensed version on network television.

DOLORES GRAY (1924–   ), a brash and talented singer-actress on Broadway and in London, never got the right kind of vehicle to launch her to stardom but she always got enthusiastic reviews. Gray made her Broadway debut in *Seven Lively Arts* (1944) and appeared in *Are You with It?* (1945) but her big break came playing Annie Oakley in the West End production of *ANNIE GET YOUR GUN* in 1947. Her Broadway credits include the musical revue *TWO ON THE AISLE* (1951), the short-lived *Carnival in Flanders* (1953), the delectable Frenchie in *DESTRY RIDES AGAIN* (1959) and the predatory actress Lorraine Sheldon in *Sherry!* (1967).

GREASE (1972), the phenomenally popular "fifties" musical, began Off Broadway but audience demand moved it to Broadway, where it stayed for 3,388 performances, the longest running musical at the time. Jim Jacobs and Warren Casey wrote the book, music and lyrics for the show that captured the sounds, attitudes and vernacular of the "greaser" era. The slight plot is set in Rydell High in Chicago where a class reunion sparks memories of the good old days. Danny (BARRY BOSTWICK) loves the virtuous Sandy (Carole Demas) but is attracted to the more worldly Betty Rizzo (Adrienne Barbeau). The songs were mostly parodies of 1950s pop but "Alone at a Drive-In Movie" and "There Are Worse Things I Could Do" were commendable character numbers. *Grease* continues to be one of the most produced musicals for schools and amateur groups.

ADOLPH GREEN (1915–   ) has written librettos and lyrics with his partner BETTY COMDEN for over fifty years, the longest collaboration in the American theatre. Green was born in the Bronx and attended New York University where he met Comden. Their dream was to become musical comedy performers and they started writing songs in order to come up with new performance material. After providing lyrics for various supper clubs and

revues, the team appeared on Broadway in *ON THE TOWN* (1944) as performers and authors of the book and lyrics for LEONARD BERNSTEIN's music.
When their next show, *Billion Dollar Baby* (1945), failed to run, the team went
out to Hollywood. Over the years they would write the scripts for several movie
musicals, most memorably *Singin' in the Rain* (1952). Back in New York they
worked with composer JULE STYNE for the first time on the musical revue
TWO ON THE AISLE (1951). Reunited with Bernstein for *WONDERFUL
TOWN* (1953), Comden and Green wrote what is arguably their finest set of
lyrics. The team then collaborated with Styne on seven more musicals: *PETER
PAN* (1954) in which they wrote about half of the score, *BELLS ARE RINGING*
(1956), *Say, Darling* (1958), *DO RE MI* (1960), *SUBWAYS ARE FOR SLEEP-
ING* (1961), *FADE IN–FADE OUT* (1964) and *HALLELUJAH, BABY!* (1967).
They wrote the libretto for the popular LAUREN BACALL vehicle *AP-
PLAUSE* (1970) and supplied some new lyrics for the CAROL CHANNING
vehicle *Lorelei* (1974). In 1978 Comden and Green wrote a vivacious libretto
and lyrics for *ON THE TWENTIETH CENTURY* with composer CY COLE-
MAN but it failed to find an audience. *A Doll's Life* (1982), the team's musical
about what happened to Ibsen's heroine Nora after the events of *A Doll's House*,
was an intriguing project with music by Larry Grossman but it quickly closed.
With their lyrics for Coleman's music in *THE WILL ROGERS FOLLIES*
(1991), the team once again had a hit on Broadway. Comden and Green are not
the most innovative of musical theatre writers but they are masters at joyous
musical comedy and unpretentious fun.

ELLEN GREENE, an unconventional leading lady in Off-Broadway musicals,
played Jenny in the 1976 Lincoln Center revival of *THE THREEPENNY
OPERA* and the dizzy Audrey in *LITTLE SHOP OF HORRORS* (1982). Greene
was also featured in the sci-fi musical *Weird Romance* (1992).

GREENWICH VILLAGE FOLLIES (1919–1928) was one of the revue rivals of
the *ZIEGFELD FOLLIES* and a fairly competent rival at that. JOHN MURRAY
ANDERSON, in his professional debut, directed the first edition in 1919 at the
Greenwich Village Theatre downtown and it was popular enough to move
uptown. Annual editions followed and, despite the series' title, all were
eventually seen on Broadway. Although not as elaborate as Ziegfeld's shows,
the *Greenwich Village Follies* boasted clever sketches, popular orchestras,
celebrated female impersonators and high-class ballet versions of famous
literary works.

GREENWILLOW (1960) was FRANK LOESSER's only unsuccessful Broadway musical yet it is a charming and underrated work with a superb score.
Samuel Lesser and Loesser co-authored the atmospheric libretto, based on B.
J. Chute's novel, about a young man from a sleepy town called Greenwillow
who fears falling in love because of a family superstition that he is cursed to

wander. The musical was decidedly uncommercial and too slight for most tastes but *Greenwillow* had a lovely score that captured the spirit of rural America with its customs and simple pleasures. Anthony Perkins gave a delicate and winning performance as the young hero and he was ably supported by PERT KELTON, Cecil Kelloway and Ellen McCown. "Faraway Boy," "The Music of Home," "Summertime Love" and "Never Will I Marry" were some of the perceptive and enjoyable numbers in the Loesser score. (95 performances)

CHARLOTTE GREENWOOD (1893–1978) was a leggy dancer-comedienne who appeared in several films and had an on- and off-Broadway musical career that lasted nearly fifty years. Greenwood started in vaudeville and then made her Broadway debut in 1905 in *The White Cat*. She went on to appear in some two dozen forgettable musicals up until the 1930s. In 1950 she returned to Broadway to play the goddess Juno in *Out of This World*.

CLIFFORD GREY (1887–1941), the British lyricist-librettist who wrote many shows on both sides of the Atlantic, collaborated with the top composers of his day, including JEROME KERN, RUDOLF FRIML, Ivor Novello, GEORGE GERSHWIN, VINCENT YOUMANS and SIGMUND ROMBERG. His best-remembered Broadway musicals are *SALLY* (1920), *HIT THE DECK!* (1927), *THE THREE MUSKETEERS* (1928) and editions of *Artists and Models* in 1924 and 1925.

JOEL GREY (1932–) is a spry singer-dancer-actor whose small stature makes him ideal for unusual roles but keeps him from becoming a conventional leading man. Grey made his musical debut in *The Littlest Revue* (1956) but didn't achieve recognition until his brilliant performance as the Master of Ceremonies in *CABARET* (1966), a role he reprised on Broadway in 1987. His other outstanding credit was as GEORGE M. COHAN in *GEORGE M!* (1968). Grey also played King Charles VI of France in *Goodtime Charley* (1975) and the Jewish refugee Jacobowski in *THE GRAND TOUR* (1979).

ROBERT GRIFFITH (1907–1961) was HAROLD PRINCE's producing partner from 1953 until his death in 1961. The celebrated Prince–Griffith musicals were *THE PAJAMA GAME* (1954), *DAMN YANKEES* (1955), *NEW GIRL IN TOWN* (1957), *WEST SIDE STORY* (1957), *FIORELLO!* (1959) and *TENDERLOIN* (1960).

TAMMY GRIMES (1934–), the fuzzy-voiced actress-singer who has done dramas, musicals, drawing room comedies and the classics, is mostly remembered by Broadway musical audiences for her performance as the indomitable heroine in *THE UNSINKABLE MOLLY BROWN* (1960). Her other musical credits include *The Littlest Revue* (1956), the ghostly Elvira in *High Spirits* (1964) and the temperamental star Dorothy Brock in *42ND STREET* (1980).

HARRY GROENER (1951–), a singer-actor-dancer on Broadway since his debut as Will Parker in the 1979 revival of *OKLAHOMA!*, originated the role of Munkustrap in the New York production of *CATS* (1982) and the happy-go-lucky Bobby Child in *CRAZY FOR YOU* (1992). Groener's other musical credits include *Oh, Brother!* (1981), *Is There Life after High School?* (1982) and *Harrigan 'n Hart* (1985).

HARRY GUARDINO (1925–), a leading man in several plays on Broadway, played the psychiatrist Hapgood in *ANYONE CAN WHISTLE* (1964) and the cartoonist Sam Craig in *WOMAN OF THE YEAR* (1981).

BOB GUNTON (1945–), a singer-actor who appeared in the Broadway musicals *Happy End* (1977), *WORKING* (1978), *King of Hearts* (1978), *Roza* (1987) and others, is most remembered as Juan Peron in the New York production of *EVITA* (1979) and the rascally King in *BIG RIVER* (1985).

GUYS AND DOLLS (1950) is perhaps the most durable of all musical comedies. It is so tightly written, has such vibrant characters and the score is so expert that the show never fails to please regardless of who is presenting it. Producers CY FEUER and ERNEST MARTIN had the idea of turning some of Damon Runyon's stories into a musical and hired FRANK LOESSER to score it and Jo Swerling to write the libretto. Not pleased with the script, the producers called in several other librettists to work on it but it was ABE BURROWS, starting from scratch, that captured Runyon's slick but affectionate style in one of the American theatre's best musical comedy librettos. The two love stories in *Guys and Dolls* are equally interesting, a rarity in the RODGERS and HAMMERSTEIN model. Gambler Sky Masterson (Robert Alda) falls for the Salvation Army-type reformer Sarah Brown (Isabel Bigley) that he takes out on a date only to win a bet. Nightclub singer Adelaide (VIVIAN BLAINE) has been engaged to bookie Nathan Detroit (SAM LEVENE) for fourteen years, causing her to have a psychosomatic cold that has lasted just as long. Both couples are brought to the altar in the end but not until horseplayer Nicely-Nicely Johnson (STUBBY KAYE) sings a rousing "Sit Down, You're Rocking the Boat" at the Save-a-Soul Mission. Other outstanding songs in the Loesser score include "My Time of Day," "Adelaide's Lament," "Fugue for Tinhorns," "If I Were a Bell," "I've Never Been in Love Before," "Luck Be a Lady" and the title song. GEORGE S. KAUFMAN directed the superior cast and MICHAEL KIDD provided the sparkling choreography that included the "Runyonland" opening, which cleverly depicted the sweetly sinful lowlife of Times Square. The original production ran for 1,200 performances and there have been two notable Broadway revivals: an all-black production in 1976 with James Randolph, Norma Donaldson, Robert Guillaume and ERNESTINE JACKSON and a 1992 production directed by JERRY ZAKS that featured Peter Gallagher, FAITH PRINCE, Nathan Lane and Josie de Guzman. *Guys and Dolls* is an enduring classic in which Loesser and Burrows created a fabled New York City that never was, peopled with characters who could never be. Musical theatre was the ideal medium to capture such a dream existence and *Guys and Dolls* remains the finest example of the idyllic musical comedy.

GYPSY (1959) is one of the American musical theatre's greatest achievements with a story, characters, songs and a theatricality that have rarely been equalled. *Gypsy* is a show business biography but its focus goes far beyond the usual backstage tale. ARTHUR LAURENTS, adapting GYPSY ROSE LEE's autobiography for the stage, came up with one of the musical theatre's finest librettos. Instead of simply telling the story of Lee's rise to stardom, Laurents wrote an episodic "fable" with Lee's mother, Rose, as the central figure. Seen through the eyes of this brash, even unpleasant stage mother, the show took on a gritty yet amusing quality that few musicals have. Rose leaves the quiet life in Seattle and tours the country, pushing her two daughters into vaudeville. When the talented June elopes and abandons the act, Rose concentrates on the performance-shy Louise. As vaudeville slowly dies, Rose grabs onto burlesque in a final desperate attempt to make Louise a star. Ironically, she succeeds but Rose is still left frustrated, a woman whose dreams are too big for this small world. JULE STYNE (music) and STEPHEN SONDHEIM (lyrics) provided a score that echoed the hilarity and heartbreak of the libretto: "Some People," "Little Lamb," "Together," "You Gotta Have a Gimmick," "Small World," "Let Me Entertain You," "Everything's Coming Up Roses," "If Momma Was Married" and "Rose's Turn," the last a devastating stream-of-consciousness musical soliloquy that is one of the theatre's unforgettable tour de forces. ETHEL MERMAN's Rose revealed a complexity and power never before seen in her many topflight performances. Also in the strong cast were Jack Klugman, Sandra Church, Lane Bradbury and MARIA KARNILOVA. JEROME ROBBINS directed and choreographed the musical, which ran 702 performances. *Gypsy* has remained popular with revivals in New York and across the country. ANGELA LANSBURY gave a masterful interpretation of Rose in London and in the 1974 Broadway revival and Tyne Daly scored a truimph in the role in 1989.

H

JONATHAN HADARY (1948–), a character actor seen in musicals and plays on and off Broadway, played Herbie in the 1989 revival of *GYPSY* and the religious fanatic Charles Guiteau in *ASSASSINS* (1990). Hadary's other musicals include *God Bless You, Mr. Rosewater* (1979), *Scrambled Feet* (1981) and *Weird Romance* (1992).

HAIR (1968) was an important musical landmark because it brought rock music and a counter culture sensibility to Broadway and, for a time at least, opened up new possibilities for the musical theatre. The almost-plotless show originated Off Broadway in 1967, played at a nightclub for a while, then was remounted as a full-scale Broadway production. TOM O'HORGAN gave the piece a colorful, grandiose staging that ran 1,750 performances but most agreed that the smaller Off-Broadway production was more coherent and effective. Gerome Ragni and James Rado wrote the book and lyrics that followed a group of flower children in contemporary New York City. GALT MACDERMOT provided the vibrant music that used pop, rock and traditional ballad forms. "Good Morning Starshine," "Aquarius," "Easy to Be Hard" and "Let the Sunshine In" all became hits on the charts but there was also commendable work in "Frank Mills," "Where Do I Go?" "Ain't Got No" and other songs. The energetic cast included Ragni and Rado as well as Lynn Kellogg, Steve Curry, Sally Eaton, MELBA MOORE, Lamont Washington and Diane Keaton. The brief nude scene at the end of Act I was a first for musicals and gave the show a provocative reputation that only enhanced business. *Hair*'s superior score still holds up today while much of the rest quickly dated itself. (A 1977

Broadway revival lasted only a month.) But the effect that *Hair* had on breaking barriers and celebrating the pure theatricality of musicals cannot be dismissed.

JACK HALEY (1902–1979), a vaudeville singer who was featured in many films, appeared on Broadway in eight musicals, most notably *FOLLOW THRU* (1929), *TAKE A CHANCE* (1932), *Higher and Higher* (1940) and *INSIDE U.S.A.* (1948).

HALF A SIXPENCE (1965) was a successful BRITISH IMPORT that featured its West End star, Tommy Steele, for whom the musical was written. Beverly Cross adapted H. G. Wells' novel *Kipps* and the predictable rags-to-riches story played well on the musical stage. Arthur Kipps, a working-class lad in Folkstone, is in love with the honest working girl Ann but when he inherits a fortune he is drawn to the wealthy Helen. Later, because of a business bust, Kipps loses most of his money and settles down to a life as a bookseller with Ann as his wife. The score by David Heneker was tuneful and lively, with "Money to Burn," "If the Rain's Got to Fall" and the title song as the show's standouts. (512 performances)

ADELAIDE HALL (1895–   ), a powerful black singer who had a successful nightclub career in America and England, appeared in a handful of musicals on Broadway and the West End. Hall made her Broadway debut as a member of the chorus of *SHUFFLE ALONG* (1921) and came into prominence in *BLACKBIRDS OF 1928*, where she introduced "I Can't Give You Anything but Love." Her last Broadway role was Grandma Obeah in *JAMAICA* (1957).

BETTINA HALL (1906–   ), a leading lady of Broadway musicals in the 1930s, played ingenues Shirley Sheridan in *THE CAT AND THE FIDDLE* (1931) and Hope Harcourt in *ANYTHING GOES* (1934).

JUANITA HALL (1901–1968) was a distinctive singer-character actress who was very effective playing various ethnic characters, most memorably Bloody Mary in *SOUTH PACIFIC* (1949). Hall started out on Broadway in the singing chorus of *Sing Out, Sweet Land* (1944), the 1946 revival of *SHOW BOAT* and in *STREET SCENE* (1947). Her character roles included Leah in *ST. LOUIS WOMAN* (1946), the enterprising Madame Tango in *HOUSE OF FLOWERS* (1954) and the meddling Madam Liang in *FLOWER DRUM SONG* (1958).

HALLELUJAH, BABY! (1967) was an ambitious attempt to capture sixty years of black culture in an episodic musical in which the major characters didn't age from decade to decade. ARTHUR LAURENTS wrote the original libretto, which had its bright moments but too often wavered between earnest social commentary and brassy Broadway entertainment. LESLIE UGGAMS played Georgina, who moves from a ghetto dweller to a jazz singer to a civil rights worker, and she was given some agreeable songs to sing by JULE STYNE (music) and BETTY COMDEN and ADOLPH GREEN (lyrics): "My Own

Morning," "Feet Do Yo' Stuff" and "Now's the Time." *Hallelujah, Baby!* was adventurous and occasionally satisfying but not quite up to the challenging task it set for itself. (293 performances)

MARVIN HAMLISCH (1944–), the popular composer who has written music for everything from films to Las Vegas acts to television, has contributed to only a few Broadway musicals but has found tremendous success there, especially with *A CHORUS LINE*. Hamlisch was born in New York and demonstrated such remarkable musical ability that he studied at Juilliard when he was only seven years old. As a teenager he was writing and selling pop songs and soon was arranging vocal and dance music for Broadway shows such as *FUNNY GIRL* (1964) and *Henry, Sweet Henry* (1967). After graduating from Queens College he found himself scoring movies in Hollywood and had collected three Academy Awards when MICHAEL BENNETT asked Hamlisch to score his experimental Off-Broadway musical about a dancing audition. *A Chorus Line* opened at the Public Theatre in 1975 and moved to Broadway later that year and stayed for fourteen years. Hamlisch collaborated with lyricist Carole Bayer Sager on the NEIL SIMON-scripted *THEY'RE PLAYING OUR SONG* (1979) and it was also a popular hit. *Smile* (1982), the musical Hamlisch wrote with lyricist-librettist HOWARD ASHMAN, had much to recommend but it never quite came together and soon closed. Hamlisch's London musical *Jean* (1983) closed before coming to Broadway. Much of Hamlisch's work may sound more pop than Broadway but it has a vitality and sense of melody that the musical theatre surely needs.

ARTHUR HAMMERSTEIN (1872–1955), the successful producer of Broadway operettas, was the uncle of OSCAR HAMMERSTEIN II. The elder Hammerstein produced his nephew's first musical effort, *Always You* (1920), as well as other early shows written with collaborator OTTO HARBACH. Arthur Hammerstein's most memorable musicals included *THE FIREFLY* (1912), *Tickle Me* (1920), *Wildflower* (1923), *ROSE-MARIE* (1924), *Song of the Flame* (1925) and *SWEET ADELINE* (1929).

OSCAR HAMMERSTEIN II (1895–1960) was the most influential lyricist-librettist in the American musical theatre. During a Broadway career of forty-one years he played a major role in the development of American operetta, musical comedy and the musical play. Hammerstein was born in New York City to a notable theatrical family. His grandfather and namesake was the most colorful and innovative opera impressario of his day. His father, William, was a theatre manager and his uncle, Arthur, was a celebrated Broadway producer. Hammerstein entered Columbia College in 1912 to study law but he left school to work as a stage manager for his uncle's productions. His dream was to write for the theatre, and after a non-musical play of his folded out of town, he teamed up with composer Herbert Stothart to write musicals. They had a few Broadway shows to their credit when the two collaborators were joined by veteran OTTO HARBACH for *Tickle Me* (1920). Harbach became Hammerstein's mentor and taught him about lyric structure and the possibility of an integrated musical play. The two men attempted these ideas in VINCENT YOUMANS' *Wildflower* (1923) but it was in the operetta *ROSE-MARIE* (1924), with music by RUDOLF FRIML, and *THE DESERT SONG* (1926), with music by SIGMUND ROMBERG, that they were able to successfully integrate song and story together. With *SHOW BOAT* (1927) Hammerstein was able to take Harbach's ideas and write the first musical play. JEROME KERN's music and Hammerstein's libretto and lyrics blended together in a way not yet seen on Broadway. Hammerstein contributed to other hits in the 1920s, such as *SUNNY* (1925), *THE NEW MOON* (1928) and *SWEET ADELINE* (1929), but his career declined during the Depression when operettas fell out of favor. *MUSIC IN THE AIR* (1932) and *May Wine* (1935), his only profitable shows in the 1930s, were throwbacks to earlier days and were far from innovative. With Kern out in Hollywood, Hammerstein needed a collaborator who was willing to attempt bolder projects. He found such a partner in composer RICHARD RODGERS, and with *OKLAHOMA!* (1943) the new team began a series of musical plays that brought together powerful drama, lyrical scores and vivid characters. *CAROUSEL* (1945), with arguably their finest score, the experimental *ALLEGRO* (1947), *SOUTH PACIFIC* (1949) and *THE KING AND I* (1951) revealed Rodgers and Hammerstein at their peak. The unsuccessful musicals *ME AND JULIET* (1953) and *PIPE DREAM* (1955) were followed by their moderate success *FLOWER DRUM SONG* (1958). Hammerstein had written the librettos as well as the lyrics for all his shows but illness made him turn over the book writing duties for *THE SOUND OF MUSIC* (1959) to HOWARD LINDSAY and RUSSEL CROUSE. Hammerstein died soon after the musical opened, and for the first time in history, every light on Broadway and in London's West End was blacked out in tribute. Throughout his career Hammerstein also directed his musicals on occasion and, with Rodgers, co-produced musicals and plays. Hammerstein even experimented with opera, writing the libretto–lyrics for *CARMEN JONES* (1943), the all-black adaptation of Bizet's work. In addition to his achievements in libretto writing, Hammerstein was a master at simple, heart-felt lyrics that emphasized character rather than cleverness or sophistication.

CAROL HANEY (1924–1964), a vivacious dancer-turned-choreographer, is mostly remembered for her sexy and sassy secretary Gladys in *THE PAJAMA GAME* (1954). Haney then went on to become a first-rate choreographer, doing the dances for *FLOWER DRUM SONG* (1958), *SHE LOVES ME* (1963), *FUNNY GIRL* (1964) and other shows before her untimely death.

THE HAPPY TIME (1968) was a domestic musical play about a French-Canadian family and the pains of growing up. N. Richard Nash adapted Samuel

Taylor's 1950 play of the same name and JOHN KANDER and FRED EBB provided a gentle, truthful score. The material was fragile and low-key but GOWER CHAMPION directed the piece like a circus attraction and added slides, projections and filmed sequences. Consequently, the show seemed hollow and audiences lost interest in the characters. ROBERT GOULET was splendid as the black sheep of the family who returns to his hometown and mesmerizes his young nephew Bibi (MICHAEL RUPERT). Also in the cast were DAVID WAYNE as the family patriarch, Charles Durning, Julie Gregg and GEORGE S. IRVING. The Kander and Ebb score had several praiseworthy songs—"Tomorrow Morning," "I Don't Remember You," "Seeing Things," "The Life of the Party" and the lyrical title song—but they got buried in the misconceived production. (286 performances)

OTTO HARBACH (1873–1963), the prodigious lyricist-librettist not widely known today, was largely responsible for bringing respectability to lyricwriting and for pioneering the integrated musical play. Harbach was born in Salt Lake City and studied to become an English teacher. He taught at Whitman College in the state of Washington until 1901 when he moved to New York to pursue graduate work at Columbia. When his money ran out, he left school and started writing for small newspapers and, eventually, the theatre. Harbach's first collaborator was the composer KARL HOSCHNA and together they wrote six musicals, most memorably *Three Twins* (1908) and *MADAME SHERRY* (1910). After Hoschna's untimely death at the age of thirty-four, Harbach collaborated with RUDOLF FRIML on ten operettas over the years, starting with *THE FIREFLY* (1912). Other composers that he worked with during his long career included Louis Hirsch, SIGMUND ROMBERG, JEROME KERN, Herbert Stothart, GEORGE GERSHWIN and VINCENT YOUMANS. In 1920 Harbach teamed with the young OSCAR HAMMERSTEIN II for the first time and their collaboration as fellow lyricist-librettists would influence the direction of the musical play on Broadway. Both men believed that story and song should be more closely integrated and in their succeeding operettas and musicals they sought to create a true musical play. *Wildflower* (1923), with Youmans' music, was a first try but *ROSE-MARIE* (1924), with music by Friml, and *THE DESERT SONG* (1936), with music by Romberg, were more successful attempts to integrate the operetta form. Meanwhile Harbach contributed to several musical comedy hits in the 1920s: *MARY* (1920), *NO, NO, NANETTE* (1925), *SUNNY* (1925), *Criss-Cross* (1926) and others. His last two Broadway successes were *THE CAT AND THE FIDDLE* (1931) and *ROBERTA* (1932), both with Kern. Harbach's twenty-five years of success finished when the Depression gradually ended operetta and Harbach's lyricwriting was considered old-fashioned. More than any other writer of musicals before him, Harbach sought for strong story structure, songs that continued plot and character, and lyrics that were polished and refined. It was Hammerstein who would later carry these ideas to fruition but Harbach was the man who first saw the possibilities for a more substantial kind of musical theatre.

E. Y. HARBURG (1898–1981), the lyricist-librettist who consistently tackled experimental and controversial ideas in his musicals, was the American musical theatre's master of fantasy, satire and passionate dreams. Harburg was born of poor Russian immigrant parents on Manhattan's East Side and held various jobs as a young boy. He started writing light verse as a high school student and, using the pen name Yip, he sold some of his work to local newspapers. Harburg worked for an electrical supply business but hated it; when the 1929 crash destroyed the firm, he gladly devoted all his time to writing. His first collaborator was composer Jay Gorney and some of their songs were interpolated into *Earl Carroll's Sketch Book* (1929) and *Americana* (1932), in which their song "Brother, Can You Spare a Dime?" first appeared and became one of the most popular songs of the Depression. Harburg also worked with composer VERNON DUKE on the book musical *Walk a Little Faster* (1932) and the *ZIEGFELD FOLLIES* (1934); and with HAROLD ARLEN on *LIFE BEGINS AT 8:40* (1934) and *HOORAY FOR WHAT!* (1937), the last an experimental satire about an inventor who tries to end all wars with laughing gas. Harburg had also been writing songs for Hollywood since 1929 and in 1939 he and Arlen scored their best film, *The Wizard of Oz*. Back on Broadway, Harburg collaborated with BURTON LANE for the first time on *Hold On to Your Hats* (1940), a satire on radio westerns. With Arlen he wrote *BLOOMER GIRL* (1944), a slice of Americana that dealt with women's rights and slavery. Harburg's most famous musical was *FINIAN'S RAINBOW* (1947) with Lane providing the music for this puckish fantasy that has one of the finest scores in the American theatre. With composer SAMMY FAIN, Harburg wrote *FLAHOOLEY* (1951), an outrageous satire on big business and modern consumerism. *JAMAICA* (1957), a sly musical set in the Caribbean with music by Arlen, boasted a strong score. Harburg's last two Broadway shows—*The Happiest Girl in the World* (1961), using Offenbach music, and *Darling of the Day* (1968) with JULE STYNE music—were not successful and he retired. Harburg was a socially conscious lyricist who used light-hearted musical comedy to write about uncomfortable issues. Few lyricists could be so provocative and, at the same time, so charming.

SHELDON HARNICK (1924–) is one of the American theatre's finest character lyricists, and with his composer-collaborator JERRY BOCK, he has given Broadway a handful of memorable musicals. Harnick was born in Chicago and studied violin as a child, later making his living as a violinist for local orchestras. He wrote both music and lyrics for college shows as a student at Northwestern and for the USO while in the Army. In 1950 he moved to New York and soon his songs were appearing in *NEW FACES OF 1952* and *John Murray Anderson's Almanac* (1953). At the suggestion of E. Y. HARBURG,

Harnick decided to concentrate on lyricwriting only and looked for a collaborator. He met Bock in 1956 and in 1958 their first Broadway musical, *The Body Beautiful*, had a short run. The team's next effort, *FIORELLO!* (1959), brought them fame and a Pulitzer Prize. *TENDERLOIN* (1960) was an exceptional piece about "little old New York" but it only had a modest run, as did their enchanting *SHE LOVES ME* (1963). The team's *FIDDLER ON THE ROOF* (1964), their greatest hit and one of Broadway's most beloved musicals, was a masterwork of restraint: comedy, pathos, ethnic folklore and simple dignity all came together beautifully. *THE APPLE TREE* (1966) was an amusing but forgettable musical that did not show Bock and Harnick at their best. Their *THE ROTHSCHILDS* (1970) had moments of power but its Jewish saga suffered in comparison to *Fiddler on the Roof*. The team broke up in 1970 and Harnick's career since has been sporadic. He provided excellent lyrics for RICHARD RODGERS' short-lived *Rex* (1976), English lyrics for Michel Legrand's *The Umbrellas of Cherbourg* (1979), a new translation for the Peter Brook production of *Carmen* (1983), some librettos for opera and a musical version of *It's a Wonderful Life*, which was presented regionally in 1991. Harnick is an expert craftsman with a highly poetic sense of character. He is more subtle and gentle than most Broadway lyricists but his words are uncompromising and powerful.

EDWARD HARRIGAN (1844–1911) wrote, directed, produced and appeared in a series of musical comedies with his acting partner TONY HART between 1878 and 1885. Their most memorable efforts were the *MULLIGAN GUARD MUSICALS* (1878–1880), seven knockdown musical farces about brawling immigrants in the slums of New York. Perhaps Harrigan's finest musical comedy was *Cordelia's Aspirations* (1883), written after the *Mulligan Guard* shows but utilizing some of the same characters. Harrigan was a versatile comic actor who played a variety of broad ethnic types but he often found a touching, sympathetic note in each of his characterizations. He appeared in musicals up until 1893. The lives and works of the famous team were the subject of the unsuccessful 1985 musical *Harrigan 'n Hart*.

BARBARA HARRIS (1937–   ), the atypical leading lady of films, stage and television, created the role of super-psychic Daisy Gamble in *ON A CLEAR DAY YOU CAN SEE FOREVER* (1965) and received plaudits for her three diverse characterizations in the musical *THE APPLE TREE* (1966).

SAM HARRIS (1872–1941) produced Broadway musicals by the top songwriters of the American theatre, from GEORGE M. COHAN to IRVING BERLIN to the GERSHWINS to KURT WEILL. Harris started as Cohan's business partner and together they produced eighteen musicals on Broadway, including *LITTLE JOHNNY JONES* (1904), *GEORGE WASHINGTON, JR.* (1906), *The Man Who Owns Broadway* (1909) and the two *Cohan Revues* (1916 and 1917). Together with Berlin, Harris presented the *MUSIC BOX REVUES* (1921–1924) as well as Berlin's *THE COCOANUTS* (1925), *FACE THE MUSIC* (1931) and *AS THOUSANDS CHEER* (1933). Harris produced the Gershwins' *OF THEE I SING* (1931) and its sequel *LET 'EM EAT CAKE* (1933), COLE PORTER's *JUBILEE* (1935), RODGERS and HART's *I'D RATHER BE RIGHT* (1937) and Weill's *LADY IN THE DARK* (1941). Harris was one of the most respected and beloved producers of his day.

REX HARRISON (1908–1990), the distinguished British actor of modern and classical roles, made such an impact with his only musical role, Henry Higgins in *MY FAIR LADY* (1956), that the character is still identified with him. Harrison reprised Higgins in the London production in 1958, on film and in the 1979 Broadway revival.

LORENZ HART (1895–1943), the ingenious lyricist who worked with composer RICHARD RODGERS, is considered one of Broadway's most clever and agile songwriters. Hart was born in New York City and showed literary promise at a young age. After graduating from Columbia he made his living writing and translating. He collaborated on and off with various composers but it was not until he met Rodgers in 1918 that his lyricwriting talents emerged. Songs of theirs were interpolated into Broadway shows as early as 1918 but it was not until their full score for *THE GARRICK GAIETIES* (1925) that the team became popular. In the 1920s they scored a series of light-hearted musical comedies, many of which were written by librettist HERBERT FIELDS: *DEAREST ENEMY* (1926), *PEGGY-ANN* (1926), *A CONNECTICUT YANKEE* (1927), *Present Arms* (1928) and others. In the 1930s the team became more experimental and had great success with such unique musicals as *JUMBO* (1935), *ON YOUR TOES* (1936), *BABES IN ARMS* (1937), *I'D RATHER BE RIGHT* (1937), *I MARRIED AN ANGEL* (1938), *THE BOYS FROM SYRACUSE* (1938) and *TOO MANY GIRLS* (1939). Rodgers and Hart's finest creation was *PAL JOEY* (1940), a musical very much ahead of its time. Despite the team's success, Hart had a drinking problem and suffered severe depression in which he would disappear for days. The strain on the writing relationship got too great and in 1943 Rodgers moved on to a collaboration with OSCAR HAMMERSTEIN II. Hart did assist in the rewrites for the 1943 revival of *A Connecticut Yankee* then died a few days after its opening. Hart was a master of all kinds of songs, from comic ditties to bittersweet torch songs. His use of complex rhyme, highly original phrasing and acerbic wit have rarely been equaled.

MOSS HART (1904–1961) was half of the acclaimed playwriting team of Kaufman and Hart but he also wrote several musical librettos and revue sketches by himself and directed some of Broadway's landmark productions. Hart was born in New York and struggled with his writing career until he collaborated with GEORGE S. KAUFMAN on the comedy *Once in a Lifetime*

(1930). He wrote sketches for IRVING BERLIN's *AS THOUSANDS CHEER* (1933), the libretto for COLE PORTER's *JUBILEE* (1935) and with Kaufman co-wrote the book for *I'D RATHER BE RIGHT* (1937). Hart's libretto for *LADY IN THE DARK* (1941) was one of the most provocative of its time and he co-directed the show as well. His superb direction of *MY FAIR LADY* (1956) helped make that production the success it was. Hart's final Broadway credit was as director and co-producer of *CAMELOT* (1960).

TONY HART (1855–1891) was an inspired comic actor who appeared with his partner EDWARD HARRIGAN in a series of musical comedies in the late nineteenth century. Hart and his partner produced the popular *MULLIGAN GUARD* MUSICALS (1878–1880) and played a variety of characters in each edition. Hart's short stature and feminine face made him ideal for drag roles and he excelled at playing women of various ethnic types. One of his most memorable roles was Rebecca Allup, which he played in all the *Mulligan Guard* shows as well as in *Cordelia's Aspirations* (1883) and *Dan's Tribulations* (1884). Hart and his partner were the subject of the short-lived Broadway musical *Harrigan 'n Hart* (1985).

HAROLD HASTINGS (1917–1973), one of Broadway's most talented MUSIC DIRECTORS, arranged the music for many musicals produced by HAROLD PRINCE: *THE PAJAMA GAME* (1954), *DAMN YANKEES* (1955), *NEW GIRL IN TOWN* (1957), *FLORA, THE RED MENACE* (1965), *Baker Street* (1965), *CABARET* (1966), *COMPANY* (1970), *FOLLIES* (1971) and *A LITTLE NIGHT MUSIC* (1973).

JUNE HAVOC (1916–   ), an actress-singer in vaudeville as a child and later in Broadway musicals and plays, appeared in *Forbidden Melody* (1936), *PAL JOEY* (1940), *Sadie Thompson* (1944) and *MEXICAN HAYRIDE* (1944). She returned to Broadway as a replacement in *ANNIE* in 1982. Havoc is the sister of GYPSY ROSE LEE and the inspiration for Baby June in *GYPSY* (1959).

TIGER HAYNES (1907–   ), a black character actor and dancer, impersonated BILL "Bojangles" ROBINSON in *FADE IN–FADE OUT* (1964) and played the Tinman in *THE WIZ* (1975). Haynes' other musicals include *New Faces of 1956*, *A Broadway Musical* (1978) and *Comin' Uptown* (1979).

LELAND HAYWARD (1902–1971), a talent agent-turned-producer, presented several dramas, comedies and musicals on Broadway. His musical successes included *SOUTH PACIFIC* (1949), *CALL ME MADAM* (1950), *WISH YOU WERE HERE* (1952), *GYPSY* (1959) and *THE SOUND OF MUSIC* (1959).

GEORGE HEARN (1934–   ), a versatile leading man in classical pieces as well as musicals, was featured in *A Time for Singing* (1966), *I Remember Mama* (1979), *A Doll's Life* (1982), *Meet Me in St. Louis* (1989) and other shows.

Hearn is most remembered for his performance as the drag queen Albin in *LA CAGE AUX FOLLES* (1983).

ANNA HELD (1873–1918), one of the great beauties of the stage at the turn of the century, became a Broadway star in a handful of musicals, most of them produced by her husband FLORENZ ZIEGFELD. Held was born in Poland and raised in Paris but began her performing career singing in British music halls. She was the toast of all Europe when Ziegfeld brought her to New York, where she made her Broadway debut in *A Parlor Match* (1896). Held subsequently appeared in eight more musicals, mostly forgotten today, and usually played the coquettish French mademoiselle with flashing eyes. Her final Broadway appearance was in *Follow Me* (1916).

HELLO, DOLLY! (1964) was the epitome of big, brassy 1960s escapism but the musical is so tightly crafted that it has remained a favorite over the years. MICHAEL STEWART adapted Thornton Wilder's delightful period piece *The Matchmaker* with few changes and made turn-of-the-century New York the happiest and most optimistic place on earth. Matchmaker Dolly Levi (CAROL CHANNING) promises to find Yonkers businessman Horace Vandergelder (DAVID BURNS) a wife but plans on marrying him herself. The subplots deal with Vandergelder's niece trying to elope with an artist and the misadventures of two Yonkers clerks (CHARLES NELSON REILLY and Jerry Dodge) out on the town in Manhattan. All three plots converge at the swank Harmonia Gardens Restaurant, where music, dance and farce overflow in a delicious manner before all ends happily. JERRY HERMAN's score was tuneful and bright, with the title song becoming a major hit single. The song's purpose in the musical is contrived but GOWER CHAMPION staged the number so effectively that it became one of Broadway's most treasured moments. Also in the score were "It Only Takes a Moment," "Put On Your Sunday Clothes," "Ribbons Down My Back," "So Long, Dearie" and "Before the Parade Passes By." Channing was a triumph as the irresistibly funny Dolly but many replacements also had success with the role: GINGER ROGERS, Martha Raye, PEARL BAILEY, Betty Grable, ETHEL MERMAN and (in London) MARY MARTIN. *Hello, Dolly!* ran a happy 2,844 performances, making it the longest-running musical for a while.

HELLZAPOPPIN (1938) was a show that owed its long run (1,404 performances) to the clowning of Olsen and Johnson and the unabashed plugging it got from Walter Winchell's newspaper columns rather than from any artistic merit. Vaudevillians OLE OLSEN and CHIC JOHNSON produced (with the SHUBERT BROTHERS), wrote the sketches and starred in the zany revue, which combined sight gags, audience participation and topical jokes about Hitler and Mussolini. None of the songs, written by various people, attracted much attention then or since.

FLORENCE HENDERSON (1934–   ), the cheerful singer-actress of stage, television and nightclubs, is most remembered by Broadway audiences for her gentle performance in the title role of *FANNY* (1954). Henderson's other New York credits include *WISH YOU WERE HERE* (1952), *The Girl Who Came to Supper* (1963), and as Nellie Forbush in the 1967 revival of *SOUTH PACIFIC*.

LUTHER HENDERSON (1919–   ), an orchestrator, arranger, MUSIC DIRECTOR and sometime composer for many Broadway musicals, television shows and recordings, adapted the music of Thomas "Fats" Waller for *AIN'T MISBEHAVIN'* (1978) and of Jelly Roll Morton for *JELLY'S LAST JAM* (1992). Henderson's other Broadway credits include *FUNNY GIRL* (1964), *HALLELUJAH, BABY!* (1967), *PURLIE* (1970), the 1971 revival of *NO, NO, NANETTE*, *Lena Horne: The Lady and Her Music* (1981) and *BLACK AND BLUE* (1989).

RAY HENDERSON (1896–1970) was the composer for the successful team of DeSylva, Brown and Henderson who scored a series of delightfully spirited musicals and revues during the 1920s. Henderson was born in Buffalo and learned to play the piano as a pre-school child from his mother. He studied music at the Chicago Conservatory then went to New York where he worked as a dance band pianist and song plugger. Henderson had a few of his songs performed by AL JOLSON and EDDIE CANTOR but fame did not come until producer GEORGE WHITE formed the team of DeSylva, Brown and Henderson to score his annual *Scandals* revues. B. G. DeSylva and Lew Brown wrote the lyrics and Henderson provided the music. Their first Broadway show, *GEORGE WHITE'S SCANDALS* (1925), had a modest run but their extraordinary score for the 1926 edition helped make it the longest-running show of all the *Scandals*. In addition to other revues in the series, the trio had great success with book musicals, most notably *GOOD NEWS!* (1927), *HOLD EVERYTHING!* (1928), *FOLLOW THRU* (1929) and *FLYING HIGH* (1930). The team separated in 1930 when DeSylva went to Hollywood but Brown and Henderson wrote an excellent score for the 1931 *Scandals*. Working with other lyricists, Henderson composed for Broadway shows until 1943. His music was often tuneful and carefree but Henderson could utilize blues and jazz in his work as well.

KATHARINE HEPBURN (1907–   ), the renowned film actress who often returned to Broadway, appeared in only one musical, *COCO* (1969), in which she played fashion designer "Coco" Chanel.

VICTOR HERBERT (1859–1924) was not only America's premiere composer of operetta but he was also the first important composer for the Broadway stage. Herbert raised the standards of theatre music to levels not previously seen in this country and greatly influenced the direction of musical theatre during the early decades of this century. Herbert was born in Dublin, Ireland, but at a young age he and his widowed mother moved to England, where he was educated. When the family moved again to Stuttgart, Germany, Herbert began studying the cello and eventually played for the Stuttgart Opera. He fell in love with and married soprano Theresa Forster and came to New York with her when she was contracted to sing with the Metropolitan Opera, and he was hired for the orchestra. Herbert became a renowned cellist and eventually was made director of the 22nd New York National Guard Band but he wanted to compose and the stage seemed the ideal milieu. By 1894 his first effort, *Prince Ananias*, was produced but caused no sensation. It was *Serenade* (1897) that established Herbert as a creative force of importance. He followed this with thirty-nine musicals that included such beloved favorites *THE FORTUNE TELLER* (1898), *BABES IN TOYLAND* (1903), *MLLE. MODISTE* (1905), *THE RED MILL* (1906), *NAUGHTY MARIETTA* (1910) and *SWEETHEARTS* (1913). Herbert's most frequent collaborators were HARRY B. SMITH and Henry Blossom. Herbert's last musical was *The Dream Girl* in 1924, the year he died of a heart attack. Although Herbert's music was strictly in the Viennese tradition, he brought such vitality to theatre music that the American operetta genre grew and flourished under his influence.

HERE'S LOVE (1963) was a competent but undistinguished musical version of the beloved film *Miracle on 34th Street* (1947) with book, lyrics amd music by MEREDITH WILLSON. The story, about a little girl who comes to believe in Santa Claus when the real Kris Kringle gets involved in a lawsuit, still pleased audiences but there was not much that was improved on in the musical except MICHAEL KIDD's spirited choreography. Lackluster performances and forgettable songs did not stop *Here's Love* from running 334 performances.

JERRY HERMAN (1932–) is the composer-lyricist of two megahits of the 1960s and one of Broadway's masters of singable melodies. Herman was born in New York City and raised in New Jersey, where he began playing piano at a young age. While studying drama at the University of Miami, he wrote music and lyrics for college revues, one of them, *I Feel Wonderful*, transferring to Off Broadway in 1954. Herman contributed to a handful of revues in New York but his first complete score heard on Broadway was *MILK AND HONEY* (1961), a musical about tourists in Israel that had a modest run. With *HELLO, DOLLY!* (1964), Herman provided a bright, tuneful score that matched the big, brassy production that became one of Broadway's longest-running shows. He followed it with *MAME* (1966), a less polished score but a show that was almost as successful. Herman tackled more challenging projects when he scored *DEAR WORLD* (1969), *MACK AND MABEL* (1974) and *THE GRAND TOUR* (1979) and there was much to recommend in each of them but all three shows failed at the box office. *LA CAGE AUX FOLLES* (1983) gave Herman a big Broadway hit again but it was not up to the quality of his other works. *Jerry's Girls*, a musical revue of his songs from different shows, played on Broadway in 1985. Herman is unabashedly old-fashioned in his music and lyrics but he has a talent for optimistic musical comedy that few have equaled.

DAVID HERSEY (1939–), an American-born lighting designer who has worked in London since 1968, did the impressive lighting for the BRITISH IMPORTS *CATS* (1982), *LES MISÉRABLES* (1987), *Starlight Express* (1987), *Chess* (1988) and *MISS SAIGON* (1991).

HIGH BUTTON SHOES (1947) was a carefree period musical that introduced composer JULE STYNE to Broadway and launched PHIL SILVERS' career as a successful top banana. The libretto was by Stephen Longstreet, who adapted his autobiographical novel with the help of director GEORGE AB-BOTT and star Silvers. Set in New Brunswick, New Jersey, in 1913, con man Harrison Floy insinuates himself into the Longstreet family and sets off a series of misadventures that takes everyone on a merry chase to Atlantic City and back again for a highly wagered Rutgers–Princeton football game. Silvers was ably supported by NANETTE FABRAY, JACK MCCAULEY, Joey Faye, Lois Lee, HELEN GALLAGHER and Mark Dawson. Styne and Hollywood lyricist SAMMY CAHN came up with a delectable score that included "Papa, Won't You Dance with Me?" "On a Sunday by the Sea," "There's Nothing Like a Model T," "I Still Get Jealous" and "Nobody Ever Died for Poor Old Rutgers." Abbott's razor-sharp direction was complimented by JEROME ROBBINS' brilliant choreography that featured the justly famous Keystone Kops chase-ballet. (727 performances)

GREGORY HINES (1946–), a black actor-dancer intermittently on Broadway since 1954, was featured in the musicals *Eubie* (1978), *Comin' Uptown* (1979), *SOPHISTICATED LADIES* (1981) and as Jelly Roll Morton in *JELLY'S LAST JAM* (1992). Hines was a child performer on television and in nightclubs and later appeared in several movies. He is also one of the most accomplished tap dancers in America.

HIT THE DECK (1927) is mainly remembered for its VINCENT YOUMANS score that included "Sometimes I'm Happy" and "Hallelujah." HERBERT FIELDS wrote the libretto about a coffee shop owner who follows her sailor love all the way to China to get him to marry her. CLIFFORD GREY, LEO ROBIN and IRVING CAESAR provided the lyrics for Youmans' engaging music. (352 performances)

HOLD EVERYTHING! (1928) was a carefree musical about professional boxing with a frolicsome score by DESYLVA, BROWN and HENDERSON but the show is mostly remembered for making a star of BERT LAHR. The negligble libretto by B. G. DeSylva and John McGowan was about a pro boxer and his romantic tangles and the top-notch cast included VICTOR MOORE, JACK WHITING, Ona Munson and Betty Compton. But Lahr, as the comic punch-drunk Gink Schiner, stole the show and began his long career as one of Broadway's favorite clowns. The standout hit song from the score was "You're the Cream in My Coffee." (413 performances)

GEOFFREY HOLDER (1930–) is a versatile black actor, dancer and choreographer who is also an accomplished director and costume designer. The Trinidad-born Holder provided the stunning direction and costumes for *THE WIZ* (1975) and *Timbuktu* (1978). As a dancer he has performed for the Metropolitan Opera and in the Broadway musical *HOUSE OF FLOWERS* (1954).

RONALD HOLGATE (1937–), a full-voiced leading man in Broadway musicals and plays, gave memorable performances as the braggart soldier Miles Gloriosus in *A FUNNY THING HAPPENED ON THE WAY TO THE FORUM* (1962), the boastful delegate Richard Henry Lee in *1776* (1969) and the aristocratic Polish colonel in *THE GRAND TOUR* (1979).

JUDY HOLLIDAY (1922–1965) captivated theatre and film audiences during her brief but memorable acting career. Holliday was born in New York and began her association with the theatre as a switchboard operator for Orson Welles' Mercury Theatre. With BETTY COMDEN and ADOLPH GREEN she founded The Revuers, a nightclub act that brought her to the attention of producers and soon she was being featured in films. Holliday's Broadway musical debut was several years later in *BELLS ARE RINGING* (1956) in which she played Ella Peterson, a switchboard operator. She also starred in the short-lived musical *Hot Spot* (1963) before her untimely death at the age of forty-three.

STANLEY HOLLOWAY (1890–1982), a raucous character actor who delighted London theatregoers in some two dozen shows, only made one Broadway appearance, as the philosophical dustman Alfred P. Doolittle in *MY FAIR LADY* (1956).

HOLLYWOOD has, for the most part, been a subject of ridicule on the stage and musicals are no exception. From *Goldilocks* (1958) to *FADE IN–FADE OUT* (1964) to *CITY OF ANGELS* (1989), moviemakers were more to be laughed at than applauded. There were some exceptions, though. *MACK AND MABEL* (1974) was an ultimately somber view of its main characters and of the fleeting success of Hollywood, *WHAT MAKES SAMMY RUN?* (1964) was about the back-stabbing side of the business of moviemaking, and *NINE* (1982) was a surrealistic view of the workings of a film director.

CELESTE HOLM (1919–), a striking actress equally at home on stage and in films, created two memorable Broadway musical roles: the boy-crazy Ado Annie in *OKLAHOMA!* (1943) and the unconventional Evelina in *BLOOMER*

GIRL (1944). Holm's most recent Broadway musical was the short-lived *The Utter Glory of Morrissey Hall* (1979).

HANYA HOLM (1893–1992), a German-born choreographer who staged the dances for a dozen musicals on Broadway and in London, is best known for her work in *KISS ME, KATE* (1948), *THE GOLDEN APPLE* (1954), *MY FAIR LADY* (1956) and *CAMELOT* (1960).

LIBBY HOLMAN (1906–1971) was one of the finest torch singers of the 1920s and 1930s with a career that included Broadway musicals, recordings and concerts. Holman made her New York debut in *THE GARRICK GAIETIES* (1925) and appeared in other revues before gaining recognition in *THE LITTLE SHOW* (1929), where she introduced "Moanin' Low." She was featured in the revue *THREE'S A CROWD* (1930) and had major roles in the book musicals *REVENGE WITH MUSIC* (1934) and *You Never Know* (1938).

HOORAY FOR WHAT! (1937) was the first important musical by librettist-lyricist E. Y. HARBURG and one that foreshadowed his talent for fantastical satire. The plot was about a ridiculous scientist who invents a poison gas for worms. The invention falls into the hands of spies for war purposes but luckily the formula gets reversed and ends up as laughing gas. The story was rich with social commentary but much of it got toned down by added librettists HOW-ARD LINDSAY and RUSSEL CROUSE when ED WYNN was cast as the scientist and the star insisted on a less controversial vehicle for his special talents. The HAROLD ARLEN–Harburg score was entertaining and witty all the same with a satirical flag-waver called "God's Country," the anti-romantic "Down with Love" and "Moanin' in the Morning." Also in the cast were JACK WHITING, VIVIAN VANCE and Paul Haakon. AGNES DE MILLE, in her Broadway debut, choreographed a stunning anti-war ballet but much of it was cut before the opening night. *Hooray for What!* was offbeat and ahead of its time (it even referred to an atom bomb-like invention) but with Wynn's popularity it was able to run 200 performances.

BOB HOPE (1903–   ), one of America's most beloved entertainers, appeared in several Broadway musicals before starting his film career in 1938. The British-born Hope made his Broadway debut in 1926 in *The Ramblers* and appeared in a handful of forgotten musicals before attracting attention as band leader-sidekick Huckleberry Haines in *ROBERTA* (1933). He was featured in *Say When* (1934), the 1936 *ZIEGFELD FOLLIES* and *RED, HOT AND BLUE!* (1936) before leaving for Hollywood.

LINDA HOPKINS (1925–   ), a celebrated blues singer who has appeared in a handful of musicals on Broadway, played Bessie Smith in *Me and Bessie* (1974). Hopkins was also featured in *PURLIE* (1970), *Inner City* (1972) and *BLACK AND BLUE* (1989).

DEWOLF HOPPER (1858–1935) was a full-voiced basso who played comic roles in many Gilbert and Sullivan operettas and in musicals on Broadway. The most notable of his many shows were *The Black Hussar* (1885), *Castles in the Air* (1890), *WANG* (1891), *EL CAPITAN* (1896), *Fiddle-Dee-Dee* (1900) and *The Passing Show* (1917).

LENA HORNE (1917–   ), the classy black song stylist of records, nightclubs, television and films, started as a dancer in Harlem's Cotton Club and appeared on Broadway in *Blackbirds of 1939*. Her busy film and concert career kept her from Broadway until 1957 when she played Savannah, the Caribbean beauty who longs for Manhattan, in *JAMAICA*. Horne returned to Broadway again in 1981 for her sensational one-woman show *Lena Horne: The Lady and Her Music*.

KARL HOSCHNA (1877–1911) was a composer most known for his collaborations with librettist-lyricist OTTO HARBACH. Their most remembered shows together are *Three Twins* (1908) and *MADAME SHERRY* (1910), both exuberant musical comedies that pointed to a brilliant new team. But Hoschna's untimely death at the age of thirty-four ended the promising collaboration.

HOUSE OF FLOWERS (1954) was an unsuccessful musical that had so many wonderful things in it that it is fondly remembered today even though subsequent revivals and revisions were also failures. Truman Capote wrote the libretto, based on a short story of his, as well as the lyrics, and he proved to be quite accomplished on his first and only Broadway musical. HAROLD ARLEN provided the music that complimented Capote's wry, tender words. Such songs as "A Sleepin' Bee," "Two Ladies in da Shade of de Banana Tree," "I Never Has Seen Snow" and the title number were superior and when delivered by PEARL BAILEY, DIAHANN CARROLL and JUANITA HALL, they were unforgettable. The plot of the musical is about two rival brothels on a West Indies isle and an ambitious madam's efforts to sell her finest "flower" to a rich merchant. Also in the cast were GEOFFREY HOLDER, RAY WALSTON, Rawn Spearman and Alvin Ailey. The stunning production's sets and costumes were by Oliver Messel and the show went through a handful of directors, Peter Brook getting the final credit. (165 performances)

HOW TO SUCCEED IN BUSINESS WITHOUT REALLY TRYING (1961) was an entertaining satire on big business that was also one of the least romantic musicals ever to become a hit. Jack Weinstock and Willie Gilbert wrote a comedy based on Shepherd Mead's tongue-in-cheek manual of the same name but it was librettist ABE BURROWS who turned it into a brash, cynical and strangely delightful musical comedy. FRANK LOESSER provided the traditional Broadway-sounding songs and BOB FOSSE came up with some unusual dances for this non-dancing show. The plot is a send-up on the old Horatio Alger success story as J. Pierpont Finch (ROBERT MORSE) rises from window washer to chairman of the board of the World Wide Wickets Company. The romantic involvement along the way is minor since Finch's relationship with the company president (RUDY VALLEE), his obnoxious nephew (CHARLES NELSON REILLY) and others in the business world is the real substance of the piece. Morse and Vallee had the roles of their careers but it was Burrows' libretto that was the real star of the show. Loesser's songs were pleasant but not very memorable except for "I Believe in You," which, taken out of the musical's context, became a popular love song of sorts. *How to Succeed...* ran 1,417 performances and was awarded the PULITZER PRIZE.

KEN HOWARD (1944–   ), a personable leading man on Broadway and on television, played Thomas Jefferson in *1776* (1969), the Nebraska lawyer Jerry Ryan in *SEESAW* (1973) and several presidents in *1600 PENNSYLVANIA AVENUE* (1976).

WILLIE HOWARD (1886–1949) was an inspired clown who, often with his brother Eugene, starred in vaudeville and on Broadway for fifty years. Howard made his Broadway debut as a boy soprano in *The Little Duchess* (1901) and later appeared in five editions of *The Passing Show* and seven editions of *GEORGE WHITE'S SCANDALS*. His other musical credits included *The Whirl of the World* (1914), *Sky High* (1925), *GIRL CRAZY* (1930), *Ballyhoo of 1932*, the 1934 *ZIEGFELD FOLLIES*, *My Dear Public* (1943) and the 1948 revival of *SALLY*. Willie Howard usually played a troublemaker with a Yiddish dialect while his brother was the stuffy straight man.

SALLY ANN HOWES (1930–   ), a leading lady in a handful of musicals on Broadway and in London, is most known in this country for her major roles in *KWAMINA* (1961) and *WHAT MAKES SAMMY RUN?* (1964). The London-born singer-actress also played Eliza Doolittle later in the run of *MY FAIR LADY* and Anna Leonowens in the 1973 revival of *THE KING AND I*.

RON HUSMANN (1937–   ), a leading man in musicals in the 1960s, played journalist Tommy Howatt in *TENDERLOIN* (1960). Husmann's other musicals include *FIORELLO!* (1959), *GREENWILLOW* (1960), *ALL AMERICAN* (1962), *Lovely Ladies, Kind Gentlemen* (1970) and the 1973 Broadway revival of *IRENE*.

WALTER HUSTON (1884–1950), the durable actor in many films, made a lasting impression with his only Broadway musical, *KNICKERBOCKER HOLIDAY* (1938), in which he played Pieter Stuyvesant and introduced "September Song."

I

I CAN GET IT FOR YOU WHOLESALE (1962) was a hard-boiled musical about the cut-throat garment business and it made few concessions to the conventional rules of musical comedy. JEROME WEIDMAN adapted his own novel about an ambitious businessman named Harry Bogan who uses his partners, family and lovers to manipulate his way to the top, only to have his greed bring on his own bankruptcy. HAROLD ROME wrote the score, and like his songs for *PINS AND NEEDLES* (1937), he captured the language and sentiments of the urban working class of the 1930s. ELLIOTT GOULD, LILLIAN ROTH, MARILYN COOPER, HAROLD LANG and Sheree North headed the cast but it was BARBRA STREISAND in the small role of an office secretary who stopped the show nightly with her comic lament "Miss Marmelstein." Other songs in the score included "The Sound of Money," "Too Soon," "A Funny Thing Happened" and "Have I Told You Lately?" (300 performances)

I DO! I DO! (1966) was a competently done musical version of Jan de Hartog's *The Fourposter* (1951), a sentimental play about fifty years of a marriage. The adaptation by TOM JONES was pretty straightforward, utilizing the original's single setting and a cast of only two actors; it was a bold move for a Broadway musical in the 1960s. But the two actors were MARY MARTIN and ROBERT PRESTON, whose personal charm and fine-tuned interaction often outshone the material. The songs by Jones and HARVEY SCHMIDT were more commercial sounding than their previous tender scores for *THE FANTASTICKS* (1960) and *110 IN THE SHADE* (1963) but they served the stars well. GOWER

CHAMPION directed, DAVID MERRICK produced and *I Do! I Do!* ran for 560 performances.

I LOVE MY WIFE (1977) was a second-rate musical comedy about a less than gripping subject: two New Jersey couples decide to try mate swapping to add some zest to their suburban lives. The four likeable performers—Lenny Baker, JOANNA GLEASON, JAMES NAUGHTON and Ilene Graff—kept the comedy pleasant and they were aided by a small onstage band that acted as a Greek chorus of sorts. The songs by CY COLEMAN (music) and MICHAEL STEWART (lyrics) were often much better than the libretto (also by Stewart) and "Hey There, Good Times" even became somewhat popular. (872 performances)

I MARRIED AN ANGEL (1938) featured not only a score but also a libretto by RICHARD RODGERS and LORENZ HART, who based their silly tale on a Hungarian play. A Budapest banker wishes for a celestial mate and once he gets her various complications arise. But all ends happily when the banker's sister teaches the angel the worldly ways of the female species. The dynamic cast included DENNIS KING, VIVIENNE SEGAL, WALTER SLEZAK, Audrey Christie and, in her Broadway debut, VERA ZORINA as the angel. The Rodgers and Hart score featured the hit song "Spring Is Here" but the musical highlight of *I Married an Angel* was GEORGE BALANCHINE's satiric ballet "At the Roxy's Music Hall," which, everyone admitted, had nothing to do with the rest of the show but was sensational. JOSHUA LOGAN, in his Broadway debut, directed the musical, which ran 338 performances.

I'D RATHER BE RIGHT (1937) marked the return of GEORGE M. COHAN to the musical stage after a ten-year absence; but it was as a performer in someone else's musical, the first time in his long career that he consented to such a thing. RODGERS and HART provided the songs and GEORGE S. KAUFMAN and MOSS HART wrote the witty book about Franklin D. Roosevelt appearing in a dream and trying to help two young lovers. Aside from the gentle ribbing of the current president and his programs, the show had fun with all branches of government and recalled Kaufman's earlier political satire *OF THEE I SING* (1931). The only hit song to come from the Rodgers and Hart score was "Have You Met Miss Jones?" but also enjoyable were "Off the Record," "We're Going to Balance the Budget" and the title song. (290 performances)

I'M GETTING MY ACT TOGETHER AND TAKING IT ON THE ROAD (1978) was the finest musical by the songwriting team of GRETCHEN CRYER and NANCY FORD. This Off-Broadway hit was about a thirty-nine-year-old singer who auditions her new nightclub act for her manager, hoping to convince him that she should present a more honest portrayal of herself instead of the glossy, fanciful one he insists is more lucrative. Cryer herself played the heroine and the songs she sang were alternately satiric and painfully revealing. "Dear Tom," "Old Friend," "Strong Woman Number" and "Natural High" were standouts in a score that was always involving. The musical was often described as a feminist show but Cryer and Ford's work was too complex and self-aware to be reduced to such a simple label. (1,165 performances)

IN DAHOMEY (1903) was the first musical comedy written and performed by black artists to be presented at a Broadway theatre. BERT WILLIAMS and George Walker, known to audiences from their delightful vaudeville acts together, were the stars of this adventurous farce about some black Bostonians who try to colonize Africa with unemployed American blacks. J. A. Shipp wrote the libretto and the songs were by Will Marion Cook (music) and the celebrated black poet Paul Laurence Dunbar (lyrics). *In Dahomey* ran for a significant fifty-nine performances and in 1904 played successfully in London.

REX INGRAM (1895–1969), an imposing black singer and actor who made many films, played the devil's assistant Lucifer, Jr., in the Broadway musical *CABIN IN THE SKY* (1940) and saloon owner Biglow Brown in *ST. LOUIS WOMAN* (1946).

INSIDE U.S.A. (1948) was a musical revue that used a tour of the nation as the springboard for its songs and sketches. ARTHUR SCHWARTZ and HOWARD DIETZ wrote the songs and MOSS HART and others provided the skits, which used locales from San Francisco to New Orleans to Pittsburgh. The multi-talented cast included BEATRICE LILLIE, JACK HALEY, John Tyers, Carl Reiner, Herb Shriner and JACK CASSIDY and the score introduced the lovely "Haunted Heart." (399 performances)

INTO THE WOODS (1987) was one of STEPHEN SONDHEIM's less accomplished musicals but one that was exceedingly popular, running 764 performances. JAMES LAPINE directed and wrote the libretto that combined several fairy tales—some legendary, others original—and let them all occur at the same time in the same woods. The first act followed the traditional plots, while the second act went beyond the happy endings to explore the consequences of the characters' actions. BERNADETTE PETERS, JOANNA GLEASON, CHIP ZIEN, Tom Aldredge and ROBERT WESTENBERG played the major characters and the Sondheim score featured "Children Will Listen," "Giants in the Sky," "No More," "Agony" and "No One Is Alone."

IRENE (1919) held the record as the longest-running Broadway musical for eighteen years and became one of America's most beloved shows as its numerous companies toured nationwide. The libretto by James Montgomery was straightforward and simple but still is engaging. Irene O'Dare is a poor shop girl who is sent to a Long Island mansion to reupholster cushions but falls in love with the wealthy son of the estate's owner. Through the help of a male couturier, Irene poses as a socialite, wins the heart of high society and marries her true love. "Alice Blue Gown" was the hit of the score by Harry Tierney (music) and Joseph McCarthy (lyrics), which also featured "The Last Part of Ev'ry Party," the title song and the Chopin-inspired "Castle of Dreams." EDITH DAY originated the role of Irene but during its 670 performances the part was also played by Irene Dunne, Jeanette MacDonald and others. With major book revisions, *Irene* was revived on Broadway in 1973 with Debbie Reynolds and it ran a surprising 604 performances.

IRMA LA DOUCE (1960) was a 1956 French musical that was translated and produced in London for a long run before producer DAVID MERRICK brought the production to Broadway. Marguerite Monnot wrote the music and Alexandre Breffont's book and lyrics were adapted by Julian Moore, David Heneker and Monty Norman. The tale is that of Paris prostitute Irma who is loved by a young student. The youth decides to disguise himself as a wealthy old man who can support Irma and keep her off the streets. Elizabeth Seal and Keith Michell repeated their West End performances and Peter Brook directed. Also in the cast were CLIVE REVILL, GEORGE S. IRVING, Stuart Damon, Fred Gwynne and ELLIOT GOULD. The serviceable score included the lovely ballad "Our Language of Love." (524 performances)

GEORGE S. IRVING (1922–), a favorite character actor in Broadway plays and musicals, made his debut in *OKLAHOMA!* (1943) and was featured in the original casts of *CALL ME MISTER* (1946), *ME AND JULIET* (1953), *BELLS ARE RINGING* (1956), *IRMA LA DOUCE* (1960), *THE HAPPY TIME* (1968), *Copperfield* (1981), *ME AND MY GIRL* (1986) and many others. Irving was also featured in the Broadway revivals of *IRENE* in 1973 and *ON YOUR TOES* in 1983.

IT'S A BIRD, IT'S A PLANE, IT'S SUPERMAN (1966) was an agreeable musical comedy suggested by the popular comic strip. The show derived its pleasure from earnestly capturing the fun of the original rather than merely camping it up. David Newman and Robert Benton wrote the libretto about the Man of Steel's rivalry with a mad scientist who hopes to blow up the world in revenge for not receiving the Nobel Prize. Bob Holiday played Superman/Clark Kent, Michael O'Sullivan was his nemesis and there was also fine work from Patricia Marand, JACK CASSIDY, Don Chastain and Linda Lavin, under the clever direction of HAROLD PRINCE. The CHARLES STROUSE–LEE ADAMS score featured the hit song "You've Got Possibilities" as well as such enjoyable numbers as "So Long, Big Guy," "The Woman for the Man," "What I've Always Wanted" and "Ooh, Do You Love You!" Curiously, the musical only ran 129 performances.

J

ERNESTINE JACKSON, a black actress-singer on Broadway since 1963, played Ruth Younger in *RAISIN* (1973) and Sarah Brown in the 1976 revival of *GUYS AND DOLLS*. Jackson's other Broadway musical credits include *Sophie* (1963), *APPLAUSE* (1970) and *JESUS CHRIST SUPERSTAR* (1971).

JAMAICA (1957) was a tropical musical with a less than inspired libretto but its sparkling score and a glittering performance by LENA HORNE more than compensated. Librettists E. Y. HARBURG and FRED SAIDY set the story on a small Caribbean island near Jamaica where the humble fisherman Koli loves the beautiful Savannah, who yearns for a life in the more up-to-date island of Manhattan. An enterprising hustler offers to take Savannah to America but when Koli rescues her little brother during a hurricane she decides to stay with the man who loves her. This limp tale was enlivened by several HAROLD ARLEN (music) and Harburg (lyrics) songs, notably "Push the Button," "Cocoanut Sweet," "Napoleon," "Monkey in the Mango Tree" and "Leave the Atom Alone." In addition to Horne's Savannah, the cast boasted strong performances by Ricardo Montalban as Koli, ADELAIDE HALL, Josephine Premice, Ossie Davis, Erik Rhodes, Joe Adams, Alvin Ailey and Billy Wilson. (558 performances)

JELLY'S LAST JAM (1992) is the musical biography of jazz artist Jelly Roll Morton with the electric GREGORY HINES in the title role. George C. Wolfe directed and wrote the libretto for this ambitious CONCEPT MUSICAL that featured Morton's music adapted by LUTHER HENDERSON (and some original music by Henderson) and with lyrics by Susan Birkenhead. The action of the piece takes place at the decaying nightclub the Jungle Inn on the eve of Morton's death, where he is forced by his guide, the Chimney Man, to review his life and seek a place among the jazz greats. In a series of musical and dramatic scenes, Morton's own prejudices and self-delusions are explored and the result is a BLACK MUSICAL with more bite than a handful of jazz and blues musicals. Also in the vivid cast were SAVION GLOVER as the younger Morton, Keith David, Tonya Pinkins and Stanley Wayne Mathis. (still running as of 3/1/93)

JESUS CHRIST SUPERSTAR (1971) was the first ANDREW LLOYD WEBBER–TIM RICE musical to play on Broadway but it was known to Americans first as a hit single "Superstar," then as a record album and a series of concert tours. The Broadway version was a noisy and gaudy spectacle directed by TOM O'HORGAN and it was greeted with mixed reviews. But the score was already so popular that the show managed to run 720 performances. Like their later works, *Jesus Christ Superstar* was all sung with Rice writing the libretto–lyrics for Webber's music. The rock opera told the story of the last seven days of Christ's life with no excuses for anachronisms or up-to-date references. "I Don't Know How to Love Him" and the title song were the established hits but Rice's wit was more evident in such numbers as "What's the Buzz?" "King Herod's Song" and "Heaven on Their Minds." From the large cast, BEN VEREEN was singled out for his vibrant Judas.

JOHNNY JOHNSON (1936) was composer KURT WEILL's first Broadway assignment after emigrating to America and it contained the bite and fervor that had been seen in his European works. Leftist playwright Paul Green wrote the libretto and lyrics for this anti-war folk tale that bordered on allegory. The title hero, a pacifist stonecutter, is drafted into World War I, where he undergoes a series of misadventures that are both funny and frightening. The musical only ran sixty-eight performances and none of the songs became popular because of Weill's sardonic harmonics and unusually lengthy musical passages. But *Johnny Johnson* was a bold and brilliant experiment that not only introduced Weill to Broadway but also some outstanding actors who would later gain fame for their non-musical work: Lee J. Cobb, Luther Adler, Jules (John) Garfield, Elia Kazan, Morris Carnovsky and Russell Collins as Johnny. The musical was also the first Broadway credit for the distinguished musical director LEHRMAN ENGEL.

CHICK JOHNSON (1891–1962) was a raucous comic who, with OLE OLSEN, starred in vaudeville and in a handful of Broadway musicals, most notably *HELLZAPOPPIN* (1938).

AL JOLSON (1886–1950), arguably America's greatest all-around entertainer, was one of Broadway's most magnetic stars even though his vehicles were usually passable at best. Jolson was born in Russia and emigrated as a young boy to America. He sang in his father's synagogue then joined the circus and ended up as a black-faced minstrel singer with Lew Dockstader's Minstrels. Jolson maintained many of these elements in his vaudeville act and later in his Broadway shows and on film. He appeared in a handful of musicals beginning in 1911 and had his two greatest Broadway successes with *SINBAD* (1918) and *BOMBO* (1921). Jolson's film career and the talking picture business both took off with *The Jazz Singer* in 1927 but he occasionally returned to Broadway, the last time in 1940 for *Hold On to Your Hats*.

TOM JONES (1928–), the lyricist-librettist who works exclusively with his composer partner HARVEY SCHMIDT, made his musical theatre debut with the Off-Broadway phenomenon *THE FANTASTICKS* (1960). The team's first Broadway musical was *110 IN THE SHADE* (1963) and it was followed by the MARY MARTIN–ROBERT PRESTON hit *I DO! I DO!* (1966). Jones scored and directed the adventurous *CELEBRATION* (1969) then returned to Off Broadway, where the team presented a series of experimental musicals at the Portfolio Theatre Workshop, the most memorable being *Philemon* (1975). Jones and Schmidt's musicalization of *Our Town*, called *Grover's Corners*, toured the country in the 1980s. Jones' lyrics and librettos are highly poetic, elegantly simple and, at their best, magically indelible.

JOSEPH AND THE AMAZING TECHNICOLOR DREAMCOAT (1982) took fourteen years to travel from its initial presentation in a London school to its appearance on Broadway. The unpretentious musical about biblical Joseph and his eleven jealous brothers was the first collaboration between ANDREW LLOYD WEBBER and TIM RICE and it played briefly Off Broadway in 1976. After the Broadway success of the team's *JESUS CHRIST SUPERSTAR* (1971) and *EVITA* (1979), the songwriters wrote some additional songs for their Old Testament cantata and it opened Off Broadway in 1981 in a sparkling production directed by Tony Tanner. The joyous musical comedy moved to Broadway in 1982 and stayed for 747 performances. The all-sung show has a score that is a cheery collection of various musical styles, from rock to French cabaret to calypso, and it makes no attempt to blend the divergent musical forms together. Webber and Rice even turned the Pharoh into an Elvis Presley impersonator and had great fun with all the anachronisms throughout. *Joseph and the Amazing Technicolor Dreamcoat* may not be Webber and Rice's most challenging work but it is irresistibly fun at times.

JUBILEE (1935) was one of COLE PORTER's less profitable shows but it did boast a strong cast and some unforgettable songs. MOSS HART wrote the libretto about a fictional royal family who gladly mix among the commoners when an uprising strikes their kingdom. MARY BOLAND, Melville Cooper, CHARLES WALTERS and Margaret Adams were the royal foursome who had romantic or comic dalliances with June Knight, Derek Williams and others.

The engaging Porter score included "Begin the Beguine," "Just One of Those Things," "A Picture of Me without You" and "Why Shouldn't I?" *Jubilee* was filled with sophistication and in jokes that audiences didn't warm up to but the popularity of Boland kept the show alive; when she had to return to Hollywood, *Jubilee* quickly closed with only 169 performances to its credit.

RAUL JULIA (1940–   ), a dashing leading man of films, Broadway musicals and classical pieces, played many roles for the NEW YORK SHAKESPEARE FESTIVAL before appearing on Broadway. The Puerto Rican-born Julia's musical credits include the outlaw MacHeath in the 1977 Lincoln Center revival of *THE THREEPENNY OPERA*, the less than noble Proteus in *TWO GENTLEMEN OF VERONA* (1971), *Via Galactica* (1972), film genius Guido Contini in *NINE* (1982) and Cervantes/Don Quixote in the 1992 Broadway revival of *MAN OF LA MANCHA*.

JUMBO (1935) was probably the biggest spectacle ever to call itself a Broadway musical, for BILLY ROSE's mammoth production was staged at the Hippodrome rather than at a conventional Broadway theatre. The Ben Hecht–Charles Mac-Arthur libretto about two quarreling circus managers allowed plenty of room for circus acts and RODGERS and HART provided a score that offered three hit songs: "Little Girl Blue," "My Romance" and "The Most Beautiful Girl in the World." JIMMY DURANTE led the large cast and Paul Whiteman's Orchestra served as the accompaniment. Although *Jumbo* ran 233 performances, it was not enough to recoup the show's unprecedented $340,000 investment.

JUNO (1959) was an ambitious, beautifully scored musical drama that could not survive its belligerently negative reviews and closed after only sixteen performances. But unlike most quick flops, *Juno* is still hauntingly powerful and will not go away. The musical was adapted from Sean O'Casey's esteemed drama *Juno and the Paycock* (1924) by JOSEPH STEIN who remained faithful to the original but played up the melodrama at the expense of the Irish wit and jocularity. Set in the troubled Dublin of the 1920s, the story concerns "Captain" Boyle (Melvyn Douglas), his long-suffering wife Juno (SHIRLEY BOOTH), his drinking buddy Joxer (Jack MacGowran) and his children, Johnny (Tommy Rall) and Mary (Monte Amundsen). The struggle between the Irish Republican Army and the British invades the lives of the family as Johnny is killed for betraying an Irish soldier and Mary is left pregnant by an unscrupulous lawyer. The tale was indeed grim and audiences, used to seeing Booth in comic roles, were disappointed. But the near-operatic score by MARC BLITZSTEIN put *Juno* in a musical class by itself with such memorable numbers as "We're Alive," "I Wish It So," "One Kind Word" and "Bird upon the Tree." AGNES DE MILLE choreographed the show and her "Johnny" ballet was outstanding. *Juno* has been revised and revived on a few occasions but it has yet to achieve the success it deserves.

K

MADELINE KAHN (1942–), a comic actress with an operatic singing range, created the role of the temperamental movie star Lily Garland in *ON THE TWENTIETH CENTURY* (1978). Kahn's other Broadway musical credits include featured roles in *New Faces of 1968*, *Promenade* (1969) and *TWO BY TWO* (1970).

BERT KALMAR (1884–1947), with his librettist-composer partner HARRY RUBY, wrote the book and lyrics for *Helen of Troy, New York* (1923), *No Other Girl* (1924), *The Ramblers* (1926), *The Five O' Clock Girl* (1927) and *ANIMAL CRACKERS* (1928). Kalmar started out as a child magician and later appeared in vaudeville. In 1929 he and Ruby went to Hollywood and scored several films in the 1930s. Kalmar returned to Broadway in 1941 with *High Kickers*.

JOHN KANDER (1927–) and his partner FRED EBB are the most intriguing songwriting team to come out of the 1960s. Kander provides the music while Ebb writes the lyrics and sometimes the libretto; together they create witty, intelligent and enjoyable scores. Kander was born in Kansas City, Missouri, and studied music at Oberlin College and Columbia University. His early jobs included conducting pit orchestras, writing dance arrangements and acting as rehearsal pianist. His Broadway debut was *A Family Affair* (1962) with James and William Goldman writing the libretto and lyrics. That same year Kander started working with Ebb and they had a few hit singles on the charts. Their first Broadway score together was *FLORA, THE RED MENACE* (1965) with producer HAROLD PRINCE, who would bring the team fame with his

CABARET (1966), arguably Kander and Ebb's finest score. In a gentler mode was Kander's music for *THE HAPPY TIME* (1968), his Greek-sounding rhythms for *ZORBA* (1968) and a vivacious vaudeville-style score for *70, GIRLS, 70* (1971). The team returned to a darker, more cynical tone for *CHICAGO* (1975). The scores for the LIZA MINNELLI vehicle *THE ACT* (1977) and the LAUREN BACALL vehicle *WOMAN OF THE YEAR* (1981) were not as impressive but *THE RINK* (1984) afforded the team the opportunity to write a passionate and engaging score once again. Kander and Ebb's *The Kiss of the Spider Woman* has undergone tryouts and revisions out of town since 1990 but has yet to come to Broadway. The 1991 Off-Broadway revue *And the World Goes 'Round* was a celebration of Kander and Ebb's songs for the theatre, movies and television. Kander's music is adventurous and unpredictable but securely in the Broadway tradition.

MARIA KARNILOVA (1920–   ), the accomplished dancer-turned-character actress, has given Broadway many superb performances, most memorably the role of Golde in *FIDDLER ON THE ROOF* (1964). Karnilova appeared in the dancing chorus of *Stars in Your Eyes* (1938), *Hollywood Pinafore* (1945) and *Out of This World* (1950), as well as featured parts in *MISS LIBERTY* (1949) and *Two's Company* (1952). Her comic striptease as Tessie Tura in *GYPSY* (1959) brought her recognition and *Fiddler on the Roof* was the highlight of her long career. Karnilova also played the faded courtesan Hortense in *ZORBA* (1968) and the motherly Inez Alvarez in the Broadway version of *Gigi* (1973).

GEORGE S. KAUFMAN (1889–1961), the prolific comic playwright who mastered several areas of show business, provided sketches and librettos for many Broadway musicals. Kaufman was born in Pittsburgh and began his writing career as a journalist, providing reviews and humorous pieces for New York newspapers. He collaborated with several different playwrights, most notably with MOSS HART. His most famous musical theatre librettos, all written in collaboration with others, include *THE COCOANUTS* (1925), *ANIMAL CRACKERS* (1928), *STRIKE UP THE BAND* (1930), *OF THEE I SING* (1931), *I'D RATHER BE RIGHT* (1937) and *SILK STOCKINGS* (1955). Kaufman was also an accomplished director of plays and musicals, his most memorable productions being *Of Thee I Sing* and *GUYS AND DOLLS* (1950).

HERSHY KAY (1919–1981), a respected and talented orchestrator and musical arranger for musicals on Broadway beginning in 1944, worked with LEONARD BERNSTEIN on the music for *ON THE TOWN* (1944), *CANDIDE* (1956) and *1600 PENNSYLVANIA AVENUE* (1976) and with CY COLEMAN on *ON THE TWENTIETH CENTURY* (1978) and *BARNUM* (1980). Kay's other musical credits included *PETER PAN* (1954), *MILK AND HONEY* (1961), *COCO* (1969), *A CHORUS LINE* (1975) and *EVITA* (1979).

DANNY KAYE (1913–1987), the rubber-faced, fast-talking comic who conquered stage, film, nightclubs and television, only appeared in four Broadway musicals but he made a lasting impression in each. Kaye was born in Brooklyn and worked his way through the "borscht" circuit in the Catskills and in vaudeville before making his Broadway debut in *The Straw Hat Revue* (1939). In *LADY IN THE DARK* (1941) he stopped the show nightly with his tongue-twisting rendition of "Tschaikovsky" and became a star. He played the amorous GI Jerry Walker in *LET'S FACE IT!* (1941) then went to Hollywood. Kaye returned to Broadway as the ancient but frisky Noah in the musical *TWO BY TWO* (1970).

JUDY KAYE (1948–), a dynamic leading lady with a highly theatrical voice, is most remembered for playing movie star Lily Garland during most of the run of *ON THE TWENTIETH CENTURY* (1978) and for her performance as the temperamental prima donna Carlotta in the New York production of *THE PHANTOM OF THE OPERA* (1988). Kaye's other musical credits include *Oh, Brother!* (1981) and several Off-Broadway revivals.

STUBBY KAYE (1918–), the rotund character actor seen in many plays and films and on television, created two memorable Broadway musical roles: bookie Nicely-Nicely in *GUYS AND DOLLS* (1950) and Marryin' Sam in *LI'L ABNER* (1956). Kaye's most recent Broadway musical appearance was in *Grind* (1985).

GENE KELLY (1912–), one of the giants of film musicals, started as a dancer on Broadway, making his debut in the chorus of *LEAVE IT TO ME!* (1938). After appearing in *One for the Money* (1939), Kelly was cast as the disreputable Joey Evans in *PAL JOEY* (1940) and became a star. He choreographed *BEST FOOT FORWARD* (1941) then went to Hollywood in 1942 and began his remarkable movie musical career. Kelly returned to Broadway in 1958 to direct *FLOWER DRUM SONG*.

PATSY KELLY (1910–1981), a dowdy, wisecracking comedienne, appeared in Broadway musicals in the 1920s and 1930s, made several films in the 1930s and 1940s, then returned triumphantly to the stage in the 1970s. Kelly made her Broadway debut in *Harry Delmar's Revels* (1927) and was featured in *Three Cheers* (1928), *Earl Carroll's Sketch Book* (1929), *EARL CARROLL VANITIES* (1930), *The Wonder Bar* (1930) and *FLYING COLORS* (1932). Thirty-nine years later she won acclaim as the housekeeper Pauline in the popular 1971 revival of *NO, NO, NANETTE*. Her final Broadway performance was as Mrs. O'Dare in the 1973 revival of *IRENE*.

PERT KELTON (1907–1968), a warm character actress in plays and musicals and on film, played Mrs. Paroo in *THE MUSIC MAN* (1957). Kelton's

Broadway debut was in *SUNNY* (1925) and she was featured in *Five O'Clock Girl* (1927) and as Gramma Briggs in *GREENWILLOW* (1960).

JEROME KERN (1885–1945), the pioneering composer who brought sophistication and lyricism to American theatre music, did much to create theatre scores that offered an elegance usually seen only in operetta. Kern was born in New York City and was taught piano by his mother. He studied at the New York College of Music and at conservatories in Europe before beginning his career as a songwriter in London. Returning to New York in 1904, Kern worked as a song plugger on Tin Pan Alley and as a rehearsal pianist with the notable songwriters of the day. Individual songs by Kern were interpolated into Broadway shows and London imports and his first full score appeared in 1912 with *The Red Petticoat. THE GIRL FROM UTAH* (1914) brought Kern recognition but it was with the PRINCESS THEATRE MUSICALS that Kern's true talent emerged. This series of witty, modern musicals, done on a small scale at the intimate Princess Theatre, were very American in character and temperament and audiences loved them. The first two musicals in the series, *Nobody Home* (1915) and *VERY GOOD EDDIE* (1915), had librettos by GUY BOLTON and lyrics by Schulyer Greene and others. When P. G. WODEHOUSE took over the lyricwriting in 1917, the musicals gained a merry, sophisticated quality that was delectable. Bolton, Wodehouse and Kern became the most influential triumvirate in the American theatre and their shows—*Have a Heart* (1917), *OH, BOY!* (1917), *LEAVE IT TO JANE* (1917) and *OH, LADY! LADY!* (1918)—inspired the next generation of songwriters to move the Broadway musical in the direction of witty and intelligent shows. Kern also scored musicals with other writers in the 1920s and had major hits with *SALLY* (1920), *SUNNY* (1925), *Criss-Cross* (1926) and *SWEET ADELINE* (1929). With OSCAR HAMMERSTEIN II he explored the idea of an integrated musical, and in *SHOW BOAT* (1927), they created America's first musical play. Kern had success in the 1930s with two shows with lyricist-librettist OTTO HARBACH—*THE CAT AND THE FIDDLE* (1931) and *ROBERTA* (1933)—and two with Hammerstein—*MUSIC IN THE AIR* (1932) and *VERY WARM FOR MAY* (1939). But Kern left Broadway in 1940 and spent the rest of his career in Hollywood where he scored several memorable film musicals. In addition to his accomplished theatre scores, Kern is important for the great influence he had on GEORGE GERSHWIN, RICHARD RODGERS and other major composers who followed in his footsteps.

LARRY KERT (1930–1991), a talented leading man whose career was plagued by FLOP MUSICALS, got to create the role of Tony in *WEST SIDE STORY* (1957), his one major hit show. Kert began his musical career appearing in the chorus of *Tickets Please* (1950) and *John Murray Anderson's Almanac* (1953) before landing the lead in *West Side Story*. In 1970 he replaced Dean Jones as Bobby in *COMPANY* (1970) soon after the opening and made the role his own.

The rest of Kert's Broadway career consisted of short-run musicals, such as *A Family Affair* (1962), *La Strada* (1969), *Into the Light* (1986) and *RAGS* (1986), and replacing other actors in long runs and on tour.

MICHAEL KIDD (1919–), the stage and film choreographer-director, was a soloist for the Ballet Theatre before making his Broadway choreographer debut with *FINIAN'S RAINBOW* (1947). Kidd then went on to choreograph *LOVE LIFE* (1948), *GUYS AND DOLLS* (1950), *CAN-CAN* (1953) and other musicals. He was also an accomplished director and staged a handful of shows in addition to choreographing them: *LI'L ABNER* (1956), *DESTRY RIDES AGAIN* (1959), *WILDCAT* (1960), *SUBWAYS ARE FOR SLEEPING* (1961), *THE ROTHSCHILDS* (1970) and others.

RICHARD KILEY (1922–), an imposing, distinguished leading man with a full voice, is mostly remembered for creating the roles of Cervantes/Don Quixote in *MAN OF LA MANCHA* (1965) but he has given several impressive performances throughout his career. Chicago-born Kiley began as a radio actor and played heavies on film during the 1950s. His Broadway musical career began with *KISMET* (1953), where he played the Caliph and introduced "Stranger in Paradise." Kiley's other musical credits include the sleuthing Tom Baxter in *REDHEAD* (1959), David Jordan, the American abroad, in *NO STRINGS* (1962) and the short-lived musicals *I Had a Ball* (1964) and *Her First Roman* (1968).

WILLA KIM, a costume designer for stage, opera, film and television, has done the costumes for Broadway musicals since *Goodtime Charley* (1975). Kim's other musical credits include *DANCIN'* (1978), *SOPHISTICATED LADIES* (1981), *Song and Dance* (1985), *Legs Diamond* (1988) and *THE WILL ROGERS FOLLIES* (1991).

THE KING AND I (1951) was RODGERS and HAMMERSTEIN's first venture into a property that was not American in either setting or character, but using the honesty and integrity with which they approached their previous work, they came up with a Broadway version of the Orient that was tasteful, exotic and very moving. Hammerstein's libretto, based on the Margaret Landon novel *Anna and the King of Siam,* which was drawn from actual events, is set in Bangkok in the 1860s, where the English governess Anna Leonowens arrives to serve as instructor for the King's many children. The events of the story center on the battle of egos between the teacher and her sovereign employer but soon rivalry turns to respect and, in a restrained fashion, to affection. The King dies at the end of the musical but Anna's democratic ideas blossom in his eldest son and successor. There is also a tragic subplot about the unhappy slave Tuptim and her lover who are destroyed for rebuking the old ways of Siam. *The King and I* was intended as a vehicle for GERTRUDE LAWRENCE and she was marvelous in the role of Anna but newcomer YUL BRYNNER's incomparable performance as the King dominated the show, as he has the role itself ever since. The lush, highly operatic score included several Rodgers and Hammerstein standards, among them "Hello, Young Lovers," "Getting to Know You," "Shall We Dance?" "I Have Dreamed," as well as the Rodgers instrumental favorite "March of the Siamese Children" and the brilliant "The Small House of Uncle Thomas" sequence that was choreographed by JEROME ROBBINS. (1,246 performances)

DENNIS KING (1897–1971), a captivating baritone and dashing leading man, created three of operetta's most famous roles: heroic Jim Kenyon in *ROSE-MARIE* (1924), the poet-outlaw François Villon in *THE VAGABOND KIND* (1925) and the swashbuckling D'Artagnan in *THE THREE MUSKETEERS* (1928). The British-born King made his West End debut in 1919 and settled in America in 1924, where he became a popular matinee idol for his musical, dramatic and classical roles. His other Broadway musical credits included Gaylord Ravenal in the 1932 revival of *SHOW BOAT*, Count Palaffi in *I MARRIED AN ANGEL* (1938), the 1951 revival of *MUSIC IN THE AIR* and *Shangri-La* (1956).

LISA KIRK (1925–1990), a personable singer-actress prevalent in nightclubs, appeared in a few Broadway musicals, most memorably *KISS ME, KATE* (1948), where she played Lois Lane/Bianca. Kirk's other musical credits included Emily in *ALLEGRO* (1947) and Lottie in *MACK AND MABEL* (1974).

KISMET (1953) was the most successful and bewitching of the series of musicals ROBERT WRIGHT and GEORGE FORREST adapted from classical music themes, in this case Alexander Borodin. *Kismet* had been a popular play by Edward Knoblock in 1911 and the libretto by Charles Lederer and Luther Davis retained the old-fashioned and highly romantic plot devices. In ancient Baghdad, a wily poet disguises himself as a beggar and over the next twenty-four hours experiences a series of bravura adventures: he unites his daughter with the dashing Caliph, destroys the evil Wazir, romances the Wazir's wife and becomes Emir of the city. ALFRED DRAKE was the delightful poet-beggar and he was ably supported by the fine voices of JOAN DIENER, DORETTA MORROW and RICHARD KILEY. Wright and Forrest found plenty of comic and romantic material in Borodin's music and wrote some imaginative lyrics as well. "Stranger in Paradise" and "Baubles, Bangles and Beads" were the standout hits of the score but also of high quality were "Sands of Time," "Rhymes Have I," "Night of My Nights," "Not Since Ninevah," "Gesticulate" and the expansive quartet "And This Is My Beloved." The lavish production was staged by ALBERT MARRE and choreographed by JACK COLE, running 583 performances. *Kismet* has since been added to the repertory of various opera companies. An all-black version, retitled *Timbuktu*, opened on Broadway in 1978 and ran for 221 performances.

KISS ME, KATE (1948) is COLE PORTER's greatest musical for various reasons: It has the finest libretto (by BELLA and SAMUEL SPEWACK) ever offered Porter, it has his best score and, most significantly, its songs and characters are tied together in a double-plot construction that still amazes. *Kiss Me, Kate* is more than a musicalized version of Shakespeare's *The Taming of the Shrew*; the musical cleverly recreates the original through excerpts even as it comments on Shakespeare's plot and its contemporary parallels. The story is confined to one day in a Baltimore theatre, where a company of actors is in out-of-town tryouts with a new musical. The feuding between producer/star Fred Graham and his leading lady/ex-wife Lili Vanessi is not dissimilar to the Elizabethan tale being staged and the subplots in each story are also similar. Further complications arise when Lili decides to quit the show to marry a wealthy Washingtonian and Fred utilizes two gangsters on the scene to keep her in the theatre. The two plays end with similar reconciliations as Shakespeare's words are used to echo modern sentiments. ALFRED DRAKE was alternately charming and comic as Fred, and PATRICIA MORISON was a melodic but demanding Lili. Also featured in the cast were HAROLD LANG, LISA KIRK, Harry Clark and Jack Diamond. Porter's score was divided between those songs in the play-within-the-play—"I've Come to Wive It Wealthily in Padua," "I Hate Men," "Were Thine That Special Face," "Where Is the Life That Late I Led?"—and those sung by the contemporary characters: "Why Can't You Behave?" "Wunderbar," "Too Darn Hot," "Always True to You in My Fashion" and "Brush Up Your Shakespeare." All were expert and revealed Porter's unknown talents for strong character lyrics. *Kiss Me, Kate* ran 1,077 performances, rightfully the biggest hit of Porter's career.

ROBERT KLEIN (1942–), a stand-up comic and actor in nightclubs, in concerts and on television, created the role of songwriter Vernon Gersch in *THEY'RE PLAYING OUR SONG* (1979). Klein's other musical credits include *THE APPLE TREE* (1966) and *New Faces of 1968*.

KEVIN KLINE (1947–), the high-energy film actor, has appeared in plays, musicals and classical pieces on and off Broadway. Kline's Broadway musical credits include movie idol Bruce Granit in *ON THE TWENTIETH CENTURY* (1978) and the Pirate King in the 1981 revival of *The Pirates of Penzance*.

FLORENCE KLOTZ, the highly acclaimed costume designer on Broadway since 1961, has created costumes for many musicals, most notably those for producer-director HAROLD PRINCE: *IT'S A BIRD, IT'S A PLANE, IT'S SUPERMAN* (1966), *FOLLIES* (1971), *A LITTLE NIGHT MUSIC* (1973), *PACIFIC OVERTURES* (1976), *ON THE TWENTIETH CENTURY* (1978), *A*

Doll's Life (1982), *Grind* (1985) and *Roza* (1987). Klotz's other musical designs include *RAGS* (1986) and *CITY OF ANGELS* (1989).

KNICKERBOCKER HOLIDAY (1938) brought the distinguished verse playwright MAXWELL ANDERSON to the musical theatre to write the libretto and lyrics for KURT WEILL's engaging music. The scene is seventeenth-century New Amsterdam where the new governor Pieter Stuyvesant arrives and gets involved in political, romantic and philosophic matters surrounding a condemned patriot and his true love. The story was playful on the surface but the subtext was a bit alarming as dictatorships and even Roosevelt himself were the implied villains. WALTER HUSTON, in his only Broadway musical, was more charming than villainous as the governor, and when he sang the haunting "September Song," the show's issues got a bit muddled. Also in the notable score were "How Can You Tell an American?" "It Never Was You," "There's Nowhere to Go but Up" and "All Hail the Political Honeymoon." The cast also included Richard Kollmar, Jeanne Madden, ROBERT ROUNSEVILLE and RAY MIDDLETON, who played the show's narrator, Washington Irving. *Knickerbocker Holiday* was not a critical or financial success but Huston's rendition of "September Song" is one of the American musical theatre's most enduring fond memories. (168 performances)

KWAMINA (1961) was an unconventional musical with a challenging subject, perhaps too challenging for audiences in the early 1960s. Robert Allan Aurthur's libretto tells of the bittersweet romance between a white doctor (SALLY ANN HOWES) and the black son of a tribal chief (Terry Carter) in a West African country on the verge of independence from Britain. RICHARD ADLER provided a score that was rich in native rhythms and yet had a pleasureable Broadway sound to it. AGNES DE MILLE came up with some novel dances and ROBERT LEWIS directed competently but the whole project was a bit too foreign for most tastes and *Kwamina* closed after thirty-two performances.

L

LA CAGE AUX FOLLES (1983) was the first Broadway musical to have homosexual characters in major roles but it was otherwise a very old-fashioned crowd pleaser with plenty of glitter and hummable songs. Harvey Fierstein adapted the French play and popular film of the same name and ARTHUR LAURENTS directed with all the appropriate flash and skill. Although the musical lacked the subtlety and gentleness of the originals, it did boast strong performances from GEORGE HEARN and Gene Barry as Albin and Georges, a pair of middle-aged lovers in St. Tropez who must try to convince a straight-laced politician that theirs is a normal home so that Georges' son can marry into the respectable family. JERRY HERMAN's songs were labored but accessible and the whole production seemed more safe than carefree. But *La Cage aux Folles* had wide audience appeal and ran for 1,761 performances.

LADY, BE GOOD! (1924) was the first Broadway musical GEORGE and IRA GERSHWIN worked on together and it turned ADELE and FRED ASTAIRE into bona fide Broadway stars. The book, by GUY BOLTON and Fred Thompson, concerns a brother–sister vaudeville act on the skids after they are evicted. Sister helps brother to avoid a bad marriage by posing as a Spanish heiress and all ends happily as true identities are revealed. Although there was some of the old Bolton wit in the libretto, it was the Gershwins' score that triumphed as it introduced jazz rhythms to the Broadway musical. "Fascinating Rhythm," "Little Jazz Bird," "Oh, Lady Be Good!" "The Half of It Dearie Blues" and "So Am I" were the standouts in a superior score. (330 performances)

LADY IN THE DARK (1941) was one of the most experimental musicals of its era and, in retrospect, one of the musical theatre's landmark productions. MOSS HART's libretto employed the often-used dream device but this time the imaginary sequences were psychological studies into the main character rather than excuses for dance or diversion. Magazine editor Liza Elliott is a success in a man's world but her indecision about the four men in her life leads her to seek a psychiatrist's aid. Running throughout the story are snatches of a song called "My Ship" that Liza recalls from her childhood and only when the whole song is completed by her sardonic advertising manager Charley does she make up her mind. Though an overly simple approach to a complex science, *Lady in the Dark* was highly intelligent, witty and fascinating. KURT WEILL (music) and IRA GERSHWIN (lyrics) provided the score, and the songs (other than "My Ship") occurred only in the dream sequences, where Liza sees herself as the star of a circus, as the center of a Ziegfeld-type spectacle, at her wedding and as a child. "This Is New," "The Saga of Jenny" and "Girl of the Moment" were the highlights in a production directed by Hart and HASSARD SHORT and choreographed by Albertina Rasch. GERTRUDE LAWRENCE triumphed as Liza and the four men in her life were played by MacDonald Carey, Bert Lytell, Victor Mature and DANNY KAYE, who stopped the show each night with the tongue-twisting song "Tschaikowsky." The musical ran for 467 performances and then returned in 1943 for 83 more.

BERT LAHR (1895–1967), one of America's most inspired clowns, delighted Broadway and film audiences with his snarling voice and rubber face. Lahr was born in New York and began his career in vaudeville and burlesque before making his Broadway musical debut in *Harry Delmar's Revels* (1927). He first stole the show in *HOLD EVERYTHING!* (1928) as the punch-drunk Gink Schiner and pulled the same stunt in *FLYING HIGH* (1930) as the incompetent airplane mechanic Rusty Krause. Lahr's finest Broadway musical performance was as the washroom attendant Louis Blore in *DuBARRY WAS A LADY* (1939), who wakes up to find himself in the court of King Louis XV. That same year he gave his greatest screen performance, as the Cowardly Lion in *The Wizard of Oz*. Lahr's other Broadway musical credits included *Hot-Cha!* (1932), *LIFE BEGINS AT 8:40* (1934), *THE SHOW IS ON* (1936), *Seven Lively Arts* (1944), *TWO ON THE AISLE* (1951) and *The Boys Against the Girls* (1959). Lahr's last musical was the unsuccessful *Foxy* (1964), in which he played a Volpone-like miser.

HEIDI LANDESMAN (1951–) is a scenic and costume designer as well as a Broadway producer. With her husband Rocco Landesman she presented *BIG RIVER* (1985), *INTO THE WOODS* (1987) and *THE SECRET GARDEN* (1991) on Broadway. Landesman also designed the award-winning sets for *Big River* and *The Secret Garden*.

BURTON LANE (1912–   ), a Hollywood composer who scored a half-dozen Broadway musicals, is mostly remembered for his score for *FINIAN'S RAIN-BOW* (1947). Lane's first songs were being heard on Broadway when he was a teenager. He collaborated with HOWARD DEITZ on songs for *THREE'S A CROWD* (1930) and later with Harold Adamson and E. Y. HARBURG on other revues. Lane went to Hollywood in 1933 but he returned to Broadway for *Finian's Rainbow* with Harburg in 1947, *ON A CLEAR DAY YOU CAN SEE FOREVER* with ALAN JAY LERNER in 1965 and again with Lerner for *CARMELINA* in 1979. Lane is a tuneful and accomplished songwriter and in *Finian's Rainbow* he gave Broadway one of its finest scores.

HAROLD LANG (1923–1985), the energetic actor-dancer and sometimes ballet performer, never got the recognition he deserved for his many and varied talents. Lang started on Broadway in the dancing chorus of *Mr. Strauss Goes to Boston* (1945) and was featured in *Look, Ma, I'm Dancin'* (1948) but did not attract attention until his misbehaving Bill Calhoun in *KISS ME, KATE* (1948). Lang's other musical credits included *Make a Wish* (1951), as Joey Evans in the acclaimed 1952 revival of *PAL JOEY*, *Shangri-La* (1956), the 1959 revival of *ON THE TOWN* and *I CAN GET IT FOR YOU WHOLESALE* (1962).

PHILIP J. LANG (1912–1986), an accomplished orchestrator of over fifty Broadway musicals, did the ORCHESTRATIONS for such renowned musicals as *ANNIE GET YOUR GUN* (1946), *CAN-CAN* (1953), *MY FAIR LADY* (1956), *CARNIVAL* (1961), *HELLO, DOLLY!* (1964), *MAME* (1966), *42ND STREET* (1980) and many more. Lang also orchestrated for the Metropolitan Opera and composed scores for film, television and ballet.

ANGELA LANSBURY (1925–   ), one of the theatre, television and filmdom's most gifted actresses, began her Broadway musical career late in life but with only a half-dozen shows she has become one of the great ladies of the American musical. Lansbury was born in London to a theatrical family and trained for the stage as a child. During World War II she studied acting in New York but was signed by MGM, where she made several movies in the 1940s and 1950s, usually playing evil women or mothers much older than her real age. Although Lansbury had appeared on Broadway in dramas, her musical debut did not come until 1964 with her conniving mayoress Cora Hoover Hoople in *ANY-ONE CAN WHISTLE*. It was her sparkling performance as Mame Dennis in *MAME* (1966), however, that really launched her new career. She played the wistful Countess Aurelia in the short-lived *DEAR WORLD* (1969) then scored a triumph as Mama Rose in *GYPSY* in London in 1973 and on Broadway in 1974. Arguably, Lansbury's most brilliant performance was as the enterprising Mrs. Lovett in *SWEENEY TODD* (1979). In 1983 she revived her Mame on Broadway.

JAMES LAPINE (1949–), a playwright, librettist and director, wrote the librettos for the STEPHEN SONDHEIM musicals *SUNDAY IN THE PARK WITH GEORGE* (1984) and *INTO THE WOODS* (1987), as well as *Falsettoland* (1990) with WILLIAM FINN. Lapine also directed all of the above, as well as the compilation of the Finn musicals called *FALSETTOS* (1992).

PETER LARKIN (1926–), a scenic designer intermittently on Broadway since 1952, did the sets for the musicals *PETER PAN* (1954), *GREENWILLOW* (1960), *DANCIN'* (1978), *Doonesbury* (1983), *THE RINK* (1984) and others.

THE LAST SWEET DAYS OF ISAAC (1970) was the first ROCK MUSICAL to suggest that strong characterization, adept narrative and even wit could be found in the new sound. GRETCHEN CRYER wrote the libretto for the two related one-act musicals about the loss of opportunity and the lack of communication in the modern world. The playlets were wise and funny, and the songs by NANCY FORD (music) and Cryer (lyrics) were astute as well as enjoyable. In the first act, a man and a woman are trapped in an elevator and slowly learn to shed their inhibitions. In the second, the hero is now in jail and tries to communicate with a blonde inmate by way of a television screen. AUSTIN PENDLETON and Fredricka Weber were agreeable as the central characters and the score highlights included "A Transparent Crystal Moment," "Love, You Came to Me" and "Somebody Died Today." The offbeat but lovable show ran Off Broadway for 485 performances.

JOHN LATOUCHE (1917–1956) was one of Broadway's most inventive librettist-lyricists but he never had an all-out hit during his sixteen-year career. Latouche wrote three musicals with composer VERNON DUKE, including the imaginative *CABIN IN THE SKY* (1940), and adapted Chopin's music for *Polonaise* (1945). He provided the lyrics for Duke Ellington's *Beggar's Holiday* (1946), an updated jazz version of John Gay's *The Beggar's Opera*. His finest theatre work was the ingenious book and lyrics for *THE GOLDEN APPLE* (1954) with music by Jerome Moross. Latouche's last contribution before his untimely death was a few lyrics for LEONARD BERNSTEIN's *CANDIDE* (1956). Highly respected by his peers and receiving critical praise for his efforts, Latouche consistently wrote lyrics of high-level craftsmanship, versatility and humor.

ARTHUR LAURENTS (1918–) wrote librettos for two of Broadway's finest post-war musicals, *WEST SIDE STORY* (1957) and *GYPSY* (1959). Laurents' other libretto credits include *ANYONE CAN WHISTLE* (1964), *DO I HEAR A WALTZ?* (1965), *HALLELUJAH, BABY!* (1967) and *Nick and Nora* (1991). Laurents is also a playwright and a much sought after director who staged *I CAN GET IT FOR YOU WHOLESALE* (1962), *Anyone Can Whistle*, *LA CAGE AUX FOLLES* (1983) and the 1974 and 1989 Broadway revivals of *Gypsy*.

CAROL LAWRENCE (1932–), an attractive singer-actress seen in night-clubs and on television, is most remembered on Broadway for creating the role of Maria in *WEST SIDE STORY* (1957). Lawrence made her Broadway debut in *NEW FACES OF 1952* and appeared in the short-lived *Shangri-La* (1956) before getting the role of Maria. Her other musical credits include the ambitious Creole Clio Delaine in *SARATOGA* (1959) and the inquiring writer Angela McKay in *SUBWAYS ARE FOR SLEEPING* (1961).

GERTRUDE LAWRENCE (1898–1952) was one of the theatre's most luminous stars with great success in plays and musicals on both sides of the Atlantic. Lawrence was born in London and was dancing professionally by the time she was twelve. She made her West End debut in 1916 and her first Broadway appearance in *Andre Charlot's Revue of 1924*, captivating New York audiences with her rendition of "Limehouse Blues." Lawrence returned to America for the 1926 edition of *Charlot's Revue* and stayed to do her first Broadway book musical, *OH, KAY!* (1926). While maintaining her London theatre career, she appeared in the New York productions of *Treasure Girl* (1928), *International Revue* (1930) and *Tonight at 8:30* (1936), which she revived in 1948. Her most challenging role was the imaginative executive Liza Elliott in *LADY IN THE DARK* (1941) but her most fondly remembered character was the governess Anna Leonowens in *THE KING AND I* (1951). Lawrence was perhaps the most beloved of all British stars who appeared on Broadway.

JOE LAYTON (1931–) is a director-choreographer who has managed to turn thin musicals into dazzling entertainment by the sheer ingenuity of his staging. Layton started as a dancer in Broadway shows and later choreographed *ONCE UPON A MATTRESS* (1959), *THE SOUND OF MUSIC* (1959), *GREENWILLOW* (1960), *TENDERLOIN* (1960) and *Sail Away* (1962). He made his directing debut with *NO STRINGS* (1962) and followed it with a series of short-lived musicals such as *The Girl Who Came to Supper* (1963), *Drat! The Cat!* (1965), *Sherry!* (1967), *DEAR WORLD* (1969) and *Platinum* (1980). Layton's two triumphs were the clever stagings he gave *GEORGE M!* (1968) and *BARNUM* (1980), two lame BIOGRAPHICAL MUSICALS disguised with exuberant dance and direction.

LEAVE IT TO JANE (1917), although not technically a PRINCESS THEATRE MUSICAL because it did not play at the Princess Theatre, had the same creators as the famous musical series and personified all of its goals to present literate musical comedies with contemporary American characters. GUY BOLTON and P. G. WODEHOUSE wrote the libretto with Wodehouse providing the lyrics for JEROME KERN's music. *Leave It to Jane* was one of the first shows to use that most serviceable of musical settings, the college campus. Everyone is concerned about Atwater College's upcoming football game and it is up to the president's daughter Jane to win the heart and loyalty of an all-American halfback who is thinking of playing for the rival team. In addition to the lively title song, the score included "Just You Watch My Step," "The Siren's Song," "Wait Till Tomorrow" and the comic "Cleopatterer." In many ways *Leave It to Jane* represents the creative trio of Bolton, Wodehouse and Kern at their best. (167 performances)

LEAVE IT TO ME! (1938) was a COLE PORTER musical mostly remembered for introducing MARY MARTIN to Broadway. Singing "My Heart Belongs to Daddy" to a male quartet in a Siberian railroad station, Martin captivated audiences for the first time. She was ably assisted by VICTOR MOORE, WILLIAM GAXTON, SOPHIE TUCKER, TAMARA and, in a small role, GENE KELLY. The libretto, by BELLA and SAMUEL SPEWACK, was a light-hearted political satire about an unwilling American ambassador to Russia and his vain attempts to get sent back to the States. Other memorable Porter songs in the musical included "Get Out of Town," "From Now On" and "Most Gentlemen Don't Like Love." (291 performances)

EUGENE and FRANNE LEE (1939– ; 1941–) are designers who collaborated together on unusual projects when they were married, he doing sets and she doing costumes. Their two most memorable Broadway musical credits were the environmental design for the 1974 revival of *CANDIDE* and the massive factory design for *SWEENEY TODD* (1979).

GYPSY ROSE LEE (1914–1970), the world-famous striptease artist, began in vaudeville and later appeared in a handful of Broadway musicals: *Hot-Cha!* (1932), *Melody* (1933), the 1936 edition of the *ZIEGFELD FOLLIES* and *Star and Garter* (1942). Lee's autobiography *Gypsy* was the basis for the 1959 musical.

MICHELE LEE (1942–), a statuesque leading lady on stage and television, played Gittel Mosca in *SEESAW* (1973). Lee also appeared in the musicals *HOW TO SUCCEED IN BUSINESS WITHOUT REALLY TRYING* (1961) and *Bravo Giovanni* (1962).

CAROLYN LEIGH (1926–1983), the lyricist who often collaborated with composer CY COLEMAN, provided lyrics for *WILDCAT* (1960), *LITTLE ME* (1962) and *How Now Dow Jones* (1967) but is most remembered for the songs she contributed to *PETER PAN* (1954). Leigh started her career in advertising and then wrote scripts for television operettas before teaming up with Coleman on several popular singles. With composer Mark Charlap she wrote some of *Peter Pan*'s most vivacious songs, such as "I'm Flying" and "I've Gotta Crow." Her lyrics for *Little Me* captured the flavor of NEIL SIMON's libretto accurately and playfully. At its best, Leigh's work was inspired fun and her lyrics had a brassy, confident tone that matched Coleman's music beautifully.

LEND AN EAR (1948), one of the last of the truly clever original musical revues, offered sketches, music and lyrics by Charles Gaynor. Although the score was not exceptional, there was a hilarious spoof of 1920s musical comedy called "The Gladiola Girl," which eclipsed the similar British *THE BOY FRIEND* (1954) by several years. *Lend an Ear* is also noteworthy for two famous debuts: it was CAROL CHANNING's first Broadway show and it provided GOWER CHAMPION with his first choreography credit. (460 performances)

LOTTE LENYA (1900–1981) was an international singing star of cabarets and concerts whose few musical theatre appearances were striking and memorable. The Austrian-born Lenya performed in four of the KURT WEILL–Bertolt Brecht musicals in Berlin, including *The Threepenny Opera* in 1928, in which she created the role of the prostitute Jenny. She married Weill and the two of them fled Nazi Germany and settled in America in 1935. Lenya played the Duchess in Weill's *The Firebrand of Florence* (1945) then retired. But after her husband's death in 1950 she began a new career performing and recording his songs and recreating the role of Jenny in the long-running Off-Broadway revival of *THE THREEPENNY OPERA* (1954). Lenya returned to Broadway to play the pragmatic Fraulein Schneider in *CABARET* (1966). With her hardened and expressive voice and her Teutonic theatrics, Lenya was one of the most unique performers to appear on the New York stage.

ALAN JAY LERNER (1918–1986), the celebrated lyricist-librettist who is most remembered for his partnership with composer FREDERICK LOEWE, collaborated with several composers in a career filled with glory and disappointment. Lerner was born in New York City into a wealthy family, the founders of a chain of women's clothing stores, the Lerner Shops. The family saw to it that Lerner received the best education: exclusive private schools in England and America, Juilliard, Harvard and Oxford. From an early age Lerner knew he wanted to make the theatre his life and he started writing lyrics for the Hasty Pudding shows at Harvard. After graduation he wrote many scripts for radio and contributed lyrics to revues at the Lambs Club, where he met Loewe in 1942. The new team's first Broadway musicals, *What's Up?* (1943) and *The Day Before Spring* (1945), had a witty, playful quality that impressed some but neither show ran very long. Their first success was *BRIGADOON* (1947) in which Lerner wrote an original libretto filled with whimsey and charm and lyrics that matched Loewe's evocative music. Despite the success of *Brigadoon*, Lerner did not plan to write with Loewe exclusively and in 1948 he collaborated with composer KURT WEILL on *LOVE LIFE*, the most experimental show of the lyricist's career and one of Broadway's first CONCEPT MUSICALS. Lerner next went to Hollywood where he scored *Royal Wedding* (1951) with BURTON LANE and wrote the screenplay for *An American in Paris* (1951). With *PAINT YOUR WAGON* (1951), the team of

Lerner and Loewe were reunited on Broadway and the result was a raucous musical that still had some room for lovely ballads. The team's greatest hit, *MY FAIR LADY* (1956), was unlike their previous work but it was the show that best displayed their talents for wit, elegance, comic character and romance. *CAMELOT* (1960) was another success for the team but it was to be their last. Loewe retired in 1961 and only returned to Broadway once in 1973 to collaborate on a few songs for the stage version of their earlier film musical *Gigi*. Undaunted by his partner's retirement, Lerner collaborated with other composers for the next twenty-five years but rarely did he ever meet with any success. *ON A CLEAR DAY YOU CAN SEE FOREVER* (1965) had a lovely score with Burton Lane but a troubled book. *COCO* (1969), with music by André Previn, only ran as long as its star KATHARINE HEPBURN stayed with the show. The promising *1600 PENNSYLVANIA AVENUE* (1976), with LEONARD BERNSTEIN returning to Broadway to provide the music, was a one-week disaster. *CARMELINA* (1979), again with Lane, had a superior score but book problems again, and *DANCE A LITTLE CLOSER* (1983), with composer CHARLES STROUSE, closed on opening night despite a strong cast and some delightful songs. Lerner was slated to write the lyrics–libretto for ANDREW LLOYD WEBBER's *THE PHANTOM OF THE OPERA* but illness prevented him from doing so. Lerner died in 1986, one of Broadway's most respected artists but a man who for twenty years had had nothing but flops. Lerner wrote the librettos for just about all of his musicals but it was his lyric power that always remained at a high point. Even the most troubled later shows had expert lyric craftsmanship. Few in the musical theatre have combined romance, intelligence and wit in the way Lerner did.

LES MISÉRABLES (1987) had originated as a musical pageant in France and was a London hit before its arrival on Broadway, where it quickly became a sensation. French pop composer Claude-Michel Schonberg and librettist Alain Boubil wrote the all-sung show but Herbert Kretzmer, who wrote the English lyrics, and the directors TREVOR NUNN and John Caird, the designer JOHN NAPIER and the producer CAMERON MACKINTOSH were all British. Victor Hugo's classic tale of poverty, revenge and love got an operatic treatment but the characters remained vivid and the visual images were stunning. Colm Wilkinson recreated his moving portrayal of the central character, Jean Val Jean, from the West End production but an American cast filled the rest of the many roles. *Les Misérables* continues to please audiences worldwide and, despite its old-fashioned grand opera approach, has done much to make Broadway musicals appealing to the younger generations. (still running as of 3/1/93)

LET 'EM EAT CAKE (1933) was a sequel to the celebrated musical satire *OF THEE I SING* (1931) and it reunited librettists GEORGE S. KAUFMAN and MORRIE RYSKIND with the GERSHWINS, as well as the three principal actors recreating their original characters: WILLIAM GAXTON as John P. Wintergreen, VICTOR MOORE as Alexander Throttlebottom and Lois Moran as Mary. The plot for *Let 'Em Eat Cake* again dealt with the political situation in the United States, but there was a less than amusing subtext in the development of an American Fascist party called the "blueshirts" and a revolution that threatened to send the vice president to the guillotine. Audiences in 1933, facing the Fascist buildup in Europe and deeper into the Depression, could not warm up to the show and it closed after ninety performances. George Gershwin's music was as accomplished as that of the original and Ira Gershwin's lyrics were equally skillful but only one song, "Mine," became popular. It would be fifty years before the complete score would be discovered and finally recorded and *Let 'Em Eat Cake* would be appreciated for the exceptional piece it is.

LET'S FACE IT! (1941) was a war-time COLE PORTER musical that featured the clowning of DANNY KAYE to distract from a silly story about men in uniform gallivanting with patriotic Southampton matrons. DOROTHY and HERBERT FIELDS wrote the libretto and Kay's wife, songster Sylvia Fine, added specialty numbers to Porter's score. The cast was top notch—EVE ARDEN, Benny Baker, Edith Meiser, VIVIAN VANCE, Mary Kay Walsh and NANETTE FABRAY—and Porter's score was best when it was comic: "Farming," "Let's Not Talk About Love" and "Ace in the Hole." (547 performances)

SAM LEVENE (1905–1980), the first-rate character actor who appeared in Broadway comedies from 1927, is most remembered by musical theatre audiences as the original Nathan Detroit in *GUYS AND DOLLS* (1950). Levene's two other musical efforts were the short-lived shows *Let It Ride* (1961) and *Cafe Crown* (1964).

HERMAN LEVIN (1907–1990) is mostly known as the producer who struggled for years to bring *MY FAIR LADY* (1956) to the Broadway stage. Levin's other musicals include *CALL ME MISTER* (1946), *GENTLEMEN PREFER BLONDES* (1949), *The Girl Who Came to Supper* (1963) and *Lovely Ladies, Kind Gentlemen* (1970).

ROBERT LEWIS (1909–   ), a theatre and film director, staged the Broadway musicals *BRIGADOON* (1947), *REGINA* (1949), *JAMAICA* (1957), *KWAMINA* (1961), *Foxy* (1964) and *ON A CLEAR DAY YOU CAN SEE FOREVER* (1965). Lewis is an eminent director of plays, a respected theatre educator and co-founder of the Group Theatre.

LIFE BEGINS AT 8:40 (1934) was another inspired musical revue to come from that genre's golden age in the 1930s. IRA GERSHWIN and E.Y. HARBURG provided lyrics for HAROLD ARLEN's music and they came up with such song favorites as "What Can You Say in a Love Song?" and "You're a

Builder-Upper." BERT LAHR led the cast with his ingenious impersonations of a newly elected Fiorello LaGuardia, a snotty Englishman, a suicidal Frenchman and a gushing concertgoer. Also in the show were Luella Gear, Frances Williams, Brian Donlevy and, in his first major Broadway assignment, RAY BOLGER, who did a nimble dance interpretation of a prize fight. (237 performances)

LI'L ABNER (1956) had the cartoonish quality of the Al Capp comic strip it was based on but it also boasted a fine score by Gene de Paul (music) and JOHNNY MERCER (lyrics) and jubilant choreography by MICHAEL KIDD. Librettists Norman Panama and Melvin Frank set their story in Dogpatch, U.S.A., and included several of the Capp regulars: easy-going Abner Yokum, ever-hopeful Daisy Mae, Mammy and Pappy Yokum, Marryin' Sam, General Bullmoose, Senator Phogbound and the seductive Appassionata Von Climax. The plot involves Daisy Mae's continual efforts to marry Li'l Abner as well as the government's plan to turn Dogpatch into a testing ground for the atom bomb. PETER PALMER, EDIE ADAMS, STUBBY KAYE, Charlotte Rae and Tina Louise led the spirited cast and among the songs were "Namely You," "The Country's in the Very Best of Hands," "If I Had My Druthers" and "Jubilation T. Cornpone." Director-choreographer Kidd's Sadie Hawkins Day chase was the show's highlight. *Li'l Abner* was not the sharp satire that its source was but it was a well-crafted musical that ran for 693 performances.

BEATRICE LILLIE (1894–1989), one of the world's great clown ladies, entertained audiences on both sides of the Atlantic for over fifty years. Lillie was born in Toronto, Canada, and began her career in London revues starting in 1914. She first appeared on Broadway in the BRITISH IMPORT *Andre Charlot's Revue of 1924* and returned on several occasions, usually in musical revues where her distinctive caricatures and outrageous comic bits could be more easily incorporated. Lillie's Broadway credits included *She's My Baby* (1928), *Walk a Little Faster* (1932), *AT HOME ABROAD* (1933), *THE SHOW IS ON* (1936), *Seven Lively Arts* (1944), *INSIDE U.S.A.* (1948) and as the wacky medium Madam Arcati in *High Spirits* (1964).

HAL LINDEN (1931–), an affable leading man of stage and television, is most remembered by Broadway audiences for his powerful performance as the family patriarch Mayer Rothschild in *THE ROTHSCHILDS* (1970). Linden's other musical credits include *WILDCAT* (1960); Billy Cocker in the 1962 Off-Broadway revival of *ANYTHING GOES*; and the short-lived musicals *Something More* (1964), *Illya, Darling* (1967) and *The Education of H*Y*M*A*N K*A*P*L*A*N* (1968).

HOWARD LINDSAY (1888–1968), the senior member of the successful playwriting team of Lindsay and Crouse, wrote nine musical librettos, most of them with his partner RUSSEL CROUSE. They provided the books for *ANYTHING*

GOES (1934), *RED, HOT AND BLUE!* (1936), *HOORAY FOR WHAT!* (1937), *CALL ME MADAM* (1950), *Happy Hunting* (1956), *THE SOUND OF MUSIC* (1959) and *MR. PRESIDENT* (1962). Lindsay was also a valued director and staged the original productions of *GAY DIVORCE* (1932), *Anything Goes, Red, Hot and Blue!* and others.

LITTLE JOHNNY JONES (1904) was the multitalented GEORGE M. COHAN's third Broadway effort and his first of many musical hits. Cohan wrote the libretto, music and lyrics for *Little Johhny Jones* as well as directing it and playing the title character. The plot, about an American jockey wrongly accused of throwing a race in England, was a well-crafted melodrama filled with emotional cliffhangers. (Cohan billed the show as a "musical play.") The most famous scene in the musical is Jones' rendition of "Give My Regards to Broadway" on the Southampton pier when he hears that criminal charges have been dropped. The vibrant score also introduced "The Yankee Doodle Boy" and "Life's a Funny Proposition After All," a sly talk-song that expresses the hero's philosophy of life. The musical ran fifty-two performances in its initial engagement but returned to New York from touring in 1905 and ran another four months.

LITTLE MARY SUNSHINE (1959) was a long-running Off-Broadway PAS-TICHE MUSICAL that spoofed the old operetta form, most obviously *ROSE-MARIE* (1924). Rick Besoyan wrote the libretto, music and lyrics and in all three he captured the highly stylized grandeur of the genre even if the whole burlesque got a bit repetitous at times. Besoyan and Ray Harrison directed a delightful cast that included Eileen Brennan and JOHN MCMARTIN and the show ran a surprising 1,143 performances.

LITTLE ME (1962) was a vehicle for television star SID CAESAR but the musical had much more to offer than just a star turn. NEIL SIMON, in his first musical assignment, adapted Patrick Dennis' novel of the same name and CY COLEMAN (music) and CAROLYN LEIGH (lyrics) provided a lively score. The episodic story tells of low-born Belle from Venezuela, Illinois, as she climbs up in the world utilizing a series of valuable husbands and lovers, all played by Caesar. The talented comic got to play a sixteen-year-old snob, a German Hollywood director, an old miser, a European prince and other fun characters, whereas the part of Belle was played at different ages by VIRGINIA MARTIN and Nancy Andrews. Two songs from the Coleman–Leigh score later became popular, "Real Live Girl" and "I've Got Your Number," but all the numbers were bright and amusing, including "Boom Boom," "Be a Performer," "I Love You" and the title number. BOB FOSSE choreographed and his "Rich Kids Rag" was the dancing highlight of the show. (257 performances)

A LITTLE NIGHT MUSIC (1973) was perhaps the most charming and accessible of the STEPHEN SONDHEIM-scored musicals. HUGH WHEELER adapted Ingmar Bergman's film *Smiles of a Summer Night* (1955) into an enchanting musical that bordered on operetta and Sondheim composed a score completely in 3/4 time or multiples thereof. The story is a comedy of manners set during a summer in turn-of-the-century Sweden. Lawyer Fredrik (LEN CARIOU) has regrets about his marriage to the young Anne (Victoria Mallory) and is drawn to his former mistress, the actress Desirée (Glynis Johns), despite her new lover, Count Carl-Magnus (Laurence Guittard). Complicating the romantic triangles are Fredrik's son, Henrik (Mark Lambert), who is falling in love with his young stepmother, and the Count's wife, Charlotte (Patricia Elliott), who is determined to get her husband back. Overseeing and commenting on the follies of all these lovers is Desirée's mother, Madame Armfeldt (HERMIONE GINGOLD), and a quintet of singers who also act as a chorus. The whole project was witty, gentle and intoxicating. Sondheim provided warm melodies and ever-skillful lyrics, the most memorable being "Every Day a Little Death," "Remember?" "The Miller's Son," "Now/Later/Soon" and the popular "Send in the Clowns." HAROLD PRINCE directed the splendid cast with a delicate touch and *A Little Night Music* pleased audiences for 600 performances.

LITTLE SHOP OF HORRORS (1982), the long-running Off-Broadway camp musical, was offbeat enough to be different and yet engaging enough to be appealing. HOWARD ASHMAN wrote the libretto, lyrics and directed the little musical and ALAN MENKEN provided the 1960s-like music. Based on the 1960 cult film of the same name, the story tells of the nerdy Seymour (Lee Wilkof) who stumbles upon a blood-dependent plant that will make his fortune if he promises to keep supplying the botanical monster with fresh blood. This odd premise was humanized with a love triangle between Seymour, his beloved but masochistic Audrey (ELLEN GREENE) and her sadistic dentist-boyfriend (Franc Luz). The plant grows with each scene until it has devoured all the main characters and starts on the audience itself. *Little Shop of Horrors* was finely crafted and the songs were more than parodies of the period's pop music. "Skid Row," "Somewhere That's Green," "Grow for Me" and "Suddenly Seymour" were among the exceptional musical numbers. (2,209 performances)

THE LITTLE SHOW (1929) was not little by today's standards but it was much more intimate and cerebral than the revues FLORENZ ZIEGFELD and GEORGE WHITE were presenting at the time. *The Little Show* was the first collaboration of composer ARTHUR SCHWARTZ and lyricist HOWARD DIETZ, perhaps the finest team to score musical revues in the 1930s. "I Guess I'll Have to Change My Plan," "Hammacher-Schlemmer, I Love You" and "A Little Hut in Hoboken" were their offerings in the show, which also introduced "Moanin' Low" (music by Ralph Rainger). Dietz and GEORGE S. KAUFMAN wrote the sketches, including the famous one-act comedy "The Still Alarm," and the talented cast included CLIFTON WEBB, LIBBY HOLMAN,

BETTINA HALL, FRED ALLEN, JACK McCAULEY and Constance Cummings. Webb had been appearing on Broadway for over a decade but it was his performance in this revue than established his popularity. *The Little Show* ran for 321 performances and inspired sequels in 1930 and 1931.

LOCATIONS FOR MUSICALS have ranged from Tibet (*Shanrgi-La* in 1956) to *Timbuktu* (1978) and back again but far and away the most popular location has always been New York City, where approximately one-third of all book musicals are set. From the pre-Revolutionary days of *KNICKERBOCKER HOLIDAY* (1938) when it was called New Amsterdam to the "with it" ROCK MUSICAL *YOUR OWN THING* (1968), where it was called Illyria, New York is the location of choice. Some of the many musicals that used the city itself as an integral part of the show include *ON THE TOWN* (1944), *A TREE GROWS IN BROOKLYN* (1951), *TENDERLOIN* (1960), *WONDERFUL TOWN* (1953), *THE NEW YORKERS* (1930), *FIORELLO!* (1959), *SEESAW* (1973), *UP IN CENTRAL PARK* (1945) and *COMPANY* (1970). The closest runner-up city is Paris, COLE PORTER's favorite town and the location for his *SILK STOCKINGS* (1951), *CAN-CAN* (1953), *FIFTY MILLION FRENCHMEN* (1929) and, of course, *Paris* (1928). Among the many other musicals set in Paris are *MLLE. MODISTE* (1905), *DEAR WORLD* (1969), *ROBERTA* (1933), *IRMA LA DOUCE* (1960), *THE VAGABOND KING* (1925) and *SUNDAY IN THE PARK WITH GEORGE* (1984). Most of the major world cities have been useful locations for musicals, including the unlikely Baghdad (*KISMET* in 1953), Johannesburg (*LOST IN THE STARS* in 1949), Budapest (*I MARRIED AN ANGEL* in 1938), Bangkok (*THE KING AND I* in 1951), Buenos Aires (*EVITA* in 1979) and even ancient Ephesus (*THE BOYS FROM SYRACUSE* in 1938). The most remote places have also been used, such as Siberia (*LEAVE IT TO ME!* in 1938), the Sahara Desert (*THE DESERT SONG* in 1926), the Canadian Rockies (*ROSE-MARIE* in 1924), the Klondike wilderness (*Foxy* in 1964) and an asteroid in outer space (*Via Galactia* in 1972). Among the musicals that eschewed just one location and gallivanted across a continent or two were *CANDIDE* (1956), *THE UNSINKABLE MOLLY BROWN* (1960), *THE ROTHSCHILDS* (1970), *EVANGELINE* (1874), *Oh, Captain!* (1958), *GYPSY* (1959), *NO STRINGS* (1962) and *ANNIE GET YOUR GUN* (1946). Fictitious locations have always been popular and sometimes entertaining in themselves. *FINIAN'S RAINBOW* (1946) is set in "Missitucky, USA" while *THE RED MILL* (1906) takes place in Katwykaan-Zee, Holland. *ROSALIE* (1928) was set in Romanza, *THE GOLDEN APPLE* (1954) in the two cities of Angel's Roost and Rhododendron, and the folks in *MEXICAN HAYRIDE* (1944) went to Xochimilco and other unpronounceable places. And, finally, there was the delightful location for *CALL ME MADAM* (1950), which took place in "two mythical countries, one is Lichtenburg, the other the United States of America."

FRANK LOESSER (1910–1969), the composer-lyricist who was associated with only six Broadway shows, was one of the most versatile artists Broadway has ever seen. Each of his musicals is different from the others and all are superior works. Loesser was born in New York City to a family involved with classical music. But Loesser loved popular music and wrote songs while he worked as a newspaper reporter and a sketch writer for vaudeville and radio. A few of his songs were heard on Broadway in *The Illustrators' Show* (1936) then he went to Hollywood where he wrote lyrics for movie musicals with many famous composers. Loesser wrote both music and lyrics for "Praise the Lord and Pass the Ammunition," a song that became a World War II favorite, and from then on he always wrote solo. He returned to Broadway with the delightful musical farce *WHERE'S CHARLEY?* (1948) and then followed it with the sly and funny *GUYS AND DOLLS* (1950). Loesser used Italianate opera techniques for his *THE MOST HAPPY FELLA* (1956), a gentle folklore quality in *GREENWILLOW* (1960) and urban satire in *HOW TO SUCCEED IN BUSINESS WITHOUT REALLY TRYING* (1961). Loesser's talent for capturing in words and music so many different kinds of settings and situations has kept his work fresh and accessible for each new generation to rediscover him.

FREDERICK LOEWE (1904–1988), the composer of some of Broadway's most romantic music, worked exclusively with lyricist-librettist ALAN JAY LERNER after 1942, forming one of the great musical collaborations of the American theatre. Loewe was born in Berlin to a musical family and became a child prodigy, playing with the Berlin Symphony at the age of thirteen. At fifteen he wrote a song called "Katrina," which became one of the most popular songs in Europe. Loewe moved to America when he was twenty so that he could make his mark in the New World but met with bitter disappointment. His musical abilities were not recognized so to survive he worked as a nightclub pianist, boxer, bus boy, cow puncher and even a gold prospector out West. Returning to New York in 1935 he started writing songs with Earle Crooker and the team had a few songs interpolated into Broadway revues as well as scoring a forgotten opera called *Great Lady* (1938). In 1942 Loewe met Lerner and his fortunes changed. Their first two musicals, *What's Up?* (1943) and *The Day Before Spring* (1945), were not hits but pointed to a team of promise. Their *BRIGADOON* (1947), though, was a sensation and made Loewe's reputation for highly romantic music. *PAINT YOUR WAGON* (1951) was quite different from *Brigadoon* in setting, character and temperament but again the score had evocative ballads and rousing chorus numbers. The team's *MY FAIR LADY* (1956) was another new direction for Lerner and Loewe as they turned a British drawing room comedy into one of the most beloved musicals of the American theatre. *CAMELOT* (1960), despite its troublesome preparation and flawed script, was also very popular but the rigors of working for Broadway had taken their toll and Loewe retired. He did collaborate with Lerner on a few songs when their 1958 film *Gigi* was adapted for Broadway in 1973 but Loewe's career was virtually over and one of Broadway's greatest collaborations ended. Loewe was a versatile composer who could create a variety of musical styles but his genius lay in his soaring romantic songs.

JOSHUA LOGAN (1908–1988) directed numerous plays, musicals and films, as well as co-authoring four Broadway musicals. Born in Texarkana, Texas, Logan was educated at Princeton and studied theatre at the Moscow Art Theatre under Stanislavky. He directed the Broadway productions of *I MARRIED AN ANGEL* (1938), *KNICKERBOCKER HOLIDAY* (1938), *THIS IS THE ARMY* (1942), *ANNIE GET YOUR GUN* (1946), *SOUTH PACIFIC* (1949), *FANNY* (1954), *ALL AMERICAN* (1962) and others. He contributed to the librettos of *Higher and Higher* (1940), *South Pacific*, *WISH YOU WERE HERE* (1952) and *Fanny*.

WILLIAM IVEY LONG (1947–), a costume designer for stage and opera, provided the superb costumes for *NINE* (1982), *THE TAP DANCE KID* (1984), *Smile* (1986), *ASSASSINS* (1990), *CRAZY FOR YOU* (1992) and the 1992 revival of *GUYS AND DOLLS*.

PRISCILLA LOPEZ (1948–), a character actress in Broadway musicals since 1966, played the Puerto Rican Diana in *A CHORUS LINE* (1975) and HARPO MARX in *A Day in Hollywood–A Night in the Ukraine* (1980). Lopez's other musical credits include *Henry, Sweet Henry* (1967), *Her First Roman* (1968) and *What's a Nice Country Like You...* (1973).

LILLIAN LORRAINE (1892–1955), a statuesque singer and a favorite of producer FLORENZ ZIEGFELD, appeared in five editions of his *Follies* between 1909 and 1918. Lorraine's other musicals included *Miss Innocence* (1908), *Over the River* (1912), *The Whirl of the World* (1914), *The Little Blue Devil* (1919) and *The Blue Kitten* (1922).

LOST IN THE STARS (1949) was, sadly, KURT WEILL's last completed musical and possibly his most passionate. Playwright MAXWELL ANDERSON adapted Alan Paton's novel *Cry, the Beloved Country* and wrote the powerful lyrics for Weill's music. Set in South Africa, the story centers on two families, one white and the other black, in a small village. The black minister's son has gone to Johannesburg and disappeared into a life of crime while the white planter's liberal son goes to the same city to work for improving the social ills. The minister goes searching for his son, finds his pregnant girlfriend and learns that the son has been arrested for an attempted robbery in which the planter's son was accidentally killed. As the son is convicted to hang, the two fathers are drawn together in grief and understanding. This grim but enlightening tale was enhanced by an excellent score that included "Thousands of Miles," "Train to

Johannesburg," "Trouble Man," "Cry, the Beloved Country" and the gentle but moving title song. ROUBEN MAMOULIAN directed a first-rate cast that included TODD DUNCAN, Leslie Banks, Julian Mayfield and Inez Matthews. Like Weill's *STREET SCENE* (1947), *Lost in the Stars* today is occasionally included in the repertory of opera companies. (273 performances)

DOROTHY LOUDON (1933–), a character actress in many plays and musicals, finally achieved stardom as the villainous Miss Hannigan in *ANNIE* (1977). Loudon's other musical credits include *The Fig Leaves Are Falling* (1969), *Ballroom* (1978) and *Jerry's Girls* (1985).

LOUISIANA PURCHASE (1940) was one of IRVING BERLIN's best book musicals with a funny libretto by B. G. DESYLVA and MORRIE RYSKIND and a delightful score that has been sadly neglected over the years. The corruption in Huey Long's Louisiana politics inspired this story about a naive senator who is sent to New Orleans to investigate shady business practices at the Louisiana Purchasing Company. The firm's shrewd lawyer tries to put the senator in a compromising position first with a sexy Viennese lady and then with a seductive French madame but all ends in justice and marriage. The superb cast included VICTOR MOORE, WILLIAM GAXTON, VERA ZORINA, IRENE BORDONI and CAROL BRUCE, and the melodic score featured "It's a Lovely Day Tomorrow," "What Chance Have I?" "Fools Fall in Love," "You're Lonely and I'm Lonely" and the cheery title song. (444 performances)

LOVE LIFE (1948) is considered one of the first CONCEPT MUSICALS of the American theatre and a fascinating experiment that foreshadowed the creative musicals of the 1960s and 1970s. The show was the only collaboration of ALAN JAY LERNER and KURT WEILL and the result was as unconventional as it was beguiling. Lerner's libretto was an expressionistic chronicle of the United States from 1791 to the present as seen through one married couple who progress through the decades without aging. The story was more episodic than linear and was interrupted by vaudeville acts that commented on the action. (The same device would later be used in *CABARET*, *FOLLIES*, *CHICAGO* and other shows.) *Love Life* wavered between brilliance and pretentiousness but the score was exemplary with "Economics," "Progress" and "This Is the Life" working effectively within the narrative but unsalable on their own. "Here I'll Stay" and "Green-Up Time" enjoyed some popularity and the show managed to run 252 performances. RAY MIDDLETON and NANETTE FABRAY played the central couple, BORIS ARONSON designed the imaginative sets and Elia Kazan directed.

PATTI LUPONE (1949–), one of the most dynamic musical theatre stars to emerge since the 1970s, gave thrilling performances as the misguided Genevieve in *THE BAKER'S WIFE* (1976), Eva Peron in *EVITA* (1979), and Reno

Sweeney in the 1987 Broadway revival of *ANYTHING GOES*. LuPone also originated the role of Fantine in the London production of *LES MISÉRABLES* (1985). Her other musical credits include the first Broadway version of *THE ROBBER BRIDEGROOM* (1975), *WORKING* (1978) and the 1984 revival of *OLIVER!*

PAUL LYNDE (1926–1982), the giggling television comic actor, made two memorable Broadway appearances: *NEW FACES OF 1952* and as the harried father Mr. McAfee in *BYE BYE BIRDIE* (1960).

M

GALT MACDERMOT (1928–) is an eclectic composer mostly known for his music for *HAIR* (1968). MacDermot was born in Montreal, the son of a diplomat, and studied music in Capetown, South Africa, where he started writing operas. He settled in New York in the late 1960s and met Gerome Ragni and James Rado, his collaborators on *Hair*. MacDermot next worked with playwright John Guare on the musical *TWO GENTLEMEN OF VERONA* (1971) before reuniting with Rado and Ragni for the two notorious Broadway flops *Dude* (1972) and *Via Galactica* (1972). His Off-Broadway *The Karl Marx Play* (1973), written with Rochelle Owens, was also a failure. MacDermot scored a series of musicals in Trinidad with playwright Derek Walcott during the 1970s but returned to the Public Theatre in New York with *The Human Comedy* (1983), a gentle and engaging near-opera version of William Sayroyan's novel. The musical was a hit Off Broadway but, despite favorable reviews, did not last long when it moved to Broadway. MacDermot is a versatile composer who uses everything from African rhythms to pop to opera in his work.

MACK AND MABEL (1974) was not a hit for composer-lyricist JERRY HERMAN but it did contain his most accomplished score. The stormy romance between movie pioneer Mack Sennett (ROBERT PRESTON) and his comic star Mabel Normand (BERNADETTE PETERS) was dramatized by MICHAEL STEWART, and GOWER CHAMPION staged the production with wit and care, but audiences didn't like the down ending and the show closed after sixty-five performances. What remains are some of Herman's finest songs: "I Won't Send Roses," "Hundreds of Girls," "Tap Your Troubles Away," "Wherever He Ain't," "Look What Happened to Mabel" and "Time Heals Everything." *Mack and Mabel* eventually found new life in revivals and summer theatre productions.

CAMERON MACKINTOSH (1946–), the celebrated British producer, has brought his biggest London blockbuster musicals to Broadway with great success: *CATS* (1982), *LES MISÉRABLES* (1987) and *MISS SAIGON* (1991). Mackintosh co-produced *LITTLE SHOP OF HORRORS* (1982) Off Broadway and then moved it to the West End, where he has presented other American musicals as well. In 1992 he presented the London revue *Five Guys Named Moe* on Broadway.

MADAME SHERRY (1910) was the most famous of the six collaborations between composer KARL HOSCHNA and lyricist-librettist OTTO HAR-BACH. Edward Sherry heads a dance school of the Isadora Duncan style but has lied to his millionaire uncle that he is married and has two children. When the uncle unexpectedly arrives, Ed must try to convince his wealthy relative that the Irish landlady is Ed's wife and that two of the dancing pupils are his kids. The plot had shown up earlier in musicals produced in London, Brussels and Paris but the Hoschna–Harbach version was the sharpest and ran for 231 performances. The whole score was bright and melodic but the only songs known today are "Every Little Movement (Has a Meaning All Its Own)" and the later-interpolated "Put Your Arms Around Me, Honey" by Albert Von Tilzer and Junie McCree.

THE MAGIC SHOW (1974) ran for 1,920 performances despite reviews that continued to lambast the show during its four-year run. The chief attraction was illusionist Doug Henning, whose spectacular magic feats made this musical a hit with families and groups. The libretto, by Bob Randall, was about a down-and-out nightclub in Passaic, New Jersey, that, hoping to avoid bankruptcy, books a magic act. STEPHEN SCHWARTZ wrote his least interesting score for the little musical but no one minded because all the magic came from elsewhere.

MAKE MINE MANHATTAN (1948), one of the last in the era of original Broadway revues, had sketches and lyrics by Arnold B. Horwitt and music by Richard Lewine but the show was a success because of the inspired antics of SID CAESAR, Joshua Shelley and DAVID BURNS. The skits and musical numbers were thematically tied together by the fact that they all took a satiric view toward life in New York City. One song from the score, "Saturday Night in Central Park," enjoyed some popularity. (429 performances)

RICHARD MALTBY, JR. (1937–), is a lyricist and director who finally found big time success in the musical theatre after nearly twenty-five years of quality work. Maltby was educated at Yale, where he met fellow student DAVID SHIRE, who would become his most frequent composer-collaborator. Their Off-Broadway musical *The Sap of Life* (1961) was short lived but gained some attention. They did better with their revue *STARTING HERE, STARTING NOW* (1977), a refreshingly romantic celebration of life and love in the 1970s. Maltby conceived, directed and wrote some lyrics for *AIN'T MISBEHAVIN'* (1978), an intimate little revue of Thomas "Fats" Waller's songs. It opened Off Broadway then later transferred to Broadway, where it became the most successful revue of the decade. Teaming up with Shire again, Maltby wrote the musical *BABY* (1983) for Broadway but it was a small show at heart and it failed in the big theatre. He next adapted the British lyrics for and directed ANDREW LLOYD WEBBER's *Song and Dance* when the American version opened on Broadway in 1985. Back off Broadway, Maltby and Shire scored the revue *CLOSER THAN EVER* (1989), an updating of the ideas explored in their earlier *Starting Here, Starting Now*. Major recognition as a lyricist finally came to Maltby in 1989 when *MISS SAIGON* opened in London and then on Broadway in 1991. His next musical, *Nick and Nora* (1991), was a quick flop on Broadway. Maltby is an incisive lyricist with a very strong sense of character and an acute ear for the American vernacular.

MAME (1966) was a splashy, broadly played musical comedy built around the talents of a star, in this case ANGELA LANSBURY, who became one of Broadway's musical theatre favorites with this show. Patrick Dennis' novel *Auntie Mame* had already been a popular play and film so there were few surprises in *Mame*. Jerome Lawrence and Robert E. Lee adapted their own play version and JERRY HERMAN provided a vivacious if less than inspired score. "Open a New Window," "It's Today," "We Need a Little Christmas," "That's How Young I Feel" and the title song were among the optimistic numbers with "If He Walked into My Life" as the title character's weakly motivated torch song. Lansbury was everything audiences expected in the zany, lovable aunt and more and she was ably supported by BEATRICE ARTHUR, Charles Braswell, JANE CONNELL, Frankie Michaels and Jerry Lanning. The musical was unsuccessfully revived on Broadway in 1983. (1,508 performances)

ROUBEN MAMOULIAN (1898–1987), the distinctive stage and film director, only staged a handful of Broadway musicals but his innovative ideas and lyrical direction have left an indelible mark on the American musical. Mamoulian was born in the Russian province of Georgia and grew up in Paris. After studying criminology at the University of Moscow, he trained under Vakhtangov at the Moscow Art Theatre. He started his own theatre company and toured England where he began directing plays in the impressionistic style that would become his trademark. Mamoulian came to America in 1923 and soon was directing plays for the THEATRE GUILD. In 1927 he directed the drama *Porgy* on Broadway and in 1935 he made his musical directing debut with *PORGY AND*

BESS. His direction of *OKLAHOMA!* (1943) for the Guild and his subsequent *CAROUSEL* (1945) for them secured his reputation as one of the most distinguished directors of his day. Mamoulian's other musical credits include *Sadie Thompson* (1944), *ST. LOUIS WOMAN* (1946), *LOST IN THE STARS* (1949) and *Arms and the Girl* (1950). Mamoulian's stylized approach to story and his lyrical use of movement paved the way for many directors and choreographers to follow.

MAN OF LA MANCHA (1965) was an unlikely musical hit that originated at the GOODSPEED OPERA HOUSE in Connecticut, played Off Broadway, and went on to Broadway for 2,328 performances. With no stars, its unknown writers and a weighty subject matter, *Man of La Mancha* slowly caught on and eventually became one of the most revived musicals from the 1960s. Dale Wasserman adapted Cervantes' *Don Quixote* for the musical stage by having the author himself in the story, telling the tale of the knight errant who pursues villains who are not there and sees beauty and glory where there is only squalor. RICHARD KILEY had the role of his career as Cervantes/Quixote and Joan Diener played the sluttish Aldonza whom the hero imagines to be the lady Dulcinea. Also in the beautifully sung show were Irving Jacobson, RAY MIDDLETON and ROBERT ROUNSEVILLE, directed by ALBERT MARRE and choreographed by JACK COLE. The score, which ranged from the highly poetic to conventional Broadway character songs, was by Mitch Leigh (music) and Joe Darion (lyrics) and featured the popular "The Impossible Dream" (called "The Quest" in the show). Also in the score were "To Each His Own Dulcinea," "What Does He Want with Me?" "Dulcinea" and the title song. *Man of La Mancha* was revived on Broadway twenty-five years later with RAUL JULIA and Sheena Easton in the lead roles.

MAN WITH A LOAD OF MISCHIEF (1966) was an enchanting off-Broadway musical with a European air to it. The intimate piece was based on a forgotten play of the same name by Ashley Dukes about six characters at a nineteenth-century English inn: a lady of high society running away from a prince, a lord who pursues her, his manservant who loves her, a maid who accompanies them and the innkeeper and his wife. Ben Tarver wrote the libretto that was at times a comedy of manners and at other times romantic operetta. John Clifton provided the engaging music and he and Tarver wrote the succinct lyrics. The score was sweeping in its imagery but never excessive or grandiose. "Goodbye, My Sweet," "Little Rag Doll," "Make Way for My Lady," "Come to the Masquerade" and "Hulla-Baloo-Balay" are exemplary songs in a score that never disappoints. The expert cast consisted of REID SHELTON, VIRGINIA VESTOFF, Alice Cannon, Lesslie Nicol, Tom Noel and Raymond Thorne. *Man with a Load of Mischief* was that rare thing in the 1960s: a small chamber piece that embraced the romanticism of past styles. (240 performances)

TERRENCE MANN (1945–), an actor-singer on Broadway since *BARNUM* (1980), created the role of Rum Tum Tugger in *CATS* (1982) and police inspector Javert in *LES MISÉRABLES* (1987) in the New York versions of those shows. Mann also appeared in *RAGS* (1986), and *Jerome Robbins' Broadway* (1989) and played immigrant-assassin Leon Czolgosz in *ASSASSINS* (1990).

ALBERT MARRE (1925–), a director of plays as well as musicals, is most remembered for his direction of *KISMET* (1953) and *MAN OF LA MANCHA* (1965). Marre's other Broadway musicals include *MILK AND HONEY* (1961), *Cry for Us All* (1970) and *Home Sweet Homer* (1975).

HOWARD MARSH (?–1969) was a romantic leading man on Broadway who created the characters of Baron Schober in *BLOSSOM TIME* (1921), princely Karl Franz in *THE STUDENT PRINCE* (1924) and gambler Gaylord Ravenal in *SHOW BOAT* (1927).

ERNEST MARTIN (1919–), a producer who worked exclusively with co-producer CY FEUER, presented several distinguished musicals beginning in the late 1940s. The most notable Feuer and Martin shows include *WHERE'S CHARLEY?* (1948), *GUYS AND DOLLS* (1950), *CAN-CAN* (1953), *THE BOY FRIEND* (1954), *SILK STOCKINGS* (1955), *HOW TO SUCCEED IN BUSINESS WITHOUT REALLY TRYING* (1961), *LITTLE ME* (1962) and *THE ACT* (1977).

HUGH MARTIN (1914–), a composer-lyricist-singer who scored many Hollywood films, collaborated with RALPH BLANE on a few Broadway musicals, including the successful *BEST FOOT FORWARD* (1941). The team's most celebrated movie score was for *Meet Me in St. Louis*, which they adapted into a Broadway musical in 1989.

MARY MARTIN (1913–1990), the eminent leading lady of Broadway musicals, introduced more beloved characters in musicals than any other actress in the American theatre. With her sparkling personality, theatrical singing voice and appealing sense of coyness and playfulness, Martin captivated the audience through her characters rather than through showmanship or glamour. The Texas-born singer started her career in nightclubs and gained recognition on Broadway with her debut performance as Dolly Winslow singing "My Heart Belongs to Daddy" in *LEAVE IT TO ME!* (1938). Her first starring role was the amorous goddess in *ONE TOUCH OF VENUS* (1943) followed by *Lute Song* (1946) and the touring *ANNIE GET YOUR GUN* in 1947. Martin then played the nurse Nellie Forbush in *SOUTH PACIFIC* (1949), arguably her finest performance. Because of its later television version, Martin's *PETER PAN* (1954) became her most famous role. It was followed by her Maria Von Trapp in *THE SOUND OF MUSIC* (1959) and the actress Jennie Malone in the short-lived *Jennie* (1963). She starred in *HELLO, DOLLY!* on tour and in

London in 1965 then returned to Broadway in 1966 playing Agnes in *I DO! I DO!*. Along with ETHEL MERMAN, Martin epitomized the Broadway musical star during the 1940s and 1950s.

VIRGINIA MARTIN (1932–   ), a singer-actress in musicals on and off Broadway, played the sexy Hedy in *HOW TO SUCCEED IN BUSINESS WITHOUT REALLY TRYING* (1961) and the younger Belle in *LITTLE ME* (1962). Martin's other musical credits include *Ankles Aweigh* (1955), *New Faces of 1956* and *CARMELINA* (1979).

THE MARX BROTHERS were America's craziest and sometimes surrealistic comedy team. The performing brothers consisted of Chico (1886–1961), Harpo (1888–1964), Groucho (1890–1977) and Zeppo (1901–1979), all born in New York and performing on the stage as youngsters. In 1917 they began in vaudeville and by 1924 they appeared on Broadway in *I'll Say She Is*, an extended musical version of their act. The brothers starred in two more hysterical musicals, *THE COCOANUTS* (1925) and *ANIMAL CRACKERS* (1928), before going to Hollywood. All of the team's trademarks, from Groucho's painted-on mustache to Chico's Italian accent to Harpo's curly wig, were all developed in vaudeville and utilized in their three Broadway musicals.

MARY (1920) was a typically silly and romantic 1920s musical comedy with a delightful score by Louis Hirsch (music) and OTTO HARBACH (lyrics). Frank Mandel and Harbach wrote the rather prophetic story about a man who seeks to make his fortune selling "portable houses." The score contained the hit song "The Love Nest," which, thanks to the extensive pre-Broadway tour, was a top-selling song by the time *Mary* opened. (219 performances)

DANIEL MASSEY (1933–   ), a British leading man in plays and musicals, played Georg in *SHE LOVES ME* (1963) and Gaston in the Broadway version of *Gigi* (1973).

MAYTIME (1917) was such a popular operetta in war-time New York that the producing SHUBERT BROTHERS had to open a second company in a theatre across the street from the original in order to handle the demand. SIGMUND ROMBERG's music and RIDA JOHNSON YOUNG's libretto and lyrics combined gracefully in this bittersweet tale that told the fate of two lovers over a sixty-year period. The wealthy Ottillie is kept from marrying her beloved Richard because he is too poor. The decades pass, Ottillie marries another man, fortunes reverse, a tree planted in Act I grows then withers and dies, the lovers age and pass away and the musical ends with their grandchildren falling in love during Maytime. PEGGY WOOD and Charles Purcell played both the lovers and their grandchildren beautifully and the score was filled with romantic favorites: "The Road to Paradise," "Will You Remember?" and "In Our Little Home, Sweet Home." (492 performances)

MARY MCCARTY (1923–1980), a nightclub singer who was intermittently on Broadway from 1948, appeared in a few musicals, most memorably as the old hoofer Stella Deems in *FOLLIES* (1971) and the prison Matron in *CHICAGO* (1975).

JACK MCCAULEY (1900–1980) was a durable leading man in Broadway musicals who appeared in such favorites as *HIT THE DECK* (1927), *THE LITTLE SHOW* (1929), *THE SHOW IS ON* (1936) and others. McCauley got his two best roles much later in his career with "Papa" Longstreet in *HIGH BUTTON SHOES* (1947) and button tycoon Gus Esmond in *GENTLEMEN PREFER BLONDES* (1949).

JOAN MCCRACKEN (1922–1961), a dancer-actress with a background in ballet, played dream Laurie in the original *OKLAHOMA!* (1943). McCracken's other musical credits include *BLOOMER GIRL* (1944), *Billion Dollar Baby* (1945), *Dance Me a Song* (1950) and *ME AND JULIET* (1953).

HOWARD MCGILLIN (1953–), a leading man in musicals on and off Broadway since 1984, played the dastardly Jasper in *THE MYSTERY OF EDWIN DROOD* (1985) and Billy Crocker in the 1987 revival of *ANYTHING GOES*. McGillin's other musical credits include the Public Theatre's 1984 *La Bohème* and *SUNDAY IN THE PARK WITH GEORGE* (1984).

JIMMY MCHUGH (1894–1969) was primarily a film composer but he started out writing Cotton Club shows and Broadway revues. McHugh's early collaborations with lyricist DOROTHY FIELDS included *BLACKBIRDS OF 1928* and *International Revue* (1930), which introduced their "On the Sunny Side of the Street." Several of McHugh's songs were used in the 1979 Broadway revue *SUGAR BABIES*.

DONNA MCKECHNIE (1944–), a vibrant dancer-singer on Broadway since 1961, played Kathy in *COMPANY* (1970) and Cassie in *A CHORUS LINE* (1975). McKechnie's other Broadway musicals include *HOW TO SUCCEED IN BUSINESS WITHOUT REALLY TRYING* (1961) and *PROMISES, PROMISES* (1968).

JOHN MCMARTIN, a durable leading man in Broadway musicals, is most remembered for his neurotic Oscar Lindquist in *SWEET CHARITY* (1966) and the embittered Ben in *FOLLIES* (1971). McMartin's other musical credits include *LITTLE MARY SUNSHINE* (1959) and *Happy New Year* (1980).

ME AND JULIET (1953) was an atypical RODGERS and HAMMERSTEIN show in that it was more musical comedy than musical play; it is also, arguably, their most uninspired effort. Hammerstein's original libretto uses a familiar backstage setting to tell the story of a chorus girl who falls in love with an assistant stage manager. While some of the more obvious backstage clichés were avoided, the tale was routine at best. The score did contain one hit, "No Other Love," but GEORGE ABBOTT's direction and a likable cast, including Isabel Bigley, Bill Hayes, JOAN McCRACKEN and RAY WALSTON, could not keep the musical running beyond 348 performances, disappointing for a Rodgers and Hammerstein show.

ME AND MY GIRL (1986) was a 1937 West End hit that was so successfully revived in London in 1985 that the production came to Broadway, where it stayed for 1,420 toe-tapping performances. The original L. Arthur Rose and Douglas Furber libretto was revised by Stephen Fry and director Mike Ockrent and the tuneful music was by Noel Gay. The predictable but merry plot tells of Cockney Bill Snibson who inherits a title and happily turns high society topsy turvy. But Bill is torn between his girlfriend Sally from Lambeth and the sensual but predatory Lady Carstone, a predicament shared by the hero of the very similar BRITISH IMPORT *HALF A SIXPENCE* (1965). Robert Lindsay was the toast of Broadway playing Bill and American Maryann Plunkett made a fine Cockney Sally. Also in the cast were Jane Summerhays, JANE CONNELL and GEORGE S. IRVING. The songs were cheerfully old-fashioned and the contagious "Lambeth Walk" number was a musical highlight of the season.

THE ME NOBODY KNOWS (1970) was an uncommonly poignant musical that voiced the concerns and dreams of children and young adults in contemporary urban society. The show was more a revue than a conventional book musical, with vignettes and songs thematically tied together. Stephen M. Joyce adapted his anthology of the same name in which he presented the writings of ghetto schoolchildren between the ages of seven and eighteen. Gary William Friedman (music) and Will Holt (lyrics) fashioned some of these writings into songs, including the commendable "Dream Babies," "If I Had a Million Dollars" and "Light Sings." The young and talented cast was splendid and two of the kids, Irene Cara and Northern J. Calloway, went on to notable careers. The most effective aspects of *The Me Nobody Knows* were its innocence, its lack of sermonizing and its hopefulness. (586 performances)

KAY MEDFORD (1920–1980), a veteran actress of many films, turned to Broadway in 1951 and appeared in several comedies and musicals, usually playing mothers, as in *BYE BYE BIRDIE* (1960) and *FUNNY GIRL* (1964). Medford's other musical credits included *PAINT YOUR WAGON* (1951), *Two's Company* (1952), *John Murray Anderson's Almanac* (1953) and *Mr. Wonderful* (1956).

ALAN MENKEN, the theatre and film composer who worked with lyricist-librettist HOWARD ASHMAN, started his career Off Broadway with the short-run musical *God Bless You, Mr. Rosewater* (1979) and the long-running *LITTLE SHOP OF HORRORS* (1982). Menken's concentration since then has been on films and his scores for Disney have brought him acclaim, most notably for *The Little Mermaid* (1989), *Beauty and the Beast* (1991) and *Aladdin* (1992). In 1992 he scored the Off-Broadway musical *Weird Romance* with lyrics by David Spencer.

JOHNNY MERCER (1909–1976), the Hollywood lyricist and sometime composer, returned to Broadway on occasion and rarely had any success but his theatre work was exceptionally potent. Born in Savannah, Georgia, Mercer worked his way to New York in order to become a singer. But he had more success selling his lyrics, and songs of his started appearing in Broadway revues in the 1930s. Hollywood beckoned and he didn't return to Broadway until 1947 with *ST. LOUIS WOMAN*, providing lyrics for HAROLD ARLEN's music. The score was enchanting but the show was less than a hit. Mercer was back on Broadway with *Texas, Li' l Darlin'* (1949), with music by Robert Emmett Dolan, and *Top Banana* (1951), in which he wrote his own music. His only all-out theatre hit was *LI'L ABNER* (1956) with music by Gene de Paul. The ambitious but failed *SARATOGA* (1959), written with Arlen, and the disappointing *Foxy* (1964), written with Dolan, concluded his theatre career. Mercer had a marvelous talent for regional sounds, ethnic idioms and poetic, evocative character songs. His Broadway career was scattered but unforgettable.

ETHEL MERMAN (1909–1984), the celebrated musical comedy star who was the very definition of a Broadway belter, usually played variations of the same character: a brash, confident woman with plenty of guts and humor. Yet Merman was so dynamic on stage that each role and each performance seemed new. She was born in Astoria, New York, and by the age of twenty-one was stealing the show on Broadway, singing "I Got Rhythm" in *GIRL CRAZY* (1930). Merman appeared in *GEORGE WHITE'S SCANDALS* (1931) and *TAKE A CHANCE* (1932) before her first starring role, the swinging evangelist Reno Sweeney in *ANYTHING GOES* (1934). This was followed by her Nails Duquesne in *RED, HOT AND BLUE!* (1936), *Stars in Your Eyes* (1939) and *DUBARRY WAS A LADY* (1939). Merman's biggest hit was *ANNIE GET YOUR GUN* (1946) in which she played Annie Oakley, a role she revived as late as 1966. Hostess Sally Adams in *CALL ME MADAM* (1950) and Liz Livingstone in the less successful *Happy Hunting* (1965) followed. Merman's most accomplished performance was that of stage mother Rose in *GYPSY* (1959), a role that revealed Broadway's favorite comedienne was also one of its finest actresses. Merman's final musical was in 1970 in *HELLO, DOLLY!* in which she played Dolly Levi late in that show's long run.

DAVID MERRICK (1911–   ), the most flamboyant and celebrated Broadway producer of the post-war American theatre, became as famous as any of his shows because of his flair for publicity, controversy and long-running hits. Merrick was born in St. Louis and studied to become a lawyer before producing his first Broadway musical, *FANNY* (1954). His other early shows include

DESTRY RIDES AGAIN (1959), *GYPSY* (1959), *TAKE ME ALONG* (1959), *IRMA LA DOUCE* (1960), *DO RE MI* (1960) and *SUBWAYS ARE FOR SLEEPING* (1961). Merrick's first musical with director-choreographer GOWER CHAMPION was *CARNIVAL* (1961) and the two worked together again on *HELLO, DOLLY!* (1964), *I DO! I DO!* (1966), *THE HAPPY TIME* (1968), *SUGAR* (1972), *MACK AND MABEL* (1974) and *42ND STREET* (1980). Other Merrick musicals include *I CAN GET IT FOR YOU WHOLE-SALE* (1962), *110 IN THE SHADE* (1963), *Foxy* (1964), *How Now, Dow Jones* (1967) and *PROMISES, PROMISES* (1968), as well as the revivals of *VERY GOOD EDDIE* in 1975 and the all-black version of *OH, KAY!* in 1990. Merrick also produced several non-musicals and imported plays from London; his musical imports include *STOP THE WORLD—I WANT TO GET OFF* (1962), *OLIVER!* (1962), *Oh, What a Lovely War* (1964), *THE ROAR OF THE GREASEPAINT—THE SMELL OF THE CROWD* (1965) and *Pickwick* (1965). Merrick is generally considered the last of Broadway's great showmen. He made producing theatre a passion rather than merely a business venture.

BOB MERRILL (1921–), the composer-lyricist who scored five Broadway hits, started his career writing silly ditties and doggerel pop songs. But his first Broadway musical was an adventurous adaptation of Eugene O'Neill's *Anna Christie* called *NEW GIRL IN TOWN* (1957). Merrill then provided the score for *TAKE ME ALONG* (1959), another O'Neill adaptation, this time of *Ah! Wilderness*. Merrill's finest work for the theatre was his music and lyrics for *CARNIVAL* (1961) and the lyrics he contributed to *FUNNY GIRL* (1964) with music by JULE STYNE. He did both music and lyrics again for the unsuccessful *Henry, Sweet Henry* (1967) but had another hit with his lyrics for *SUGAR* (1972), music again with Styne. In 1990 Merrill scored the Off-Broadway *Hannah... 1939*. Although his lyric work is sometimes uneven, Merrill's music is usually very melodic and his scores have a grace and style not always found in big Broadway musicals.

MERRILY WE ROLL ALONG (1981) was a short-lived musical that was beset with libretto and production problems but boasted a superb score by STEPHEN SONDHEIM. George Furth adapted and updated the 1934 problematic play of the same name by GEORGE S. KAUFMAN and MOSS HART in which the story of an artist's compromises with life and art is told in reverse order. In the musical version, the hero is a crass Hollywood producer who once dreamed of writing innovative musicals for Broadway and the plot follows (backward) his gradual selling out to money and fame. The shaky production and uneven cast never overcame the inherent difficulties of the piece and *Merrily We Roll Along* closed after only sixteen performances. But the Sondheim score, recorded after the closing, revealed extraordinary music and lyric work: "Not a Day Goes By," "Now You Know," "Good Thing Going," "Opening Doors" and "Our

Time." It is a remarkable score that has caused *Merrily We Roll Along* to be revised and revived on several occasions.

MEXICAN HAYRIDE (1944) was a popular war-time diversion that had much to recommend it: Latin-flavored COLE PORTER songs; a spectacular production by producer MIKE TODD, which featured a cast of 89; a long chorus line of girls in tantalizing costumes; and the buffoonish genius of BOBBY CLARK. The libretto, by HERBERT and DOROTHY FIELDS, was a silly concoction about a fugitive racketeer in Mexico, a lady bullfighter named Montana and a chase that took the characters through the ancient cities south of the border. Clark got to doff a series of disguises, from a mariachi musician to an Indian squaw, and he was ably assisted in his shenanigans by JUNE HAVOC, George Givot, Wilbur Evans and Corina Mura. The Porter ballad "I Love You" was the hit of the score but also delightful were "There Must Be Someone for Me," "Carlotta" and "Count Your Blessings." (481 performances)

RAY MIDDLETON (1907–1984), a full-voiced leading man who began his career as an opera singer, originated some notable musical theatre roles. Middleton made his Broadway debut in a featured part in *ROBERTA* (1933). After appearing as Washington Irving in *KNICKERBOCKER HOLIDAY* (1938) and the 1939 edition of *GEORGE WHITE'S SCANDALS*, he landed the prize role of sharpshooter Frank Butler in *ANNIE GET YOUR GUN* (1946). Middleton also played the ageless hero of *LOVE LIFE* (1948) and the bewildered innkeeper in *MAN OF LA MANCHA* (1965).

JO MIELZINER (1901–1976), one of the American theatre's most prolific and influential scenic designers, created memorable sets on Broadway for fifty years and designed some of the most outstanding plays and musicals of the century. Mielziner's most accomplished musical scenic designs include the cartoonish sets for *OF THEE I SING* (1931), the fanciful merry-go-round for *CAROUSEL* (1945), the posterboard style scenery for *ANNIE GET YOUR GUN* (1945), the evocative South Seas settings for *SOUTH PACIFIC* (1949), the romanticized Times Square locales for *GUYS AND DOLLS* (1950) and the tawdry sets for *GYPSY* (1959). His other musical credits include *ON YOUR TOES* (1936), *THE BOYS FROM SYRACUSE* (1938), *BEST FOOT FORWARD* (1941), *FINIAN'S RAINBOW* (1947), *THE KING AND I* (1951), *THE MOST HAPPY FELLA* (1956), *ALL AMERICAN* (1961) and *Look to the Lilies* (1970). Mielziner also designed lights for many of his productions and, on occasion, the costumes as well.

MILK AND HONEY (1961), a musical that used Israel as its setting, was the first Broadway score for composer-lyricist JERRY HERMAN. Don Appell wrote the original libretto about two middle-aged American tourists in Israel and their bittersweet romance. There were also subplots about a young married couple on a kibbutz and a New York yenta looking for a suitable husband for herself. Opera singers ROBERT WEEDE and Mimi Benzell were the primary couple and Molly Picon was the comic husband-hunter. Herman's score was a lovely mixture of ethnic and traditional Broadway sounds, with "Shalom," "Independence Day Hora," "I Will Follow You," "There's No Reason in the World" and the stirring title song being the most pleasing songs. (543 performances)

MARILYN MILLER (1898–1936) was Broadway's brightest and most beloved musical theatre star of the 1920s. Miller was slight of build and not much of a belter, but she managed to shine on stage and endear audiences in a way rarely seen since. Born in Evansville, Indiana, to a theatrical family, Miller was appearing in vaudeville and touring shows at a young age. Her Broadway musical debut came in the SHUBERT BROTHERS' 1914 edition of *The Passing Show* and she appeared in two subsequent editions as well as two editions of the *ZIEGFELD FOLLIES*. But it was her performance as Sally Green in *SALLY* (1920) that made her a star and she captivated audiences as the title heroines in *SUNNY* (1925), *ROSALIE* (1928) and *Smiles* (1930), all vehicles created for her. Miller's last Broadway appearance, before her untimely death at the age of thirty-seven, was in the revue *AS THOUSANDS CHEER* (1933).

LIZA MINNELLI (1946–), the high-energy singer-actress who has dazzled audiences on stage, television, film and nightclubs, made her professional theatre debut in the 1963 Off-Broadway revival of *BEST FOOT FORWARD*. Minnelli first showed her stellar powers as Flora in *FLORA, THE RED MENACE* (1965) then went on to a film career. She appeared as a replacement in *CHICAGO* in 1975 and then returned for *THE ACT* (1977) and *THE RINK* (1984). Minnelli is the daughter of Judy Garland and VINCENTE MINNELLI and brings an acute sense of theatricality to whatever media she performs in.

VINCENTE MINNELLI (1910–1986), the eminent director of film musicals, started his career as a theatre designer and later a Broadway director before going to Hollywood. Minnelli made his Broadway debut as costume designer for *EARL CARROLL VANITIES* in 1931. He later designed sets and/or costumes for *AT HOME ABROAD* (1935), *THE SHOW IS ON* (1936), *HOORAY FOR WHAT!* (1937), *VERY WARM FOR MAY* (1939), all of which he also directed, as well as some editions of the *ZIEGFELD FOLLIES* and shows at Radio City Music Hall.

MISS LIBERTY (1949) was one of IRVING BERLIN's gentler, more evocative musicals but not one of his more successful ones. Playwright Robert Sherwood provided the flawed libretto about two rival newspapers and a search for the model for the Statue of Liberty. MOSS HART directed and JEROME ROBBINS choreographed the musical expertly but the whole affair was too solemn for the audience's tastes and only the large advance sale let the show run 308 performances. Sadly neglected was an enchanting score that approached operetta at times. "Paris Wakes Up and Smiles," "Just One Way to Say I Love You," "Only for Americans" and "Let's Take an Old-Fashioned Walk" were exceptional with only the last gaining any popularity. A song cut from the musical, "Mr. Monotony," did become a cult favorite later and was finally heard on Broadway in *Jerome Robbins' Broadway* (1989).

MISS SAIGON (1991), the eagerly awaited hit musical from London, arrived on Broadway with a record-breaking advance sale and a whirlwind of controversy but it won audiences over by its powerful narrative and striking production values. The story is basically that of *Madame Butterfly* adapted to a Vietnam War setting and addressing social and moral issues that were neglected in the turn-of-the-century tale. The Marine Chris falls in love with the young Saigon prostitute Kim and they plan to go back to America together. But before they can process the necessary papers, the South Vietnam regime falls and the Americans quickly abandon Saigon. The lovers are separated in the confusion and do not meet until three years later when Kim, a refugee in Bangkok, contacts Chris and he learns that they have a son. But when Kim finds out that Chris has married, she kills herself so that her son will be taken back and raised in the States by Chris and his wife. Involved in the lovers' story from the start is the sly Engineer who cynically comments on the events throughout and acts as a unifying force in the musical's many themes. Claude-Michel Schonberg composed the all-sung score and RICHARD MALTBY, JR., adapted Alain Boublil's original French lyrics. Lea Salonga as Kim and Jonathan Pryce as the Engineer repeated their West End performances, despite pressure from Actors Equity that an Asian actor should be cast as the Engineer. Among the score's highlights were "I Still Believe," "The Movie in My Mind," "If You Want to Die in Bed," "The American Dream" and "The Last Night of the World." The admirable staging by Nicholas Hytner emphasized character and theme but the talk of all Broadway was designer JOHN NAPIER's celebrated helicopter used during the evacuation of Saigon scene. *Miss Saigon* succeeds because it is poignant musical drama rather than mere stage spectacle and it is one of the few megahits to have substantial content and integrity. (still running as of 3/1/93)

DAVID MITCHELL (1932–) is a scenic designer whose most notable sets were the New York City scenery for *ANNIE* (1977) and the clever circus design for *BARNUM* (1980). Mitchell's other Broadway musical credits include *I LOVE MY WIFE* (1977), *WORKING* (1978), *I Remember Mama* (1979), *Bring Back Birdie* (1981), *LA CAGE AUX FOLLES* (1983) and *Legs Diamond* (1989).

JULIAN MITCHELL (1854–1926) was a director-choreographer who staged over seventy Broadway musicals during his forty-year career, the most prolific director in the American musical theatre. Beginning his career as a dancer, Mitchell's first directing credit came in 1886 with *The Maid and the Moonshiner*. The most remembered musicals that he staged include *A TRIP TO CHINATOWN* (1891), *THE FORTUNE TELLER* (1898), *THE WIZARD OF OZ* (1903), *BABES IN TOYLAND* (1903), *Hitchy-Koo* (1917), *Little Nelly Kelly* (1922) and nine editions of the *ZIEGFELD FOLLIES*. Mitchell's final Broadway credit was as choreographer for the hit *SUNNY* (1925).

MLLE. MODISTE (1905) was the VICTOR HERBERT operetta that boasted the best-written libretto of all his shows. Henry Blossom wrote the book as well as the lyrics and both had a sophistication and sassiness too rarely seen in operetta. The story is set in a Paris hat shop where salesgirl Fifi must overcome various obstacles in order to wed the aristocratic Captain de Bouvray. When Fifi becomes a singing sensation, the barriers tumble and both stardom and romance are hers. The waltz "Kiss Me Again" is the most famous song from the score but also distinctive are "If I Were on the Stage," "I Want What I Want When I Want It," "The Time and the Place and the Girl" and "The Mascot of the Troop." Prima donna Fritzi Scheff scored a triumph as Fifi and repeated the role in New York on five different occasions over the next twenty-four years. (202 performances)

LILIANE MONTEVECCHI (1933–　), a Paris-born singer-dancer from the Folies Bergères, played the sly producer Liliane La Fleur in *NINE* (1982) and the faded ballerina Grushinskaya in *GRAND HOTEL* (1989).

DAVID MONTGOMERY (1870–1917) was a comic actor who, with his partner FRED STONE, starred in vaudeville and on Broadway. His most famous roles were the Tin Woodsman in *THE WIZARD OF OZ* (1903) and Kid Connor in *THE RED MILL* (1906).

MELBA MOORE (1945–　), a black singer-actress on Broadway and in nightclubs, played Lutiebelle in the original *PURLIE* (1970), singing "I Got Love" and securing her career. Moore's other musical credits include *HAIR* (1968) and *Timbuktu* (1978).

ROBERT MOORE (1928?-1984), an actor-turned-director, staged several Broadway comedies and musicals. Moore's musical directing credits included *PROMISES, PROMISES* (1968), *Lorelei* (1974), *THEY'RE PLAYING OUR SONG* (1979) and *WOMAN OF THE YEAR* (1981).

VICTOR MOORE (1876–1962), the beloved character actor who played several memorable comic roles in Broadway musicals, was often paired with actor WILLIAM GAXTON for comedic effect. Moore usually played bumbling, innocent characters who are taken advantage of by more worldly types (i.e., Gaxton). He started in vaudeville and made an impressive Broadway debut as Kid Burns in *FORTY-FIVE MINUTES FROM BROADWAY* (1906), a role that he repeated in the sequel *The Talk of the Town* (1907). Moore's comic talents were seen in *OH, KAY!* (1926), *HOLD EVERYTHING!* (1928), *Heads Up!* (1929) and other shows before being teamed up with Gaxton for the first time in *OF THEE I SING* (1931). He played Vice President Alexander Throttlebottom to Gaxton's President Wintergreen and they both reprised their roles in the sequel *LET 'EM EAT CAKE* (1933). Moore's other musical credits included the big-hearted gangster "Moonface" in *ANYTHING GOES* (1934), incompetent U.S. Ambassador Alonzo P. Goodhue in *LEAVE IT TO ME!* (1938) and righteous U.S. Senator Oliver P. Loganberry in *LOUISIANA PURCHASE* (1940). His last Broadway musical was *Nellie Bly* (1946).

FRANK MORGAN (1890–1949), the veteran actor of many films, appeared in featured roles on Broadway, most notably in the musicals *ROSALIE* (1928) and *THE BAND WAGON* (1931).

HELEN MORGAN (1900–1941), one of America's greatest torch singers, is most remembered by theatre patrons for creating the role of Julie in *SHOW BOAT* (1927). Morgan sang in vaudeville, nightclubs and Broadway musicals such as *GEORGE WHITE'S SCANDALS* (1925), *SWEET ADELINE* (1929) and the 1931 *ZIEGFELD FOLLIES*. Morgan introduced "Bill," "Can't Help Lovin' Dat Man" and "Why Was I Born?"—torch songs that were always identified with her.

PATRICIA MORISON (1915–), a leading lady in films and a few Broadway musicals, played the original Lilli Vanessi/Kate in *KISS ME, KATE* (1948).

DORETTA MORROW (1928–), a dark-haired soprano who played romantic leads in some Broadway musicals, introduced "I Have Dreamed" as the slave Tuptim in *THE KING AND I* (1951). Morrow also created the roles of Kitty Verdun in *WHERE'S CHARLEY?* (1948) and Marsinah in *KISMET* (1953).

ROBERT MORSE (1931–), a puckish leading man with a bad boy persona, has been on the Broadway stage from 1955 and made his musical debut in *Say, Darling* (1958). Morse played the juvenile Richard in *TAKE ME ALONG* (1959), the corporate climber J. Pierpont Finch in *HOW TO SUCCEED IN BUSINESS WITHOUT REALLY TRYING* (1961) and the musician-in-drag Jerry in *SUGAR* (1972). His last Broadway musical to date was *So Long, 174th Street* (1976).

JOE MORTON (1947–), a black leading man on television and films, appeared in a handful of musicals on Broadway, most memorably as the eager Walter Younger in *RAISIN* (1973). Morton's other musical credits include *HAIR* (1968), *TWO GENTLEMEN OF VERONA* (1971) and *Oh, Brother!* (1981).

THE MOST HAPPY FELLA (1956) was FRANK LOESSER's adventurous, inconsistent and highly operatic musical version of Sidney Howard's 1924 melodrama *They Knew What They Wanted*. Loesser did the adaptation himself and somewhat improved on the improbable tale of Tony, an aging Italian vineyard owner in the California Napa Valley, who proposes by letter to a waitress, Rosabella, that he saw briefly in San Francisco. Surprisingly, Rosabella accepts but has a one-night affair with Tony's foreman, getting pregnant and trying to pass off the child as Tony's. The musical ends with Tony and Rosabella reconciled to the truth and to each other. ROBERT WEEDE and Jo Sullivan were in fine form as the mismatched lovers and Joe Lund played the unlikeable foreman competently enough but it was Susan Johnson and Shorty Long as the comic sidekicks that were more interesting as they sang the show's two liveliest numbers, "Big D" and "Standing on the Corner." Also in the ambitious score's thirty-some musical numbers were "Joey, Joey, Joey," "My Heart Is So Full of You" and "Somebody Somewhere." *The Most Happy Fella* fluctuated uneasily between opera and musical comedy and it asked its audience to accept the heavy sentiment and the Broadway jokes side by side. But there were soaring moments in the show and Loesser's music was never finer. The original production ran 676 performances and there were Broadway revivals in 1979 with Giorgio Tozzi and in 1991 with Spiro Malas. *The Most Happy Fella* also shows up in the repertory of opera companies on occasion.

ZERO MOSTEL (1915–1977), the large and expressive actor who appeared on stage in musicals and dramas, created two of the American theatre's favorite musical roles: the sly slave Pseudolus in *A FUNNY THING HAPPENED ON THE WAY TO THE FORUM* (1962) and the beleaguered father Tevye in *FIDDLER ON THE ROOF* (1964). Mostel started his career in nightclubs and made his Broadway debut in *Beggar's Holiday* (1946) playing Mr. Peachum.

MOTLEY, the trade name for the three British costume designers Margaret Harris, Sophia Devine and Elizabeth Montgomery, provided the costumes for a number of Broadway musicals, including *SOUTH PACIFIC* (1949), *MISS LIBERTY* (1949), *PAINT YOUR WAGON* (1951), *CAN-CAN* (1953), *PETER PAN* (1954), *THE MOST HAPPY FELLA* (1956), *KWAMINA* (1961) and *Baker Street* (1965).

MR. PRESIDENT (1962) was IRVING BERLIN's last Broadway musical and more a major disappointment than a major flop. HOWARD LINDSAY and RUSSEL CROUSE wrote the original libretto, about a fictitious First Family with personal and political problems, that was likeable but hardly exciting. Robert Ryan and NANETTE FABRAY were also likeable but the songs they sang seemed like pale versions of earlier Berlin hits. Although the songwriter tried to keep up to date (he even included a number called "The Washington Twist"), the First Lady said it all with her song "Let's Go Back to the Waltz."

The huge advance sale let *Mr. President* run 265 performances but with this show Berlin retired and his long and astonishing career came to an end.

THE MULLIGAN GUARD MUSICALS were a series of seven antic musical comedies at the end of the nineteenth century written, produced and performed by EDWARD HARRIGAN and TONY HART with music by David Braham. The shows were outrageous farces that related the misadventures of the Irish Mulligan Guards, a boisterous, hard-drinking social and military club in the slums of New York. The characters in the musicals were Irish, German, Italian and Jewish immigrants and the way Harrigan and Hart utilized ethnic idioms and street vernacular would later greatly influence GEORGE M. COHAN. The series began as a vaudeville sketch in 1873 but in 1878 *The Mulligan Guards' Picnic* ran a month on Broadway. It was followed by *The Mulligan Guards' Ball* in 1879, considered the best of the series, and five more farces ending with *The Mulligans' Silver Wedding* (1880), although some of the characters reappeared in later musicals.

MUSIC BOX REVUES (1921–1924), a series of musical revues featuring IRVING BERLIN songs, did not last as long as other series in the 1920s or 1930s but it was a much-loved project and had distinctions of its own. Producers SAM HARRIS and Berlin built the Music Box Theatre in 1921 to house a series of revues that would be more intimate than the lavish extravaganzas by FLORENZ ZIEGFELD and GEORGE WHITE. The shows emphasized strong musical scores but witty sketches and personable performers also played a major role in their success. The first edition in 1921 offered the song "Say It with Music," the theme for the series. Several notable songs came from the four editions, including "Everybody Step," "Pack Up Your Sins and Go to the Devil," "All Alone" and "What'll I Do?" Of the many sketches presented in the *Music Box Revues*, the most famous was Robert Benchley's "The Treasurer's Report," which he performed himself in the 1922 edition.

MUSIC DIRECTORS and vocal/dance arrangers are perhaps the least understood creative jobs in the musical theatre. A show's composer rarely does the ORCHESTRATIONS for a musical and almost always turns over the music's arrangements to a musical director. Many of the important elements of the score are created during rehearsals by the musical director working with the pianist, choreographer and sometimes the stage director. How the song will be routined, what rhythms will be used, what key and what harmonies will the piece have, and even when singers will sing and dancers will dance are decided at these rehearsals under the supervision of the music director. It is only after this is done that the score can be turned over to the orchestrator for notation for orchestral parts. Broadway's most accomplished music directors and arrangers have done much to shape the sound that we associate with certain musicals and composers. ROBERT RUSSELL BENNETT, for example, was the music director and orchestrator for most of the RODGERS and HAMMERSTEIN shows and much of what is sometimes attributed to Rodgers was the work of Bennett. Other distinguished music directors are: LEHRMAN ENGEL, who conducted many Broadway musicals and arranged such shows as *ANNIE GET YOUR GUN* (1946) and *GUYS AND DOLLS* (1950); HAROLD HASTINGS, who was music director for most of the musicals produced by HAROLD PRINCE; DONALD PIPPIN, who arranged many musicals in the 1970s and 1980s, including *APPLAUSE* (1970) and *LA CAGE AUX FOLLES* (1983); and MILTON ROSENSTOCK, whose many Broadway shows include *BELLS ARE RINGING* (1956) and *GYPSY* (1959). Other outstanding Broadway music directors and arrangers include Franz Allers, Salvatore Dell'isola, Herbert Greene, Peter Howard and Elliot Lawrence. The most notable of the new generation of Broadway music directors includes PAUL GEMIGNAMI and Wally Harper.

MUSIC IN THE AIR (1932), like JEROME KERN's *THE CAT AND THE FIDDLE* with OTTO HARBACH two years before, was an attempt to create a gentle modern operetta that moved away from the slick musicals and revues of the 1930s. Kern's collaborator this time was OSCAR HAMMERSTEIN II, who wrote an endearing tale of a Bavarian girl and her sweetheart who travel across the countryside to Munich in order to get a music publisher interested in her father's song, "I've Told Ev'ry Little Star." Once involved in the professional music business, however, she leaves the big city to return to a simpler life. Kern's music and Hammerstein's lyrics were captivating with both of them writing some of the most lyrical work of their careers: "There's a Hill Beyond a Hill," "I'm Alone," "One More Dance," "The Song Is You," "And Love Was Born," "In Egern on the Tegren Sea" and "We Belong Together." (342 performances)

THE MUSIC MAN (1957), one of Broadway's most beloved musicals, was a big, corny, funny show that was also very innovative and unique. The charm of the piece came not just from the nostalgia it evoked but also from the sly humor that looked at small-town life with cockeyed amusement. MEREDITH WILLSON, who grew up in an Iowa town not unlike the one featured in the show, wrote the libretto (with help from Franklin Lacey), music and lyrics. The story covers the events that occur in River City one summer when the traveling salesman/con man Professor Harold Hill arrives and gets the town all worked up about starting a marching boys band. The local librarian, Marian Paroo, is the only one who sees through the fraudulent professor but she finds herself falling in love with him. When the jig is up, Hill decides to stay with Marian instead of skipping out and the musical ends with the town going into raptures as they listen to the discordant sounds of their young citizens trying to play musical instruments. ROBERT PRESTON, in his Broadway musical debut, gave the American theatre one of its most cherished performances as Hill. The rest of the cast, under the direction of Morton Da Costa, brought the various characters to life with humor and affection: BARBARA COOK as Marian, DAVID BURNS, PERT KELTON, Iggie Wolfington, Eddie Hodges and the singing Buffalo Bills. HOWARD BAY's sets and ONNA WHITE's choreography were also superior but it was Willson's story and score that made *The Music Man* so special. In addition to the standard musical comedy songs, such as the popular "Till There Was You," Willson also provided barbershop quartet pieces, stirring marches, rhythmic dialogue scenes and fast-talking monologues. "Seventy-Six Trombones" and "Goodnight, My Someone" (both of which used the same melody) were the standouts but no less accomplished were "Rock Island," "Marian the Librarian," "Trouble," "My White Knight" and "Lida Rose." *The Music Man*, like *GUYS AND DOLLS* (1950), is a timeless musical comedy because it recreates a world that exists only in the vivid imagination of its creators. (1,375 performances)

THARON MUSSER (1925–   ), one of the American theatre's most prolific and talented lighting designers, has lit plays and musicals on Broadway since 1956. Among her many musical credits are *Shinbone Alley* (1957), *GOLDEN BOY* (1964), *FLORA, THE RED MENACE* (1965), *MAME* (1966), *HALLELUJAH, BABY!* (1967), *APPLAUSE* (1970), *FOLLIES* (1971), *A LITTLE NIGHT MUSIC* (1973), *MACK AND MABEL* (1974), *A CHORUS LINE* (1975), *THE WIZ* (1975), *PACIFIC OVERTURES* (1976), *42ND STREET* (1980), *DREAMGIRLS* (1981), *Teddy and Alice* (1987) and *THE SECRET GARDEN* (1991). Musser has made several innovations in lighting design technique and was the first designer to use a computer lighting system on Broadway.

MY FAIR LADY (1956) was LERNER and LOEWE's most triumphant musical as well as one of the glories of the American theatre. Lerner adapted George Bernard Shaw's *Pygmalion* and wrote the lyrics in such an expert Shavian style that few could tell where the musical digressed from the original. Loewe's music captured both the elegance and bawdiness of Edwardian England and MOSS HART's direction combined the British temperament and Broadway showmanship in a grand manner. The story of phonetician Henry Higgins and his attempt to pass off the Cockney flower girl Eliza Doolittle as a lady by improving her speech and manner is really just one more variation on the old Cinderella tale. But Shaw's wit and social commentary remain in the musical version and are heightened by the songs in such a way that *My Fair Lady* remains one of the most intelligent musicals ever devised. "I Could Have Danced All Night" and "On the Street Where You Live" became the biggest hits from a score in which every song is distinctive and memorable, including "Get Me to the Church on Time," "Wouldn't It Be Loverly?" "I've Grown Accustomed to Her Face," "Show Me," "Why Can't the English?" "I'm an Ordinary Man," "A Hymn to Him" and "The Rain in Spain." REX HARRISON as Higgins, JULIE ANDREWS as Eliza and STANLEY HOLLOWAY as Alfred Doolittle gave extraordinary performances that they are identified with forever. OLIVER SMITH's sets and CECIL BEATON's costumes contributed greatly to this esteemed production that ran for 2,717 performances, a new record at the time. All of which seems remarkable when one considers that *My Fair Lady* has no overt love story, the action is that of a drawing room comedy, there is too much talk and not enough dancing, the major characters are more comic than romantic and there is absolutely nothing American about it. *My Fair Lady* is not only one of the best musicals ever written, it is also one of the bravest and most exceptional.

MY ONE AND ONLY (1983) retained a handful of the GERSHWINS' songs from *FUNNY FACE* (1927) but the new libretto shared nothing in common with the original except that the hero was an aviator. The plot, by PETER STONE and Timothy S. Mayer, was an agreeable piece of nonsense about a barnstorming pilot (TOMMY TUNE) who falls for a British swimming champion (Twiggy) but gets involved with a bootlegging minister and a Russian spy. Also in the cast were Charles "Honi" Coles, Denny Dillon and Roscoe Lee Browne with choreography by Tune and Thommie Walsh. The musical had a stormy out-of-town tryout with director Peter Sellars being replaced by Mike Nichols, then MICHAEL BENNETT and finally Tune himself, who turned the muddled show into one of the brightest musicals of the season. Among the Gershwin songs interpolated into the *Funny Face* score were "Strike Up the Band," "'S Wonderful," "Blah, Blah, Blah," "Sweet and Low-Down" and "How Long Has This Been Going On?" (767 performances)

THE MYSTERY OF EDWIN DROOD (1985) was an unusual musical on several fronts: It was a whodunnit that asked the audience to decide who the murderer was; it was an American work in the style of British music hall entertainment; and its libretto, music, lyrics and even ORCHESTRATIONS were written by one man, Rubert Holmes. Charles Dickens' unfinished novel of the same title allowed Holmes to create an audience participation piece that fit in well with the direct performance techniques of British variety. In the English town of Cloistertram, the youth Edwin Drood is betrothed to the beautiful Rosa Bud. But one night Drood mysteriously disappears and various characters become likely suspects in the crime. The cast let the audience vote on who the culprit was and Holmes wrote six different musical climaxes, one for each of the possible conclusions. British veteran GEORGE ROSE acted as master of ceremonies and a talented cast of American actors had great fun with the different character types. BETTY BUCKLEY, in pantomime fashion, played the youth Edwin and HOWARD McGILLIN, Cleo Laine and PATTI COHENOUR were among the prime suspects. Holmes' score ranged from music hall sing-alongs to flowery Victorian ballads, with some exceptional songs such as "Moonfall," "Perfect Strangers," "The Wages of Sin," "Don't Quit While You're Ahead" and "Writing on the Wall." During its run of 608 performances the producers shortened the show's official title to *Drood*.

N

JOHN NAPIER (1944–), the award-winning British scenic designer, has been occasionally represented on Broadway, including four London musicals, *CATS* (1982), *LES MISÉRABLES* (1987), *Starlight Express* (1987) and *MISS SAIGON* (1991), all of which he designed for the original West End productions. Napier's designs are known for their spectacular effects but they are also expertly detailed and very stageworthy.

JAMES NAUGHTON (1945–), a leading man in Broadway plays and musicals since 1971, played the wife-swapping Wally in *I LOVE MY WIFE* (1977) and the fictional private eye Stone in *CITY OF ANGELS* (1989).

NAUGHTY MARIETTA (1910) was not composer VICTOR HERBERT's biggest hit but it is probably his finest operetta and remains popular to this day. RIDA JOHNSON YOUNG wrote the libretto and lyrics and producer Oscar Hammerstein cast it with opera singers from his financially troubled Manhattan Opera. The story is set in 1780s Louisiana, where noblewoman Marietta has arrived, escaping from an unhappy marriage in France. Also in New Orleans is Captain Dick and his rangers seeking out the pirate Bras Pique, whose identity is unknown. Marietta is attracted to Etienne, the lieutenant governor's son, but it is Captain Dick who realizes he loves her. When it is discovered that Etienne is the notorious pirate, Mariette and Captain Dick are united as they revel in the "sweet mystery of life." The full-voiced cast included EMMA TRENTINI as Marietta, Orville Harrold and Edward Martindel. Perhaps because he was writing for opera singers, Herbert came up with his richest and most enthralling score. Among the highlights are "Tramp! Tramp! Tramp!" "'Neath the Southern Moon," "Italian Street Song," "I'm Falling in Love with Someone," "Ah, Sweet Mystery of Life" and the title song. (136 performances)

GENE NELSON (1920–), a dancer-singer on stage and in films, made his Broadway debut in *THIS IS THE ARMY* (1942) and appeared in the revue *LEND AN EAR* (1948). Nelson played the self-deceptive Buddy in *FOLLIES* (1971) and was featured in the 1974 revival of *GOOD NEWS!*

RICHARD NELSON (1938–), a lighting designer for dance and Broadway musicals and plays, lit *THE MAGIC SHOW* (1974), *Oh, Brother!* (1981), *THE TAP DANCE KID* (1983), *SUNDAY IN THE PARK WITH GEORGE* (1984), *Harrigan 'n Hart* (1985), *INTO THE WOODS* (1987) and others.

NEW FACES OF 1952 was the best of the seven editions of the series produced by LEONARD SILLMAN. The new faces (Ronny Graham, Eartha Kitt, PAUL LYNDE, CAROL LAWRENCE, Alice Ghostly, Robert Clary and others) were inspired comics and their material, written by a variety of songwriters and playwrights, was highly original and literate. Mel Brooks wrote a spoof of *Death of a Salesman*, Ghostly lamented of lost romance in "The Boston Beguine," the Lizzie Borden tale got a hoedown treatment, Graham imitated Truman Capote and Kitt purred about her "Monotonous" life. The popular revue ran for 365 performances.

NEW GIRL IN TOWN (1957) was a successful musical with a very unlikely source: Eugene O'Neill's gloomy drama *Anna Christie*. GEORGE ABBOTT did the adaptation and BOB MERRILL, in his Broadway debut, wrote the songs. Despite its rousing musical comedy approach, *New Girl in Town* was rather faithful to the original source. The story is set in New York's waterfront area where Anna, a former prostitute, has returned from St. Paul to join her father, a crusty old barge captain. She meets the sailor Matt Burke and they fall in love but the truth about her past is revealed and the two lovers must reconcile themselves to each other's faults. GWEN VERDON played Anna and, with BOB FOSSE's choreography, her dancing was the highlight of the show. Cameron Prud'homme and George Wallace played the father and Matt, and Thelma Ritter was memorable as the sly alcoholic friend, Marthy. None of the Merrill songs became popular but there were some competent character numbers in the score: "Flings," "On the Farm," "It's Good to Be Alive" and "Sunshine Girl." Abbott also directed and the show ran for 431 performances.

THE NEW MOON (1928) is considered the last of the great American operettas; the era dominated by VICTOR HERBERT, RUDOLF FRIML and SIGMUND ROMBERG would soon end with the Depression. *The New Moon* featured music by Romberg and lyrics by OSCAR HAMMERSTEIN II. The libretto, by Hammerstein and others, was a complicated tale set in eighteenth-century New Orleans. It included a French nobleman in disguise, a revolt of "stouthearted" men, a spy from the French king, a ship called *The New Moon*, a mutiny, an island colony of free citizens and even the French Revolution itself. But what really mattered was the score that contained operetta favorites "Lover, Come Back to Me," "One Kiss," "Softly, as in a Morning Sunrise" and "Stouthearted Men." (509 performances)

THE NEW YORK SHAKESPEARE FESTIVAL, the official title of an ambitious and all-encompassing theatre organization founded by JOSEPH PAPP in 1954, seeks to develop and produce new plays and musicals, presents reconsidered revivals of old works and offers free Shakespeare productions in Central Park and other locations. The Off-Broadway, non-profit organization has presented some notable new musicals during its existence, some of which moved to Broadway. The most memorable New York Shakespeare Festival musicals include *HAIR* (1968), *TWO GENTLEMEN OF VERONA* (1971), *A CHORUS LINE* (1975), *I'M GETTING MY ACT TOGETHER AND TAKING IT ON THE ROAD* (1978), *Runaways* (1978), *The Human Comedy* (1984) and *THE MYSTERY OF EDWIN DROOD* (1985).

THE NEW YORKERS (1930) was a cynical and even bitter view of upper-class Manhattan that was palatable to audiences because of its COLE PORTER songs and its libretto, by HERBERT FIELDS, that set the whole story in a dream. A high-society dame is in love with a gangster-murderer-bootlegger but her philandering parents and their friends are no better. From Park Avenue to Harlem, the city is portrayed as a dangerous, romantic nightmare. Porter's "I Happen to Like New York" and "Take Me Back to Manhattan" continued this theme but the hit song was "Let's Fly Away." Also in the score was the provocative "Love for Sale" sung by a prostitute but the song was considered too wicked for radio broadcast so the general public never heard it. The cast included Hope Williams, ANN PENNINGTON, Charles King and JIMMY DURANTE as a comic gangster. Coming only weeks after the stock market crash, *The New Yorkers*' satire on the wealthy was ill-timed but the show still managed to run 168 performances.

ANTHONY NEWLEY (1931–), the singing actor and author of London musicals, appeared on Broadway as Littlechap in *STOP THE WORLD—I WANT TO GET OFF* (1961) and as Cocky in *THE ROAR OF THE GREASE-PAINT—THE SMELL OF THE CROWD* (1965), both of which he co-wrote with Leslie Bricusse.

PHYLLIS NEWMAN (1935–), an actress-singer of stage, nightclubs and television, made her Broadway debut in *WISH YOU WERE HERE* (1953) and played the towel-clad Martha in *SUBWAYS ARE FOR SLEEPING* (1961). Newman's other musical credits include *BELLS ARE RINGING* (1956), *First*

Impressions (1959), *The Madwoman of Central Park West* (1979) and various replacement roles on and off Broadway.

NINE (1982), a musicalization of Federico Fellini's film classic *8 1/2*, may not have been what devotees of the original wanted but it was a spectacular CONCEPT MUSICAL that was continually fascinating. Director-choreographer TOMMY TUNE took the uninspired libretto, worked on by Mario Fratti and then Arthur Kopit, and turned it into a highly stylized showcase for imaginative musical theatre. Guido Contini, a Fellinilike filmmaker and the only adult male in the show, is wrapped up in his psychological confusion over his art and the various women in his life, past and present. Everyone from his wife to his mistress to his mother to his star are conjured up in Guido's mind until he is eventually confronted with his younger self at the age of nine. Tune staged the whole production in a surreal spa in Venice and used the women in the hero's life as an orchestra, chorus and even scenery. Composer-lyricist MAURY YESTON made his Broadway debut with his scintillating score for *Nine*. Some of the memorable musical numbers included "Be Italian," "Only with You," "Be on Your Own" and "My Husband Makes Movies." RAUL JULIA led the gifted cast that included KAREN AKERS, LILIANE MONTEVECCHI, Anita Morris and Kathi Moss, and Lawrence Miller and WILLIAM IVEY LONG provided the stunning scenery and costumes. Thommie Walsh and Tune did the choreography, which included an expressionistic version of the Folies Bergère. *Nine* may have been a bit lean on content but was rich with theatrical creativity. (732 performances)

NO, NO, NANETTE (1925) is the musical that immediately comes to mind when 1920s musical comedy is mentioned. This silly but endearing show was a hit nationwide and its signature song, "Tea for Two," is still one of the most easily recognized songs in American popular culture. The plot of *No, No, Nanette*, by OTTO HARBACH and Frank Mandel, revolves around a bible publisher named Jimmy and his innocent ward Nanette. Jimmy has been giving financial support to three women in three different cities without his wife's knowledge. The three damsels converge on Jimmy's Atlantic City cottage along with Nanette and her romantic troubles, a screwball housemaid and a couple whose marriage is on the rocks. Composer VINCENT YOUMANS provided the finest score of his career with lyrics by Harbach and IRVING CAESAR. In addition to the idiotically optimistic "Tea for Two," the song "I Want to Be Happy" was also a hit. Included in the light-hearted score was "Too Many Rings around Rosie," "You Can Dance with Any Girl at All" and " 'Where Has My Hubby Gone?' Blues." *No, No, Nanette* ran 321 performances in New York, over a year in Chicago and spawned numerous road companies. A 1971 Broadway revival ran an unbelievable 861 performances and put the show back into the repertory of producible musicals.

NO STRINGS (1962) was an unusual musical on several accounts: It was the only show in which RICHARD RODGERS provided both music and lyrics; it used simple, suggestive scenery that was changed by the actors in full view of the audience; it put the musicians backstage and sometimes on stage; and, as the title announced, the ORCHESTRATIONS used no string instruments. Although all of these elements were commonplace by the end of the decade, they were quite innovative for 1962. Samuel Taylor wrote the original libretto about an American writer in Europe (RICHARD KILEY) who falls in love with a highly paid black fashion model (DIAHANN CARROLL) and they travel the continent together until the American decides he must return to Maine to write again. Financial and racial barriers discourage her from going with him and the lovers part. JOE LAYTON directed and choreographed the bittersweet show and Kiley and Carroll gave warm and thoughtful performances. Rodgers' "The Sweetest Sounds" thematically unified the story and the song became popular. Also in the score were "Loads of Love," "Look No Further," "Nobody Told Me" and the title song. (580 performances)

TREVOR NUNN (1940–), the renowned British director of classical theatre, directed four London musical hits that transferred to Broadway: *CATS* (1982), *LES MISÉRABLES* (1987), *Starlight Express* (1987) and *Aspects of Love* (1990).

NUNSENSE (1985), the inexplicably popular Off-Broadway musical about dancing and singing nuns, was the brainchild of Dan Goggin who wrote the libretto, music and lyrics for this silly show that seems to break records everywhere it is produced. The setting is a Catholic high school gymnasium in New Jersey where the "Little Sisters of Hoboken" are holding a benefit performance. The songs are sometimes pleasurable if mostly on a one-joke track and the five-character cast uses a lot of audience participation to keep the evening lively. (still running as of 3/1/93)

RUSSELL NYPE (1924–), a bespectacled singer-actor, was featured in the Broadway musicals *REGINA* (1949), *CALL ME MADAM* (1950), *Goldilocks* (1958) and others.

O
___

OF THEE I SING (1931), one of the boldest and most brilliant of all musicals, was closer to comic operetta than standard musical comedy. It utilized extended musical passages and rhymed recitative even as it maintained a very modern tone. The satire in *Of Thee I Sing* encompassed politics, love, beauty contests, diplomacy and even motherhood yet the show was more delectable than malicious. GEORGE S. KAUFMAN and MORRIE RYSKIND, who had previously worked on different versions of the Gershwins' satirical *STRIKE UP THE BAND* (1930), wrote the libretto and GEORGE and IRA GERSHWIN provided the nearly non-stop score. The story follows presidential candidate John P. Wintergreen who gets the popular vote riding on a platform of love. Once elected, Wintergreen runs into trouble with the French government because he married his humble secretary Mary Turner rather than, as previously announced, the beauty contest winner Diana Deveraux, who is illegitimately descended from Napoleon. After an impeachment hearing and the birth of twins, all ends well as Diana marries the hapless Vice President Throttlebottom and Wintergreen remains president. Kaufman directed the musical with razor-sharp proficiency and the cast included WILLIAM GAXTON and VICTOR MOORE as president and vice president. Because of the continuous nature of the score, individual songs could not be easily lifted from the show but "Love Is Sweeping the Country," "Who Cares?" and the title song became well known. *Of Thee I Sing* brought a new level of satirical writing to the American musical and seemed to link Gilbert and Sullivan operetta with the most up-to-date sassy musical comedy. The writers were awarded the PULITZER

PRIZE for Drama, the first ever bestowed on a musical, and the script was the first musical to be published as a hardcover book. The show ran 441 performances and became the standard by which all musical satires were later judged. A sequel to *Of Thee I Sing*, called *LET 'EM EAT CAKE* (1933), reunited the same authors and leading performers but, despite a superb score, it was too bitter for mid-Depression audiences and soon closed.

OH, BOY! (1917) was one of the PRINCESS THEATRE MUSICALS by the celebrated team of Bolton, Wodehouse and Kern. The story is one of mistaken identity with an eloped couple, a country club full of fun-loving friends, a lecherous judge and a Quaker aunt all tangled together in delightful confusion. GUY BOLTON wrote the libretto with P. G. WODEHOUSE, who also provided lyrics for JEROME KERN's scintillating music. "Till the Clouds Roll By" was the show's biggest hit but the entire score was superb with such standouts as "An Old-Fashioned Wife," "Nesting Time in Flatbush," "The Land Where the Good Songs Go" and "You Never Knew About Me." *Oh, Boy!* ran for 463 performances and helped establish the emerging new form of American musical comedy.

OH, CALCUTTA! (1969) was a notorious revue that explored humankind's sexual hangups through the ages and did it with a cast that was nude for sections of the evening. It was a show everyone heard about but few realized that it was a musical. Kenneth Tynan "devised" the revue and Jacques Levy "conceived" and directed it, using sketches by writers as diverse as Jules Feiffer, Sam Shepard, John Lennon and Samuel Beckett. (Actually, Beckett withdrew his playlet before the opening but the producers kept his name in the credits since the program never identified who wrote what.) The songs were by the Open Window, which consisted of Stanley Walden, Robert Dennis and Peter Schickele. None of the score was of much interest except, in retrospect, a number called "Coming Together, Going Together," in which a group of theatre auditionees reveal their anxieties, hopes, ambitions and even love of ballet à la *A Chorus Line* but six years earlier. *Oh, Calcutta!*'s initial Off-Broadway engagement ran 397 performances but it was revived on Broadway in 1976 and ran a disconcerting 5,959 performances.

OH, KAY! (1926) has one of the best of all the GERSHWINS' musical comedy scores with "Clap Yo' Hands," "Maybe," "Do, Do, Do" and "Someone to Watch over Me" as the standouts. GUY BOLTON and P. G. WODEHOUSE, reunited from their PRINCESS THEATRE MUSICALS days, wrote the libretto, which found wonderful comic possibilities in Prohibition and bootlegging. At a Long Island estate, an English heiress named Kay has disguised herself as a cook to keep an eye on the illegal liquor that her brother has hidden in the cellar. The owner of the house returns and falls in love with Kay and they are united after some romantic and legal tangles are cleared up. GERTRUDE LAWRENCE had appeared on Broadway earlier in a British revue but *Oh, Kay!* was her first American vehicle and it made her a Broadway favorite. Lawrence's rendition of "Someone to Watch over Me," quietly sung to a rag doll, is one of the musical theatre's most endearing images. (256 performances)

OH, LADY! LADY! (1918) was the last of the Bolton–Wodehouse–Kern collaborations for the PRINCESS THEATRE MUSICALS series and all the familiar elements were there in top form. GUY BOLTON and P. G. WODEHOUSE's libretto concerned an impending wedding that is upset by the arrival of a long-lost love. VIVIENNE SEGAL led a sparkling cast for 219 performances and the JEROME KERN–Wodehouse score included "When the Ships Come Home," "Before I Met You," "Moon Song," "Not Yet" and "Greenwich Village." The best song in the show, "Bill," had to be discarded because it did not fit the production's Bill; the song would show up nine years later in Kern's *SHOW BOAT* (1927).

JILL O'HARA (1947–   ), an actress-singer who was featured in Broadway musicals in the 1960s, appeared as Sheila in the Off-Broadway *HAIR* (1967) and as Agnes Nolan in *GEORGE M!* (1968). O'Hara's best role was the suicidal Fran Kubelik in *PROMISES, PROMISES* (1968).

TOM O'HORGAN (1928–   ), the director of highly theatrical and often controversial plays, staged a handful of Broadway musicals, most notably *HAIR* (1968) and *JESUS CHRIST SUPERSTAR* (1971).

OKLAHOMA! (1943) is not only one of the American theatre's most beloved shows, it is also one of its most influential. *Oklahoma!* changed the direction of the Broadway musical and affected the way musicals were written for the next two decades. The story of how the show came to be is one of accidents, surprises and longshots. OSCAR HAMMERSTEIN II thought that Lynn Riggs' 1931 play *Green Grow the Lilacs* would make a good musical and suggested to JEROME KERN that they collaborate. RICHARD RODGERS had the same hunch and approached his partner LORENZ HART. Both Kern and Hart didn't like the idea so when Rodgers mentioned it to Hammerstein, and he immediately accepted, the new team was born. The impending product, initially titled *Away We Go!*, did not look very promising to theatre insiders. Rodgers had never worked with anyone but Hart whose witty, urbane lyrics gave their shows a sassy verve that audiences adored. To team Rodgers with the unclever, sentimental Hammerstein, who had several years of Broadway and Hollywood flops to his credit, seemed like courting disaster. Also, Riggs' play was unlikely musical theatre material and the producers, the THEATRE GUILD, had had a very unsuccessful track record of late. But Rodgers and Hammerstein persevered, avoided using stars in their cast and got ROUBEN MAMOULIAN to direct with his characteristic sincerity and lack of razzle-dazzle. Hammerstein wrote the libretto, keeping to *Green Grow the Lilacs* faithfully and using some of Riggs' dialogue and stage directions as inspiration for the lyrics. Rodgers eschewed the sophisticated, brash sounds of his Hart musicals and used more subtle musical phrasing and even folk song structure. Out-of-town reports were negative, but when the show, now retitled *Oklahoma!*, opened in New York, the acclaim from critics and audiences alike was unanimous. The plot is rather straightforward, using two sets of lovers, one romantic and the other comic. In the midwestern Indian territory, the likeable cowhand Curly (ALFRED DRAKE) loves Laurie (Joan Roberts), who is being pursued by the menacing Jud Fry (HOWARD DA SILVA). After a brief lovers' spat with Curly, Laurie tells Jud that she will acccept his invitation to the box social but immediately regrets it and her fears are revealed in a dream ballet. Curly and Laurie eventually get engaged but on their wedding day Jud pulls a knife on the groom and in the fight is killed by Curly. A judge finds Curly innocent and the couple ride off happily in a surrey. The secondary plot involves man-hungry Ado Annie (CELESTE HOLM) and her indecision regarding her two beaux, the peddler Ali Hakim (Joseph Buloff) and the cowboy Will Parker (Lee Dixon). In telling the simple but engaging tale of *Oklahoma!* the creators hit upon an honest, homespun style of presentation that seemed like a breath of fresh air amid all the phoney sophistication of shows that centered on jokes, chorus girls and spectacle. The Rodgers and Hammerstein score is one of the American theatre's very best not only for the masterful quality of each song but also for the way the whole ensemble is closely integrated with character and story. "Oh, What a Beautiful Mornin'," "I Cain't Say No," "Poor Jud Is Daid," "People Will Say We're in Love," "The Surrey with the Fringe on Top," "Out of My Dreams" and the rousing title song are among the show's highlights. Added to the warm and perceptive performances by the young cast was AGNES DE MILLE's famous choreography that revealed character and emotion rather than simply giving the show movement. *Oklahoma!* ran an unprecedented 2,212 performances and has been revived on a regular basis by all levels of performing groups. In addition to establishing the musical theatre's most influential collaborative team, *Oklahoma!* pushed Broadway toward a more rural, innocent kind of musical. For the next twenty years, musicals, by and large, would shun urbane wit for a more honest type of characters and situations. Earthy American values would rank above educated, worldly ones. Character songs would become the expected instead of the exception. Not since *SHOW BOAT* (1927) had a show revealed the exciting possibilities of the musical play.

OLIVER! (1963) held the record as the most successful West End musical on Broadway (774 performances) until the British invasion in the 1970s. Lionel Bart wrote the music and lyrics and adapted Charles Dickens' *Oliver Twist* into a lively family entertainment that seemed to celebrate Victorian London rather than castigate it as the novel had. Clive Revill recreated his audacious performance as Fagin and GEORGIA BROWN was an expert Nancy. Also in the cast were Bruce Prochnik as the orphan Oliver, Willoughby Goddard, Hope Jackman and David Jones. Bart's score offered the rousing "Consider Yourself" and the ballad "As Long as He Needs Me," as well as other tuneful songs.

OLE OLSEN (1892–1963) was a member of the outrageous comic team of Olsen and Johnson that headlined in vaudeville and was featured on Broadway in seven musicals, most notably *HELLZAPOPPIN* (1938). Olsen and his partner CHICK JOHNSON also co-produced most of their Broadway shows.

ON A CLEAR DAY YOU CAN SEE FOREVER (1965) was a less-than-satisfying musical about extrasensory perception that boasted a fine score by ALAN JAY LERNER (lyrics) and BURTON LANE (music) and a delightful performance by BARBARA HARRIS. Lerner wrote the original libretto about Daisy, a chain-smoking New Yorker with extrasensory perception who seeks help from a doctor. Under hypnosis Daisy can recall a previous life as Melinda, an eighteenth-century British femme fatale, and soon the doctor is in love with the past as Daisy is falling for the doctor. The script had too many loose ends and never quite worked but Harris was a delectable Daisy and the songs were pleasurable: "Hurry! It's Lovely Up Here," "She Wasn't You," "Come Back to Me," "What Did I Have That I Don't Have?" and the soaring title song that remained popular long after the show's 280 performances.

ON THE TOWN (1944), besides being a fanciful musical comedy that utilized more dance than usually seen in a Broadway show, is notable as the debut of four of the American theatre's major creative talents: composer LEONARD BERNSTEIN, librettists-lyricists BETTY COMDEN and ADOLPH GREEN and choreographer JEROME ROBBINS. *On the Town* was an extended version of Bernstein's "Fancy Free," a dance piece Robbins had previously done at the Ballet Theatre. Three sailors on twenty-four-hour leave in New York City find romance with three girls as their adventures take them from the top of the Empire State Building to Coney Island. Comden and Green wrote the libretto and lyrics and also played major roles in the musical. Bernstein's music was jazzy, romantic and very contemporary. "I Get Carried Away," "Lucky to Be Me," "I Can Cook, Too," "Lonely Town," "Come Up to My Place," "Some Other Time" and the recurring "New York, New York" were standouts in an impeccable score. GEORGE ABBOTT directed but it was Robbins' "Miss Turnstiles" and other dance pieces that made *On the Town* so unique. Also in the cast were Cris Alexander, John Battles, Sono Osato and, as a hilarious cab driver, NANCY WALKER. (463 performances)

ON THE TWENTIETH CENTURY (1978) was a superb musical farce with outstanding production values and a cheerful cast of characters, all under the astute direction of HAROLD PRINCE. The libretto by BETTY COMDEN and ADOLPH GREEN was based on the 1932 Ben Hecht–Charles MacArthur comedy *Twentieth Century*. The flamboyant Broadway producer Oscar Jaffe needs to make a big comeback and, while traveling by train from Chicago to New York, tries to convince the movie star (and his former lover) Lily Garland to star in his musical version of *The Passion of Mary Magdalene*. Also on the train is Lily's new lover Bruce Granit and a religious fanatic posed as a philanthropist. The score by CY COLEMAN (music) and Comden and Green (lyrics) was mock opera at times and relished the bravura of the characters and situations. None of the songs were as effective outside of the show's context but "Veronique," "Never," "Our Private World" and the title song were laudable. JOHN CULLUM was a wildly funny Oscar, MADELINE KAHN played Lily with her multiranged voice doing all sorts of acrobatics, KEVIN KLINE made a brash debut as Bruce and IMOGENE COCA delighted as the daffy religious zealot. (JUDY KAYE replaced Kahn early in the run and it secured her career.) Perhaps the biggest star in the show, though, was ROBIN WAGNER's sleek art deco train set that amused audiences from various angles and perspectives. (449 performances)

ON YOUR TOES (1936) was one of the most inventive of all the RODGERS and HART musicals and did much to redefine the ways dance could be utilized in the musical theatre. GEORGE ABBOTT collaborated with Rodgers and Hart on the libretto, which dealt with the rivalry between classical ballet and modern tap and jazz. Junior Dolan is a former vaudeville dancer now teaching music at Knickerbocker University. He uses a society matron to enlist a Russian ballet troupe to perform a jazz ballet called "Slaughter on Tenth Avenue" and soon he is torn between his girlfriend and the exotic Russian prima ballerina. The musical's climax is the new ballet in which Junior must keep dancing until the police can arrest the ballerina's jealous boyfriend. GEORGE BALANCHINE choreographed both the classical and modern dance sections, including a mock romantic ballet called "Princess Zenobia" and the justly famous "Slaughter on Tenth Avenue." Rodgers and Hart wrote a dazzling score that included "There's a Small Hotel," "It's Got to Be Love," "Glad to Be Unhappy" and the toe-tapping title song. RAY BOLGER played Junior and established himself as Broadway's top singer-dancer-comic. And the whole enterprise was held together by Abbott who was becoming Broadway's most influential director of musical comedy. *On Your Toes* ran for 315 performances, was revived unsuccessfully in 1954, then revived again in 1983 for an astonishing 505 performances; Abbott directed all three productions.

ONCE ON THIS ISLAND (1990) was a simple, evocative musical that utilized folklore and a Caribbean temperament with pleasing effect. The all-sung musical was based on the novel *My Love, My Love* by Trinidadian Rosa Guy. It told the tale of a peasant girl named Ti Moune, an orphan considered a gift of the gods, who leaves her village to seek her love Daniel. But when she finds the wealthy heir, he is contracted to marry another and Ti Moune mystically is transformed into a tree that forever reminds the locals of the power of true love. Lynn Ahrens did the adaptation and provided the lyrics for Stephen Flaherty's music and GRACIELA DANIELE directed and choreographed the enchanting production. Among the many praiseworthy numbers in the score were "We Dance," "Waiting for Life," "Mama Will Provide" and "A Part of Us." *Once on This Island* workshopped Off Broadway at the PLAYWRIGHTS HORIZONS then successfully moved to Broadway in 1990, proving there was an audience for small, intimate musicals amid all the spectaculars currently in vogue.

ONCE UPON A MATTRESS (1959) was a serviceable musical comedy version of the fairy tale *The Princess and the Pea* with a routine score but an unpretentious sprightly manner. Jay Thompson, Dean Fuller and Marshall Barer wrote the silly libretto and Mary Rodgers (music) and Barer (lyrics) provided the score. Princess Winnifred (CAROL BURNETT) arrives at the castle as a possible bride for Prince Dauntless the Drab (Joseph Bova) but first must endure a series of tests laid out by the dictatorial Queen Agravain (Jane White). The secondary couple in the musical were the romantic lovers while the clowning was left to the principals, including the pantomime role of the king (JACK GILFORD). The Rodgers–Barer score was pleasant enough and Burnett's debut performance was bright and jocular. GEORGE ABBOTT directed and JOE LAYTON did the choreography. (460 performances)

110 IN THE SHADE (1963) was a gentle and affecting musical that couldn't survive on Broadway in a season that offered big spectacles and glamorous stars. N. Richard Nash adapted his own 1954 play *The Rainmaker* and songwriters TOM JONES and HARVEY SCHMIDT came up with a tender and warm score in the temperament of their *THE FANTASTICKS* (1960). The story concerns a con man named Starbuck (Robert Horton) who comes to a drought-striken midwestern town and promises rain for a fee of $100. The Curry family takes on Starbuck's offer and the spinster daughter Lizzie (INGA SWENSON), although complaining that he is a fake, falls in love with the magnetic confidence man because of the hopes he awakens in her. In the end, Lizzie gains the self-confidence to reject Starbuck and take up with the local sheriff (STEPHEN DOUGLASS) who has always loved her as, to the surprise of everyone, rain begins to fall. The score offered no hits but a lovely collection of songs that included "Love, Don't Turn Away," "Melisande," "Little Red Hat," "Simple Little Things" and "Everything Beautiful Happens at Night." (330 performances)

ONE TOUCH OF VENUS (1943) was much lighter and carefree than other musicals associated with composer KURT WEILL but it was a piece of superb craftsmanship aided by the talents of humorists Ogden Nash and S. J. Perelman. The story is yet another variation on the Pygmalion legend, this time a statue of Venus coming to life and falling in love with a henpecked barber named Rodney. Venus is well on the way to winning Rodney from his domineering fiancée until the goddess realizes that life as a barber's wife would be unbearably humdrum. She returns to stone but Rodney immediately meets an art student who resembles Venus and a new romance begins. The libretto by Nash and Perelman was refreshingly witty and Nash's lyrics were as entertaining as his famous light verse. "How Much I Love You," "That's Him" and "The Trouble with Women" were exceptional but the hit of the show was the romantically haunting "Speak Low." MARY MARTIN, in her first starring role, played Venus with a sly coyness that was infectuous and Kenny Baker was a delightful Rodney. Elia Kazan directed and AGNES DE MILLE choreographed, adding two memorable ballets—"Forty Minutes for Lunch" and "Venus in Ozone Heights"—to her outstanding dance achievements. (567 performances)

OPERETTA is no longer with us in name but the effects of this seemingly antique form of musical theatre are still present on Broadway. By definition, operetta refers to a light form of opera that utilizes dialogue and tends toward the amusing rather than the thought provoking. Such a general definition would include most musical comedies and even a good portion of musical plays. But the true American operetta flourished from the 1890s until the Depression and patterned itself on the cheery, lyrical works coming from Europe in the nineteenth century. American operetta grew out of opéra bouffe and opéra comique from France, ballad opera and comic opera from England and the waltzing Viennese operas. These forms had been coming across the Atlantic early in the century and by the 1860s were a stronghold in legitimate theatres as well as opera houses. The popularity of the Gilbert and Sullivan comic operettas during the Victorian era secured operetta a place on Broadway and from the time of *THE BLACK CROOK* (1866) American composers were pursuing the form. Perhaps the earliest native product of note was REGINALD DE KOVEN's *ROBIN HOOD* (1891), a purely European piece in many ways. *EL CAPITAN* (1896), by the all-American composer John Philip Sousa, used a South American setting in keeping with the "foreign" quality that audiences expected in operetta. America's three outstanding masters of operetta, VICTOR HERBERT, RUDOLF FRIML and SIGMUND ROMBERG, also tended toward non-American locales at first but soon the foreign flavor was transferred to French Louisiana, the Canadian Rockies and other regional settings. Herbert's talent for melodic and romantic themes was first fully recognized with *THE FORTUNE TELLER* (1898) and he reached his artistic peak in such operetta favorites as *MLLE. MODISTE* (1905), *NAUGHTY MARIETTA* (1910) and *SWEETHEARTS* (1913). Friml made a smashing debut with *THE FIRE-FLY* (1912) and went on to compose such masterworks of the genre as *ROSE-MARIE* (1924), *THE VAGABOND KING* (1925) and *THE THREE*

MUSKETEERS (1928). Romberg had the longest career and was the only one of the three to also have some success outside of operetta. *MAYTIME* (1917), *THE STUDENT PRINCE* (1924) and *THE DESERT SONG* (1926) were his greatest accomplishments and are part of the reason that the 1920s became the golden age of American operetta. Romberg's *THE NEW MOON* (1929) is considered the last of the breed for the stock market crash indirectly ended the era. Few composers would label their work "operetta" after 1930 yet many of them still were writing similar products. In fact, most "modern" American composers have attempted the genre sometime during their careers but called it something else. JEROME KERN did it with *THE CAT AND THE FIDDLE* (1931) and *MUSIC IN THE AIR* (1932), the GERSHWINS' *STRIKE UP THE BAND* (1930) and *OF THEE I SING* (1931) were nothing short of comic operetta, RODGERS and HART toyed with the genre in *DEAREST ENEMY* (1925) while even IRVING BERLIN, that most un-operatic of composers, found the style useful in *MISS LIBERTY* (1949). Later on, RODGERS and HAMMERSTEIN relied on operetta techniques for *CAROUSEL* (1945), LERNER AND LOEWE in *BRIGADOON* (1947), FRANK LOESSER in *THE MOST HAPPY FELLA* (1956) and LEONARD BERNSTEIN in *CANDIDE* (1956). It is much the same today. No producer would bill his show as an operetta but how else to describe BOCK and HARNICK's *SHE LOVES ME* (1963), STEPHEN SONDHEIM's *A LITTLE NIGHT MUSIC* (1973), CY COLEMAN's *ON THE TWENTIETH CENTURY* (1978) or Lucy Simon's *THE SECRET GARDEN* (1991)? The European-style American operetta is long gone but the light-hearted, lyric aspects of operetta are still very much a part of the Broadway scene.

JERRY ORBACH (1935–), a solid musical theatre leading man, usually plays characters with a dark, brooding side to them. Orbach originated the role of El Gallo in the Off-Broadway *THE FANTASTICKS* (1960), introducing the song "Try to Remember." He played the embittered puppeteer Paul in *CARNIVAL* (1961) and featured roles in the revivals of *THE CRADLE WILL ROCK* in 1964 and *ANNIE GET YOUR GUN* in 1966. Orbach's personable Chuck Baxter in *PROMISES, PROMISES* (1968) was a lighterweight part but just as skillfully done. His mature roles on Broadway were shyster lawyer Billy Flynn in *CHICAGO* (1975) and theatrical producer Julian Marsh in *42ND STREET* (1980).

ORCHESTRATIONS on Broadway are done by talented and trained composers who take the musical arrangements set by the MUSIC DIRECTOR or musical arrangers and then turn them into notated parts for the orchestra. In the world of concert music and opera, the original composer usually does the orchestrations but on Broadway, where few composers can even notate, the job is done by orchestrators. LEONARD BERNSTEIN, STEPHEN SCHWARTZ, ANDREW LLOYD WEBBER, KURT WEILL and a few other Broadway composers have written or assisted in writing the orchestrations for their shows but they are the exception. Among the American theatre's most distinguished orchestrators are: ROBERT RUSSELL BENNETT, who did hundreds of shows including most of the RODGERS and HAMMERSTEIN musicals and the LERNER and LOEWE works; HERSHY KAY, who worked with Bernstein on his musicals and orchestrated *A CHORUS LINE* (1975), *EVITA* (1979), and other hits; PHILIP J. LANG, who did such classics as *ANNIE GET YOUR GUN* (1946), *MY FAIR LADY* (1956) and *HELLO, DOLLY!* (1964); and DON WALKER, who orchestrated *FINIAN'S RAINBOW* (1947), *THE MUSIC MAN* (1957) and many of the HAROLD PRINCE-produced musicals. Other outstanding Broadway orchestrators include Ralph Burns, LUTHER HENDERSON, Irwin Kostal, Peter Matz, Sid Ramin, Eddie Sauter and Harold Wheeler. The most notable of the newer generation of Broadway orchestrators include JONATHAN TUNICK, who did many of the STEPHEN SONDHEIM musicals, and MICHAEL STAROBIN, who orchestrated *ONCE ON THIS ISLAND* (1990) and the *FALSETTOS* musicals.

ORIGINAL CAST RECORDINGS of Broadway musicals are a relatively recent innovation. Today one expects a musical's recording to have the same performers, songs and ORCHESTRATIONS that were heard on the stage but such recreations did not exist before 1943. The invention of the phonograph in 1877 coincides nicely with the developing American musical theatre but the earliest recordings of songs from Broadway shows on cylinders and 78–rpm disks rarely used the stage performers. It was felt that recording artists were more suited for these records and often the house band for the recording company played their own orchestrated version of the song. Once in a while a performer of renown would get to record his or her hit song but rarely did it resemble the manner in which it was done in the theatre. In Britain, on the other hand, recording companies felt differently and in 1900 the complete score for the musical *Floradora* was recorded on 78s. On several occasions the British would record the West End versions of American musicals and the earliest and most accurate recordings of *ROSE-MARIE* (1924), *LADY, BE GOOD!* (1924), *NO, NO, NANETTE* (1925) and other shows were made this way. The first American to try to preserve stage scores accurately on records was Jack Kapp who took selections from *BLACKBIRDS OF 1928* and the 1932 revival of *SHOW BOAT* and recorded them with the original artists on the Brunswick label in 1932. Kapp was also responsible for putting all of the songs and some narration from *THE CRADLE WILL ROCK* (1938) on six 78s, using the original cast as well as composer MARC BLITZSTEIN as narrator. The first complete cast recording of a full-scale Broadway musical was Kapp's 78s of *OKLAHOMA!* (1943) on the Decca label. When the long-playing (LP) record, capable of having twenty-five minutes of music on each side, was introduced in 1948, the concept of original cast recordings became even more practical.

The first major hit on the LP format was *SOUTH PACIFIC* (1949) on the Columbia label. LP recordings did have one drawback: musicals originally issued on several 78s were now forced to edit the score to fit within fifty minutes. The Broadway show album as we know it today was mostly developed by Goddard Lieberson, a record producer and president of Columbia Records from 1956 to 1966. It was Lieberson who tried to recapture the stage experience on the recording by adding lead-in dialogue for songs and editing longer musical passages in order to include their essence on the LP. Using these techniques, almost every Broadway musical in the late 1950s and 1960s, successful or not, was recorded for posterity. But the rise of rock music and the new directions the music industry was taking in the late 1960s made original cast albums less profitable and too many shows in the 1970s and 1980s went unrecorded. The introduction of the compact disc (CD) in the 1980s meant that the scores for Broadway musicals could be recorded with fewer omissions but CDs did not manage to make show recordings popular enough to compete with mainstream popular music. CDs do allow for older, previously recorded musicals to be reissued with additional tracks and CDs are ideal for recording complete scores of classic shows from the past with contemporary performers. But the original cast recording is still not big business in the eyes of record companies. Perhaps the most blatant example of this was the hit musical *GRAND HOTEL* that opened on Broadway in November 1989 but was not recorded until April 1992 because of legal complications and the recording industry's reservations about its practicality.

P

PACIFIC OVERTURES (1976) was an uncompromising experiment that attempted to musicalize the history of the Westernization of Japan from the arrival of Commodore Perry in 1859 to the present day. To make the experiment even bolder, the story was told from the Japanese point of view using Kabuki theatre techniques, haikulike lyrics and Asian-influenced music. But in the hands of composer-lyricist STEPHEN SONDHEIM and producer-director HAROLD PRINCE, *Pacific Overtures* was a deeply moving theatrical piece rather than a mere curiosity. JOHN WEIDMAN wrote the unconventional libretto and Mako led an all-Asian cast that played a variety of characters in this ambitious chronicle. "Someone in a Tree," "Poems," "Welcome to Kanagawa," "Please, Hello" and "Pretty Lady" were standouts in a masterful score though none of them could possibly survive outside of the context of the musical. Another memorable aspect of *Pacific Overtures* was BORIS ARONSON's brilliant scenic design, which viewed the West with Asian eyes, turning ships into dragons and admirals into lions. It was Aronson's final Broadway credit and one of his greatest achievements. (193 performances)

KEN PAGE (1954–   ) is a black singer-actor who made his Broadway debut as Nicely-Nicely in the 1976 revival of *GUYS AND DOLLS*. Page was one of the nimble quintet of performers in *AIN'T MISBEHAVIN'* (1978) and originated the role of Old Deuteronomy in the New York production of *CATS* (1982).

PAINT YOUR WAGON (1951) was a robust and engaging musical set during the California gold rush with a superior score by LERNER and LOEWE. Alan

Jay Lerner wrote the original libretto about an old prospector and his daughter who discover gold on their land and watch their property become a boom town. But the lode dwindles, the town goes bust and the prospector quietly dies with all his dreams of wealth fondly remembererd. "I Talk to the Trees" and "They Call the Wind Maria" were the hit songs from the show but also effective were "I Still See Elisa," "Wand'rin' Star," "What's Goin' on Here?" and the title song. *Paint Your Wagon* is a splendid musical but receives fewer revivals than it deserves, due partly to the dreadful 1969 film version, which retained only the setting and a few of the songs. (289 performances)

THE PAJAMA GAME (1954) was an unpretentious musical comedy that, aside from being a rousing good time, introduced a handful of talents in their first major Broadway effort: producers Frederick Brisson, ROBERT GRIFFITH and HAROLD PRINCE; JEROME ROBBINS as co-director; choreographer BOB FOSSE and the songwriting team of RICHARD ADLER and JERRY ROSS. The slight but entertaining libretto was by GEORGE ABBOTT and Richard Bissell, based on Bissell's novel *7½ Cents*. The new plant superintendent (JOHN RAITT) at the Sleep-Tite Pajama Factory is attracted to a union activist (Janis Paige) but their romance is hindered by a workers' strike for a 7 ½-cent raise. The secondary lovers in the show were a time-efficiency manager and a flirtatious bookkeeper, played with comic verve by EDDIE FOY, JR., and CAROL HANEY. The Adler–Ross score was zestful and appealing: "I'm Not at All in Love," "Hernando's Hideaway," "I'll Never Be Jealous Again," "Once a Year Day," "Steam Heat" and "Hey, There," the last a unique love song in which Raitt accompanied his own voice on the office dictaphone. Fosse's choreography was dazzling and, as usual, Abbott's direction was brisk and expert. *The Pajama Game* was conventional and familiar; but what it lacked in subtlety or depth it made up for with irresistible fun. (1,063 performances)

PAL JOEY (1940), possibly the first adult musical because of its uncompromising look at its seedy and cynical characters, is arguably RODGERS and HART's finest work. *Pal Joey* is bold and intoxicating even as it retains the lyrical quality that distinguishes the team's other musicals. Joey Evans is a self-serving Chicago entertainer who drops his naive girlfriend Linda in order to secure his own nightclub through a relationship with a wealthy, knowing woman named Vera. After dealing with some blackmailers from his past, Joey loses his grip on Vera and both women send him packing. The libretto by John O'Hara (with uncredited help from director GEORGE ABBOTT) was based on his *New Yorker* stories and it was unsentimentally potent. Such a two-timing, self-reliant character had only shown up previously in musicals in minor comic roles or as secondary villains. The Rodgers and Hart songs picked up on the libretto's true-to-life, non-romantic style and are even sharper than the team's usual fare. "You Mustn't Kick It Around," "Bewitched, Bothered and Bewildered," "Zip," "I Could Write a Book," "Den of Iniquity" and "Take Him" were among the vivid songs. GENE KELLY played Joey, VIVIENNE SEGAL was Vera and the cast also featured JUNE HAVOC, Jack Durant, Leila Ernst and Van Johnson. Critics were divided on the tough-as-nails show but it still managed to run 354 performances. A 1952 revival with HAROLD LANG as Joey and Segal recreating the role of Vera received better reviews and ran for 540 performances.

LELAND PALMER (1945–), a singer-dancer on and off Broadway since 1966, played the boyish Viola in *YOUR OWN THING* (1968) and the lusty mother Fastrada in *PIPPIN* (1972). Palmer's other musical credits include *A Joyful Noise* (1966) and *APPLAUSE* (1970).

PETER PALMER (1931–), a leading man in musicals, originated the role of Abner Yokum in *L'IL ABNER* (1956) and played the wealthy Gus Esmond in *Lorelei* (1974).

PANAMA HATTIE (1940) was not top drawer COLE PORTER but it was enjoyable enough to entertain audiences for 501 performances on a Broadway slowly recovering from the Depression. ETHEL MERMAN was the star and librettists B. G. DeSYLVA and HERBERT FIELDS called her Hattie Maloney, a brassy bar girl in Panama City who wishes to marry a Philadelphia blue blood but must befriend his eight-year-old daughter first. Merman was supported by a likable cast that included Arthur Treacher, James Dunn, Joan Carroll, Rags Ragland, Betty Hutton, June Allyson, Lucille Bremer, VERA-ELLEN and Betsy Blair. The highlight of the show was Merman and Carroll's "Let's Be Buddies" and the score also featured "I've Still Got My Health," "I'm Throwing a Ball Tonight" and "Make It Another Old-Fashioned, Please."

JOSEPH PAPP (1921–1991), the tireless producer who founded and guided the NEW YORK SHAKESPEARE FESTIVAL for thirty-five years, presented several musicals at his Public Theatre, many of which later moved to Broadway for successful runs. Among Papp's most memorable shows are *HAIR* (1968), *TWO GENTLEMEN OF VERONA* (1971), *A CHORUS LINE* (1975), *Runaways* (1978), *I'M GETTING MY ACT TOGETHER AND TAKING IT ON THE ROAD* (1978), *The Human Comedy* (1983) and *THE MYSTERY OF EDWIN DROOD* (1985), as well as the popular revivals of *THE THREEPENNY OPERA* in 1976 and *The Pirates of Penzance* in 1981.

THE PASSING SHOW (1894) is generally agreed upon to be the first American musical revue, although its producers called it a "review" at the time. The show spoofed the recent plays by Arthur Wing Pinero, offered acrobatics and ballet pieces, "reviewed" the events of the day and even did a send-up of several operas in a number called "Round the Opera in Twenty Minutes." With a cast of one hundred performers, *The Passing Show* was also a pleasing spectacle and ran for 110 performances. Throughout the subsequent decades the title would be used by various producers for other musical revues.

PASTICHE MUSICALS imitate and usually spoof musical styles of earlier eras. Many a modern musical has included a pastiche nightclub act or a show-within-a-show number for atmospheric effect or variety: *FUNNY GIRL* (1964), *GYPSY* (1959), *THE WILL ROGERS FOLLIES* (1991), *FLORA, THE RED MENACE* (1965), *GUYS AND DOLLS* (1950), *ON THE TWENTIETH CENTURY* (1978) and on and on. But a true pastiche musical consistently echoes a previous style throughout. *LITTLE MARY SUNSHINE* (1959) spoofed the *ROSE-MARIE*-type operettas and "The Gladiola Girl" section of *LEND AN EAR* (1948) and *THE BOY FRIEND* (1954) took off on the 1920s musical comedies. *Curly McDimple* (1967) lampooned Shirley Temple and, like *DAMES AT SEA* (1968), had fun with the Hollywood musical. *Charlotte Sweet* (1982) and *THE MYSTERY OF EDWIN DROOD* (1985) imitated British music hall entertainment. All of the songs in *CHICAGO* (1975) and many of those in *LOVE LIFE* (1948) pastiched vaudeville numbers. Surely the most interesting use of serious pastiche were the many period songs STEPHEN SONDHEIM wrote for the flashback sections of *FOLLIES* (1971).

MANDY PATINKIN (1952–), an intense singer and leading man in plays, musicals, films and the concert stage, first gained recognition with his mesmerizing portrayal of Che in the New York production of *EVITA* (1979). Patinkin created the roles of the two artists named George in *SUNDAY IN THE PARK WITH GEORGE* (1984) and the moody Uncle Archibald in *THE SECRET GARDEN* (1991). His one-man show, *Mandy Patinkin in Concert: Dress Casual*, played on Broadway in 1989.

PEGGY-ANN (1926) boasted a score by RODGERS and HART but it was HERBERT FIELDS' libretto that made this show distinctive. Fields constructed a long elaborate dream sequence that took the heroine, poor little Peggy-Ann, from Glens Falls, New York, on exotic adventures to Fifth Avenue, her wedding on a yacht, a mutiny in the Caribbean and the high life in Havana. There were no musical numbers in the early scenes and only when Peggy-Ann entered her dream world of talking animals and other distortions was music used. Another innovative touch: The audience could see all the costume and scenery changes. Although no standards came from the Rodgers and Hart score, audiences kept *Peggy-Ann* alive for 333 performances. Many of the experiments in this musical would surface fifteen years later in the more polished *LADY IN THE DARK* (1941).

AUSTIN PENDLETON (1940–), an offbeat actor and sometime director, created two memorable musical theatre roles: Motel the tailor in *FIDDLER ON*

THE ROOF (1964) and the hyperactive Isaac in *THE LAST SWEET DAYS OF ISAAC* (1970).

ANN PENNINGTON (1894?–1971), a diminutive, flashy dancer on Broadway between 1913 and 1931, was a favorite in lavish revues, including six editions of the *ZIEGFELD FOLLIES* and five of *GEORGE WHITE'S SCANDALS*, introducing the "Black Bottom" in the 1926 edition.

PETER PAN (1954) was intended as a non-musical vehicle for MARY MARTIN with a few songs by Mark Charlap (music) and CAROLYN LEIGH (lyrics). But as it grew into a full-scale musical, veterans JULE STYNE, BETTY COMDEN and ADOLPH GREEN were brought in. The result, under JEROME ROBBINS' direction, was pure magic. The musical follows James M. Barrie's classic play somewhat faithfully with allowances for the charming talents of Martin and CYRIL RITCHARD's delightfully unthreatening Captain Hook. The score was just as engaging, featuring the songs "I've Gotta Crow," "Mysterious Lady," "I Won't Grow Up," "I'm Flying" and the lovely ballad "Neverland." The original Broadway production ran an unimpressive 152 performances but its subsequent television version has made the musical a beloved classic in the eyes of many. SANDY DUNCAN and Cathy Rigby are among the revival Peter Pans to score success on Broadway and across the country.

BERNADETTE PETERS (1948–   ), one of Broadway's brightest and most unique leading ladies in the 1970s and 1980s, is one of the musical theatre's best actresses as well. Peters started her career playing cute, bubbling ingenues but later graduated to more complex and revealing character roles. She first gained attention as Alice in the Off-Broadway spoof *Curly McDimple* (1967) then moved up to Broadway to play Cohan's sister Josie in *GEORGE M!* (1968). Peters' first starring role was the Ruby Keeler-like heroine in *DAMES AT SEA* (1968) followed by the short-lived musical *La Strada* (1969) and the 1971 revival of *ON THE TOWN*. Tragic film star Mabel Normand in *MACK AND MABEL* (1974) and the artist's model Dot in *SUNDAY IN THE PARK WITH GEORGE* (1984) were challenging roles fully realized on stage and her British Emma in *Song and Dance* (1985) was a one-woman tour de force. Peters also played the Witch in the fairy tale-like *INTO THE WOODS* (1987).

IRRA PETINA (1900–   ), a singer-actress who sang at the Metropolitan Opera, has been featured in many Broadway musicals. Petina played the indomitable Old Lady in *CANDIDE* (1956) as well as roles in *SONG OF NORWAY* (1944), *Magdalena* (1948), *Anya* (1965) and others.

THE PHANTOM OF THE OPERA (1988), the London musical version of the famed Gaston Leroux story, came to Broadway with the same director, stars and production team from the West End and, despite mixed reviews, became just as popular in America as it was in England. The ANDREW LLOYD WEBBER score, with lyrics by Charles Hart and Richard Stilgoe, was highly romanticized and unabashedly operatic. HAROLD PRINCE staged the elaborate production with intelligence and strong emphasis on the visuals, letting Maria Bjornson's sets and costumes become more than mere background. Michael Crawford and Sarah Brightman were the original Phantom and his protégée Christine and they were backed by a large and talented singing ensemble that featured Steve Barton and JUDY KAYE. As in the previous Webber musicals, the show was entirely sung but individual songs became well known: "Think of Me," "The Music of the Night," "All I Ask of You" and the title number. (still running as of 3/1/93)

THE PINK LADY (1911), a now forgotten musical that was the biggest hit of the 1910–1911 season, was the most engaging of the fourteen musicals composer Ivan Caryll wrote for Broadway. The complicated plot, based on a French play, dealt with a satyr in the woods, a fiancé out on one last romantic fling, a fancy dress ball filled with nymphs and a heroine who wears only pink. The show ran for 312 performances, made a star of Hazel Dawn and produced three hit songs: "On the Saskatchewan," "Donny Didn't, Donny Did" and "My Beautiful Lady," the last remaining popular for several years.

PINS AND NEEDLES (1937), one of the longest-running musical revues on record, started as a one-weekend entertainment by and for members of the International Ladies Garment Workers Union. Despite lackluster reviews and skepticism about the non-professional performers, audiences cheered and word of mouth turned *Pins and Needles* into a surprise hit, running for 1,108 performances in its various versions. The sketches and songs in the show dealt with a variety of labor–management issues but the whole affair was surprisingly light-hearted and witty at times. HAROLD ROME, in his Broadway debut, wrote the songs that ranged from the wistful ("Chain Store Daisy" and "Sunday in the Park") to the comic ("Nobody Makes a Pass at Me" and "It's Not Cricket to Picket") to the romantic reactionary ("One Big Union for Two" and "It's Better with a Union Man"). "Sing Me a Song of Social Significance," the signature song for the revue, became somewhat popular and the sly "Four Little Angels of Peace" was the show's satiric highlight as it parodied current world dictators. *Pins and Needles* did not have the polish of other 1930s revues but it often struck home with honesty and accuracy.

ENZIO PINZA (1892–1957), the acclaimed Italian opera singer who turned to Broadway musicals late in his career, originated the roles of the French planter Emile de Becque in *SOUTH PACIFIC* (1949) and the café owner Cesar in *FANNY* (1954).

PIPE DREAM (1955), a RODGERS and HAMMERSTEIN musical that even the team's fans forget about, was an unsuccessful attempt to musicalize the aimless, amiable characters in John Steinbeck's novels *Cannery Row* and *Sweet Thursday*: a warm-hearted brothel keeper, a pretty drifter, a poor marine biologist and so on. This was not typical musical fare and not something suited to Rodgers and Hammerstein's talents. Opera star Helen Traubel, Bill Johnson and Judy Tyler led the cast, which was directed by the unlikely Harold Clurman. The mediocre score did have one admirable ballad, "All at Once You Love Her," but *Pipe Dream* closed after 246 performances, the shortest run in the team's career.

PIPPIN (1972) was as much a grand hocus-pocus act as a musical for it seemed to pull dazzling entertainment out of thin air. The principal musician behind its success was director-choreographer BOB FOSSE who took Roger O. Hirson's lame libretto and made the show seem like gold. The story is an anachronistic retelling of Prince Pippin, son of Charlemagne, and his quest for fulfillment. Having tried war, sex and politics, Pippin settles for domestic bliss. John Rubenstein played the naive hero but BEN VEREEN as the demonic Leading Player turned out to be more interesting. Also in the cast were LELAND PALMER, Irene Ryan, Eric Berry and Jill Clayburgh. Lost in all of Fosse's sensational dancing and commedia del l'arte staging was a fine score by STEPHEN SCHWARTZ. "Magic to Do," "Morning Glow," "No Time at All," "On the Right Track" and other songs used a variety of styles and rhythms and were a splendid example of the emerging kind of score that utilized the old and the new musical sounds. (1,944 performances)

DONALD PIPPIN, an accomplished MUSIC DIRECTOR and arranger on Broadway, did the music for such memorable shows as *MAME* (1966), *APPLAUSE* (1970), *SEESAW* (1973), *A CHORUS LINE* (1975), *LA CAGE AUX FOLLES* (1983) and many others.

PLAIN AND FANCY (1955) was a musical that used an Amish community in Pennsylvania Dutch country as its setting. Two worldly New Yorkers arrive in Bird-in-Hand, Pennsylvania, to sell a farm they have inherited and get involved with local events. The show took an unprejudiced view of the Amish way of life but allowed room for a romantic triangle between a young girl, her pre-arranged husband-to-be and her true love. JOSEPH STEIN and Will Glickman wrote the sensitive libretto and the songs were by Albert Hague (music) and Arnold B. Horwitt (lyrics). Morton Da Costa staged the musical that included a rousing barn raising and choreographer HELEN TAMIRIS provided a lovely carnival ballet. The score was pleasant and appropriately simple with one song, "Young and Foolish," becoming well known. (461 performances)

PLAYWRIGHTS HORIZONS, an Off-Broadway theatre organization dedicated to developing and producing new American plays and musicals, has brought a number of notable musicals to fruition. These products were all presented in their intimate little theatre and some of them then moved on to larger Broadway or Off-Broadway houses. The most memorable Playwrights Horizons musicals were *March of the Falsettos* (1981), *SUNDAY IN THE PARK WITH GEORGE* (1984), *ONCE ON THIS ISLAND* (1990), *Falsettoland* (1990) and *ASSASSINS* (1990).

POLITICS, that alternative American form of mass entertainment, has provided the subject matter for many musicals, most of them comic or satiric rather than somber or grave. Political satire is as old as politics itself and some of Broadway's most incisive musical satires have used government, elections and diplomacy as its targets: *OF THEE I SING* (1931), *FACE THE MUSIC* (1932), *STRIKE UP THE BAND* (1930), *RED, HOT AND BLUE!* (1936), *I'D RATHER BE RIGHT* (1937), *LOUISIANA PURCHASE* (1940), *KNICKERBOCKER HOLIDAY* (1938), *LET 'EM EAT CAKE* (1933), *LEAVE IT TO ME!* (1938) and others. Less satirical but still within the range of musical comedy were *MR. PRESIDENT* (1962), *GEORGE WASHINGTON, JR.* (1906), *Ben Franklin in Paris* (1964), *FIORELLO!* (1959), *FLORA, THE RED MENACE* (1965), *Jimmy* (1969), *Teddy and Alice* (1987), *1776* (1969) and others. On a much more serious level were *THE CRADLE WILL ROCK* (1938), *EVITA* (1979), *Cry for Us All* (1970), *ASSASSINS* (1990) and *1600 PENNSYLVANIA AVENUE* (1976).

POPPY (1923) was a silly rags-to-riches musical comedy that gained distinction as W. C. FIELDS' ticket to stardom. Fields played Professor Eustace McGargle, a juggler-con man who tried to pass his foster daughter off as an heiress. It was the type of character that he would continue to play throughout his stage and film career. (346 performances)

PORGY AND BESS (1935) was GEORGE GERSHWIN's last work for the stage and a high point of accomplishment for his brother Ira and himself, as well as for librettist-lyricist DuBose Heyward. Much discussion still continues over whether *Porgy and Bess* is an opera or a musical play. Its creators called it "an American folk opera" and, although it uses recitative and extended musical sequences, it also has the dramatic structure and intricate lyrics of a musical drama. *Porgy and Bess* is so rich and so encompassing that it must be appreciated for the unique work that it is. The story follows Heyward's novel and non-musical play *Porgy* with minor alterations. In a black tenement in Charleston, South Carolina, called Catfish Row, the cripple Porgy loves the seductive Bess who is the girlfriend of the violent Crown. When he kills a man in a gambling fight, Crown flees Catfish Row and Porgy and Bess declare their mutual love for each other. But Crown soon returns and Porgy kills him in self-defense, going to jail and leaving Bess under the influence of the slick drug dealer Sportin' Life. The musical ends with Porgy released from jail and setting off to New York where Sportin' Life has taken Bess. George Gershwin not only composed the music for *Porgy and Bess* but orchestrated it as well, a rarely done practice at the time and today. Ira Gershwin and Heyward shared the lyricwriting, with Heyward writing many of the haunting, painful songs, such as "Summertime," "My Man's Gone Now," "I Loves You, Porgy" and "I'm on My Way," and the sly, cynical ones, such as "It Ain't Neccessarily So" and "There's a Boat Dat's Leavin' Soon for New York," by Gershwin. Also in the superlative score is "A Woman Is a Sometime Thing," "I Got Plenty o' Nuthin' " and "Bess, You Is My Woman Now." ROUBEN MAMOULIAN directed a cast that included TODD DUNCAN, Anne Brown, John Bubbles and Ford Buck, and the show was greeted with respectful reviews but was not a commercial success, playing only 124 performances. Disappointed with the response to what he considered his best stage work, George Gershwin went to Hollywood where he died two years later. Over the past fifty years *Porgy and Bess* has been revived on Broadway several times and has entered the repertory of many major opera companies as well.

COLE PORTER (1891–1964), the celebrated composer-lyricist known for the sophisticated wit he brought to the Broadway musical, was one of the most distinctive of songwriters with an easily identifiable style. Porter was born in Peru, Indiana, to a family of wealth who expected him to go into law. He was educated at Yale and Harvard for a law career but his interest in writing songs grew stronger so he quit school and spent several years traveling in Europe and writing. Although some of his songs were heard in various Broadway shows as early as 1916, it was not until *Paris* (1928) and *FIFTY MILLION FRENCH-MEN* (1929) that Porter's reputation as an urbane lyricist and elegant composer became widespread. He had several hits in the 1930s, most notably *GAY DIVORCE* (1932), *ANYTHING GOES* (1934), *JUBILEE* (1935), *RED, HOT AND BLUE!* (1936), *LEAVE IT TO ME!* (1938) and *DuBARRY WAS A LADY* (1939). In 1937 one of Porter's legs was crushed in a horse-riding accident. He would spend the next twenty years undergoing dozens of operations to save the leg. But he continued to write for Broadway and Hollywood at a steady pace and his songs maintained their high levels of charm, romance and humor. *PANAMA HATTIE* (1940), *LET'S FACE IT!* (1941), *SOMETHING FOR THE BOYS* (1943) and *MEXICAN HAYRIDE* (1944) were all popular but his finest work was *KISS ME, KATE* (1948), in which BELLA and SAM SPEWACK provided Porter with the best libretto of his career. He had two successes in the 1950s, *CAN-CAN* (1953) and *SILK STOCKINGS* (1955), but in 1958 his damaged leg had to be amputated and Porter retired from public life. Among the many innovative features of Porter's work are an insistent, Latin-sounding rhythm in his love songs, the bold and sometimes censored sexual imagery in his lyrics and a playful and almost acrobatic dexterity with rhyming. Only a handful of the Porter shows can be easily revived today because of weak librettos but his repertoire of songs is timeless and his music and lyrics are rediscovered with joy by each new generation.

ELEANOR POWELL (1910–1982), the tap-dancing star of film musicals, appeared in six Broadway musicals before going to Hollywood. Powell's most remembered stage performances were in *FOLLOW THRU* (1929), *FINE AND DANDY* (1930) and *AT HOME ABROAD* (1935).

ROBERT PRESTON (1918–1987), a durable film actor who became one of Broadway's favorite leading men later in his career, will always be most remembered for his Broadway debut as Professor Harold Hill in *THE MUSIC MAN* (1957). Preston gave a winning performance as diplomat Franklin in the short-lived *Ben Franklin in Paris* (1964) and co-starred with MARY MARTIN in the marital musical *I DO! I DO!* (1966). His last Broadway musical was *MACK AND MABEL* (1974), in which he played film pioneer Mack Sennett.

GILBERT PRICE (1942–1991), a full-voiced black singer-actor, made an impressive Broadway debut singing "Feeling Good" in *THE ROAR OF THE GREASEPAINT—THE SMELL OF THE CROWD* (1965). Price's other musical credits included *Promenade* (1969), the 1972 revival of *LOST IN THE STARS*, the never-aging servant Lud in *1600 PENNSYLVANIA AVENUE* (1976) and the Mansa of Mali in *Timbuktu* (1978).

LONNY PRICE (1959–   ), a juvenile actor in plays and musicals and sometime director, played the high-strung Charlie in *MERRILY WE ROLL ALONG* (1981) and the enterprising immigrant Ben in *RAGS* (1986). Price directed the long-running Off-Broadway revival of *THE ROTHSCHILDS* in 1990.

FAITH PRINCE (1957–   ), a character actress in musicals on and off Broadway, appeared in *Scrambled Feet* (1981) and *Olympus on My Mind* (1986) before gaining attention playing various roles in *Jerome Robbins' Broadway* (1989). Prince was the frustrated Trina in *Falsettoland* (1990), was featured in the short-lived *Nick and Nora* (1991) and played Miss Adelaide in the 1992 Broadway revival of *GUYS AND DOLLS*.

HAROLD PRINCE (1928–   ) has had two theatre careers of equal importance and renown: as the producer of some of the finest post-war Broadway musicals and as the highly creative director of some of the most admired shows of the 1960s and 1970s. Prince began as an assistant to director GEORGE ABBOTT. In 1953 he teamed up with ROBERT GRIFFITH and together they produced *THE PAJAMA GAME* (1954), *DAMN YANKEES* (1955), *NEW GIRL IN TOWN* (1957), *WEST SIDE STORY* (1957), *FIORELLO!* (1959) and *TENDERLOIN* (1960). After Griffith's death in 1961, Prince went on to produce *A FUNNY THING HAPPENED ON THE WAY TO THE FORUM* (1962), *FIDDLER ON THE ROOF* (1964) and *FLORA, THE RED MENACE* (1965). Having worked with JEROME ROBBINS and Abbott on several occasions, Prince had become more interested in directing and he made his Broadway directing debut with the short-lived musical *A Family Affair* (1962). His directing–producing effort *SHE LOVES ME* (1963) revealed Prince's talents as a director, as did *IT'S A BIRD, IT'S A PLANE, IT'S SUPERMAN* (1966), but both shows failed to run despite strong reviews. It was with *CABARET* (1966) that Prince emerged as a major force in creating musical theatre. *ZORBA* (1969) and the 1974 revitalized *CANDIDE* further illustrated his talents but it was a series of five musicals with STEPHEN SONDHEIM that made Prince the premiere director of his day: *COMPANY* (1970), *FOLLIES* (1971), *A LITTLE NIGHT MUSIC* (1973), *PACIFIC OVERTURES* (1976) and *SWEENEY TODD* (1979). His staging of *ON THE TWENTIETH CENTURY* (1978) was spectacular but largely ignored while his direction of *EVITA* (1979) was justly acclaimed and is arguably his finest directing achievement. Prince had a series of short-runs in the 1980s—*MERRILY WE ROLL ALONG* (1981), *A Doll's Life* (1982), *Grind* (1985) and *Roza* (1987)—but he was back on top by the end of the decade with *THE PHANTOM OF THE OPERA* (1988), which he staged in London and on Broadway. In addition to his Broadway work, Prince has also directed operas, London versions of his shows and regional tryouts, the most notable being *The Kiss of the Spider Woman* (1990). Prince has no easily recognizable style because he is continually experimenting with new forms. He has proven to be a deft master of the CONCEPT MUSICAL, sung-through operatic shows, musical camp, highly romantic operetta and gritty, dark musical drama.

THE PRINCESS THEATRE MUSICALS (1915–1919) were a series of shows that aimed to create literate, intimate and modern musical comedies that were alternatives to operettas or lavish revues. The series drew its name from its home, the Princess Theatre, a 299–seat house that was considered too small for musicals. Literary agent Elisabeth Marbury and theatre owner F. Ray Comstock had an idea for a series that would feature small, contemporary musicals by new composers, performed by a resident company of actors; in fact, they wanted to create the world's first musical repertory theatre. Because of the small stage, the shows would not have chorus lines, large casts or opulent scenery. The size of the orchestra pit limited ORCHESTRATIONS to eleven musicians. The first offering was *Nobody Home* (1915) with music by JEROME KERN, libretto by GUY BOLTON and lyrics by Schuyler Greene. This delightful little musical about young lovers and mistaken identity did not differ greatly from the standard fare of the day except in its size. But the same team's *VERY GOOD EDDIE* (1915) made efforts to integrate the songs into the plot and the comedy grew from the characters rather than from comic bits or clowning performers. *Go to It* (1916), the next musical in the series, had a score by John Golden and ANNE CALDWELL but it was not successful. P. G. WODEHOUSE took over the lyricwriting duties for the next Princess musical, *OH, BOY!* (1917), and the illustrious team of Bolton, Wodehouse and Kern was born. The series would reach its goal of expert modern musical comedy in the shows by this trio who blended character, song and story together in a charming and literate way. Although not a part of the series, *LEAVE IT TO JANE* (1917) by the same team, had all the qualities that the Princess musicals celebrated. *OH, LADY! LADY!* (1918) was another hit in the series but the last by Bolton, Wodehouse and Kern. Louis Hirsch took over the composing for *Oh, My Dear!* (1918) and, although the show was fairly popular, Kern's music was greatly missed. The final Princess Theatre musical, *Toot Sweet* (1919), with a score by Richard Whiting and Ray Egan, was an unsuccessful revue that departed from the series' initial intention. The bold experiment ended after only seven shows in four years but the Princess musicals would inspire the next generation of songwriters, such as RODGERS and HART and COLE PORTER, to develop the ideas first presented in the series.

PROMISES, PROMISES (1968) was the only Broadway musical by the popular 1960s songwriting team of Burt Bacharach (music) and Hal David (lyrics). NEIL SIMON adapted the film *The Apartment* for the musical stage with few changes and JERRY ORBACH triumphed as the young executive who climbs the corporate ladder by loaning his apartment key to higher-ups needing a trysting place. Also in the cast were JILL O'HARA, Edward Winter, Norman Shelly and A. Larry Haines, directed by ROBERT MOORE and choreographed by MICHAEL BENNETT. The title song and "I'll Never Fall in Love Again" became hits on the charts but also pleasing were "Whoever You Are," "She Likes Basketball," "Knowing When to Leave" and other pop-sounding songs typical of the era. (1,281 performances)

The PULITZER PRIZE in drama, presented by Columbia University, has always been considered a distinguished award but also a controversial one as well. The Pulitzer committee started presenting the awards in 1918 but it wasn't until 1932 that a musical was so honored. *OF THEE I SING* (1931) was the first recipient but the award was given only to librettists MORRIE RYSKIND and GEORGE S. KAUFMAN and lyricist IRA GERSHWIN; GEORGE GERSHWIN's music was not considered "literary" and was not included. The committee would later change their policy on this matter. To date, six musicals have received the Pulitzer Prize in drama: *Of Thee I Sing*, *SOUTH PACIFIC* (1949), *FIORELLO!* (1959), *HOW TO SUCCEED IN BUSINESS WITHOUT REALLY TRYING* (1961), *A CHORUS LINE* (1975) and *SUNDAY IN THE PARK WITH GEORGE* (1984).

PURLIE (1970) was a joyous musical comedy that was alternately rousing and touching, utilizing gospel and folk sounds within a conventional Broadway framework. PHILIP ROSE, PETER UDELL and Ossie Davis adapted Davis' 1961 racial comedy *Purlie Victorious*, turning much of the show into an invigorating celebration of black culture. The unconventional preacher Purlie comes to rural Georgia to found a church but must deal with the bigoted Cap'n who runs the territory. Armed with optimism, enthusiam and the help of the Cap'n's liberal-minded son, Purlie succeeds and even wins the love of the shy but passionate Lutiebelle. Cleavon Little was a dandy Purlie and MELBA MOORE was radiant as Lutiebelle. Also in the cast were John Hefferman, Sherman Hemsley, Novella Nelson and George Faison, directed by Rose and choreographed by Louis Johnson. The songs by GARY GELD (music) and Udell (lyrics) were first-rate all around: "Walk Him Up the Stairs," "I Got Love," "First Thing Monday Mornin'," "New Fangled Preacher Man" and the affectionate title song were the most memorable numbers. *Purlie* managed to cover racism and the frustrations of racial injustice all in the guise of a musical comedy that pleased both black and white audiences. (688 performances)

R

RAGS (1986) was one of those much-anticipated musicals that quickly closed on Broadway but refuses to die because of its superb score. JOSEPH STEIN wrote the original libretto about various immigrants on the Lower East Side of New York in 1910 and CHARLES STROUSE (music) and STEPHEN SCHWARTZ (lyrics) provided a rich score that encompassed period music, ethnic temperaments and traditional Broadway ballads. But the whole enterprise refused to come together and with each rewrite and staff change the already complicated libretto got more disjointed. The Strouse–Schwartz score contained such commendable songs as "Blame It on the Summer Night," "Three Sunny Rooms," "Children of the Wind" and the gripping title number. *Rags* was also memorable for its stunning cast that featured opera star Teresa Stratas, Judy Kuhn, LONNY PRICE, LARRY KERT, Dick Latessa and Marcia Lewis. Although *Rags* only lasted four performances on Broadway, the score was later recorded and revivals with book and song revisions continue to surface.

RAISIN (1973) was a warm and honest musical play based on Lorraine Hansberry's 1959 black drama *A Raisin in the Sun.* Robert Nemiroff and Charlotte Zaltsberg wrote the libretto that faithfully stuck to the original and Judd Woldin (music) and Robert Brittan (lyrics) provided the workable if not memorable score. The musical is set in a Chicago ghetto in the 1950s where widow Lena Younger tries to keep her family together, despite hard times and personal discouragement. Her son Walter wants to use his father's life insurance money to buy a liquor store but Lena hopes to buy a house in a better neighborhood. Family friction is increased by Walter's troubled marriage and his young sister's growing awareness of her African heritage. Virginia Capers was terrific as Lena and there was impressive work by JOE MORTON as Walter, ERNESTINE JACKSON, Ralph Carter, DEBBIE ALLEN and Ted Ross. Donald McKayle directed and choreographed the show, which ran 847 performances.

JOHN RAITT (1917–), a strong-voiced leading man of musicals, is best remembered for his Broadway debut as Billy Bigelow in *CAROUSEL* (1945) and for his genial factory manager Sid Sorokin in *THE PAJAMA GAME* (1954). Raitt's other Broadway credits include the short-lived musicals *Magdalena* (1948), *Three Wishes for Jaime* (1952), *Carnival in Flanders* (1953) and *A Joyful Noise* (1966).

ROBERT RANDOLPH (1926–), a scenic and lighting designer on Broadway since 1954, did both sets and lights for *HOW TO SUCCEED IN BUSINESS WITHOUT REALLY TRYING* (1961), *LITTLE ME* (1962), *Foxy* (1964), *FUNNY GIRL* (1964), *IT'S A BIRD, IT'S A PLANE, IT'S SUPERMAN* (1966), *Golden Rainbow* (1968), *70, GIRLS, 70* (1971), the 1974 revival of *GYPSY* and others.

LEE ROY REAMS (1942–), a personable actor-dancer on Broadway since 1966, played the gay hairdresser Duane in *APPLAUSE* (1970) and the high-stepping Billy Lawlor in *42ND STREET* (1980). Reams' other musical credits include *SWEET CHARITY* (1966), *Lorelei* (1974) and various revivals on and off Broadway.

RED, HOT AND BLUE! (1936) was a silly political satire with some memorable COLE PORTER songs and superb clowning by its three stars ETHEL MERMAN, JIMMY DURANTE and BOB HOPE. The team of HOWARD LINDSAY and RUSSEL CROUSE wrote the libretto, which dealt with a lottery to pay off the national debt, a former manicurist named Nails O'Reilly Duquesne (Merman), her amorous lawyer (Hope) and Policy Pinkle (Durante), a parolee who misses playing polo at Larks Nest Prison. This agreeable nonsense didn't have the satirical bite it sought but it did have Porter's "It's De-Lovely," "Ridin' High," "Down in the Depths" and the rousing title song. (183 performances)

THE RED MILL (1906) was much lighter fare than VICTOR HERBERT's other operettas and much of the time it resembled musical comedy. Con Kidder and Kid Conner are two Americans taking the grand tour of Europe who end up penniless in Katwyk-aan-Zee, Holland. There the two comic characters get involved in helping the romance of a sea captain and the beautiful innkeeper's daughter. Their misadventures include disguising themselves as Italian musicians and as Sherlock Holmes and Watson, and they even get to rescue the heroine who is locked inside the red mill. Henry Blossom provided the clever libretto and lyrics, and comics FRED STONE and DAVID MONTGOMERY were hilarious as Con and Kid. The Herbert score included the songs "Moonbeams," "The Streets of New York," "The Isle of Our Dreams," "Every Day Is Ladies Day with Me" and "Because You're You." *The Red Mill* ran 274 performances, the longest run of Herbert's career.

REDHEAD (1959) was a vehicle for the joyous talents of GWEN VERDON, whose dancing and sharp character acting kept the show running for 452 performances. HERBERT and DOROTHY FIELDS, Sidney Sheldon and David Shaw all contributed to the barely serviceable libretto about a Jack the Ripper-like murderer who stalks the London of the early 1900s. The murderer's identity is discovered eventually but only after two sensational dance numbers, "Pick-Pocket Tango" and "The Uncle Sam Rag," which director-choreographer BOB FOSSE devised for Verdon. RICHARD KILEY as her love interest also gave a praiseworthy performance. The songs, by Albert Hague (music) and DOROTHY FIELDS (lyrics), were satisfactory with "Merely Marvelous" being better than that.

VIVIEN REED (1947–), a black singer-dancer, was outstanding in the musical revues *DON'T BOTHER ME, I CAN'T COPE* (1972), *Bubbling Brown Sugar* (1976), *It's So Nice to Be Civilized* (1980) and *The High Rollers Social and Pleasure Club* (1992).

REGINA (1949) was as much an opera as musical theatre with its sweeping arias and extended musical passages. MARC BLITZSTEIN wrote the music, lyrics and libretto, based on Lillian Hellman's renowned drama *The Little Foxes* (1939). The story of a greedy Southern family who destroy the gentle and innocent ones around them had vivid and powerful characters and they came to life with the fine voices of Jane Pickens, Brenda Lewis, RUSSELL NYPE, George Lipton and William Warfield. Highlights in Blitzstein's score were the pragmatic "The Best Thing of All" and the tender "Birdie's Aria." Both drama and music critics reviewed the show on opening night; there was much praise for the music but there were many reservations about its success as a theatre piece and the musical closed after 56 performances. *Regina* was later added to the repertory of the New York City Opera.

CHARLES NELSON REILLY (1931–), a quirky, bespectacled character actor on Broadway since 1960, played the obnoxious Frump in *HOW TO SUCCEED IN BUSINESS WITHOUT REALLY TRYING* (1961) and the amorous clerk Cornelius Hackl in *HELLO, DOLLY!* (1964). Reilly's other musical credits include the Off-Broadway *BEST FOOT FORWARD* (1956), *BYE BYE BIRDIE* (1960) and *Skyscraper* (1965). He is also a respected director of non-musical plays.

ANN REINKING (1949–), a leggy dancer in Broadway musicals often choreographed by BOB FOSSE, played Joan of Arc in *Goodtime Charley* (1975). Reinking appeared in *COCO* (1969) and *PIPPIN* (1972) and was featured in *Over Here* (1974) and *DANCIN'* (1978).

REVENGE WITH MUSIC (1934) was the first attempt by songwriters AR-THUR SCHWARTZ and HOWARD DIETZ to write a book musical. Their success with revues had made them one of Broadway's most laudable teams but this operetta set in Spain didn't seem to fit their talents very well. LIBBY HOLMAN, Georges Metaxa and CHARLES WINNINGER starred in the tale about a provincial governor who tries to seduce a bride on her wedding day only to have her husband woo the governor's wife in revenge. Two splendid Dietz–Schwartz songs came from the score: "If There Is Someone Lovelier Than You" and "You and the Night and the Music," although, like the whole score, there was nothing remotely Spanish about them. (158 performances)

CLIVE REVILL (1930–), a British character actor intermittently on Broadway, was featured in the musical *IRMA LA DOUCE* (1960), played Fagin in *OLIVER!* (1963) and was Sheridan Whiteside in the short-lived *Sherry!* (1967).

REVUE, a genre in which a series of special components combine to create a plotless entity, has been around for centuries and musical revues first caught the fancy of the American theatre-going public in the nineteenth century. As opposed to vaudeville in which a series of individual acts are performed, the musical revue is an evening that is planned, designed, scored and directed with an eye for a unified final product. Some revues are held together thematically, others are strung together less obviously. The first distinctive American revue was *THE PASSING SHOW* in 1894; years later the SHUBERT BROTHERS would present a series of revues utilizing the name. FLORENZ ZIEGFELD started his *ZIEGFELD FOLLIES* in 1907 and they soon stood as the epitome of the lavish Broadway revue. Following in Ziegfeld's footsteps were *GEORGE WHITE'S SCANDALS* and *EARL CARROLL VANITIES* as well as IRVING BERLIN's *MUSIC BOX REVUES* and JOHN MURRAY ANDERSON's *GREENWICH VILLAGE FOLLIES*. RODGERS and HART broke onto the scene with the first *GARRICK GAIETIES* (1925), which went in for wit and charm rather than spectacle, and DOROTHY FIELDS and JIMMY McHUGH made their name with *BLACKBIRDS OF 1928*. ARTHUR SCHWARTZ and HOWARD DIETZ, arguably the finest songwriters of the American musical revue, brought the genre to an all-time high in the 1930s with such fondly remembered shows as *THE LITTLE SHOW* (1929), *THREE'S A CROWD* (1930), *THE BAND WAGON* (1931) and *AT HOME ABROAD* (1935). Berlin's *AS THOUSANDS CHEER* (1933), the zany *HELLZAPOPPIN* (1938), HAROLD ARLEN's *LIFE BEGINS AT 8:40* (1934) and HAROLD ROME's "socially significant" *PINS AND NEEDLES* (1937) were other gems during the golden age of revues. The genre started to wane after World War II and by the 1950s and 1960s revues with original scores were usually to be found Off Broadway if anywhere at all. In the 1970s a new breed of musical revue became popular: the nostalgic recollection of the work of former greats. *Eubie* (1978) celebrated EUBIE BLAKE, *SOPHISTICATED LADIES* (1981) honored Duke Ellington, *AIN'T MISBEHAVIN'* (1978) rediscovered Thomas "Fats" Waller, and on and on. Even more recent artists were revued: *Side by Side by Sondheim* (1977), *Beatlemania* (1977), *Elvis—A Musical Celebration* (1989), *Jerome Robbins' Broadway* (1989), *And the World Goes Round* (1991) saluting JOHN KANDER and FRED EBB, *Words and Music* (1974) with and about SAMMY CAHN, *A Party with Comden and Green* (1958 and again in 1977) and many more. Sometimes the party was not limited to one or two songwriters' careers. Revues such as *SUGAR BABIES* (1979), *Bubbling Brown Sugar* (1976), *BLACK AND BLUE* (1989) and *Tintypes* (1980) concentrated on a particular culture or on period music from the past. Today the revue with an original score does occasionally surface, such as MALTBY and SHIRE's *STARTING HERE, STARING NOW* (1977) and *CLOSER THAN EVER* (1989), but the age of the big-time Broadway revue is long gone. Even television abandoned the "variety" format in the 1980s. All that remains is a collection of timeless song standards and an accumulation of sketches that never read as well as they once played.

TIM RICE (1944–) is the British lyricist-librettist who collaborated with ANDREW LLOYD WEBBER on three successful London transfers: *JESUS CHRIST SUPERSTAR* (1971), *EVITA* (1979) and *JOSEPH AND THE AMAZING TECHNICOLOR DREAMCOAT* (on Broadway in 1982). Of the West End musicals he has written without Webber, only *Chess* (1988) has traveled to Broadway.

HARRY RICHMAN (1895–1972), a breezy, dapper singer-dancer who had a long career in nightclubs, appeared in a handful of Broadway revues, most notably three editions of *GEORGE WHITE'S SCANDALS*, the 1931 *ZIEGFELD FOLLIES* and *International Revue* (1930), in which he introduced "On the Sunny Side of the Street."

THE RINK (1984) was an ambitious musical play put together by first-class talents but it did not appeal to audiences looking for lightweight entertainment. Terrence McNally wrote an original libretto about a mother and her estranged daughter who are reunited at their home situated over an amusement park roller skating rink. CHITA RIVERA and LIZA MINNELLI played the mother and daughter but *The Rink* was no star vehicle; both characters were far from glamorous and the songs, by JOHN KANDER and FRED EBB, were incisive character pieces rather than talent showcases. "Colored Lights," "Blue Crystal," "Not Enough Magic," "All the Children in a Row," "Marry Me" and "The

Apple Doesn't Fall" proved that Kander and Ebb were still at the top of their songwriting skills. Audiences disliked *The Rink*'s heavy-handed plot and even the two stars could not keep the musical running any longer than 204 performances. But it was a commendable show and deserves to be revised and revived.

RIO RITA (1927), a large-scale operetta set in Texas, was one of the decade's most successful musicals. FLORENZ ZIEGFELD produced the lavish production and put a chorus of one hundred girls on JOSEPH URBAN's spectacular sets. The plot, about the Texas Rangers, a bank robber, and a flirtatious gal named Rita from across the Rio Grande, was by musical comedy veterans GUY BOLTON and Fred Thompson. Songwriters Harry Tierney (music) and Joseph McCarthy (lyrics), whose usual fare was also musical comedy, provided the operetta score, which featured "The Rangers' Song," "If You're in Love You'll Waltz" and the title song. Ethelind Terry played Rita and comics Bert Wheeler and Robert Woolsey, in their first of many appearances together, provided the laughs. *Rio Rita* was the premiere production of the ornate Ziegfeld Theatre, also designed by Urban, and ran for 494 performances.

CYRIL RITCHARD (1897–1977), a popular singer-actor who played comic roles in many West End musicals between 1925 and 1953, made a handful of memorable Broadway appearances later in his career. Ritchard is best known for his Captain Hook in the musical version of *PETER PAN* (1954) with MARY MARTIN. His other Broadway credits included Pluto in *The Happiest Girl in the World* (which he also directed) in 1961, the aristocratic Sir in *THE ROAR OF THE GREASEPAINT—THE SMELL OF THE CROWD* (1965) and the infatuated Osgood Fielding, Jr., in *SUGAR* (1972).

CHITA RIVERA (1935–   ), one of Broadway's most accomplished performers, is equally adept at singing, dancing and acting. Rivera began her career in the chorus of Broadway musicals in the 1950s and was featured in *Shoestring Revue* (1955), *Seventh Heaven* (1955) and *Mr. Wonderful* (1956) before gaining attention as Anita in *WEST SIDE STORY* (1957). Her first starring role was the amorous secretary Rose Grant in *BYE BYE BIRDIE* (1960), followed by the gypsy Anyanka in *Bajour* (1964), the murderess Velma Kelly in *CHICAGO* (1975), the evil Queen in *Merlin* (1983) and the embittered mother Anna Antonelli in *THE RINK* (1984). Rivera reprised the role of Rose in the unsuccessful sequel *Bring Back Birdie* (1981).

THE ROAR OF THE GREASEPAINT—THE SMELL OF THE CROWD (1965) was technically a BRITISH IMPORT, although it had never played in London before its Broadway premiere. ANTHONY NEWLEY and Leslie Bricusse wrote the libretto, music and lyrics for this allegorical tale about those who have, represented by Sir (CYRIL RITCHARD), and those who have not, as seen in Cocky (Newley). In a series of "games," the two symbolic characters squabble over food, love, religion, racism and revolution, a sort of musical *Waiting for Godot* with an upbeat ending. The score contained some songs that became well known: "Who Can I Turn To?" "A Wonderful Day Like Today" and "Nothing Can Stop Me Now." Also admirable in the score was "Look at That Face," "The Joker" and "Feeling Good," the last introduced by GILBERT PRICE in an impressive Broadway debut. (232 performances)

THE ROBBER BRIDEGROOM (1976) was a charming backwoods musical based on Eudora Welty's novella of the same name but, unlike *BIG RIVER* a decade later, it suffered at the box office because no one seemed to want to hear a country music score on Broadway. Songwriters Robert Waldman (music) and Alfred Uhry (lyrics) also did the excellent adaptation in which the tall tale from Mississippi was told by members of a square-dance gathering. The silly but agreeable plot is about outlaw Jamie Lockhart who captures the love of a plantation owner's daughter when he is a bandit in the woods but loses her affection when he presents himself as a respectable suitor. The songs used a lot of folk and bluegrass but had the characterization and variety of a traditional Broadway score. "Love Stolen," "Pickle Pear and Lilybud," "Ain't Nothing Up" and "Steal with Style" were among the pleasurable numbers and BARRY BOSTWICK was a jubilant Jamie Lockhart. *The Robber Bridegroom* had started out as a workshop production, had toured the country as part of the Acting Company's repertory and played briefly in New York. The show got good reviews when it reopened on Broadway but still only managed to last 145 performances. It has since found new life with regional theatres and similar producing groups.

CARRIE ROBBINS(1943–), a costume designer on Broadway since *Look to the Lilies* (1970), did the costumes for *GREASE* (1972), *Over Here* (1974), *The First* (1981), *Raggedy Ann* (1986), *Anna Karenina* (1992) and other musicals.

JEROME ROBBINS (1918–), perhaps the most famous director-choreographer of the American musical theatre, has had extensive careers in ballet and modern dance and a tremendous influence on musicals because of his unforgettable staging of some of Broadway's finest musicals. Robbins was a dancer and choreographer for the Ballet Theatre before appearing in a few forgotten Broadway musicals in the 1930s. His choreography for *ON THE TOWN* (1944) immediately established Robbins as an exciting new talent and he followed it up with memorable dances for *Billion Dollar Baby* (1945), *HIGH BUTTON SHOES* (1947), *Look, Ma, I'm Dancin'* (1948), *MISS LIBERTY* (1949), *CALL ME MADAM* (1950), *THE KING AND I* (1951) and *Two's Company* (1952). Robbins' directing career began with *THE PAJAMA GAME* (1954), which he co-directed with GEORGE ABBOTT. He went on to direct and choreograph *PETER PAN* (1954), *BELLS ARE RINGING* (1956), *WEST SIDE STORY* (1957), *GYPSY* (1959), *A FUNNY THING HAPPENED ON THE WAY TO THE*

FORUM (1962), *FUNNY GIRL* (1964), which he co-directed with Garson Kanin, and *FIDDLER ON THE ROOF* (1964). Robbins left the Broadway theatre in 1964 to work full time in the world of dance, choreographing for the Ballet Russe, New York City Ballet and his own Ballet: U.S.A. In 1989 he returned to Broadway to stage *Jerome Robbins' Broadway*, an anthology of musical numbers from his past shows. Robbins is the quintessential Broadway director-choreographer because he uses dance to illustrate character, story, atmosphere, temperament and theme. His justly famous dance/theatre sequences, such as "Teyve's Dream" from *Fiddler on the Roof* or "The Small House of Uncle Thomas" from *The King and I*, represent the post-war American musical at its best.

ROBERTA (1933) had a tired and contrived libretto that was already old-fashioned when the show opened but the JEROME KERN score was filled with lyrical charm and the sumptuous production featured such a strong cast that the musical ran 295 performances. OTTO HARBACH wrote the libretto about an American football star who inherits a Paris fashion salon and falls in love with a worker there who is really a Russian princess in disguise. The cast featured Lyda Roberti, BOB HOPE, FAY TEMPLETON, TAMARA, George Murphy, Sydney Greenstreet, RAY MIDDLETON and Fred MacMurray and the Kern–Harbach score introduced "You're Devastating," "The Touch of Your Hand," "Yesterdays" and "Smoke Gets in Your Eyes."

TONY ROBERTS (1939–), a leading man in Broadway plays and musicals since 1962, played the musician-on-the-run Joe in *SUGAR* (1972). Roberts' other musical credits include *How Now Dow Jones* (1967) and replacement roles in several musicals on Broadway.

PAUL ROBESON (1898–1976) was a dynamic black singer-actor who gave impressionable performances on stage, in film, in concert and on recordings. Robeson made his first Broadway appearance in the singing chorus of *SHUFFLE ALONG* (1921) and then went on to give some powerful performances in dramas. Although he was associated with the song "Ol' Man River" all of his career, Robeson was not in the original 1927 production of *SHOW BOAT*. But he did play Joe and sang it in the 1928 London production, in the 1932 Broadway revival and on film.

LEO ROBIN (1900–1984) provided the lyrics for a handful of musicals, most notably *HIT THE DECK* (1927) with music by VINCENT YOUMANS and *GENTLEMAN PREFER BLONDES* (1949) with music by JULE STYNE. Robin also contributed to many film scores in Hollywood.

ROBIN HOOD (1891) was one of the most popular American operettas of the nineteenth century and the most remembered work by composer REGINALD DE KOVEN. The libretto by HARRY B. SMITH adheres to the English legend rather carefully and all of the well-known characters are there, including a comic Sheriff of Nottingham and an Alan-a-Dale played by a woman. The two standouts in the score were "Song of Brown October Ale" and the interpolated "Oh, Promise Me!" *Robin Hood* was a touring production from Boston and only played forty performances in its New York stop but the show returned several times later and remained an audience favorite for decades.

BILL "BOJANGLES" ROBINSON (1878–1949), the black tap-dancing sensation of vaudeville, nightclubs and films, appeared in a handful of Broadway musicals, most memorably in *BLACKBIRDS OF 1928*, where he introduced "Doin' the New Low-Down," and *The Hot Mikado* (1939) in which he played the title role.

ROCK MUSICALS were prevalent on and off Broadway in the late 1960s and early 1970s and then seemed to fade away. But, in fact, they left quite an indelible mark on the musical theatre and, in less obvious ways, rock musicals are still affecting Broadway. It is not surprising that rock music hit the theatre so strongly in 1968; what *is* surprising is that it took so long. Rock and roll started to permeate the music business in the mid-1950s and soon movies and television caught on to the new sound. Yet the first rock musical in New York didn't occur until the Off-Broadway *HAIR* in 1967. By its very nature, a rock musical tends to be unconventional and more experimental than the traditional show, not only in subject matter but also in structure and presentation. The music is more pounding with less emphasis on lyrics and more on a free-flowing celebration of sorts. The rock shows tend to be less literary, are more anachronistic and rely on a variety of audiovisual effects. Most significantly, the ORCHESTRATIONS for rock musicals require a good deal of electronic instruments so mechanical amplification is a must. Broadway was slow to embrace the rock sentiment but *Hair* opened the floodgates and in 1969 and 1970, audiences on and off Broadway were subjected to *YOUR OWN THING*, *Salvation*, *THE LAST SWEET DAYS OF ISAAC*, *Sambo*, *Peace*, *Mod Donna*, *Stomp*, *Touch* and other shows of varying quality. *GODSPELL* (1971) was more accessible to many but at its core was a rock score. The British added to the genre with *JESUS CHRIST SUPERSTAR* (1971) and *JOSEPH AND THE AMAZING TECHNICOLOR DREAMCOAT* (Off Broadway in 1976, on Broadway in 1982). But what seemed like a new direction for musicals started to fade quickly, helped by two colossal Broadway flops, *Dude* (1972) and *Via Galactica* (1972). Although it looked like lyricism was returning to the musical theatre, the rock musical was not gone and forgotten. Many conventional shows picked up on the rock sound and, more importantly, rock orchestrations and soon almost all musicals were using electronic instruments and were being amplified. Today most musicals carry something of the rock musical's influence. And, as the rock and roll heyday becomes old enough to become nostalgia, a series of musicals about that era have appeared, including *GREASE*

(1972), *Beatlemania* (1977), *Rock and Roll: The First 5000 Years* (1983), *Buddy: The Buddy Holly Story* (1990) and others. Although few new shows today would bill themselves as a rock musical, few are not somehow affected by that short but overpowering movement.

RICHARD RODGERS (1902–1979), America's premiere composer of Broadway musicals, had a long and successful career that encompassed many important innovations and included some of the most beloved shows of the genre. Rodgers was born in New York City to a father who was a doctor and a mother who played piano. He grew up admiring operetta and the new-style musicals of JEROME KERN and was soon composing for summer camps and community shows. Rodgers met lyricist LORENZ HART in 1918 and soon their songs were being interpolated into Broadway musicals. The team's career blossomed with their first full score, *THE GARRICK GAIETIES* (1925), and they followed it with a series of delightful musical comedies, including *PEGGY-ANN* (1926), *A CONNECTICUT YANKEE* (1927), *Present Arms* (1928) and *JUMBO* (1935). Rodgers experimented with an extended dance score in the legendary *ON YOUR TOES* (1936), writing the modern ballet "Slaughter on Tenth Avenue." The team's popular *BABES IN ARMS* (1937), *I'D RATHER BE RIGHT* (1937), *I MARRIED AN ANGEL* (1938), *THE BOYS FROM SYRACUSE* (1938) and *TOO MANY GIRLS* (1939) highlighted their prime years, which climaxed with *PAL JOEY* (1940), arguably their finest musical. Despite all the success, the collaboration deteriorated as Hart's alcoholism and bouts of depression hindered their efforts. When Hart dismissed the idea of a musical version of *Green Grow the Lilacs*, Rodgers went to OSCAR HAMMERSTEIN II and they began their long and fruitful collaboration with *OKLAHOMA!* (1943). Hart died in 1943 and Rodgers worked exclusively with Hammerstein for the next sixteen years, writing a series of musical plays with diverse subjects, settings and themes: *CAROUSEL* (1945), *ALLEGRO* (1947), *SOUTH PACIFIC* (1949), *THE KING AND I* (1951), *ME AND JULIET* (1953), *PIPE DREAM* (1955), *FLOWER DRUM SONG* (1958) and *THE SOUND OF MUSIC* (1959). The two partners also produced many of their own musicals as well as musicals and plays by others. When Hammerstein died in 1960, Rodgers' career suffered from the lack of a solid collaborator. He wrote his own lyrics for *NO STRINGS* (1962) and worked with STEPHEN SONDHEIM on *DO I HEAR A WALTZ?* (1965) but neither musical was anything exceptional. *TWO BY TWO* (1970), with lyrics by MARTIN CHARNIN, only ran because of its star, DANNY KAYE, and *Rex* (1976), with lyrics by SHELDON HARNICK, and *I Remember Mama* (1979), lyrics by Charnin again, quickly closed. Rodgers was one of the theatre's most versatile composers with a seemingly endless talent for melody. No one, for example, has rivaled his proficiency for waltzes. With two great collaborations he had two distinct careers and excelled both times.

GINGER ROGERS (1911–), the popular movie singer-dancer who was partnered with FRED ASTAIRE in ten films, appeared on Broadway before going to Hollywood and she returned to the stage in the 1960s. Rogers started as a dancer and band singer before being featured in the Broadway musical *Top Speed* (1929). She gained notoriety as Molly Gray, singing "Embraceable You" and "But Not for Me" in *GIRL CRAZY* (1930) but was then off to Hollywood. In 1965 Rogers was one of the Dolly Levi replacements in *HELLO, DOLLY!* and starred in *MAME* in London in 1969.

WILL ROGERS (1879–1935), the beloved American humorist whose home-spun humor was a hit in vaudeville, on film, on the radio and in newspaper columns, appeared in ten Broadway shows, most memorably five editions of the *ZIEGFELD FOLLIES* between 1916 and 1924. Rogers was portrayed by Keith Carradine in the vague BIOGRAPHICAL MUSICAL *THE WILL ROGERS FOLLIES* (1991).

ROMANCE, ROMANCE (1988) was a pleasant twin bill of two one-act musicals about love at the turn of the century and today. Barry Harman wrote both librettos and the lyrics and Keith Hermann provided the engaging music that captured both periods. "The Little Comedy" was about an affair between two wealthy Viennese who each disguise themselves as working-class folk in order to discover some excitement in their dull lives. "Summer Share" was set in the Long Island Hamptons where two friends contemplate becoming lovers and end up examining their own marriages. Scott Bakula and ALISON FRA-SER played both sets of lovers with warmth and charm. *Romance, Romance* opened Off Broadway in 1987 and transfered to Broadway in 1988 but the musical was on too intimate a scale to compete with bigger shows and it closed after 297 performances.

SIGMUND ROMBERG (1887–1951) is the only American operetta composer who was versatile enough to successfully move into other areas of musical theatre. He was also the most prolific composer of the Broadway stage, credited with fifty-seven operettas, musical comedies and revues during his career of thirty-seven years. Romberg was born in rural Hungary and started composing as a child. His family wanted him to become an engineer so he studied both violin and engineering in Vienna. He became acquainted with Viennese operetta when he became an assistant manager of a theatre that produced Strauss and Lehar works. Romberg traveled to London and then New York, where he decided to stay, making his living as a pianist in cafés and restaurants. Producer J. J. SHUBERT heard some of Romberg's original compositions and hired him to score his lavish revue *The Whirl of the World* (1914). No one paid much attention to the music and Romberg's subsequent work for other Shubert revues also went unnoticed but *The Blue Paradise* (1915) set his career in motion with the song "Auf Wiedersehn." That show also gave Romberg his first chance to write in the rhapsodic operetta style, a genre he would master in such popular favorites as *MAYTIME* (1917), *BLOSSOM TIME* (1921), *THE STUDENT PRINCE OF HEIDELBERG* (1924), *THE DESERT SONG* (1926) and *THE NEW MOON* (1928). Romberg was also successful with musical comedy and revues and composed several versions of *The Passing Show*; star vehicles such as *SINBAD* (1918), *BOMBO* (1921) and *ROSALIE* (1928); and book musicals like *May Wine* (1935) and *UP IN CENTRAL PARK* (1945). Romberg's best work was written with librettist-lyricists OTTO HARBACH, OSCAR HAMMERSTEIN II, RIDA JOHNSON YOUNG, DOROTHY DONNELLY and DOROTHY FIELDS.

HAROLD ROME (1908–), the composer-lyricist of several musical plays and revues, is a master at capturing the persona of the working class in his shows. Rome was born in Hartford, Connecticut, and studied at Yale to become a lawyer and later an architect. He quit his job as an architectural draftsman to write songs for summer camp revues, where his work was noticed by the head of drama activities for the International Ladies Garment Workers Union. Rome was asked to write the songs for the ILGWU's revue *PINS AND NEEDLES* (1937), a satirical show about labor relations that became so popular it moved to Broadway and ran for over 1,000 performances. Rome provided similar songs for *Sing Out the News* (1948), *Let Freedom Sing* (1942) and *CALL ME MISTER* (1946). His first book musical, *WISH YOU WERE HERE* (1952), recalled his days at adult summer camp and it was followed by *FANNY* (1954), based on Marcel Pagnol stories, and *DESTRY RIDES AGAIN* (1959), which had a western setting. Rome returned to urban working-class characters with *I CAN GET IT FOR YOU WHOLESALE* (1962). His other credits include the songs for the play *The Zulu and the Zayda* (1965) and the London musical version of *Gone with the Wind* (1972). Rome's strength as a songwriter is in his ability to vividly portray common people without sentiment or cliché.

ROSALIE (1928) had a lot going for it—songs by the GERSHWINS, SIGMUND ROMBERG and P. G. WODEHOUSE; stunning sets by JOSEPH URBAN; top-notch production values by producer FLORENZ ZIEGFELD— but the only thing that really mattered was the show's star, MARILYN MILLER. The plot, by William Anthony McGuire and GUY BOLTON, was an improbable tale about a Lindbergh-like flyer who loves a Rumanian princess named Rosalie. The best song in the musical was the Gershwins' "How Long Has This Been Going On?" which at the time was completely overlooked by critics and audiences alike. (335 performances)

BILLY ROSE (1899–1966) was a celebrated producer involved in most areas of show business, from Broadway to nightclubs to expositions. Rose started as a lyricist and provided songs for some Broadway musicals in the 1920s. He produced five musicals for Broadway: *Sweet and Low* (1930), *Crazy Quilt*

(1931), *JUMBO* (1935), *CARMEN JONES* (1943) and *Seven Lively Arts* (1944).

GEORGE ROSE (1920–1988), the veteran British character actor of plays, musicals and the classics, gave memorable performances in Broadway musicals, most notably as Alfred P. Doolittle in the 1979 revival of *MY FAIR LADY* and as the Chairman in *THE MYSTERY OF EDWIN DROOD* (1985). Rose's other musical credits included *Walking Happy* (1966), *Canterbury Tales* (1969), *COCO* (1969), *DANCE A LITTLE CLOSER* (1983) and as the Major General in the 1981 revival of *The Pirates of Penzance*.

PHILIP ROSE (1921–), a director, producer and sometime librettist, has been associated with the musicals scored by PETER UDELL and GARY GELD: *PURLIE* (1970), *SHENANDOAH* (1975), *Angel* (1978), *Comin' Uptown* (1979) and *The Amen Corner* (1983).

ROSE-MARIE (1924), with its popular Broadway, London and Paris productions, as well as four road companies, was the most financially successful musical until *OKLAHOMA!* came along twenty years later. OSCAR HAMMERSTEIN II and OTTO HARBACH wrote the libretto and lyrics and RUDOLF FRIML provided the delectable music. The setting is the Canadian Rockies, where hotel singer Rose-Marie loves fur trapper Jim Kenyon. When Jim is falsely accused of murder, the Mounties, with Rose-Marie's help, get the real culprit and the lovers are reunited. The score features operetta favorites "Indian Love Call," "The Mounties," "Totem Tom-Tom" and the title song. DENNIS KING as Jim became America's most popular operatic leading man with this show and Mary Ellis played the heroine lovingly. With its highly romantic score, lush scenic background and rhapsodic lovers, *Rose-Marie* today seems like the quintessential antique operetta. But, in fact, the show made some bold advances in musical theatre structure by consciously trying to integrate book and score. Harbach and Hammerstein even included a murder plot, something very unusual on the musical stage. And Friml's music, while glowingly melodic, manages to depart somewhat from the Viennese tradition toward an American sound. *Rose-Marie* ran for 557 performances in New York, 851 in London and a record-breaking 1,250 in Paris.

MILTON ROSENSTOCK, one of Broadway's most respected and accomplished MUSIC DIRECTORS, did the music for such memorable musicals as *CAN-CAN* (1953), *BELLS ARE RINGING* (1956), *GYPSY* (1959), *FUNNY GIRL* (1964) and many others.

JEAN ROSENTHAL (1912–1969), the American theatre's premiere lighting designer, helped pioneer many of the practices and techniques that are considered standard today. She was also responsible for developing the role of the lighting designer as separate from scenic and costume designers. Rosenthal designed over 200 Broadway shows, operas and ballets. Among her musical theatre credits were *HOUSE OF FLOWERS* (1954), *JAMAICA* (1957), *WEST SIDE STORY* (1957), *REDHEAD* (1959), *SARATOGA* (1959), *THE SOUND OF MUSIC* (1959), *THE GAY LIFE* (1961), *A FUNNY THING HAPPENED ON THE WAY TO THE FORUM* (1962), *FIDDLER ON THE ROOF* (1964), *HELLO, DOLLY!* (1964), *CABARET* (1966) and *DEAR WORLD* (1969).

HERBERT ROSS (1927–   ), the Broadway choreographer-turned-film director, staged the musical numbers for *A TREE GROWS IN BROOKLYN* (1951), *HOUSE OF FLOWERS* (1954), *ANYONE CAN WHISTLE* (1964), *DO I HEAR A WALTZ?* (1965), *ON A CLEAR DAY YOU CAN SEE FOREVER* (1965), *THE APPLE TREE* (1966) and other musicals before going to Hollywood to work exclusively with movies.

JERRY ROSS (1926–1955) wrote the lyrics and music with his collaborator RICHARD ADLER, who also wrote both, for two of the most tuneful and rousing musicals of the 1950s: *THE PAJAMA GAME* (1954) and *DAMN YANKEES* (1955). Born into a poor Bronx family, Ross was on the stage from childhood, acting for Yiddish theatre groups. He started writing songs while in his teens and later took a few music courses at New York University. After teaming up with Adler in 1950 they caught the attention of FRANK LOESSER who published some of their early songs. The young team provided some of the musical numbers for *John Murray Anderson's Almanac* (1953) and then had an all-out hit with their complete score for *The Pajama Game*. Following this with *Damn Yankees* made Adler and Ross the most promising songwriting team of the decade. But Ross died suddenly of a lung ailment in 1955 at the age of twenty-nine. The songs of Adler and Ross are not subtle or even sophisticated but they have a contagious joy about them that is full of confidence and humor.

ANN ROTH, the prolific costume designer on Broadway since 1958 who excels at contemporary designs, did the costumes for the musicals *I Had a Ball* (1964), *PURLIE* (1970), *SEESAW* (1973), *THE BEST LITTLE WHOREHOUSE IN TEXAS* (1978), *THEY'RE PLAYING OUR SONG* (1979), *Singin' in the Rain* (1985) and others.

LILLIAN ROTH (1910–1980), a vaudeville and nightclub singer since childhood, appeared in editions of *Artists and Models*, *EARL CARROLL VANITIES* and other Broadway musicals in the 1920s and 1930s. Roth returned to Broadway much later in her career, featured as mature characters in *I CAN GET IT FOR YOU WHOLESALE* (1962) and *70, GIRLS, 70* (1971).

THE ROTHSCHILDS (1970) was a sensitive and expertly crafted musical about the famous banking family. Sherman Yellen's libretto tells the saga of the Rothschild family from its humble beginnings in Frankfurt to its days of power and influence, keeping the story on a personal level and exploring the relationship that patriarch Meyer Rothschild has with his five sons. JERRY BOCK and SHELDON HARNICK wrote the score and, because the Rothschild clan was Jewish, the inevitable comparisons with the team's *FIDDLER ON THE ROOF* (1964) arose. But *The Rothschilds* had its own admirable qualities: imaginative direction and choreography by MICHAEL KIDD, fine performances by HAL LINDEN, Paul Hecht, Keene Curtis, Jill Clayburgh and Leila Martin, and some memorable songs such as "One Room," "Sons" and "In My Own Lifetime." The musical ran 507 performances and an Off-Broadway revival in 1990 ran 379 performances. *The Rothschilds* was, sadly, the last collaboration between Bock and Harnick.

ROBERT ROUNSEVILLE (1914–1974) was a pure-voiced tenor who appeared in opera as well as in Broadway musicals and nightclubs. Rounseville made his Broadway debut as one of the youngsters in *BABES IN ARMS* (1937) and sang in the chorus of *The Two Bouquets* (1938), *KNICKERBOCKER HOLIDAY* (1938) and *Higher and Higher* (1940). He was featured in the 1943 revival of *The Merry Widow* and in *UP IN CENTRAL PARK* (1945) before landing the title role in *CANDIDE* (1956). Rounseville returned to Broadway as the Padre in *MAN OF LA MANCHA* (1965), where he sang "To Each His Dulcinea."

PATRICIA ROUTLEDGE (1929–   ), an accomplished British actress-singer who appeared in several plays and musicals in the West End, was superb in the leading roles in the Broadway musicals *Darling of the Day* (1968) and *1600 PENNSYLVANIA AVENUE* (1976), as well as in two musicals that closed on the road: *Love Match* (1968) and *Say Hello to Harvey* (1981). Routledge was always highly praised but all of her New York shows failed to run and she returned to London.

HARRY RUBY (1895–1974), with his lyricist-librettist partner BERT KALMAR, composed the scores for several musical comedies in the 1920s before going off to Hollywood for a successful career. The team's best-remembered Broadway musicals are *The Ramblers* (1926), *The Five O'Clock Girl* (1927) and *ANIMAL CRACKERS* (1928). Ruby also contributed to the librettos for most of his musicals.

MICHAEL RUPERT (1951–   ) is an affable leading man in musicals who played Marvin in *March of the Falsettos* (1981), *Falsettoland* (1990) and *FALSETTOS* (1992). Rupert made his Broadway debut playing the young nephew Bibi in *THE HAPPY TIME* (1968) and went on to play the neurotic Oscar in the 1986 revival of *SWEET CHARITY*. He is also the composer of the musicals *Three Guys Naked from the Waist Down* (1985) and *Mail* (1988), in which he appeared as well.

LILLIAN RUSSELL (1861–1922), the world-famous beauty with the hour-glass figure, was a favorite of comic opera audiences and the female star of WEBER and FIELDS musical burlesques. Russell first gained attention singing at Tony Pastor's Music Hall in 1883 and was soon on Broadway playing the title roles in such musicals as *Pocahontas* (1884), *Polly* (1885), *Pepita* (1886), *Dorothy* (1887) and *Anita* (1888). Her comic opera credits included *The Brigands* (1889), *The Grand Duchess* (1889) and *La Perichole* (1895). Russell's most notable Weber and Fields show was *Twirly Whirly* (1902), in which she sang "Come Down, Ma Evenin' Star." Her last Broadway show was *Hokey Pokey* (1912).

ROSALIND RUSSELL (1912–1976), the acclaimed film actress and comedienne, appeared briefly in the 1930 *THE GARRICK GAIETIES* before going to Hollywood. Russell returned to the Broadway musical twenty-three years later to play the self-deprecating Ruth Sherwood in *WONDERFUL TOWN* (1953).

MORRIE RYSKIND (1895–1985) co-authored some of Broadway's most satirical musical comedies, including *ANIMAL CRACKERS* (1928), *STRIKE UP THE BAND* (1930), *OF THEE I SING* (1931), *LET 'EM EAT CAKE* (1933) and *LOUISIANA PURCHASE* (1940).

S

DONALD SADDLER (1920–   ), a choreographer who started as a soloist with the American Ballet Company and the Harkness Ballet, made his Broadway choreographer debut with *WONDERFUL TOWN* (1953). Saddler's dozen Broadway credits include *MILK AND HONEY* (1961), *THE ROBBER BRIDE-GROOM* (1976), *THE GRAND TOUR* (1979) and *Teddy and Alice* (1987). His finest work was the dances he devised for the Broadway revivals of *NO, NO, NANETTE* (1971) and *ON YOUR TOES* (1983).

FRED SAIDY (1907–1982) provided bold and provocative librettos for five musicals written with lyricist-librettist E. Y. HARBURG: *BLOOMER GIRL* (1944), *FINIAN'S RAINBOW* (1947), *FLAHOOLEY* (1951), *JAMAICA* (1957) and *The Happiest Girl in the World* (1961).

GENE SAKS (1921–   ), the Broadway director most known for his staging of NEIL SIMON's plays, has directed a handful of musicals, including *HALF A SIXPENCE* (1965), *MAME* (1966), *I LOVE MY WIFE* (1977) and *RAGS* (1986).

SALLY (1920) was the show that made MARILYN MILLER the First Lady of musical comedy in the 1920s. Producer FLORENZ ZIEGFELD surrounded his star with the best talent in the business: a smart and funny libretto by GUY BOLTON, lavish sets by JOSEPH URBAN, ballet music by VICTOR HER-BERT and impeccable songs by JEROME KERN with various lyricists. Sally washes dishes in Greenwich Village but, through the machinations of a co-worker who is really an exiled duke, she ends up at an elegant ball disguised as a famous Russian ballerina. By the time her true identity is discovered, Sally has charmed high society and ends up starring in the *ZIEGFELD FOLLIES*. The wonderful score included "Wild Rose," "Whip-Poor-Will," "The Church 'Round the Corner" and "Look for the Silver Lining," but it was Marilyn Miller who made it all come together for 570 happy performances, one of the longest runs of the decade.

SARATOGA (1959) was more a disappointment than a flop for it seemed that, under different circumstances, the show was destined for success. This sprawling, ambitious musical epic was based on Edna Ferber's novel *Saratoga Trunk* and it might have become something akin to *SHOW BOAT* (1927) if it had a stronger libretto. Morton Da Costa provided both the libretto and direction and both were plodding and cumbersome. HAROLD ARLEN (music) and JOHNNY MERCER (lyrics) came up with a competent score and there was no question about the strong cast and CECIL BEATON's sets and costumes. The story is basically a romance between a Creole girl named Clio (CAROL LAWRENCE) in 1880s New Orleans and a Montana cowboy (Howard Keel), both set on getting revenge with the people who scorned their families in the past. The unlikely pair team up to help each other, go to Saratoga to infiltrate high society and fall in love with each other. Also in the cast were Odette Myrtil, Edith King and Carol Brice. The score had two exceptional numbers, "A Game of Poker" and "Love Held Lightly." The large advance let *Saratoga* run eighty performances; it was, sadly, Arlen's last Broadway musical.

JIMMY SAVO (1895–1960), a vaudeville comic who was featured in seven Broadway musicals and revues, is most remembered for his Dromio of Syracuse in *THE BOYS FROM SYRACUSE* (1938).

DOUGLAS SCHMIDT (1942–) is a scenic designer whose work has been presented on Broadway since 1970. Schmidt's musical theatre credits include *Over Here* (1974), *THE ROBBER BRIDEGROOM* (1976), the 1977 revival of *THE THREEPENNY OPERA*, *Runaways* (1978), *THEY'RE PLAYING OUR SONG* (1979), *Smile* (1986) and *Nick and Nora* (1991).

HARVEY SCHMIDT (1929–), the composer for *THE FANTASTICKS* (1960) and other shows, works exclusively with lyricist-librettist TOM JONES. Both partners were born in Texas and met as fellow students at the University of Texas. Their one-act musical version of Edmond Rostand's *Les Romanesques* played one summer at Barnard College in New York and was expanded into the Off-Broadway sensation *The Fantasticks*. Jones and Schmidt were represented on Broadway with *110 IN THE SHADE* (1963), *I DO! I DO!* (1966) and *CELEBRATION* (1969). In the 1970s the team returned to Off Broadway where they opened the Portfolio Studio, a theatre workshop used to try out small, intimate musicals. *Philemon* (1975), their offbeat musical about a clown in ancient Rome, was first produced there and was later broadcast on television.

Jones and Schmidt's *Grover's Corners*, a musical version of *Our Town*, toured the country in the 1980s. Schmidt's music is varied and rich, running from the wistfully simple to Broadway brassy.

ARTHUR SCHWARTZ (1900–1984) wrote music for Broadway revues and book musicals with a number of different lyricists but he is most remembered for the sparkling revues he scored with HOWARD DIETZ in the 1930s and some book musicals he collaborated with DOROTHY FIELDS on in the 1950s. Schwartz was born in Brooklyn and studied at Columbia to be a lawyer. He had written songs with little success since his student days but he gave up his law career when he teamed up with lyricist Dietz in 1929. Their first Broadway revue was the witty *THE LITTLE SHOW* (1929) and they followed it with a series of revues that are considered the finest of the genre: *THREE'S A CROWD* (1930), *THE BAND WAGON* (1931), *FLYING COLORS* (1932), *AT HOME ABROAD* (1935) and *INSIDE U.S.A.* (1948). In between Schwartz wrote scores with IRA GERSHWIN, Agnes Morgan, Al Stillman and others as well as for a handful of London musicals and film scores. His two early book musicals with Dietz, *REVENGE WITH MUSIC* (1934) and *BETWEEN THE DEVIL* (1937), were not as successful as their revues but with lyricist Dorothy Fields, Schwartz wrote commendable scores for *Stars in Your Eyes* (1939), *A TREE GROWS IN BROOKLYN* (1951) and *By the Beautiful Sea* (1954). In the 1960s Dietz and Schwartz once again attempted the book musical, but both *THE GAY LIFE* (1961) and *Jennie* (1963) failed despite some excellent songs. Schwartz's music ranges from the brooding romantic to the bright and sophisticated and, although few of his shows can be revived today, some of the songs he left behind are timeless.

STEPHEN SCHWARTZ (1948–   ) began his career as a composer-lyricist with one of the most astonishing track records in the musical theatre: By the age of twenty-seven he had three hit musicals running simultaneously in New York, each one playing over 1,000 performances. Schwartz was born in New York City and was raised on Long Island, where he took piano lessons at a young age. He studied drama at the Carnegie Institute of Technology and musical composition at Juilliard but began a career as a record producer at RCA in the 1960s. *GODSPELL*, a musical project he had worked on at Carnegie Tech, opened off Broadway in 1971 and ran for five years. Also in 1971 he provided lyrics for LEONARD BERNSTEIN's *Mass*, which opened the Kennedy Center in Washington, D.C. Schwartz's first Broadway musical was the dazzling *PIPPIN* (1972), followed by the vapid but popular *THE MAGIC SHOW* (1974); each ran nearly 2,000 performances. *THE BAKER'S WIFE*, arguably Schwartz's finest score, never made it to Broadway but closed on the road in 1976. He next directed and provided some songs for *WORKING* (1978) but it also failed to run. Schwartz wrote the lyrics for CHARLES STROUSE's music in *RAGS* (1986). Greatly respected but plagued with difficulties, *Rags* quickly closed. Schwartz's early success has sometimes been attributed to directors and performers who made him look good; but his music and lyrics are very inventive and he has a versatility that ranges from rock to vaudeville camp to the highly romantic.

THE SECRET GARDEN (1991) brought the beloved Frances Hodgson Burnett novel to the musical stage with affection and superior craftsmanship. Marsha Norman wrote the libretto and the lyrics for Lucy Simon's enchanting music and director Susan H. Schulman staged the production with a dreamlike quality that reflected the fragile mood of the original. Burnett's story tells of orphan Mary Lennox who arrives at the gloomy Yorkshire mansion of her uncle, befriends his invalid son Colin and cures him through the magical powers of nature. The musical version opened up the tale by presenting several deceased characters from the past in a ghostly fashion that commented on the actions of the surviving characters. Some of the show's most effective moments occurred during this juxtaposition of the living and the dead. Daisy Egan played Mary with MANDY PATINKIN as her uncle and they were backed by strong performances by ROBERT WESTENBERG, Rebecca Luker, ALISON FRASER and John Cameron Mitchell. Highlights of the Simon–Norman score included "Lily's Eyes," "Race You to the Top of the Morning," "Winter's on the Wing," "Where in the World" and "Come to My Garden." With HEIDI LANDESMAN's toy theatre-like sets, THEONI V. ALDREDGE's delicate costumes and THARON MUSSER's atmospheric lighting, *The Secret Garden* was one of the loveliest looking productions seen on Broadway in years. (706 performances)

SEESAW (1973) was a much-loved musical comedy that never became an all-out hit but it is fondly remembered for its CY COLEMAN (music) and DOROTHY FIELDS (lyrics) score and for MICHAEL BENNETT's skillful staging. Based on William Gibson's two-character play *Two for the See Saw* (1958), the musical was as much about New York City as it was about its two mismatched lovers. Bennett (with NEIL SIMON's uncredited help) did the adaptation, opening up the story to include a contemporary, upbeat view of Manhattan. KEN HOWARD and MICHELE LEE were both in fine form as the central characters but TOMMY TUNE stole the show as an optimistic dancer who sang and danced "It's Not Where You Start" in a clever production number. Other pleasurable songs in the score included "Welcome to Holiday Inn," "Poor Everybody Else," "My City" and "Nobody Does It Like Me." *Seesaw* was the last score by Fields who died a year later. (296 performances)

VIVIENNE SEGAL (1897–1992), a versatile leading lady, played dreamy ingenues in musical comedies and operettas in the 1910s and 1920s, then did sophisticated, worldly roles in the 1930s and 1940s. Segal made her Broadway debut in *The Blue Paradise* (1915) and had featured roles in *Miss 1917* (1917),

OH, LADY! LADY! (1918), *The Yankee Princess* (1922) and other shows. She originated the part of Margot Bonvalet in *THE DESERT SONG* (1926), Constance Bonacieux in *THE THREE MUSKETEERS* (1928) and Peggy Palaffi in *I MARRIED AN ANGEL* (1938). Segal's best role was the amoral Vera Simpson in *PAL JOEY* (1940) and her most comedic character was the deliciously evil Morgan Le Fay in the 1943 revival of *A CONNECTICUT YANKEE*. Her final Broadway musical appearance was her reprise of Vera in the 1952 revival of *Pal Joey*.

1776 (1969) was an unlikely musical hit that took Broadway by surprise and stayed for 1,217 performances. The unknown Sherman Edwards wrote the music and lyrics and PETER STONE provided the talky but always interesting libretto, which covered the events in Philadelphia during the summer of 1776 that led to the signing of the Declaration of Independence. The hero of the piece was not the unseen George Washington but the stubborn John Adams of Massachusetts (WILLIAM DANIELS) with Benjamin Franklin (HOWARD DA SILVA) tossing in bon mots to lessen the tension. Yet *1776* was actually more historically accurate than most plays and films about the period. Also in the large cast of characters were KEN HOWARD as Jefferson, RONALD HOLGATE, Paul Hecht, Clifford David, BETTY BUCKLEY and VIRGINIA VESTOFF. Edwards' score was a pleasing mixture of styles: period minuets, Broadway character songs, Gilbert and Sullivan-like choral numbers, folk ballads and even the musical patter of the auctioneer, as seen in the gripping "Molassas to Rum." Other memorable songs included "Momma Look Sharp," "Sit Down, John," "Cool, Cool Considerate Men," "He Plays the Violin" and "Is Anybody There?"

70, GIRLS, 70 (1971) was a short-lived but lively musical comedy that featured a bevy of skillful veteran performers and a vivacious score by JOHN KANDER and FRED EBB. Norman L. Martin and Ebb co-authored the libretto based on Peter Coke's geriatric comedy *A Breath of Spring*. The story of a group of senior citizens who turn to robbery in order to finance their crumbling old folks' home was offbeat and required a certain amount of silliness and fantasy on the part of the audience. Instead people didn't know how to react and sat dumbfounded as the aged cast sang and danced like spry chorus kids. Mildred Natwick, Hans Conreid, Joey Faye, LILLIAN ROTH and Henrietta Jacobson were among the seasoned performers who got to sing such cheery Kander and Ebb songs as "Broadway, My Street," "Do We?" "Coffee in a Cardboard Cup," "Go Visit Your Grandmother," "See the Light" and "Yes." *70, Girls, 70* only lasted thirty-five performances but it became a cult favorite of many who never saw it.

SHAKESPEARE MUSICALS have appeared on and off Broadway over the decades and it is not surprising to see why. Most musicals depend on previous works for plot and the Bard of Avon had a way with good plots, most of which he took from previous sources. The fact that most of Shakespeare's comedies and some of the tragedies already have songs in them has not deterred writers from musicalizing the plays. The two most popular musicals based on Shakespeare are RODGERS and HART's *THE BOYS FROM SYRACUSE* (1938) from *A Comedy of Errors* and COLE PORTER's *KISS ME, KATE* (1948) from *The Taming of the Shrew*, unless you count *WEST SIDE STORY* (1957) and its updating of *Romeo and Juliet*. The lovers of Verona also inspired a 1970 Off-Broadway musical called *Sensations. A Midsummer Night's Dream* got a jazz facelift in *Swingin' the Dream* (Louis Armstrong played Bottom) in 1939 and appeared Off Broadway as *Babes in the Wood* (1964). Even the melancholy Dane discovered rock in *Rockabye Hamlet* (1976) but it didn't last two weeks. *The Two Gentlemen of Verona* dropped the "the" and moved to New York City to become the musical *TWO GENTLEMEN OF VERONA* (1971) in Central Park and then on Broadway. *Twelfth Night* is Shakespeare's most musical play with more songs than any other so it is understandable why it has been musicalized three times: The delightful *YOUR OWN THING* (1968) spoofed the Bard and ROCK MUSICALS and had a long run Off Broadway, the lackluster *Music Is* (1976) lasted only a week on Broadway, and *Love and Let Love* (1968) did not do much better Off Broadway. And for those not content with *The Boys from Syracuse*, there was *Oh, Brother!* (1981), a silly reworking of *A Comedy of Errors* set in oil-rich Iran with the Ayatollah singing and dancing.

IRENE SHARAFF, one of the most illustrious and prolific costume designers in America, has costumed many ballets, films and Broadway shows, including thirty-three musicals beginning with the revue *AS THOUSANDS CHEER* (1933). Among her most celebrated designs were the dazzling expressionistic clothes for *LADY IN THE DARK* (1941), the exotic costumes for *THE KING AND I* (1951), and the realistic street clothes for *WEST SIDE STORY* (1957). Sharaff's other musical credits include *JUBILEE* (1935), *ON YOUR TOES* (1936), *THE BOYS FROM SYRACUSE* (1938), *BY JUPITER* (1942), *A TREE GROWS IN BROOKLYN* (1951), *CANDIDE* (1956), *FLOWER DRUM SONG* (1958), *DO RE MI* (1960), *FUNNY GIRL* (1964), *SWEET CHARITY* (1966) and the 1973 revival of *IRENE*.

OSCAR SHAW (1889–1967) was a popular leading man in Broadway musicals in the 1910s and 1920s. Among Shaw's many musical credits were *VERY GOOD EDDIE* (1915), *LEAVE IT TO JANE* (1917), *Two Little Girls in Blue* (1920), *Good Morning Dearie* (1920), *OH, KAY!* (1926), *The Five O'Clock Girl* (1927) and *FLYING HIGH* (1930).

SHE LOVES ME (1963) was a unique and thoroughly enchanting musical that offered what is arguably the finest score written by JERRY BOCK and

SHELDON HARNICK. The story was not new, having been a popular Hungarian play that Hollywood had filmed twice. But JOE MASTEROFF adapted the fragile tale about the employees of a European parfumerie into a delicately humorous musical play. The plot centers on the romance of a shop manager (DANIEL MASSEY) who has been writing love letters to an anonymous "dear friend" who turns out to be a new sales clerk (BARBARA COOK) that he has been squabbling with. Barbara Baxley, JACK CASSIDY and Nathaniel Frey were among the other employees and each had a vivid character that was brought to life with gentle skill. Producer HAROLD PRINCE directed *She Loves Me*, creating a consistently engaging production that had a distinct European air to it. But the highlight of the musical was its highly melodic score that featured traditional theatre songs, musical conversations and soliloquys. The title song later gained some popularity and "Tonight at Eight," "Will He Like Me?" "Ice Cream," "Grand Knowing You," the recurring "Dear Friend" and the rest of the score all came together in a beautifully sustained musical valentine. *She Loves Me* received generally favorable reviews but it was much too gentle for Broadway that season and only lasted 301 performances. But the show is one of the most affectionately remembered of all cult musicals and is revived on occasion.

REID SHELTON (1924–   ), an actor-singer in musicals on and off Broadway since 1952, is most remembered for his performance as Daddy Warbucks in *ANNIE* (1977). Shelton's other musical credits include *WONDERFUL TOWN* (1953), *By the Beautiful Sea* (1954), *MAN WITH A LOAD OF MISCHIEF* (1966), *Canterbury Tales* (1969), *THE ROTHSCHILDS* (1970) and *1600 PENNSYLVANIA AVENUE* (1976).

SHENANDOAH (1975) was an old-fashioned but powerful musical play in the RODGERS and HAMMERSTEIN mold that rose above its grim Civil War plot to please audiences for 1,050 performances. James Lee Barrett, PHILIP ROSE and PETER UDELL wrote the heavy-handed libretto that was based on the film of the same name. Virginia widower Charlie Anderson hopes to keep his family out of the war waging around his farm but soon his whole family is caught up in the turmoil. Udell (lyrics) and GARY GELD (music) wrote a competent score that was honest and perceptive and Rose directed the fine cast that included JOHN CULLUM as the solid hero, Donna Theodore, Penelope Milford, Joel Higgins, Ted Agress, Gordon Halliday and Chip Ford.

HIRAM SHERMAN(1908–1989), a durable comic actor of many plays and musicals, was featured in the Broadway musicals *THE CRADLE WILL ROCK* (1937), *Sing Out the News* (1938), *VERY WARM FOR MAY* (1939), *Two's Company* (1952) and *How Now Dow Jones* (1967).

BURT SHEVELOVE (1915–1982) was a director of Broadway musicals and plays who also co-authored the libretto for *A FUNNY THING HAPPENED ON*

THE WAY TO THE FORUM (1962) with LARRY GELBART. Shevelove's musical directing credits included *HALLELUJAH, BABY!* (1967), the 1971 revival of *NO, NO, NANETTE*, *So Long, 174th Street* (1976) and *Happy New Year* (1980).

HASSARD SHORT (1877–1956) was both a director and a designer of musicals and was known for his innovative blending of stage movement and visual design. The most notable of his forty-plus Broadway productions are *SUNNY* (1925), *THE BAND WAGON* (1931), *AS THOUSANDS CHEER* (1933), *RO-BERTA* (1933), *JUBILEE* (1935), *LADY IN THE DARK* (1941), *CARMEN JONES* (1943) and three editions of the *MUSIC BOX REVUE*.

SHOW BOAT (1927) was neither musical comedy nor operetta but the first true musical play and it broke rules as quickly as it set up new standards for the American musical theatre. Edna Ferber's book of the same title was a sprawling epic filled with racial conflicts, unhappy marriages and gambling addiction—hardly promising musical theatre fare. But librettist-lyricist OSCAR HAMMERSTEIN II crafted the piece into a taut, powerful drama and, together with JEROME KERN's music, heightened that drama with the musical score. The story covers nearly fifty years in the Hawkes family. The patriarch, Cap'n Andy, runs the show boat *Cotton Blossom*, which tours up and down the Mississippi. His daughter Magnolia falls in love with a gambler, they marry and move to Chicago, then separate when his luck runs out. Left with a daughter, Magnolia struggles, eventually becomes a singing star and years later is reunited with her former husband. Secondary plots involve the tragic mulatto Julie and her husband Steve and the black couple Joe and Queenie. *Show Boat* produced six song standards—"Make Believe," "You Are Love," "Can't Help Lovin' Dat Man," "Bill," "Why Do I Love You?" and "Ol' Man River"—but the entire score was superior in every way and has not lost any of its impact over the decades. Just as the Mississippi River brings unity to the story, the song "Ol' Man River" keeps returning to bring thematic unity to the score. (It must be mentioned that the lyric for "Bill" was by P. G. WODEHOUSE and "After the Ball" by Charles K. Harris was interpolated into the show.) No other single musical did more to reveal the possibilities of the musical theatre and few musicals since have achieved such a high level of music drama. *Show Boat* ran 572 performances in its initial engagement, has been revived on Broadway and in opera houses many times and inspired three movie versions.

THE SHOW IS ON (1936) was a merry musical revue that used the world of show business as its unifying gimmick. MOSS HART and David Freedman wrote the sketches that gave the superb cast plenty of opportunity to parody different entertainment styles. BERT LAHR played a Hollywood movie idol, Reginald Gardiner portrayed Shakespeare adapting his work for modern audiences and BEATRICE LILLIE spoofed "Moon" musical numbers by swinging out over the audience on a giant stage moon singing "Buy Yourself a Balloon." (This number was, in turn, spoofed thirty years later in *MAME*.) The SHUBERT BROTHERS produced the revue and got Broadway's top songwriters to contribute to the score. The GERSHWINS provided "By Strauss," Hoagy Carmichael and Stanley Adams' "Little Old Lady" was featured, RODGERS and HART wrote "Rhythm," HAROLD ARLEN and E. Y. HARBURG penned "Song of the Woodman" for Lahr and VERNON DUKE and Ted Fetter supplied several songs, including "Now" and "Casanova." *The Show Is On* was tastefully staged by VINCENTE MINNELLI and ran for 237 performances.

THE SHUBERT BROTHERS, although not the most high-minded or innovative of Broadway producers, appealed to a wider audience than anyone before them and, consequently, presented more shows in more theatres and made more money than previously seen. The three brothers were Lee (1873–1953), Sam S. (1876–1905) and J. J. (1878–1963) and all were born in Lithuania. Their father emigrated to England and later Syracuse, New York, and then sent for the family. It was Sam who first got involved in theatre as an actor but before long he and his brothers were buying theatres, producing road companies and presenting stars on Broadway. At the peak of their empire, the Shuberts owned thirty-one theatres in New York City plus another seventy across the United States and in England. They presented over 500 Broadway shows, about 125 of them musicals. All three brothers were involved in each production but it was J. J. who was in charge of the musicals. Among the many Shubert shows were *A Chinese Honeymoon* (1902), their first musical; *MAYTIME* (1917); *SINBAD* (1918); *BLOSSOM TIME* (1921); *BOMBO* (1921); *THE STUDENT PRINCE* (1924); *AT HOME ABROAD* (1935); *BETWEEN THE DEVIL* (1937); *HELLZAPOPPIN* (1938); a series of revues called *Artists and Models* (1923–1930); and twelve editions of *The Passing Show* (1912–1924), the Shuberts' answer to the *ZIEGFELD FOLLIES*. The brothers boasted that their shows were for the tired businessman and the Shuberts never presented anything of landmark status. But they brought theatre to all America and provided a sizable percentage of the musicals seen on Broadway during the first half of the twentieth century.

SHUFFLE ALONG (1921) was not only the first successful musical written, directed and performed by black artists, but it was also one of the most joyous shows of the decade. The libretto, by Flournoy Miller and Aubrey Lyles, was a silly affair about two rival candidates for mayor of Jimtown but it was the score, by EUBIE BLAKE (music) and NOBLE SISSLE (lyrics), that mattered most. "I'm Just Wild About Harry" has remained a standard for over eight decades but all the songs are contagious fun: "Love Will Find a Way," "If You've Never Been Vamped by a Brownskin" and "Bandana Days." *Shuffle Along* quietly opened uptown with meager sets and costumes and no advance ballyhoo but it soon caught on and ran for 504 performances. Other versions of *Shuffle Along* were produced in 1928, 1932 and 1952 but none were successful.

SILK STOCKINGS (1955) is more notable as COLE PORTER's last Broadway musical rather than for any distinctive features in it. The libretto, by GEORGE S. KAUFMAN and Laureen McGrath and rewritten by ABE BURROWS, was an uninspired musicalization of the superior film *Ninotchka* (1939). The plot still featured a beautiful Russian official who goes to Paris to investigate the activities of Soviet émigrés and she slowly succumbs to the charms of the City of Light and the man who falls in love with her. But what was delightful in 1939 had a sinister subtext during the Cold War and many topical jokes about Stalin and disappearing Soviet figures have soured with time. Hildegarde Neff played the lovely Russian with DON AMECHE as her enamored foe. Also in the cast were George Tobias, Philip Sterling, Julie Newmar and, as a flamboyant Hollywood starlet, GRETCHEN CRYER. The Porter score contained two memorable love songs, "All of You" and the title song, as well as "Paris Loves Lovers" and "It's a Chemical Reaction, That's All." (478 performances)

LEONARD SILLMAN (1908–1982), the producer behind the popular *New Faces* revues on Broadway, introduced dozens of performers to the American public, from Henry Fonda to PAUL LYNDE to Maggie Smith. Sillman started in vaudeville as an actor and appeared in a few Broadway musicals in the 1920s and 1930s. His first *New Faces* revue came in 1936 and was followed by editions in 1943, 1952, 1956, 1962 and 1968. Sillman directed four of the series' revues, as well as other musicals in the 1940s and 1950s.

PHIL SILVERS (1911–1985), the fast-talking comic actor who was a favorite of television audiences, appeared on Broadway intermittently during his long career. Silvers made his musical debut in *Yokel Boy* (1939) and had his first starring role in *HIGH BUTTON SHOES* (1947) where he played the flimflamming Harrison Floy. His other Broadway musical credits included *Top Banana* (1951), entrepreneur Hubie Cram in *DO RE MI* (1960) and Pseudolus in the 1972 revival of *A FUNNY THING HAPPENED ON THE WAY TO THE FORUM*.

NEIL SIMON (1927–   ), America's most popular playwright, wrote the libretto for four Broadway musicals: *LITTLE ME* (1962), *SWEET CHARITY* (1966), *PROMISES, PROMISES* (1969) and *THEY'RE PLAYING OUR SONG* (1979). Simon's librettos are known for their comic wit, engaging plots (most of which are cleverly adapted from other sources) and their lovable, self-deprecating characters. Simon is also a much respected play doctor and has provided uncredited material for several musicals, most notably *A CHORUS LINE* (1975).

SINBAD (1918) was an AL JOLSON vehicle and probably the finest musical showcase for his dynamic stage talents. The story, such as it was, moved from a dog show on Long Island to ancient Baghdad, often stopping for Jolson's specialty numbers. SIGMUND ROMBERG composed the music but all the popular songs were interpolations by others: "My Mammy," "Rock-a-Bye Your Baby with a Dixie Melody" and "Swanee," the last added during the road tour and GEORGE GERSHWIN's first hit. (388 performances)

NOBLE SISSLE (1889–1975), the first major black lyricist to be represented on Broadway, collaborated with composer EUBIE BLAKE on the landmark musical *SHUFFLE ALONG* (1921). The same team's *Chocolate Dandies* (1924) was not as popular but was just as jubilant. Later editions of *Shuffle Along* came in 1928, 1932 and 1952 but they did not compare favorably with the original. Sissle was also a performer and appeared in all his shows. His deft lyricwriting must be acknowledged not only for its own high quality but for the groundwork it laid for later black songwriters.

1600 PENNSYLVANIA AVENUE (1976) was an unanimously panned musical that lasted only seven performances on Broadway but it is a show that refuses to disappear from memory or speculation. The musical itself is probably beyond reviving since its libretto problems remain numerous but the score by LEONARD BERNSTEIN (music) and ALAN JAY LERNER (lyrics) will not be ignored and we have not heard the last of this strangely hypnotic disaster. Lerner's ambitious libretto took a servant's point of view in telling of the inhabitants of the White House from George Washington (who never lived there) to Teddy Roosevelt. KEN HOWARD played all the presidents and PATRICIA ROUTLEDGE all the first ladies, with GILBERT PRICE as the black butler who agelessly watches them all come and go. With such a large scope the story was reduced to several episodic scenes with little character development. But the songs (there were about two hours of music in the piece) were expansive and exceptional. Since the score was never recorded, it took many years for parts of it to be performed and recorded. What finally emerged was a superior collection of songs worthy of these two master songwriters. "Take Care of This House," "If I Was a Dove," "Lud's Wedding," "Seena" and "The President Jefferson Sunday Luncheon Party March" are highlights in a score that continues to fascinate and please.

THOMAS R. SKELTON (1927–), an accomplished lighting designer on Broadway since 1963, has done the lights for several dance companies and the musicals *COCO* (1969), *PURLIE* (1972), *SHENANDOAH* (1975), *DANCE A LITTLE CLOSER* (1983) and many revivals during the 1970s and 1980s.

WALTER SLEZAK (1902–1983), a film character actor who played romantic leads on Broadway in the 1930s, is best remembered by musical theatre audiences for his aging husband Panisse in *FANNY* (1954). Slezak's early

Broadway musicals included *MUSIC IN THE AIR* (1932), *May Wine* (1935) and *I MARRIED AN ANGEL* (1938).

ALEXIS SMITH (1921–), the statuesque film actress, came to Broadway late in her career and won plaudits for her cynical Phyllis in *FOLLIES* (1971). Smith also starred in the short-lived musical *Platinum* (1978).

HARRY B. SMITH (1860–1936) was a librettist and lyricist who is mostly forgotten today but, in addition to many hits, he has the distinction of being Broadway's most prolific librettist. Between 1887 and 1932 he wrote the book and/or lyrics for 123 musicals and operettas. In 1899 alone his name appeared as author on no less than eight new shows. Smith's collaborators ranged from REGINALD DE KOVEN to VICTOR HERBERT to JEROME KERN. His most notable musicals include *ROBIN HOOD* (1891), *THE FORTUNE TELLER* (1898), *SWEETHEARTS* (1913), *THE GIRL FROM UTAH* (1914), *WATCH YOUR STEP* (1914) and various editions of the *ZIEGFELD FOLLIES*.

OLIVER SMITH (1918–), one of Broadway, opera and ballet's busiest and most successful scenic designers, has also served as a Broadway producer on occasion. Smith is most remembered for his celebrated designs for *BRIGADOON* (1947), *MY FAIR LADY* (1956), *WEST SIDE STORY* (1957), *THE SOUND OF MUSIC* (1959) and *CAMELOT* (1960). Among his other Broadway musical credits are *ON THE TOWN* (1944), *HIGH BUTTON SHOES* (1947), *GENTLEMEN PREFER BLONDES* (1949), *PAINT YOUR WAGON* (1951), *CANDIDE* (1956), *JAMAICA* (1957), *FLOWER DRUM SONG* (1958), *THE UNSINKABLE MOLLY BROWN* (1960), *HELLO, DOLLY!* (1964), *Baker Street* (1965), *Darling of the Day* (1968), *DEAR WORLD* (1969) and *CARMELINA* (1979).

SOMETHING FOR THE BOYS (1943) was one of several ETHEL MERMAN shows with songs by COLE PORTER but this was not one of the best. Librettists DOROTHY and HERBERT FIELDS set the ramshackle plot in Texas with three cousins inheriting a worthless ranch. Porter's score was not memorable, although "Could It Be You?" and "Hey, Good Lookin'" were pleasant and the comic "By the Mississiniwah," about Indian bigamy, revealed Porter at his uncensored bawdiest. (422 performances)

STEPHEN SONDHEIM (1930–), the eclectic composer-lyricist who has continually experimented with various musical forms, genres and styles, is the contemporary American musical theatre's leading creative artist. Although he has enjoyed financial and popular success only occasionally, Sondheim has been Broadway's most respected songwriter for the past twenty years. Born in New York City, Sondheim was educated at the George School in Pennsylvania where he met James Hammerstein, the son of the master lyricist-librettist OSCAR HAMMERSTEIN II. Sondheim was drawn to writing musicals at an early age and the elder Hammerstein served as his mentor who guided the precocious teenager in his early efforts. After schooling at Williams College and studying composition with avant-garde composer Milton Babbitt, Sondheim wrote television scripts while working on various musical projects. His early effort *Saturday Night* was slated for Broadway until the unexpected death of the producer brought the venture to a halt. Sondheim was invited to join the team writing *WEST SIDE STORY* (1957) and his Broadway debut was as lyricist for that landmark musical. He next provided an impeccable set of lyrics for *GYPSY* (1959) but a full score by Sondheim, music and lyrics, was not heard on Broadway until *A FUNNY THING HAPPENED ON THE WAY TO THE FORUM* in 1962. His highly experimental *ANYONE CAN WHISTLE* (1964) quickly closed and the lyrics he wrote for RICHARD RODGERS' *DO I HEAR A WALTZ?* (1965) got little attention. Sondheim's reputation as an innovative and challenging artist was secured with *COMPANY* (1970), produced and directed by HAROLD PRINCE. Sondheim and Prince would work together on a series of shows that represented the boldest and most exciting musical theatre to be seen in the 1970s: *FOLLIES* (1971), *A LITTLE NIGHT MUSIC* (1973), *PACIFIC OVERTURES* (1976), *SWEENEY TODD* (1979) and *MERRILY WE ROLL ALONG* (1981). Few of these musicals returned their financial investment but they were as admired as they were ambitious. Sondheim won a PULITZER PRIZE for his score for *SUNDAY IN THE PARK WITH GEORGE* (1984), written and directed by JAMES LAPINE. Sondheim and Lapine teamed up again in 1987 for *INTO THE WOODS*, one of the songwriter's longest-running shows. His *ASSASSINS* had a limited run Off Broadway in 1990 and, like all his work, was intelligent and fascinating. Although Sondheim has his roots in the traditions of Broadway, he is the least commercial of songwriters. His scores are so fully integrated with plot, character, style and concept that many of the songs refuse to exist outside of the musical play. Consequently, he has had fewer hit songs than most major Broadway songwriters. Sondheim's dexterity with lyrics has rarely been matched and his musical talents, so long neglected by critics and audiences alike, are now recognized for their superb quality.

SONG OF NORWAY (1944) was one of the most successful of all the musicals utilizing classical music. Edvard Grieg's compositions were adapted by ROBERT WRIGHT and GEORGE FORREST into an operetta score that told, without much concern for historical accuracy, the story of Grieg's life and loves. The most memorable musical moment of the evening was "Strange Music," a romantic duet based on Grieg's "Wedding Day in Troldhaugen." With its lilting melodies and strong operatic cast, *Song of Norway* ran 860 performances.

SOPHISTICATED LADIES (1981) offered thirty-six Duke Ellington songs in a musical revue that followed in the footsteps of the popular *AIN'T*

MISBEHAVIN' (1978). Donald McKayle conceived the show as a nightclub floor show but it was director Michael Smuin who took over and made the revue one of the most glittering productions of the decade. In addition to the wonderful Ellington music, the musical boasted sprightly dancing by GREGORY HINES, HINTON BATTLE, Gregg Burge, Judith Jamison and others. (767 performances)

THE SOUND OF MUSIC (1959), arguably the most well-known RODGERS and HAMMERSTEIN musical, was the team's final collaboration. For one of the few times in his career, Hammerstein had no hand in writing the libretto; the task fell to HOWARD LINDSAY and RUSSEL CROUSE who adapted Maria Von Trapp's autobiography. The story tells of the young religious postulant Maria (MARY MARTIN), who is sent to become governess to widower Captain Von Trapp's seven children. Maria befriends the neglected offspring, falls in love and marries the Captain and helps them all escape out of Nazi Austria. It was the kind of highly romantic tale seen only in operetta but the characters had humor and honesty and the Rodgers and Hammerstein score was more than pleasing. "Edelweiss," "My Favorite Things," "Climb Ev'ry Mountain," "Do-Re-Mi" and the title song were among the show's well-known songs. Also in the cast were Theodore Bikel as the Captain, Patricia Neway, Kurt Kaszner, Marion Marlowe and BRIAN DAVIES. *The Sound of Music* ran for 1,443 performances but Hammerstein died nine months after it opened and the American musical theatre's most influential songwriting collaboration ended.

SOUTH PACIFIC (1949) is perhaps the most adult of the RODGERS and HAMMERSTEIN musicals because its story is not dictated merely by romance but also by prejudice and fear. JOSHUA LOGAN and Hammerstein adapted two stories from James Michener's *Tales of the South Pacific* into a cohesive plot with parallel themes. Set on an American-occupied Pacific island during World War II, the story follows the unlikely romance between a Navy nurse, Nellie Forbush (MARY MARTIN), and an older French planter, Emile de Becque (ENZIO PINZA). Although they are of very different cultures, their love sustains the relationship until Nellie learns that de Becque has two Polynesian children from a former marriage. In a tragic subplot, Lieutenant Joe Cable (WILLIAM TABBERT) has fallen in love with Liat, a native girl, through the machinations of her sly mother, "Bloody Mary" (JUANITA HALL). Having lost Nellie, de Becque volunteers to join Cable on a dangerous mission, during which Cable is killed. De Becque returns to find Nellie beginning to overcome her prejudices as she is drawn to his children. Martin and Pinza gave perceptive and gripping performances as the unusual romantic leads and they were ably supported by a first-rate cast under the direction of Logan. The Rodgers and Hammerstein score contained some of their most passionate and their funniest songs: "Some Enchanted Evening," "This Nearly

Was Mine," "Bali Ha'i," "There Is Nothing Like a Dame," "I'm Gonna Wash That Man Right Out of My Hair," "A Wonderful Guy," as well as the bitter but revealing "You've Got to Be Carefully Taught." (1,925 performances)

BELLA AND SAM SPEWACK (1899–1990; 1899–1971) were a successful playwriting team who wrote the librettos for two of COLE PORTER's finest musicals, *LEAVE IT TO ME!* (1938) and *KISS ME, KATE* (1948).

SPORTS, as portrayed in musicals, have had an uneven track record. Collegiate football has been the most profitable, providing the background for musicals such as *LEAVE IT TO JANE* (1917), *ALL AMERICAN* (1962), *GOOD NEWS!* (1927) and *TOO MANY GIRLS* (1939). Baseball has proved to be less success-ful with most attempts striking out. Even the one major exception, the delightful *DAMN YANKEES* (1955), had trouble finding an audience until the producers replaced their baseball diamond ads with GWEN VERDON's legs. Boxing figured significantly in *HOLD EVERYTHING!* (1928), *GOLDEN BOY* (1964) and *The Body Beautiful* (1957), and golf was featured in *FOLLOW THRU* (1929). *LITTLE JOHNNY JONES* (1904) was based on real-life jockey Tod Sloan but musicals have usually been more interested in horse race gambling, as in *GUYS AND DOLLS* (1950) and *BELLS ARE RINGING* (1956). Basketball has never inspired a memorable musical but JERRY ORBACH sang lovingly of the sport in "She Likes Basketball" in *PROMISES, PROMISES* (1968).

ST. LOUIS WOMAN (1946) had libretto problems but was a superior musical with a dynamic score and incomparable cast. Arna Bontemps and Countee Cullen wrote the libretto, based on a novel by Bontemps, about rivalry in love and gambling in 1898 St. Louis. The brothers Harold and Fayard Nicholas led a cast that also included PEARL BAILEY, Ruby Hill, REX INGRAM and JUANITA HALL. ROUBEN MAMOUILIAN staged the evocative production and HAROLD ARLEN (music) and JOHNNY MERCER (lyrics) provided the sensational songs: "Come Rain or Come Shine," "I Had Myself a True Love," "Legalize My Name," "Ridin' on the Moon," "A Woman's Prerogative" and "Any Place I Hang My Hat Is Home." *St. Louis Woman* was a splendid period piece that was somewhat reminiscent of *PORGY AND BESS* (1935) but it only managed a run of 113 performances.

LEWIS J. STADLEN (1947–) is a character actor who played GROUCHO MARX in the musical biography *Minnie's Boys* (1970) and went on to repeat the characterization in one-man shows. Stadlen played Dr. Pangloss and a variety of other characters in the 1974 revival of *CANDIDE* and the slave Socia in *Olympus on My Mind* (1986).

JEAN STAPLETON (1923–), a durable character actress widely known from television, returns often to the stage. Stapleton was featured in the musicals

DAMN YANKEES (1955), *JUNO* (1959) and *FUNNY GIRL* (1964) and played Susan, the owner of Susanswerphone, in *BELLS ARE RINGING* (1956).

STARTING HERE, STARTING NOW (1977) was an exciting Off-Broadway musical revue that first brought recognition to songwriters RICHARD MALTBY, JR., and DAVID SHIRE. The songs were very contemporary in subject and spirit and covered a variety of topics, usually with wit and intelligence. "Crossword Puzzle," "Flair," "Watching the Parade Go By," "I Don't Remember Christmas" and the title song were among the many gems in the score and the cast, Loni Ackerman, George Lee Andrews and Margery Cohen, performed them beautifully. *Starting Here, Starting Now* ran for 120 performances and has been produced regionally many times over the years.

JOSEPH STEIN (1912–　) is a major Broadway musical librettist with an up-and-down record for success. Stein's first three Broadway librettos were written in collaboration with Will Glickman: *PLAIN AND FANCY* (1955), *Mr. Wonderful* (1956) and *The Body Beautiful* (1958). Each showed promise and had moderate runs. *JUNO* (1959), an ambitious musicalization of Sean O'Casey's *Juno and the Paycock*, deserved more attention but quickly closed. Stein's libretto for *TAKE ME ALONG* (1959) helped secure his career, and his script for *FIDDLER ON THE ROOF* (1964) put him in the top ranks of musical playwrights. He provided a competent libretto for *ZORBA* (1968) and co-authored the new version of *IRENE* in 1973. Stein's career since then has been a series of short-lived failures, some of which have much to recommend: *So Long, 174th Street* (1976), *THE BAKER'S WIFE* (closed on its pre-Broadway tour in 1976), *King of Hearts* (1978), *CARMELINA* (1979) and *RAGS* (1986). Stein may be a hit-or-miss talent but there is no question that his *Fiddler on the Roof* libretto is one of the finest in the American theatre.

MICHAEL STEWART (1929–1987) was a Broadway librettist and sometime lyricist who had a run of hit shows in the 1960s. Stewart began his career in 1951 writing sketches and lyrics for various Off-Broadway revues. He made his name on Broadway with his libretto for *BYE BYE BIRDIE* (1960) and then followed it with three more long-runs: *CARNIVAL* (1961), *HELLO, DOLLY!* (1964) and *GEORGE M!* (1968). One of Stewart's more ambitious book musicals, *MACK AND MABEL* (1974), failed to run but he had another hit with *I LOVE MY WIFE* (1977), in which he wrote the lyrics as well as the libretto. *THE GRAND TOUR* (1979) was a challenging but unsuccessful musical written with JERRY HERMAN. In 1980 he co-authored with Mark Bramble two weak librettos that became hugely popular shows because of their sensational production values: *42ND STREET* and *BARNUM*, writing lyrics again for the latter. Stewart's final Broadway musicals were the misguided flops *Bring Back Birdie* (1981) and *Harrigan 'n Hart* (1985). The finest Stewart librettos were bright and engaging examples of Broadway musical comedy at its best.

FRED STONE (1873–1959) was an extremely popular comic actor who appeared in comedies and musicals, often with his partner DAVID MONTGOMERY. Stone's most notable credits were the Scarecrow in *THE WIZARD OF OZ* (1903), Con Kidder in *THE RED MILL* (1906), *Chin-Chin* (1914) and *Criss-Cross* (1926).

PETER STONE (1930–) is one of Broadway's most reliable and ingenious librettists. Stone made his Broadway debut with the libretto for the ambitious but unsuccessful *Kean* (1961) and did not fare much better with *Skyscraper* (1965). But his libretto for *1776* (1969) launched his career. *1776* had more book than most musicals and Stone's ability to turn congressional debates into lively and entertaining musical theatre was no easy feat. Subsequent musicals by Stone include *TWO BY TWO* (1970), *SUGAR* (1972), *WOMAN OF THE YEAR* (1981), *MY ONE AND ONLY* (1983) and *THE WILL ROGERS FOLLIES* (1991). Stone is also an expert play doctor and has provided uncredited help on several musicals, such as *GRAND HOTEL* (1989).

STOP THE WORLD—I WANT TO GET OFF (1962) was a BRITISH IMPORT that was too offbeat for some tastes but some of the show's songs became so popular that the musical ran for 555 performances. ANTHONY NEWLEY directed, played the central role of Littlechap and, with Leslie Bricusse, wrote the libretto, music and lyrics. The musical is an allegorical tale about Littlechap's rise in business, his sexual conquests and his discovery that he is unfulfilled at the end of it all. Anna Quayle played Littlechap's wife as well as his various lovers from around the globe. The whole musical took place in Sean Kenny's circus tent set with all the characters in clown makeup. "Gonna Build a Mountain," "Once in a Lifetime" and "What Kind of Fool Am I?" all became standards and much of the rest of the score was rather amusing. *Stop the World...* did not start any trend toward symbolic musical theatre but it was a unique and satisfying piece.

TONY STRAIGES (1942–) is a scenic designer known to musical theatre audiences for his superb Seurat-like sets for *SUNDAY IN THE PARK WITH GEORGE* (1984). Straiges' other Broadway musicals include *Timbuktu* (1978), *Copperfield* (1981), *INTO THE WOODS* (1987) and *Dangerous Games* (1989).

STREET SCENE (1947) is arguably KURT WEILL's most ambitious project, an operatic look at a group of neighbors in a New York tenement on a hot summer day. The libretto was adapted by Elmer Rice from his 1929 play of the same name and LANGSTON HUGHES provided the conversational but powerfully expressive lyrics. The slice-of-life story centers on the dreamy

Rose, her two beaux and her discontented mother and jealous father. As in the GERSHWINS' *PORGY AND BESS* (1935), the neighbors serve as chorus, commentators and local atmosphere. Only the song "Moon-Faced, Starry-Eyed" could be easily lifted from the score and it became popular but all of Weill and Hughes' work in *Street Scene* is extraordinary, most notably "Somehow I Never Could Believe," "What Good Would the Moon Be?" "I Got a Marble and a Star" and "Lonely House." Anne Jefferys played Rose and she was ably supported by Norman Cordon, Polyna Stoska, Don Saxon, Brian Sullivan and JUANITA HALL. The challenging musical managed to run 148 performances and over the years *Street Scene* has taken its place in the repertory of many opera companies.

BARBRA STREISAND (1942–   ), the film actress-director-singer, had a brief but sensational Broadway career in the 1960s. Streisand first gained attention playing the put-upon Miss Marmelstein in *I CAN GET IT FOR YOU WHOLE-SALE* (1962). She achieved stardom as FANNY BRICE in *FUNNY GIRL* (1964), a role she played on Broadway, in London and on film.

STRIKE UP THE BAND (1930) was the first of a handful of 1930s musicals that used political and social satire to deal with the grim reality of the Depression instead of merely ignoring the situation with frivolous musical escapism. The GERSHWINS got together with librettist GEORGE S. KAUFMAN in 1927 and wrote *Strike Up the Band* but its humor was too dark and the show closed out of town. With a new and more palatable book by MORRIE RYSKIND the musical finally arrived on Broadway in 1930 and was a success at 191 performances. The plot, all set in a dream, dealt with a war between the United States and Switzerland over tariffs on imported Swiss chocolate. Everything from the White House to pacifists to Swiss yodeling came under comic attack and Ira Gershwin provided several comic lyrics, such as "A Typical Self-Made American," which parodied Gilbert and Sullivan. In addition to the rousing title number, there were two memorable love songs in the score: "Soon" and "I've Got a Crush on You." Even Red Nichols' orchestra was outstanding with the young Benny Goodman, Gene Krupa, Glenn Miller and Jimmy Dorsey in the pit. *Strike Up the Band* is not as polished as the later Gershwin satire *OF THEE I SING* (1931) but it was a bold and innovative work that forecast one of the ways Broadway would react to the difficult 1930s.

ELAINE STRITCH (1925–   ) is a character actress with a throaty singing voice who appeared in a handful of musicals on Broadway and in London. Stritch made her New York debut in *Angel in the Wings* (1947) and was featured in the revivals of *PAL JOEY* in 1952 and *ON YOUR TOES* in 1954. Her Broadway musical credits include the reluctant silent movie actress Maggie Harris in *Goldilocks* (1958), *Sail Away* (1961) and *COMPANY* (1970), in which she originated the role of the cynical Joanne and sang "The Ladies Who Lunch."

CHARLES STROUSE (1928–) is one of Broadway's most reliable and sought after composers despite the fact that he has been associated with more notable FLOP MUSICALS than any other person of unquestionable talent. Strouse was born in New York City and studied at the Eastman School of Music, with Aaron Copland at Tanglewood and with Nadia Boulanger in Paris. Seemingly destined for the concert stage, Strouse was drawn to popular music and broke into musical theatre as a rehearsal pianist. When he met lyricist LEE ADAMS in 1949, they began writing revues together and scored three shows for producer BEN BAGLEY. Their first book musical, *BYE BYE BIRDIE* (1960), was a major hit but their next three efforts, *ALL AMERICAN* (1962), *GOLDEN BOY* (1964) and *IT'S A BIRD, IT'S A PLANE, IT'S SUPERMAN* (1966), were respectable failures with superior scores. The team found success again with *APPLAUSE* (1970) but it was to be their last triumph together. In 1977 Strouse teamed up with lyricist MARTIN CHARNIN for the megahit *ANNIE* and followed it with a series of collaborations with some of the musical theatre's finest lyricists and librettists: Adams, ALAN JAY LERNER, JOSEPH STEIN, STEPHEN SCHWARTZ, ARTHUR LAURENTS and RICHARD MALTBY, JR. But in each case the result was an expensive and notorious flop: *A Broadway Musical* (1978), *Charlie and Algernon* (1980), *Bring Back Birdie* (1981), *DANCE A LITTLE CLOSER* (1983), *RAGS* (1986), *Annie 2: Miss Hannigan's Revenge* (closed out of town in 1990) and *Nick and Nora* (1991). The scores for some of these shows were exemplary and Strouse could hardly be blamed for their failure even if his choice of projects was questionable. Strouse's earlier collaborations with Adams still remain his finest work. In addition to his talent for vibrant melody and musical variety, all of Strouse's musicals have the distinction of being particularly American in setting, characters and theme.

THE STUDENT PRINCE OF HEIDELBERG (1924) is arguably SIGMUND ROMBERG's finest operetta. DOROTHY DONNELLY provided the lyrics and the libretto for this popular German tale that had enjoyed success previously as a non-musical play. Prince Karl arrives in the famed university town to complete his studies but falls in love with Kathie, a waitress at the local inn. After a series of obstacles it seems that Karl and Kathie will be united. But the old king dies suddenly and the prince must assume the throne and marry a foreign princess. There were two unusual aspects to *The Student Prince* (as it is titled today): It had a bittersweet ending with the lovers separating instead of marrying and it featured a strong male chorus instead of a line of pretty chorines. Romberg's music is among his most rapturous and ranges from the rousing "Students March Song" to the wistful "Golden Days" to the romantic "Deep in My Heart, Dear" to the ever-popular "Drinking Song." The show ran for 608 performances in New York and touring versions continued non-stop for the next twenty-five years.

JULE STYNE (1905–), the prolific Broadway and Hollywood composer, worked with a variety of different lyricists and librettists during his impressive career. Styne was born in London and moved to Chicago when he was eight years old. As a teenager he was guest piano soloist for the Chicago Symphony and later studied at the Chicago Institute of Music. Styne left the world of classical music to perform popular songs with a dance band he founded and he wrote his first compositions for the group. A contract to compose and do vocal arrangements for the movies brought him to Hollywood and throughout the 1930s and 1940s he had many individual song hits with lyricists FRANK LOESSER, SAMMY CAHN and others. Styne yearned to write for Broadway but his first show there did not open until 1947: the delightful *HIGH BUTTON SHOES* with Cahn supplying the lyrics. With LEO ROBIN, Styne had an even bigger hit with *GENTLEMEN PREFER BLONDES* (1949). For the revue *TWO ON THE AISLE* (1951), he worked with BETTY COMDEN and ADOLPH GREEN for the first time; they would collaborate together seven more times in the future, most notably on *PETER PAN* (1954), *BELLS ARE RINGING* (1956), *DO RE MI* (1960), *SUBWAYS ARE FOR SLEEPING* (1961) and *HALLELUJAH, BABY!* (1967). Styne's greatest achievement was *GYPSY* (1959), in which he worked with STEPHEN SONDHEIM for the first and only time. *FUNNY GIRL* (1964), with lyrics by BOB MERRILL, was Styne's most successful musical of the 1960s and he had a final hit with *SUGAR* (1972), again with Merrill. Styne's lesser known, and less successful, shows include *Hazel Flagg* (1953), *Darling of the Day* (1968) and *One Night Stand* (closed out of town in 1980). He has also acted as producer for several Broadway musicals, most memorably the 1952 revival of *PAL JOEY*. Styne's music is pure show business and has a confident flair to much of it but he is also capable of the tender ballad and the wistful character song.

SUBWAYS ARE FOR SLEEPING (1961) was a less than successful JULE STYNE–BETTY COMDEN–ADOLPH GREEN musical but it had its pleasurable moments and a number of agreeable songs. Comden and Green wrote the libretto based on the stories by Edward G. Love about some eccentric Manhattanites. The main love story was an unconvincing tale about a homeless but dapper man (SYDNEY CHAPLIN) who lives his life on the subway and falls for a fashion magazine writer (CAROL LAWRENCE). But much more interesting was the odd romance between a former beauty queen (PHYLLIS NEWMAN), who is reduced to wearing a towel for most of the show, and a part-time Santa Claus (ORSON BEAN). The score contained the popular "Be a Santa" as well as "Girls Like Me," "Comes Once in a Lifetime," "Ride Through the Night" and "I Just Can't Wait." MICHAEL KIDD directed and choreographed with lively skill but the reviews were not enthusiastic. More famous than the musical itself was producer DAVID MERRICK's publicity stunt in which he invited seven New Yorkers with the same last names as the critics for the seven major newspapers, treated them to the show and then printed their raves in an ad. Most of the papers caught on to the gimmick and cut the ad but the publicity stunt helped keep *Subways Are for Sleeping* alive for 205 performances.

SUGAR (1972) was one of those rare musical comedies that worked best when the libretto took over from the songs. Since the plot was adapted from the hilarious film *Some Like It Hot*, it was easy to see why. PETER STONE's serviceable adaptation retained the Depression-era setting where the two heroes disguised themselves as female musicians in order to escape from some Chicago gangsters. ROBERT MORSE and TONY ROBERTS were in fine form as the drag principals and CYRIL RITCHARD was quite splendid as the dotty millionaire who falls for one of them. The title role of Sugar Kane was a poorly written caricature that Elaine Joyce performed valiantly. The real disappointment of the show was the lackluster score by JULE STYNE (music) and BOB MERRILL (lyrics), which slowed the action down and even director-choreographer GOWER CHAMPION couldn't find a way to make the whole thing work. But audiences adored Morse and Ritchards and *Sugar* managed to run 505 performances.

SUGAR BABIES (1979) was a pleasant mixture of burlesque and nostalgia raised to the level of a Broadway musical revue. Ralph G. Allen conceived and wrote the sketches for this affectionate look at variety entertainment in the first decades of the century and included some memorable songs by JIMMY McHUGH, DOROTHY FIELDS and others. Mickey Rooney made his Broadway debut as the show's top banana and Ann Miller provided the requisite dancing. The whole affair was much more glamorous than burlesque ever was but it thrilled audiences for 1,208 performances.

SUNDAY IN THE PARK WITH GEORGE (1984) was a deeply personal musical by STEPHEN SONDHEIM (music and lyrics) and JAMES LAPINE (libretto) that explored the creative process and the need to be truthful to the art rather than to the general trend. The musical itself was far from trendy, basing its subject not on a book or a play but on a painting. Lapine's script dramatized the figures in Georges Seurat's *A Sunday Afternoon on the Island of La Grande Jatte* as well as the artist himself as he develops his new style of painting. Act I ends with Seurat finishing the painting and Act II deals with the artist's great-grandson struggling with his own self-confidence as a multimedia sculptor in 1980s Chicago. While the libretto was a bit uninvolving for some, there was little question about Sondheim's score, which was rich with imagery, warmth and intelligence. "Color and Light," "Finishing the Hat," "Putting It Together," "Children and Art" and "Move On" are as accomplished as anything Sondheim ever wrote yet they are unique and atypical of him as well. Lapine directed, TONY STRAIGES designed the pointillist-like scenery, and

MANDY PATINKIN and BERNADETTE PETERS were exceptional as Seurat and his mistress/model Dot. *Sunday in the Park With George* made no effort to be everyone's cup of tea yet it did run 604 performances and won the 1985 PULITZER PRIZE in drama.

SUNNY (1925) was an obvious attempt to recreate the magic of *SALLY* (1920) by reuniting its star MARILYN MILLER and composer JEROME KERN once again. Sunny Peters, an American bareback rider in a circus visting England, falls in love with an American tourist and must stow away on an ocean liner to follow him back to New York. OTTO HARBACH and OSCAR HAMMER-STEIN II, working with Kern for the first time, provided the libretto and lyrics and the score was wonderful: "Who?" "D'Ye Love Me?" "Let's Say Goodnight Till It's Morning" and the title song. But it was Miller's star performance that kept *Sunny* running for 517 performances.

ELIZABETH SWADOS (1951–), a composer-lyricist who utilizes a wide variety of musical forms to create a collage effect in her musicals, has provided the scores for a series of unconventional pieces such as *Nightclub Cantata* (1977), *Runaways* (1978), *Dispatches* (1979), *Alice in Concert* (1980) and *The Haggadah* (1981). Swados' most traditional musical was *Doonesbury* (1983) with libretto and lyrics by Gary Trudeau.

SWEENEY TODD, THE DEMON BARBER OF FLEET STREET (1979) was an expert musicalization of the old English tale that had existed in various forms since the mid-nineteenth century. The half-crazed barber Sweeney returns to London from an unjust imprisonment in Australia and seeks to avenge himself on the judge who sentenced him and stole his young wife. But Sweeney's insanity grows once he's back in the midst of the Industrial Revolution and soon he is indiscriminately murdering his customers and turning the bodies over to his cohort Mrs. Lovett, who makes them into meat pies. HUGH WHEELER based his libretto on a 1973 stage version of the story by Christopher Bond; it was a stylized Brechtian approach that also managed to be quite sly and entertaining. STEPHEN SONDHEIM's near-operatic score was perhaps his richest yet, employing a good deal of romanticism to offset the Grand Guignol story. "Johanna," "Worst Pies in London," "Not While I'm Around," "Pretty Women" and "A Little Priest" were standouts in the superlative score and LEN CARIOU as Sweeney and ANGELA LANSBURY as Mrs. Lovett were outstanding. Also in the cast were VICTOR GARBER, Ken Jennings and Merle Louise, under the direction of HAROLD PRINCE and staged on EUGENE and FRANNE LEE's massive industrial setting. Despite its unsavory subject matter and the extreme Englishness of the piece, *Sweeney Todd* was able to run 557 performances and has since been successfully revived by both theatre and opera companies.

SWEET ADELINE (1929) was a vehicle for HELEN MORGAN, put together after her stunning performance in *SHOW BOAT* (1927). JEROME KERN and OSCAR HAMMERSTEIN II provided the score and libretto, ARTHUR HAMMERSTEIN produced the musical and his brother Reginald Hammerstein directed. *Sweet Adeline*, as the title suggests, was a nostalgic look back at the 1890s and the story concerned a New Jersey beerhall singer and her many loves and heartbreaks. The score was lovely and provided several opportunities for Morgan to deliver the kind of wistful torch song at which she excelled, most notably "Why Was I Born?" which was forever after identified with her. Also in the score was "Here Am I," "T'was Not So Long Ago," "Don't Ever Leave Me" and "Some Girl Is on Your Mind." *Sweet Adeline* ran 234 performances and would have lasted longer but for the stock market crash two months after it opened.

SWEET CHARITY (1966) was an entertaining musical comedy with perhaps NEIL SIMON's best libretto, a sharp and sassy New York City version of Federico Fellini's film *Nights of Cabiria*. Charity Hope Valentine (GWEN VERDON) is a dance hostess at the sleazy Fan-Dango Ballroom who is ever hopeful for success and true love despite a bad track record. She finally meets the straight-laced Oscar (JOHN MCMARTIN) and they fall in love but the engagement falls apart and Charity is left characteristically alone and hopeful. CY COLEMAN (music) and DOROTHY FIELDS (lyrics) wrote a brash and witty score that had several hit songs in it: "Big Spender," "If My Friends Could See Me Now," "Baby, Dream Your Dream," "There's Gotta Be Something Better Than This" and "Where Am I Going?" Verdon gave what is arguably the finest performance of her career and director-choreographer BOB FOSSE provided her with some outstanding dance numbers. *Sweet Charity* ran for 608 performances and was successfully revived on Broadway with DEBBIE ALLEN in 1986 for 368 performances.

SWEETHEARTS (1913) had one of the most farfetched librettos of any operetta but the VICTOR HERBERT music was still top drawer. The librettist HARRY B. SMITH and Fred De Gresac claimed that the tale was based on a real fifteenth-century princess from Naples but nothing could be less plausible than the story of *Sweethearts*. A baby princess from mythological Zilania is shipped off to Bruges during a war and is raised by a laundress called Mother Goose. A prince traveling incognito falls in love with her on first sight but there is a jealous lieutenant, a trio of villains and an old family friend disguised as a monk to keep the lovers apart until the finale. The title song is the score's best but also of note is "Pretty as a Picture" and "Angelus." *Sweethearts* ran for 136 performances and a 1945 revival, retailored for the talents of comic BOBBY CLARK, ran 288 performances.

INGA SWENSON (1932–   ), a leading lady in plays, musicals and classical pieces, made her Broadway debut in *New Faces of 1956* and went on to play the spinster Lizzie in *110 IN THE SHADE* (1963) and Sherlock Holmes' romantic foil Irene Adler in *Baker Street* (1965).

T

WILLIAM TABBERT (1921–1974), a full-voiced singer who played juvenile roles in a handful of Broadway musicals, is most remembered for originating the role of the tragic Lt. Joe Cable in *SOUTH PACIFIC* (1949). Tabbert's other musical credits included *What's Up?* (1943), *Billion Dollar Baby* (1945) and the troubled Marius in *FANNY* (1954).

TAKE A CHANCE (1932) went through so many revisions on its pre-Broadway road tour that it opened with three composers providing the score: Richard A. Whiting, Nacio Brown and VINCENT YOUMANS. B. G. DESYLVA wrote the lyrics and, with co-producer Lawrence Schwab and star Sid Silvers, the contrived book about the romance of two stars appearing in a musical revue about American history. The strong cast included Silvers, JACK HALEY, June Knight, JACK WHITING and, in a supporting role, ETHEL MERMAN, who sang "Rise 'n' Shine," "Eadie Was a Lady" and "You're an Old Smoothie." *Take a Chance* was, sadly, Youmans' last Broadway score. (243 performances)

TAKE ME ALONG (1959) was a musicalization of Eugene O'Neill's only comedy, *Ah, Wilderness!* JOSEPH STEIN and Robert Russell wrote the libretto about young love in a small Connecticut town in 1910. The father–son relationship was the focal point of O'Neill's play but a subplot about the jolly alcoholic Uncle Sid and his love for the spinster Lily lent itself to music better and seemed to dominate the musical, especially with the vibrant JACKIE GLEASON playing Sid. Walter Pidgeon and ROBERT MORSE were the father and son and the cast also boasted fine performances from Eileen Herlie as Lily, Una Merkel, Peter Conlow, Susan Luckey and Valerie Harper. BOB MERRILL wrote the score and the title song enjoyed some popularity. Also impressive were "Staying Young," "Sid Ol' Kid" and "Little Green Snake." (448 performances)

TAMARA (1907–1943) was an exotic singer-actress most remembered for introducing "Smoke Gets in Your Eyes" in *ROBERTA* (1933). The Russian-born Tamara also appeared in *The New Yorkers* (1927), *Crazy Quilt* (1931), *Right This Way* (1938) and *LEAVE IT TO ME!* (1938).

HELEN TAMIRIS (1905–1966) choreographed the Broadway musicals *UP IN CENTRAL PARK* (1945), *ANNIE GET YOUR GUN* (1946), *INSIDE U.S.A.* (1948), *FLAHOOLEY* (1951), *By the Beautiful Sea* (1954), *FANNY* (1954) and others. Formerly a ballet dancer with the Metropolitan Opera, Tamiris headed the School of American Dance for twelve years.

THE TAP DANCE KID (1983) was a musical play about black dancers and dancing but with a new twist: an upper middle-class lawyer discourages his son from pursuing his dream of becoming a dancer in order to maintain the family's social acceptance. Charles Blackwell's libretto had vivid and believeable characters and the score by Henry Krieger (music) and Robert Lorick (lyrics) offered both insightful character songs and exciting opportunities for dance. HINTON BATTLE, as the uncle who encourages the young hero to follow his heart and dance, led the cast directed by Vivian Matalon and choreographed by DANNY DANIELS. (669 performances)

FAY TEMPLETON (1865–1939), a favorite Broadway leading lady at the turn of the century, appeared in musical burlesques with WEBER and FIELDS and musical comedies by GEORGE M. COHAN and others. Templeton was singing on stage at the age of three, made her New York debut in 1873 and was on Broadway from 1881. Her twenty Broadway shows included *Madame Favart* (1893), *Hurly Burly* (1898), *Fiddle-Dee-Dee* (1900), *Twirly Whirly* (1902) and *FORTY-FIVE MINUTES FROM BROADWAY* (1906). Templeton returned to Broadway after a twenty-one-year absence to play Aunt Minnie in *ROBERTA* (1933).

TENDERLOIN (1960) was a highly entertaining musical comedy that reunited most of the creators of the previous year's *FIORELLO!*—songwriters JERRY BOCK and SHELDON HARNICK, librettists GEORGE ABBOTT and JEROME WEIDMAN and producers HAROLD PRINCE and ROBERT GRIFFITH. The libretto was about a minister (MAURICE EVANS) in the 1880s who tried to clean up the corrupt Tenderloin district of New York City by enlisting the help of a yellow journalist (RON HUSMANN). Although quite different in intent than *Fiorello!*, the musical suffered from comparisons and lasted only 216 performances. There was much to recommend in *Tenderloin*:

Abbott's brash direction, a talented cast, the vivacious choreography by JOE LAYTON, CECIL BEATON's outstanding sets and costumes and a score that rivaled that for *Fiorello!* "Little Old New York," "Artificial Flowers," "The Picture of Happiness," "My Gentle Young Johnny" and "Good Clean Fun" were among the witty, agreeable Bock and Harnick songs. *Tenderloin* was a commendable show that was sadly neglected and one that deserves to be revived on occasion.

RUSS THACKER (1946–), a juvenile actor in musicals in the 1960s and 1970s, played Sebastian in *YOUR OWN THING* (1968), Collin in *THE GRASS HARP* (1971) and was featured in several Off-Broadway musical revues.

THE THEATRE GUILD, the oldest and most distinguished producing organization in the American theatre, has presented world classics, bold European imports and original American plays since 1919. The Guild has also produced some landmark musicals that might not have seen the light of day under usual commercial conditions. *THE GARRICK GAIETIES* (1925) was the Guild's first venture into musicals and it was a major hit with its sharp satire and RODGERS and HART score. Two subsequent editions followed in 1926 and 1930. *PORGY AND BESS* (1935) received its first production by the Guild, as did RODGERS and HAMMERSTEIN's *OKLAHOMA!* (1943). The Guild also produced the team's *CAROUSEL* (1945) and *ALLEGRO* (1947). Other Theatre Guild musicals include *Sing Out, Sweet Land* (1944), *Arms and the Girl* (1950), *BELLS ARE RINGING* (1956), *THE UNSINKABLE MOLLY BROWN* (1960) and *Darling of the Day* (1968). The Theatre Guild was the idea of Lawrence Langner and Theresa Helburn, who supervised its productions for many years.

LEE THEODORE (1933–1987), a dancer-turned-choreographer, created the role of Anybodys in *WEST SIDE STORY* (1957) and danced in musicals such as *GENTLEMEN PREFER BLONDES* (1949), *THE KING AND I* (1951), *DAMN YANKEES* (1955) and *TENDERLOIN* (1960). Theodore choreographed the Broadway musicals *Baker Street* (1965), *FLORA, THE RED MENACE* (1965) and *THE APPLE TREE* (1966). In 1962 she founded the American Dance Machine, a company dedicated to preserving the choreography of American musicals.

THEY'RE PLAYING OUR SONG (1979) marked NEIL SIMON's return to the Broadway musical after eleven years. His libretto about a neurotic songwriter and his professional/personal relationship with a kookie lady lyricist was less than inspired but the wisecracking Simon touch was top rate and offered a dandy vehicle for ROBERT KLEIN and Lucie Arnez. MARVIN HAMLISCH (music) and Carole Bayer Sager (lyrics) wrote the pop songs and ROBERT MOORE directed expertly. (1,082 performances)

THIS IS THE ARMY (1942) was IRVING BERLIN's contribution to the war effort just as his revue *YIP YIP YAPHANK* (1918) was his military fundraiser during World War I. *This Is the Army* was a benefit for the Army Emergency Relief Fund and featured songs and sketches about military life. Produced "by Uncle Sam," the revue's cast consisted of performers in the military and the Berlin songs included "This Is the Army, Mr. Jones," "I'm Getting Tired So I Can Sleep," "I Left My Heart at the Stage Door Canteen" and the composer himself sang "Oh, How I Hate to Get Up in the Morning" as he had in the 1918 show. *This Is the Army* ran for a sold-out 113 performances and then toured the country.

THE THREE MUSKETEERS (1928) featured DENNIS KING as the swashbuckling d'Artagnan just three years after he had performed similar derring-do as François Villon in *THE VAGABOND KING*. RUDOLF FRIML again provided the music with lyrics this time by CLIFFORD GREY and P. G. WODEHOUSE. The story followed the Alexander Dumas novel somewhat faithfully and the cast was top notch: VIVIENNE SEGAL, Joseph Macaulay, Douglass R. Dumbrille, Detmar Poppen, Lester Allen, Reginald Owen and Vivienne Osborne. Although Friml's score was not as strong as his earlier efforts, it was richly melodic and contained four standout numbers: "March of the Musketeers," "Ma Belle," "My Sword and I" and "Your Eyes." (318 performances)

THE THREEPENNY OPERA (1933, 1954), the world-renowned music drama by Bertolt Brecht (libretto and lyrics) and KURT WEILL (music), had its premiere in Berlin in 1928. The first English-language version in America was a short-lived Broadway production in 1933 that lasted only twelve performances. A new translation-adaptation by MARC BLITZSTEIN opened Off Broadway in 1954 with a superb cast (LOTTE LENYA, Scott Merrill, Jo Sullivan, Charlotte Rae, BEATRICE ARTHUR, John Astin) and ran a limited engagement of ninety-five performances. Critics and audiences demanded its return and, prompted by the popularity of the show's signature song "Mack the Knife," *The Threepenny Opera* reopened Off Broadway in 1955 and ran for an astonishing 2,611 performances. The musical's plot follows that of John Gay's *The Beggar's Opera*, the eighteenth-century ballad opera about outlaw MacHeath, who is loved by and betrayed by various women in his life. It was Blitzstein's version that made the songs accessible, from the eerie "Pirate Jenny" to the lyrical "Love Song" to the sardonic "Useless Song." A 1976 revival at Lincoln Center, using a new translation, featured RAUL JULIA and ELLEN GREENE and ran for 307 performances and there was an unsuccessful Broadway revival in 1989 with Sting, GEORGIA BROWN and Maureen McGovern that lasted only 65 performances.

THREE'S A CROWD (1930) was an ironically titled musical revue, for its three stars—CLIFTON WEBB, LIBBY HOLMAN and FRED ALLEN—were reunited from their earlier success in *THE LITTLE SHOW* (1929). Also rejoining them were songwriters HOWARD DIETZ and ARTHUR SCHWARTZ, who provided "Right at the Start of It," "The Moment I Saw You" and "Something to Remember You By." The Johnny Green song "Body and Soul" was interpolated into the show and Holman sang it sensationally. The trio of stars was supported by TAMARA GEVA, Portland Hoffa and Fred MacMurray. Other highlights of the revue were choreographer Albertina Rasch's ballets, Fred Allen's famous monologue as an explorer from Antarctica and director HASSARD SHORT's staging that used some innovative lighting techniques not previously seen on Broadway. (272 performances)

TIP-TOES (1925) was an art deco-styled musical comedy in which GUY BOLTON and Fred Thompson provided the libretto for the GERSHWINS' score, as they had in *LADY, BE GOOD!* (1924). The plot was about three down-and-out vaudevillians stranded in Florida who try to pass off "Tip-Toes" Kaye as an heiress. The George and Ira Gershwin songs included "Looking for a Boy," "These Charming People," "That Certain Feeling" and "Sweet and Low-Down." (194 performances)

JENNIFER TIPTON (1937–   ), a versatile lighting designer of theatre, opera and dance, did the lighting for the Broadway musicals *Rex* (1976), *Happy End* (1977), *Runaways* (1978), *SOPHISTICATED LADIES* (1981), *Jerome Robbins' Broadway* (1989) and others.

MICHAEL TODD (1907–1958), the high-profile impressario who involved himself in many different aspects of show business, produced a half-dozen Broadway musical hits in the 1940s: *Star and Garter* (1942), *SOMETHING FOR THE BOYS* (1943), *MEXICAN HAYRIDE* (1944), *UP IN CENTRAL PARK* (1945) and *As the Girls Go* (1948).

TOO MANY GIRLS (1939) was RODGERS and HART's obligatory college musical and, although the libretto by George Marion, Jr., held few surprises, the show was spirited and ran for 249 performances. At Pottawatomie College in Stop Gap, New Mexico, four football players are paid to spy on a millionaire's daughter. As is always the case in these shows, the big football game is the center of the plot with plenty of romance thrown in. The young and vibrant cast included Hal Le Roy, EDDIE BRACKEN, Marcy Westcott, Desi Arnez and Richard Kollmar under the tight direction of GEORGE ABBOTT. Highlights from the Rodgers and Hart score included "I Didn't Know What Time It Was," "Love Never Went to College," "Spic and Spanish" and "Give It Back to the Indians."

THE TONY AWARDS, Broadway's "Oscars" that are presented annually by the American Theatre Wing, have included musical accomplishments since their first presentation in 1947. Although no category was included for best musical that year, choreographers AGNES DE MILLE and MICHAEL KIDD were honored, as was DAVID WAYNE for his performance in *FINIAN'S RAINBOW*. In 1949 the Tony committee added categories for a musical, composer, lyricist, librettist and producer, all of which were given to COLE PORTER's *KISS ME, KATE* that year. It wasn't until 1956 that there were public announcements of the nominees in all the categories; previously only the winners' names were made public. *DAMN YANKEES* was the big winner in 1956 but the only other musical of note during the lean 1955–1956 season was *PIPE DREAM*. In 1960 there was a tie between *THE SOUND OF MUSIC* and *FIORELLO!* for best musical, so both shows were honored. Between 1949 and 1964, a Tony was given for conductor and musical director, and LEHRMAN ENGEL was the person most often nominated. The Tony Awards were first televised in 1967 and Broadway realized how potent TV was in promoting musicals. *CABARET* was the big winner that year and the broadcast helped secure that musical's success. Over the years, producer-director HAROLD PRINCE has won the most Tony Awards: fifteen, as of 1992. Although winning the Tony for best musical may be considered the ultimate recognition on Broadway, it is worth listing some of the many superb musicals since 1947 that did not win: *WEST SIDE STORY* (1956), *SWEET CHARITY* (1966), *CARNIVAL* (1961), *MISS SAIGON* (1990), *PETER PAN* (1954), *GRAND HOTEL* (1989), *BELLS ARE RINGING* (1956), *SUNDAY IN THE PARK WITH GEORGE* (1984), *THE MOST HAPPY FELLA* (1956), *FOLLIES* (1971), *GYPSY* (1959), *THE SECRET GARDEN* (1991), *WHERE'S CHARLEY?* (1948), *DREAMGIRLS* (1981) and so on.

A TREE GROWS IN BROOKLYN (1951) was a gentle, nostalgic period musical that only had a modest run (270 performances) but it is still fondly remembered for its engaging score. Director GEORGE ABBOTT assisted Betty Smith in adapting her best-selling novel for the musical stage and ARTHUR SCHWARTZ (music) and DOROTHY FIELDS (lyrics) provided the charming character songs and lovely ballads to bring the story to life. Set in turn-of-the-century Brooklyn, the plot centers on Katie Nolan, her devoted love for her alcoholic husband Johnny, their adolescent daughter Frankie and the amiable but pathetic Aunt Cissy. SHIRLEY BOOTH played Cissy with such remarkable comic tenderness that the focus of the original story was offset but there was much to recommend in the show. The Schwartz–Fields score included "I'll Buy You a Star," "Make the Man Love Me," "He Had Refinement," "Look Who's Dancing" and "Love Is the Reason."

EMMA TRENTINI (1885?–1959) was a world-famous opera singer who appeared in a few Broadway and London musicals written particularly for her. The Italian-born Trentini was brought to America by impressario Oscar Hammerstein to sing at his opera house. She created the title role in *NAUGHTY MARIETTA* (1910) and Nina in *THE FIREFLY* (1912).

A TRIP TO CHINATOWN (1891) was a merry, madcap musical comedy that for twenty-eight years held the record for the longest run: 657 performances. The libretto by the successful farcer Charles H. Hoyt is a lively tale about two young couples who enjoy a night on the town. Aside from all the comic shenanigans, audiences were also treated to a delightful score by Percy Gaunt that featured two popular favorites: "Reuben and Cynthia" and "The Bowery." Charles K. Harris' "After the Ball" was later interpolated, just as it would be again into *SHOW BOAT* thirty-seven years later. *A Trip to Chinatown* shares several plot devices with *HELLO, DOLLY!* (1964). In both shows the young lovers are encouraged by a sly widow to run away from a rich merchant. They go to an expensive restaurant in the big city and in both musicals the merchant shows up and in the confusion loses his wallet. *A Trip to Chinatown* was one of the first directing assignments for the prolific JULIAN MITCHELL.

SOPHIE TUCKER (1884–1966), the bold and brassy singer in nightclubs, recordings and stage, claimed to be "the last of the red-hot mamas" and captivated audiences everywhere during her long career. The Russian-born Tucker appeared on Broadway in the *Follies of 1909*, *EARL CARROLL VANITIES* (1924) and other shows. Her best character role was the ambassador's wife, Mrs. Goodhue, in *LEAVE IT TO ME!* (1938). The short-lived musical *Sophie* (1963) was based on her autobiography.

TOMMY TUNE (1939–), the multitalented director, choreographer and performer who became the most prominent new creator of musicals in the 1980s, has a distinctive ability for merging dance and story together in an unconventional but fully satisfying manner. Tune was born in Witchita Falls, Texas, and worked his way to New York to become a dancer on Broadway. He first gained attention with his performance as the dancing David in *SEESAW* (1973), a role he choreographed himself under MICHAEL BENNETT's direction. Tune's first directing assignment was the Off-Broadway *The Club* (1976), a play with music rather than a full-scale musical but it showed all the signs of the dazzling theatrics that would follow. He got to co-direct as well as choreograph *THE BEST LITTLE WHOREHOUSE IN TEXAS* (1978) on Broadway and the Tommy Tune style emerged fully. *A Day in Hollywood/A Night in the Ukraine* (1980) followed and, although it was on a smaller scale, Tune's direction and choreography (with Thommie Walsh) was memorable. Even more startling was his highly stylized staging of *NINE* (1982), which won further awards and plaudits. Always a performer at heart, Tune was contracted only to appear in *MY ONE AND ONLY* (1983) but, during the out-of-town difficulties, the original director was fired and Tune ended up directing and, with Walsh again, choreographing the hit musical. *GRAND HOTEL* (1989), arguably Tune's greatest accomplishment to date, brought his ideas of movement and story together in a high-concept musical in which dance and music were continuous, yet the show was not at all like opera or the British sung-through works. *THE*

WILL ROGERS FOLLIES (1991) was another award-winning success for Tune but the libretto and concept were lame and only in the dance numbers did the director-choreographer's ingenuity shine. Tune is the most potent "auteur" director in the American musical today and one whose work combines high craftsmanship with inventive ideas.

JONATHAN TUNICK (1938–), an ingenious orchestrator of Broadway musicals, has been associated with several STEPHEN SONDHEIM musicals, including *COMPANY* (1970), *FOLLIES* (1971), *A LITTLE NIGHT MUSIC* (1973), *SWEENEY TODD* (1979) and *INTO THE WOODS* (1987). Tunick has also orchestrated *PROMISES, PROMISES* (1968), *A CHORUS LINE* (1975), *NINE* (1982) and other musicals, as well as several films.

TWO BY TWO (1970) was an anxiously awaited musical by RICHARD RODGERS because it marked DANNY KAYE's return to Broadway after nearly three decades in Hollywood. The libretto, by PETER STONE, was based on Clifford Odets' sentimental comedy *The Flowering Peach* (1954) about biblical Noah and his family. Kaye's clowning kept things lively and he had a fine supporting cast with Joan Copeland, Harry Goz, MADELINE KAHN, Walter Willison and MARILYN COOPER. Rodgers' music was serviceable but MARTIN CHARNIN's lyrics were inferior; the score boasted one lovely ballad, though, called "I Do Not Know a Day I Did Not Love You." Critics roasted *Two by Two* but Kaye's ad-libbing and, after he broke his leg, cavorting in a wheelchair kept the audiences happy for 352 performances.

TWO GENTLEMEN OF VERONA (1971), a clever if substandard musical version of the dark Shakespearean comedy, was so successful at the outdoor NEW YORK SHAKESPEARE FESTIVAL that producer JOSEPH PAPP brought it to Broadway where it ran for 627 performances. John Guare and Mel Shapiro did the adaptation, which turned Milan and Verona into contemporary New York City with many ethnic and political anachronisms. GALT MACDERMOT wrote some agreeable music for the show but Guare's second-rate lyrics only came to life when a phrase or a whole passage from the Bard was used. RAUL JULIA, Clifton Davis, Diana Davila and Jonelle Allen led the talented multi-racial cast and Shapiro directed.

TWO ON THE AISLE (1951) was a spirited musical revue that marked the first of nine collaborations between composer JULE STYNE and lyricists BETTY COMDEN and ADOLPH GREEN. BERT LAHR was the star of the revue and in the Comden–Green sketches he played a confused baseballer, a neurotic Central Park street sweeper and Queen Victoria. DOLORES GRAY got to introduce the two best songs in the revue, "Give a Little, Get a Little Love" and "If You Hadn't, But You Did," in which she outlined all the reasons why she bumped off her husband. (281 performances)

U

PETER UDELL (1934–) is a lyricist-librettist who works exclusively with composer GARY GELD. The team's first Broadway venture was the rousing *PURLIE* (1970), which was popular enough to return to Broadway in 1972. Less effective but just as popular was Udell and Geld's *SHENANDOAH* (1975). There was quality work in the team's *Angel* (1978), based on Thomas Wolfe's *Look Homeward, Angel*, but it failed to run. Neither did *Comin' Uptown* (1979) and *The Amen Corner* (1983), two musicals that tried to capture the vibrant black idiom as *Purlie* had. The Udell–Geld musicals tend toward the rural and sentimental but at their best are lively and compassionate.

LESLIE UGGAMS (1943–), a vivacious black singer on television and in nightclubs, played the eager heroine Georgina in *HALLELUJAH, BABY!* (1967), Cleopatra in the short-lived musical *Her First Roman* (1968) and was featured in *Blues in the Night* (1982) and *Jerry's Girls* (1985).

THE UNSINKABLE MOLLY BROWN (1960) was a lavish musical comedy with an almost epic story that moved from the mountains of Colorado to the high life of European society. Richard Morris wrote the libretto inspired by the legendary title character, a backwoods girl who marries a prospector, makes a fortune or two, tries to crash Denver's elite society, captivates Europe, proves a hero at the sinking of the *Titanic* and gets her man. MEREDITH WILLSON wrote the agreeable songs and TAMMY GRIMES lit up Broadway with her sparkling performance as Molly. Also in the cast were Harve Presnell and Cameron Prud'homme, directed by Dore Schary and choreographed by

PETER GENNARO. "I Ain't Down Yet" and "Belly Up to the Bar, Boys" were the show's most jubilant numbers and there was the lovely ballad "I'll Never Say No." (532 performances)

UP IN CENTRAL PARK (1945) was composer SIGMUND ROMBERG's last hit, written decades after the golden age of American operetta. DOROTHY and HERBERT FIELDS provided an atmospheric libretto about a newspaper reporter trying to expose political racketeer Boss Tweed in 1870s New York City. The show had a Currier and Ives look to it and an ice skating number in Central Park staged by HELEN TAMIRIS was the highlight of the evening. Romberg's music departed somewhat from the operetta style but songs (with lyrics by Dorothy Fields) such as "Close as Pages in a Book" and "April Snow" had an old-style charm about them. (504 performances)

JOSEPH URBAN (1872–1933), the renowned theatre architect, scenic designer and illustrator, is mostly remembered for his outstanding designs for the *ZIEGFELD FOLLIES* and the original *SHOW BOAT* (1927). Born in Vienna and trained in architecture at the Art Academy there, Urban won several design awards and built a palace and the Czar Bridge in his native city. He came to America in 1901 to design the Austrian Pavilion at the 1904 St. Louis World's Fair and was invited back by the Boston Opera Company on several occasions. His Broadway debut was in 1915 when FLORENZ ZIEGFELD hired Urban to design that season's *Follies* and he would subsequently provide decor for several other editions over the years, as well as designing the Ziegfeld Theatre. Other Broadway musical credits included *SALLY* (1920), *Song of the Flame* (1925), *RIO RITA* (1927), *ROSALIE* (1928), *WHOOPEE* (1928), *FLYING HIGH* (1930) and *MUSIC IN THE AIR* (1932).

V

THE VAGABOND KING (1925), arguably composer RUDOLF FRIML's finest score, was an operetta based on the popular 1901 melodrama *If I Were King*. DENNIS KING starred as the dashing French outlaw François Villon, who replaces King Louis XI for a day, saves the crown and the city of Paris and wins the love of a beautiful aristocrat at court. Brian Hooker provided the lyrics and, with W. H. Post, the libretto for the operetta that ran 511 performances. Highlights from the lush score include "Song of the Vagabonds," "Love Me Tonight," "Some Day," "Love for Sale" and "Only a Rose."

RUDY VALLEE (1901–1986), the bandleader and singing idol of the 1920s and 1930s, appeared in editions of *GEORGE WHITE'S SCANDALS* in 1931 and 1935. Valle returned to Broadway twenty-six years later and originated the role of corporate chief J. B. Biggley in *HOW TO SUCCEED IN BUSINESS WITHOUT REALLY TRYING* (1961).

BOBBY VAN (1930–1980), a dancing-singing leading man, was seen as the high-stepping Billy in the 1971 revival of *NO, NO, NANETTE* as well as in *Alive and Kicking* (1950), the 1954 revival of *ON YOUR TOES* and *Doctor Jazz* (1975).

VIVIAN VANCE (1913–1979), the popular television actress, was featured in Broadway musicals in the 1930s and 1940s. Vance made her debut in *ANYTHING GOES* (1934) and appeared in *RED, HOT AND BLUE!* (1936), *HOORAY FOR WHAT!* (1937), *LET'S FACE IT!* (1941) and other shows.

VERA-ELLEN (1926–1987), an actress-dancer of several 1940s movie musicals, made her theatre debut in *The Grand Street Follies* (1925) and was featured in the Broadway musicals *AT HOME ABROAD* (1935) and *THE SHOW IS ON* (1936).

GWEN VERDON (1926–) is post-war Broadway's most acclaimed dancer-actress. Verdon made her Broadway debut in *Alive and Kicking* (1950) but gained stardom for her high-kicking Claudine in *CAN-CAN* (1953). She went on to play a series of flamboyant characters with hearts of gold: the devil's assistant Lola in *DAMN YANKEES* (1955), the ex-prostitute Anna Christie in *NEW GIRL IN TOWN* (1957), the sleuth-like Essie in *REDHEAD* (1959), the indomitable Charity Hope Valentine in *SWEET CHARITY* (1966) and the crafty Roxie Hart in *CHICAGO* (1975). All of Verdon's shows were tailored to her vibrant dancing talents and most of them were directed and choreographed by BOB FOSSE.

BEN VEREEN (1946–), a high-powered black dancer-actor-singer, created two memorable musical roles on Broadway: Judas in *JESUS CHRIST SUPERSTAR* (1971) and the hypnotic Leading Player in *PIPPIN* (1972). His most recent Broadway musical was *Grind* (1985).

VERY GOOD EDDIE (1915) was the second of the PRINCESS THEATRE MUSICALS and the first to fulfill the goal of the series to present literate, modern musical comedies on an intimate scale. The delightful GUY BOLTON–Philip Bartholomae plot concerns two honeymooning couples aboard a Hudson River cruise ship who realize that they love the other's spouse. The score had music by JEROME KERN and lyrics by Schuyler Greene and others. "Babes in the Woods," "Some Sort of Somebody," "Isn't It Great to Be Married?" and "If I Find the Girl" were among the musical numbers that charmed audiences for 341 performances. In 1975 *Very Good Eddie* was revived at the GOODSPEED OPERA HOUSE and on Broadway where it ran for 304 performances.

VERY WARM FOR MAY (1939) was a short-lived musical remembered today as being JEROME KERN's final Broadway show and for its enchanting score, particularly the song "All the Things You Are." OSCAR HAMMERSTEIN II provided the lyrics and libretto about a daughter of vaudevillians who, instead of going off to college, runs away to a summer theatre where she gets a part onstage and falls in love with the son of the theatre owners. The cast included JACK WHITING, EVE ARDEN, Grace MacDonald and HIRAM SHERMAN. VINCENTE MINNELLI designed the sets and costumes and directed the show. *Very Warm for May* only ran for fifty-nine performances and Kern went back to Hollywood, never to return to Broadway again.

VIRGINIA VESTOFF (1940–1982), a leading lady in Broadway musicals and plays, is most remembered for creating the role of Abigail Adams in *1776* (1969). Vestoff's other musical credits included *IRMA LA DOUCE* (1960), *Baker Street* (1965), *MAN WITH A LOAD OF MISCHIEF* (1966) and *Via Galactica* (1972).

W

ROBIN WAGNER (1933–   ) is the ingenious scenic designer who has done the sets for many of the finest Broadway musicals of the past twenty-five years. Some of his unforgettable designs include the mirrored set for *A CHORUS LINE* (1975), the clever train locales for *ON THE TWENTIETH CENTURY* (1978), the dazzling decor for *42ND STREET* (1980), the stream-lined designs for *DREAMGIRLS* (1987) and the dual color/black and white sets for *CITY OF ANGELS* (1989). Wagner's other musical credits include *HAIR* (1968), *PROMISES, PROMISES* (1968), *JESUS CHRIST SUPERSTAR* (1971), *MACK AND MABEL* (1974), *Ballroom* (1978), *Chess* (1989) and *JELLY'S LAST JAM* (1992).

DON WALKER (1907–   ), one of Broadway's most renowned orchestrators, did the music for such distinguished musicals as *FINIAN'S RAINBOW* (1947), *THE PAJAMA GAME* (1954), *THE MUSIC MAN* (1957), *SHE LOVES ME* (1963), *FIDDLER ON THE ROOF* (1964), *CABARET* (1966), *SHENAN-DOAH* (1975) and many others.

NANCY WALKER (1921–1992) was an accomplished comedienne who shone in musicals and plays and on television. The diminutive actress made a memorable Broadway debut as the Blind Date in *BEST FOOT FORWARD* (1941) and topped it with her hilarious taxi driver Brunhilde Esterhazy in *ON THE TOWN* (1944). Walker's other Broadway musical credits included Lily Malloy in *Look, Ma, I'm Dancin'* (1948), *Copper and Brass* (1957), *The Girls Against the Boys* (1959) and the adventurous housewife Kay Cram in *DO RE MI* (1960).

RAY WALSTON (1918–), a character actor on Broadway, in films and on television, is most remembered for playing the devil Applegate in *DAMN YANKEES* (1955). Walston's other musical credits include *ME AND JULIET* (1953) and *HOUSE OF FLOWERS* (1954).

CHARLES WALTERS (1911–1982), an actor-dancer who later became a choreographer, had featured roles in several musicals, including *JUBILEE* (1935), *THE SHOW IS ON* (1936), *BETWEEN THE DEVIL* (1937), *I MARRIED AN ANGEL* (1938) and *DuBARRY WAS A LADY* (1939). Walters choreographed *Sing Out the News* (1938), *LET'S FACE IT!* (1941), *ST. LOUIS WOMAN* (1946) and other shows.

TONY WALTON (1934–), the British-born scenic and costume designer of theatre and film, has provided sets for some of the American theatre's most renowned musicals of the last thirty years. Among his most memorable designs were the stylized medieval sets for *PIPPIN* (1972), the art deco design for *CHICAGO* (1975) and the expressionistic *GRAND HOTEL* (1989). Walton's other musical credits include *A FUNNY THING HAPPENED ON THE WAY TO THE FORUM* (1962), *THE APPLE TREE* (1966), *THE ACT* (1977), *SOPHISTICATED LADIES* (1981), *Leader of the Pack* (1985) and others.

WANG (1891) was a comic opera set in Siam, a sort of American answer to Gilbert and Sullivan's *The Mikado*. J. Cheever Goodwin wrote the libretto and lyrics and Woolson Morse provided the music for this strangely popular show. The plot involved the powerful regent of Siam, a prince in love with a foreigner and the French consul's widow who had enough daughters to provide the musical's chorus line. Two songs from *Wang*, "A Pretty Girl" and "Ask the Man in the Moon," were widely known at the time and the beloved comic actor DEWOLF HOPPER thrilled audiences as the conniving regent Wang. So widespread was *Wang*'s appeal that forty years later when the real king of Siam visited America he asked to hear songs from the musical. (151 performances)

WATCH YOUR STEP (1914) was a milestone on three fronts: It introduced ragtime to the musical stage, it contained IRVING BERLIN's first complete Broadway score and it was the final appearance by VERNON and IRENE CASTLE together. The show had a silly story ("plot, if any, by HARRY B. SMITH," the program read) about a millionaire who bequeaths a fortune on any male relative who has never fallen in love. The score featured several variations on ragtime and plenty of opportunities for the dancing Castles but the only songs known today are "The Syncopated Walk" and "Play a Simple Melody." (175 performances)

ETHEL WATERS (1896?-1977), the splendid black actress and blues singer, had a remarkable career on stage, in films and nightclubs and in concert. She also appeared in five Broadway musical revues, starting with *Africana* (1927).

Waters introduced several song standards in *Rhapsody in Black* (1931), *AS THOUSANDS CHEER* (1933) and *AT HOME ABROAD* (1935), the last revue being the first where a black artist was starred with a racially mixed cast. Her one book musical was *CABIN IN THE SKY* (1940), in which she played Petunia Jackson and introduced "Taking a Chance on Love."

SUSAN WATSON (1938–), a bright musical ingenue in the 1960s, played the wholesome teenager Kim McAfee in *BYE BYE BIRDIE* (1960), the ambitious Angel in *CELEBRATION* (1969) and the naive Nanette in the 1971 revival of *NO, NO, NANETTE*. Watson's other musical credits include Luisa in the original 1959 one-act version of *THE FANTASTICKS*, the 1959 revival of *LEND AN EAR*, *CARNIVAL* (1961), *Ben Franklin in Paris* (1964) and *A Joyful Noise* (1966).

NED WAYBURN (1874–1942) was a prolific director and choreographer on Broadway and in London who staged many musical revues, including six editions of the *ZIEGFELD FOLLIES* between 1916 and 1923. Wayburn's other credits included *The Belle of Broadway* (1902), *The Ham Tree* (1905), *The Midnight Sons* (1909), *The Yankee Girl* (1910), *Broadway to Paris* (1912), *The Honeymoon Express* (1913), *The Century Girl* (1916), *Miss 1917* (1917), *Hitchy-Koo* (1920), *Two Little Girls in Blue* (1921) and *Smiles* (1930).

DAVID WAYNE (1914–), the versatile character actor of films, television and the stage, brightened up a handful of Broadway musicals from 1943 to 1968. Wayne's most memorable performance was as Og, the amorous leprechaun, in *FINIAN'S RAINBOW* (1947). His other musical credits include *Park Avenue* (1946), *Say, Darling* (1958), *The Yearling* (1965), Cap'n Andy in the 1966 revival of *SHOW BOAT* and as Grandpere Bonnard in *THE HAPPY TIME* (1968).

CLIFTON WEBB (1891–1966), the elegant film star of the 1950s and 1960s, had a long and successful career as a leading man in Broadway musicals before going to Hollywood. Webb made his debut in *The Purple Road* (1913) and appeared in several musicals before gaining attention in *SUNNY* (1925). His finest stage performances were in the musical revues *THE LITTLE SHOW* (1929), *THREE'S A CROWD* (1930), *FLYING COLORS* (1932) and *AS THOUSANDS CHEER* (1933). Webb's final Broadway musical performance was as Gaston in *You Never Know* (1938).

ANDREW LLOYD WEBBER (1948–), the phenomenally successful British composer, does not write for Broadway directly but his London musicals that have transferred to New York have had a major influence on the American musical theatre. The Webber shows that have appeared on Broadway are: *JESUS CHRIST SUPERSTAR* (1971), *EVITA* (1979), *JOSEPH AND THE AMAZING TECHNICOLOR DREAMCOAT* (1981), all written with lyricist

TIM RICE; and *CATS* (1982), *Song and Dance* (1985), *Starlight Express* (1987), *THE PHANTOM OF THE OPERA* (1988) and *Aspects of Love* (1990).

JOE WEBER (1867–1942), an actor and later a producer-director, was the shorter and rounder half of Weber and Fields, the stars of a series of musical burlesques and the most popular stage comics at the turn of the century. Weber teamed up with LEW FIELDS in the 1880s and they became so successful that they bought their own theatre in 1896, where they produced their antic musical comedies for eight years. The Weber and Fields shows parodied well-known plays of the day so they are unproducible today but the titles reveal their satirical tone: *The Art of Maryland, Hoity Toity, The Merry Widow Burlesque, Fiddle-Dee-Dee, Cyranose de Bricabrac* and so on. The two comics always played the same character types, Dutch immigrants with vulgar check suits and exaggerated whiskers. Weber's recurring characters included Herr Weinschoppen, Michael Schmaltz and Herman Dillpickle. The team broke up in 1904 and, except for a few onstage reunions, Weber concentrated on producing shows on his own.

ROBERT WEEDE (1903–1972) was an opera singer who gave a moving portrayal of vineyard owner Tony in the original *THE MOST HAPPY FELLA* (1956). Weede's other Broadway musical credits were the American tourist Phil Arkin in *MILK AND HONEY* (1961) and politician Edward Quinn in *Cry for Us All* (1970).

JEROME WEIDMAN (1913–), a novelist who wrote the librettos for a handful of Broadway musicals, co-authored *FIORELLO!* (1959) and *TENDERLOIN* (1960) with GEORGE ABBOTT, as well as *I CAN GET IT FOR YOU WHOLESALE* (1962) and *Pousse-Cafe* (1966).

JOHN WEIDMAN (1946–), a television and magazine writer, wrote the librettos for two of STEPHEN SONDHEIM's most adventurous musicals, *PACIFIC OVERTURES* (1976) and *ASSASSINS* (1990). Weidman also helped revise the libretto for the 1987 Broadway revival of *ANYTHING GOES*.

KURT WEILL (1900–1950), one of the musical theatre's most passionate and ambitious composers, came to America as a seasoned creator of opera and music–drama. But few men have involved themselves in the American spirit as Weill did and his eight New York musicals are pure Broadway even though each one challenges the image of the frivolous Great White Way. Weill was born in Germany and, proving to be a child prodigy, studied music in Berlin under Humperdinck. Soon he was composing opera, ballets and, with playwright-lyricist Bertolt Brecht, powerful music–drama pieces. *THE THREE-PENNY OPERA* (1928) and *Mahogany* (1930) brought Weill and Brecht renown throughout Europe but also put them in disfavor with the rising Nazi party. Weill fled Germany in 1933 and stayed in Paris where he wrote *Marie*

Galante with French playwright Jacques Deval and the ballet "The Seven Deadly Sins" with fellow ex-patriot Brecht. Weill emigrated to America in 1935 and immediately saw the Broadway stage as a place where music, drama and expansive ideas could find a popular audience. His first Broadway musical was *JOHNNY JOHNSON* (1936), a potent anti-war piece written with Paul Green. It was greatly admired but not very popular. *KNICKERBOCKER HOLIDAY* (1938), written with playwright MAXWELL ANDERSON, was more satiric than caustic and it was a bit more successful. *LADY IN THE DARK* (1941) united Weill with librettist MOSS HART and lyricist IRA GERSHWIN and the result was a revolutionary experiment in mixing music and character. Poet Ogden Nash provided the lyrics for *ONE TOUCH OF VENUS* (1943) and Weill wrote delightfully droll music to compliment them. *The Firebrand of Florence* (1945), with Gershwin again, was a misguided failure. Weill's last three musicals were perhaps his most ambitious: *STREET SCENE* (1947), *LOVE LIFE* (1948) and *LOST IN THE STARS* (1949). Each was a bold attempt to push the parameters of the Broadway musical further than previously seen but each would only be fully appreciated after Weill's death in 1950. *The Three-penny Opera* had been produced on Broadway in 1933, before Weill came to America, and it was a quick failure. But a new translation-adaptation by MARC BLITZSTEIN opened Off Broadway in 1955 and ran for 2,611 performances. There is a distinct quality to all of Weill's music: It is hypnotic, exotic and yet engaging. Much of his work was ahead of its time but much of it has found continued life in theatres and opera companies around the world.

WEST SIDE STORY (1957) remains one of the musical theatre's perennial successes but it is often forgotten how bold and unique a work it was for 1950s audiences. Rarely had a musical attempted a story so unrelentlessly tragic, never had dance taken on such an emotional impact and tried to convey frustration as well as joy, and how extraordinary it was to hear a score that embraced both operatic loftiness and crude street talk. The idea for *West Side Story* was JEROME ROBBINS', who envisioned a modern *Romeo and Juliet* set amidst feuding Catholic and Jewish families. By the time the concept came to fruition, the tale was changed to the more recent and relevent rivalry between Puerto Rican immigrants and "American" street gangs in New York. LEONARD BERNSTEIN was slated to write the lyrics as well as the music but as the project grew in scope and more and more dance music was needed, the young STEPHEN SONDHEIM was asked to provide the lyrics. LARRY KERT and CAROL LAWRENCE played Tony and Maria, the lovers caught between the two feuding gangs, and CHITA RIVERA was Anita, the heroine's friend who acts as both go-between and catalyst in the action. ARTHUR LAURENTS' libretto was pure melodrama but in such a contemporary, fearless way that the story still plays powerfully on stage. The score utilized Latin rhythms, jazz, traditional ballads and even operatic devices as in the brilliant "Tonight" quintet. Also from the musical was "Maria," "America," "Something's Coming," "Cool," "I Feel Pretty," "Somewhere," "Gee, Officer Krupke" and "A Boy Like That/I Have a Love." Robbins directed and, with PETER GENNARO, choreographed *West Side Story*, giving the musical a ballet reality that didn't jar with the modern, anti-romantic setting. Dance, for example, heightened the tension and actually punctuated the authenticity of the situation. *West Side Story*, like *SHOW BOAT* (1927) and *OKLAHOMA!* (1943) before it, was a landmark piece that revealed new possibilities for the musical theatre and presented exciting ways to pursue those possibilities. (734 performances)

ROBERT WESTENBERG (1953–), an actor-singer in Broadway musicals, played Nikos in the 1983 revival of *ZORBA* and went on to a featured role in *SUNDAY IN THE PARK WITH GEORGE* (playing George later in the run) in 1984, the Wolf and Prince Charming in *INTO THE WOODS* (1987) and the cold-hearted Dr. Craven in *THE SECRET GARDEN* (1991).

WHAT MAKES SAMMY RUN? (1964) was a tough-as-nails musical about the cutthroat movie business. Budd and Stuart Schulberg wrote the libretto about the unscrupulous Sammy Glick (Steve Lawrence) who works his way to the top by taking up with and dropping the necessary women. Movie songwriter Erwin Drake wrote the score, which had two hit songs, "A Room without Windows" and "My Hometown." (540 performances)

HUGH WHEELER (1916–1987), the British-born playwright and screenwriter who wrote the librettos for a half-dozen Broadway shows, is best remembered for his musicals with STEPHEN SONDHEIM and HAROLD PRINCE: *A LITTLE NIGHT MUSIC* (1973), *SWEENEY TODD* (1979) and, with JOHN WEIDMAN, *PACIFIC OVERTURES* (1976). Wheeler also wrote the libretto for the 1974 revival of *CANDIDE*, the first successful production of that much-loved comic operetta. He co-authored the revised book for the 1973 revival of *IRENE* and adapted the film *Meet Me in St. Louis* into the stage version, which opened on Broadway in 1989, two years after his death.

WHERE'S CHARLEY? (1948) was the first book musical by FRANK LOESSER and it gave RAY BOLGER the stage role of his career. GEORGE ABBOTT adapted Brandon Thomas' British farce *Charley's Aunt*, retaining the original's delightful plot complications and making room for several delectable songs. "My Darling, My Darling," "Make a Miracle," "The New Ashmoleon Marching Society and Students' Conservatory Band" and "Once in Love with Amy" were standouts in a consistently pleasing score. The last became so popular that later in the run Bolger entreated the audience each evening to join him in singing it. Abbott directed, GEORGE BALANCHINE choreographed and *Where's Charley?* ran a happy 792 performances.

GEORGE WHITE (1890–1968), the producer of lavish Broadway revues that came closest to rivaling FLORENZ ZIEGFELD's shows, was also an accomplished director, dancer, sketch writer, actor and producer of Hollywood movies. *GEORGE WHITE'S SCANDALS* premiered in 1919 and there were annual editions each year until 1926 with subsequent versions in 1928, 1929, 1931, 1935 and 1939. White appeared as a dancer in a few Broadway musicals in the 1910s and later danced in some of his own shows. Unlike Ziegfeld, he personally directed all the *Scandals* as well as the popular *Manhattan Mary* (1927) and *FLYING HIGH* (1930).

MILES WHITE (1920?–), a prolific costume designer who did his first Broadway show at the age of eighteen, provided costumes for over two dozen Broadway musicals as well as for circuses and ice shows. White's most famous musicals include *OKLAHOMA!* (1943), *CAROUSEL (1945), HIGH BUTTON SHOES* (1947), *GENTLEMEN PREFER BLONDES* (1949), *JAMAICA* (1957), *TAKE ME ALONG* (1959), *BYE BYE BIRDIE* (1960) and *THE UNSINKABLE MOLLY BROWN* (1960).

ONNA WHITE has choreographed several Broadway musicals as well as films. Starting out as a dancer, White appeared in the original productions of *FINIAN'S RAINBOW* (1947), *GUYS AND DOLLS* (1950), *SILK STOCKINGS* (1955) and other shows. She came into prominence with her choreography for *THE MUSIC MAN* (1957) and went on to choreograph such Broadway successes as *IRMA LA DOUCE* (1960), *HALF A SIXPENCE* (1965), *MAME* (1966), *1776* (1969), *I LOVE MY WIFE* (1977) and others.

JACK WHITING (1901–1961), a smiling singer-dancer, played musical juveniles for many years on Broadway and in London. Whiting made his Broadway debut in the 1922 *ZIEGFELD FOLLIES* and went on to play the young lover in *The Ramblers* (1926), as well as in *HOLD EVERYTHING!* (1928), *Heads Up!* (1929), *TAKE A CHANCE* (1932), *HOORAY FOR WHAT!* (1937), *VERY WARM FOR MAY* (1939), *Hold on to Your Hats* (1940), and others. In his later career he played character roles in musicals such as the 1946 revival of *THE RED MILL*, *Hazel Flagg* (1953) and *THE GOLDEN APPLE* (1954).

WHOOPEE (1928) was a zany musical comedy built around the many talents of comedian EDDIE CANTOR. The plot, by William Anthony McGuire, was about a hypochondriac who flees to California for health reasons only to get involved with Indians, a girl on the run from an amorous sheriff and other Wild West antics. Highlights in the score by Walter Donaldson (music) and Gus Kahn (lyrics) were Cantor's rendition of "Makin' Whoopee" and RUTH ETTING's version of "Love Me or Leave Me." Both performers would be identified with the songs for the rest of their careers. (379 performances)

WILDCAT (1960) was a vehicle for television star LUCILLE BALL and the musical only ran as long as she was in it. The N. Richard Nash libretto was set in an oil drilling town in 1912 where the con artist Wildcat Jackson (Ball) arrives and tries to pull a fast one on the locals. The highlight of the show was a hoe-down number called "What Takes My Fancy" choreographed by MICHAEL KIDD but another song in the score by CY COLEMAN (music) and CAROLYN LEIGH (lyrics) titled "Hey, Look Me Over" later became well known. (171 performances)

THE WILL ROGERS FOLLIES (1991) was a popular musical biography that made little pretense of being an accurate account of the famous stage-screen-radio personality. The libretto by PETER STONE, subtitled "a life in revue," used the premise that showman FLORENZ ZIEGFELD was producing his version of Rogers' career so there were no apologies for lavish production numbers and unmotivated songs and specialty acts. Director-choreographer TOMMY TUNE kept the whole superficial affair moving with a fast, light and luscious touch. Keith Carradine was an engaging, affable Rogers with no attempt to mimic or physically resemble the familiar celebrity and he received strong support from Dee Hoty, Cady Huffman and Dick Latessa in thankless roles. CY COLEMAN (music) and BETTY COMDEN and ADOLPH GREEN (lyrics) provided the appealing if unmemorable score that featured "Willomania," "Our Favorite Son," "Give a Man Enough Rope" and "My Big Mistake." TONY WALTON designed the clever scenery, JULES FISHER came up with some unique lighting effects and WILLA KIM's costumes were alternately lavish and witty. (still running as of 3/1/93)

BERT WILLIAMS (1874?–1922) was a brilliant comic and singer who was the first black performer to star in Broadway shows, most notably eight editions of the *ZIEGFELD FOLLIES* between 1910 and 1919. Williams' trademark was a shuffling gentleman hobo who sang "Nobody" with bittersweet pathos. He began in vaudeville with his partner George W. Walker and together they appeared on Broadway in the landmark musical *IN DAHOMEY* (1903). Williams' other musical credits included *Abyssinia* (1906), *Bandanna Land* (1908) and *Broadway Brevities* (1920).

MEREDITH WILLSON (1902–1984), the composer-lyricist who wrote *THE MUSIC MAN* (1957), began his theatre career late in life but he was a veteran musician and composer by the time of his Broadway debut. Willson's background was the same as that of his most famous work. He was born in Mason City, Iowa, where his mother was the local piano teacher and he took music lessons as a boy and played in the civic band. After studying music at Juilliard, Willson played in John Philip Sousa's band and by 1924 was a member of the New York Philharmonic under Toscanini. He later became the music director at ABC and conducted on several popular radio shows. Willson wrote the libretto (with Franklin Lacey), music and lyrics for *The Music Man* and it launched his new career. He followed it with the less accomplished *THE UNSINKABLE MOLLY BROWN* (1960) and the disappointing *HERE'S LOVE* (1963). Willson's remarkable talent for sentimental yet sly characters, highly rhythmic music and mesmerizing lyrics make his work distinctive and, in the case of *The Music Man*, unforgettably unique.

DOOLEY WILSON (1894–1953), a black singer and musician on stage, in nightclubs and on film, played Little Joe Jackson in *CABIN IN THE SKY* (1940) and sang "The Eagle and Me" in *BLOOMER GIRL* (1944).

CHARLES WINNINGER (1884–1969) was a roly-poly comic actor of stage and film who appeared in some two dozen Broadway musicals. Winninger's most notable roles were the philandering Jimmy Smith in the original *NO, NO, NANETTE* (1925) and Cap'n Andy of the *Cotton Blossom* in *SHOW BOAT* (1927). He also appeared in editions of *The Cohan Revue*, the *ZIEGFELD FOLLIES* and book musicals such as *The Yankee Girl* (1910), *The Wall Street Girl* (1912), *Oh, Please!* (1926) and *REVENGE WITH MUSIC* (1934). Winninger returned to Broadway after a long absence to appear in the 1951 revival of *MUSIC IN THE AIR*.

WISH YOU WERE HERE (1952) was composer-lyricist HAROLD ROME's first book musical and, despite a lackluster libretto by Arthur Kober and JOSHUA LOGAN, it managed to please audiences for 598 performances. The story, based on Kober's play *Having Wonderful Time* (1937), was about the romantic entanglements at Camp Karefree, a Jewish summer camp for adults in the Catskills. Logan directed and choreographed, with the help of JEROME ROBBINS, and the large production even had a real swimming pool built into the stage. Patricia Marand, JACK CASSIDY, Sheila Bond, FLORENCE HENDERSON, LARRY BLYDEN, PHYLLIS NEWMAN, Harry Clark and REID SHELTON were featured in the cast. Rome's score included "Where Did the Night Go?" "Social Director," "Don Jose of Far Rockaway" and the best-selling title song.

FREDDY WITTOP (1921–), a dancer-turned-costume designer, did the distinctive costumes for *CARNIVAL* (1961), *SUBWAYS ARE FOR SLEEPING* (1961), *HELLO, DOLLY!* (1964), *ON A CLEAR DAY YOU CAN SEE FOREVER* (1965), *GEORGE M!* (1968), *DEAR WORLD* (1969) and other musicals.

THE WIZ (1975) was a clever, hip retelling of *The Wizard of Oz* in terms of contemporary black culture. William F. Brown wrote the libretto that retained the structure of the original but took a modern viewpoint toward the tale. The songs by Charlie Smalls were jubilant enough to let audiences temporarily forget the wonderful 1939 film score. "Ease on Down the Road," "Don't Nobody Bring Me No Bad News" and "Everybody Rejoice" may have been lyrically dull but the music was contagiously joyous. There were also three lovely character songs: "Be a Lion," "If You Believe" and "Home." *The Wiz* had a shaky out-of-town tryout, during which director Gilbert Moses was replaced by GEOFFREY HOLDER, who also designed the wonderous costumes. The cast was first-rate all around with Stephanie Mills as Dorothy, TIGER HAYNES as the Tinman, HINTON BATTLE as the Scarecrow, Ted Ross as the Lion, ANDRE DE SHIELDS as the Wizard, and Mabel King, Clarice Taylor and Dee Dee Bridgewater. Producer Ken Harper considered closing the show after opening night but critical and audience reaction was unanimous and *The Wiz* ran for 1,672 performances.

THE WIZARD OF OZ (1903) differed considerably from the original L. Frank Baum stories and barely resembled the 1939 film classic but it was the most successful musical of the 1902–1903 season and an audience favorite for years. Baum himself wrote the lyrics and libretto, and Paul Tietjens and A. Baldwin Sloane provided the music. But the real attractions of the show were the two vaudeville comics DAVID MONTGOMERY and FRED STONE making their legitimate stage debut as the Tin Woodsman and the Scarecrow. (The lion was a very minor character in this version.) Director-choreographer JULIAN MITCHELL's staging of the tornado was the talk of the town and the show ran an impressive 293 performances. Although the HAROLD ARLEN–E. Y. HARBURG-scored film version has been staged on occasion, Broadway would not see the Baum story musicalized again until *THE WIZ* in 1975.

P. G. WODEHOUSE (1881–1975), the lyricist and librettist who only spent a small portion of his long writing career in the musical theatre, greatly influenced the sound and shape of the Broadway musical. During his ninety-three years, Wodehouse (who was nicknamed "Plum" all his life) wrote ninety-six novels, over three hundred short stories, sixteen non-musical plays, as well as film scripts and essays. Somehow he found time to write the lyrics and/or librettos for twenty-two Broadway and London musicals as well. Wodehouse was born in Guildford, England, and pursued a banking career until his writing started to appear in print. By the age of twenty-four he had twenty novels to his name and he yearned for a career in America. Arriving in New York in 1915 he saw *VERY GOOD EDDIE* and was intrigued by the concept of the PRINCESS THEATRE MUSICALS. Wodehouse joined librettist GUY BOLTON and composer JEROME KERN to form the most influential trio of collaborators the American musical has ever seen. The team's *Have a Heart* (1917), *OH, BOY!* (1917), *LEAVE IT TO JANE* (1917) and *OH, LADY! LADY!* (1918) were witty, sophisticated musicals that helped define the style and attitude of Broadway musical comedy. The trio disbanded in 1918 to pursue individual careers but reunited in 1924 for the delightful *Sitting Pretty*. Wodehouse became disillusioned with the lack of control writers had in the musical theatre and after 1934 he concentrated on his novels and non-musical plays. His last musical contribution was as co-author of the libretto for *ANYTHING GOES* (1934). Wodehouse's most consequential work for the American musical was done between 1917 and 1928 but during that time he brought a charm and intelligence to lyricwriting that was unheard of on the Broadway stage. The lyrics of COLE PORTER, IRA GERSHWIN and LORENZ HART during the 1930s would be rooted in Wodehouse's work and all three men publicly acknowledged Plum as their idol and inspiration.

WOMAN OF THE YEAR (1981) was ostensibly a musical version of the celebrated 1942 film of the same name but in reality it was a star vehicle for LAUREN BACALL. PETER STONE reduced the clever screenplay to a one-dimensional tale about a cartoonist and an intellectual. HARRY GUARDINO was Bacall's romantic and professional foil and they made the weak material seem tolerable. The songs by JOHN KANDER and FRED EBB were well below their usual standards and a series of directors worked on the show to try and make it something special. But Bacall was special enough for audiences and *Woman of the Year* ran for 770 performances.

WONDERFUL TOWN (1953) was a sprightly musical comedy that celebrated life in New York City in the 1930s. JOSEPH FIELDS and Jerome Chodorov adapted their 1940 comedy *My Sister Eileen* (which was based on Ruth McKinney's short stories) for the musical stage and ROSALIND RUSSELL, who had been in the film version of the play, recreated the role of the smart-aleck intellectual Ruth. Having left their home in Ohio, Ruth and her sister Eileen arrive in Greenwich Village hoping to find success and romance. Neither comes very easily but after a series of misadventures that involve everyone from Brazilian sailors to the police department, the two women find happiness in the crazy but lovable city. BETTY COMDEN and ADOLPH GREEN provided the witty lyrics for LEONARD BERNSTEIN's masterful music, resulting in a superior score that included "Ohio," "A Quiet Girl," "One Hundred Easy Ways," "A Little Bit in Love," "Conga!" "It's Love" and "The Wrong Note Rag." EDIE ADAMS played Eileen and also featured in the cast were George Gaynes, Henry Lascoe, Dort Clark, Dody Goodman and Nathaniel Frey. (559 performances)

PEGGY WOOD (1892–1978) was a leading lady in operettas and plays on Broadway and in London. Wood's most famous role was the ill-fated Ottilie in *MAYTIME* (1917). She began her career in the chorus of *NAUGHTY MARIETTA* (1910) and was featured in *The Madcap Duchess* (1913), *Hello, Broadway!* (1914), *Love o' Mike* (1917), *Marjolaine* (1922) and other Broadway shows up to 1938. Wood also appeared in London musicals and was a popular favorite on television.

WORKING (1978) was a valiant little musical based on Studs Terkel's book about the jobs people have and their attitude toward them. STEPHEN

SCHWARTZ adapted the non-fiction anthology, directed the production and provided some of the songs. There were also contributions by songwriters MICKI GRANT, Mary Rodgers, CRAIG CARNELIA, Susan Birkenhead and James Taylor and the talented cast included PATTI LUPONE, Lenora Nemetz, BOB GUNTON, Lynn Thigpen and Rex Everhart. But as perceptive and engaging as the show was, it was hardly commercial enough for Broadway and only lasted twenty-five performances.

ROBERT WRIGHT (1914–) is a composer-lyricist who, with his partner GEORGE FORREST, has scored a series of Broadway musicals using CLASSICAL MUSIC. The team adapted Edvard Grieg music into *SONG OF NORWAY* (1944), VICTOR HERBERT melodies into *Gypsy Lady* (1946), Heitor Villa–Lobos compositions into *Magdalena* (1948), Alexander Borodin themes into *KISMET* (1953) and Rachmaninoff variations into *Anya* (1965). Wright and Forrest wrote their own compositions for *Kean* (1961) and provided half of the songs for *GRAND HOTEL* (1989).

ED WYNN (1886–1966) was a beloved clown who was popular on stage, in film and on the radio. Wynn began in vaudeville where he became famous for his lisping voice, high-pitched giggle and pun-filled jokes. He made his Broadway debut in 1910, appeared in the 1914 and 1915 *ZIEGFELD FOLLIES* and starred in a series of musicals tailored to his talents: *Sometime* (1918), *The Perfect Fool* (1921), *Manhattan Mary* (1927), *Simple Simon* (1930), *The Laugh Parade* (1931), *HOORAY FOR WHAT!* (1937), *Boys and Girls Together* (1940) and others. Wynn also helped write, direct and produce many of his shows.

Y

MAURY YESTON (1945–   ) is a composer-lyricist with two hit musicals to his credit. Yeston received a formal music education at Yale and at Cambridge University and began writing orchestral pieces as a student. In addition to several concert works, he has written books on music theory. Yeston made his Broadway musical debut with *NINE* (1982) and provided about half of the score for *GRAND HOTEL* (1989). He is also the composer-lyricist of the opera *Goya* and a musical version of *The Phantom of the Opera* that has been successfully produced regionally.

YIP YIP YAPHANK (1918) was more a fundraiser than a Broadway show but it had the score and the impact of a musical theatre hit. IRVING BERLIN, as a member of the military getting ready to go to France, put together the revue billed as "a military mess cooked up by the boys of Camp Upton." *Yip Yip Yaphank* had a cast of 350 members of the armed forces and a Berlin score that included "I Can Always Find a Little Sunshine in the Y.M.C.A.," "Mandy," "We're on Our Way to France" and "Oh, How I Hate to Get Up in the Morning," the last sung by the composer himself. The show ran for thirty-two performances and raised thousands of dollars for the war effort. Berlin did a similar project under the title *THIS IS THE ARMY* in 1942.

VINCENT YOUMANS (1898–1946), the Broadway composer who most typifies the musical comedies of the 1920s, had a theatre career of only ten years but in that time he worked with the best lyricists in the business and wrote three of the decade's biggest hits. Youmans was born in New York City into a business family and trained to become a Wall Street broker. While serving in the Army during World War I he started writing songs and after the war he met the GERSHWINS. With lyrics by Ira Gershwin, Youmans' music was first heard on Broadway in *Two Little Girls in Blue* (1921). He collaborated with OSCAR HAMMERSTEIN II and OTTO HARBACH on *Wildflower* (1923) and later with Harbach and IRVING CAESAR on *NO, NO, NANETTE* (1925), a major hit and often proclaimed as the epitome of 1920s musical comedy. Youmans scored nine other Broadway shows, the most notable being *HIT THE DECK* (1927) and *TAKE A CHANCE* (1932), and then retired in 1932 due to his tuberculosis. In addition to Harbach, Hammerstein, Caesar and Gershwin, Youmans collaborated with CLIFFORD GREY, BILLY ROSE, ANNE CALD-WELL, B. D. DESYLVA, Harold Adamson and other lyricists during his short career. Although Youmans' output was limited, his sense of rhythm and his use of harmony made his work distinctive. He also experimented with new variations of musical form, as in the innovative but short-lived *Rainbow* (1928).

RIDA JOHNSON YOUNG (1869?–1926) was a librettist-lyricist who collaborated with all three of America's operetta composer giants: VICTOR HERBERT, RUDOLF FRIML and SIGMUND ROMBERG. Her most famous musicals were *NAUGHTY MARIETTA* (1910) and *MAYTIME* (1917).

YOUR OWN THING (1968) was a silly but endearing Off-Broadway rock musical that spoofed Shakespeare's *Twelfth Night* as well as rock music itself. Librettist Donald Driver set the Elizabethan tale in Manhattan and put the characters into the music business. Siblings Viola and Sebastian look alike because all the boys are wearing their hair long and Viola is able to disguise herself and get a job with a male rock group, The Four Apocalypse. The usual confusions result, stopping intermittently to make sly comments on the generation gap, Shakespeare, homosexuality and love. Hal Hester and Danny Apolinar provided the derivative but humorous songs that sometimes used Shakespeare's lyrics and there was one outstanding ballad that was original called "The Middle Years." The young, likable cast featured LELAND PALMER, RUSS THACKER, Marcia Rodd and Tom Ligon under Driver's direction. (933 performances)

YOU'RE A GOOD MAN, CHARLIE BROWN (1967) was a modest little Off-Broadway musical inspired by Charles Schulz's *Peanuts* comic strip. Clark Gesner wrote the music, lyrics and libretto that followed a typical day in the life of Charlie Brown, Linus, Lucy, Schroeder, Patty and the very-human beagle Snoopy. The songs captured the Schultz temperament beautifully and the engaging performers made the show enjoyable for children and adults. The score was very simple and pleasing with "Happiness Is" becoming fairly popular. Gary Burghoff as Charlie Brown led the cast that consisted of Reva Rose, Bob Balaban, Karen Johnson, and Skip and Bill Hinnant under the direction of Joseph Hardy. The show ran for 1,597 performances and became one of the most revived musicals for amateur groups. A sequel of sorts, called *Snoopy* (1982), had a score by Larry Grossman and Hal Hackaday but it only lasted Off Broadway for 152 performances.

Z

JERRY ZAKS (1946–), an actor-turned-director, proved to be one of the most promising directors of plays and musicals in the 1980s. Zaks appeared in *GREASE* in 1973 and was featured in the musical revue *Tintypes* (1980). He made his musical directing debut with the tour of *THE TAP DANCE KID* then went on to stage the successful Broadway revivals of *ANYTHING GOES* in 1987 and *GUYS AND DOLLS* in 1992, as well as the Off-Broadway *ASSASSINS* (1990). Zaks is an endlessly inventive director equally at home with musical comedy, drama, farce and experimental projects.

FLORENZ ZIEGFELD (1867–1932), whose name is synonymous with Broadway glamour, was America's most well-known theatre producer. In addition to the twenty-one editions of the *ZIEGFELD FOLLIES*, he also produced such renowned musicals as *SALLY* (1920), *SHOW BOAT* (1927) and *WHOOPEE* (1928). His other musical productions included *The Century Girl* (1916), *Miss 1917* (1917), *Kid Boots* (1923), *RIO RITA* (1927), *ROSALIE* (1928), *THE THREE MUSKETEERS* (1928), *BITTER SWEET* (1929), *Smiles* (1930) and *Simple Simon* (1930). Ziegfeld's magnetic personality dominated Broadway just as his shows did, making him the greatest showman of his day.

THE *ZIEGFELD FOLLIES* (1907–1931), the most famous series of musical revues in the American theatre, was for many years considered the hallmark of the opulant but tasteful extravaganza. FLORENZ ZIEGFELD produced *Follies of 1907* at the rooftop theatre Jardin de Paris and it was such a hit that he moved it to Broadway. The revue emphasized beautiful girls and dazzling scenery rather than the songs and sketches; it was a pattern that was continued throughout the series. Ziegfeld presented twenty-one annual editions of the *Follies* before his death in 1932. As the shows got bigger, more girls were added and top stars were signed up. The most recurring *Follies* performers were FANNY BRICE, BERT WILLIAMS, W. C. FIELDS, ANN PENNINGTON, EDDIE CANTOR, NORA BAYES, Leon Errol and WILL ROGERS. JOSEPH URBAN, a noted architect, designed the scenery for several editions and Ben Ali Haggin created many of the famous tableau vivants. Although Ziegfeld did not put much importance on songs, IRVING BERLIN, VICTOR HERBERT, Harry Tierney and other composers wrote *Follies* scores and several popular songs came from the shows, including Berlin's "A Pretty Girl Is Like a Melody," the signature song for the series. In 1934 Ziegfeld's widow sold the rights to the series' title and there were editions produced by others in the 1930s and 1940s but they did not compare favorably to the originals. It was Ziegfeld's careful eye, his demand for high-class production values and his respectful but adoring presentation of beautiful women that made his shows unique.

CHIP ZIEN (1947–), a character actor in plays and musicals on and off Broadway, played Mendel the psychiatrist in *March of the Falsettos* (1981), *Falsettoland* (1990) and in *FALSETTOS* (1992). Zien's other musical credits include the Baker in *INTO THE WOODS* (1987) and featured roles in *Diamonds* (1984) and other Off-Broadway shows.

PATRICIA ZIPPRODT (1925–), one of Broadway's most respected and creative costume designers, has provided costumes for a very diverse selection of musicals. Zipprodt's most notable musical credits include *SHE LOVES ME* (1963), *FIDDLER ON THE ROOF* (1964), *CABARET* (1966), *ZORBA* (1968), *PIPPIN* (1972), *CHICAGO* (1975), *Big Deal* (1986), *INTO THE WOODS* (1987) with Ann Hould-Ward, *Dangerous Games* (1989) and *Shogun* (1990).

ZORBA (1968) was a well-crafted but somewhat awkward musical version of the Nikos Kazantzakis novel *Zorba the Greek* and the 1964 film based on it. JOSEPH STEIN did the adaptation and retained most of the elements of the original: the rustic Crete setting, the life-affirming Zorba (HERSCHEL BERNARDI) taking the young Nikos (John Cunningham) under his wing, the pathetically optimistic Hortense (MARIA KARNILOVA) and her illusions about love, the tragic affair with a local widow and so on. JOHN KANDER and FRED EBB wrote their most atypical score, an ethnic-sounding collection of songs that were sometimes very effective: "The First Time," "The Butterfly," "Happy Birthday," "No Boom Boom" and "Only Love." HAROLD PRINCE directed expertly and *Zorba* pleased audiences for 305 performances. A 1983 revival was even more successful with Anthony Quinn and Lila Kedrova recreating their film roles on the stage for 362 performances.

VERA ZORINA (1917–   ), a graceful ballet dancer who was featured in a handful of Broadway musicals, made her New York debut as the alluring Angel in *I MARRIED AN ANGEL* (1938). The Norwegian dancer also appeared in *LOUISIANA PURCHASE* (1940), *Dream with Music* (1944) and the 1954 revival of *ON YOUR TOES*.

Chronological List of Musicals

1866	The Black Crook
1874	Evangeline
1884	Adonis
1891	Wang
	Robin Hood
	A Trip to Chinatown
1894	The Passing Show
1896	El Capitan
1898	The Fortune Teller
1903	The Wizard of Oz
	In Dahomey
	Babes in Toyland
1904	Little Johnny Jones
1905	Mlle. Modiste
1906	Forty-Five Minutes from Broadway
	George Washington, Jr.
	The Red Mill
1910	Madame Sherry
	Naughty Marietta
1911	The Pink Lady
1912	The Firefly

1913	Sweethearts
1914	The Girl from Utah
	Watch Your Step
1915	Very Good Eddie
1917	Oh, Boy!
	Maytime
	Leave It to Jane
1918	Oh, Lady! Lady!
	Sinbad
	Yip Yip Yaphank
1919	Irene
1920	Mary
	Sally
1921	Shuffle Along
	Blossom Time
	Bombo
1923	Poppy
1924	Rose-Marie
	Lady, Be Good!
	The Student Prince of Heidelburg
1925	The Garrick Gaieties
	No, No, Nanette
	Dearest Enemy
	The Vagabond King
	Sunny
	The Cocoanuts
	Tip-Toes
1926	Oh, Kay!
	The Desert Song
	Peggy-Ann
1927	Rio Rita
	Hit the Deck
	Good News!
	A Connecticut Yankee
	Funny Face
	Show Boat
1928	Rosalie

The Three Musketeers
Blackbirds of 1928
The New Moon
Hold Everything!
Animal Crackers
Whoopee
1929   Follow Thru
The Little Show
Sweet Adeline
Fifty Million Frenchmen
1930   Strike Up the Band
Flying High
Fine and Dandy
Girl Crazy
Three's a Crowd
The New Yorkers
1931   The Band Wagon
The Cat and the Fiddle
Of Thee I Sing
1932   Face the Music
Flying Colors
Music in the Air
Take a Chance
Gay Divorce
1933   The Threepenny Opera
As Thousands Cheer
Let 'Em Eat Cake
Roberta
1934   Life Begins at 8:40
Anything Goes
Revenge with Music
1935   At Home Abroad
Porgy and Bess
Jubilee
Jumbo
1936   On Your Toes
Red, Hot and Blue!

	Johnny Johnson
	The Show Is On
1937	Babes in Arms
	I'd Rather Be Right
	Pins and Needles
	Hooray for What!
	Between the Devil
1938	The Cradle Will Rock
	I Married an Angel
	Hellzapoppin
	Knickerbocker Holiday
	Leave It to Me
	The Boys from Syracuse
1939	Too Many Girls
	Very Warm for May
	DuBarry Was a Lady
1940	Louisiana Purchase
	Cabin in the Sky
	Panama Hattie
	Pal Joey
1941	Lady in the Dark
	Best Foot Forward
	Let's Face It!
1942	By Jupiter
	This Is the Army
1943	Something for the Boys
	Oklahoma!
	One Touch of Venus
	Carmen Jones
1944	Mexican Hayride
	Follow the Girls
	Song of Norway
	Bloomer Girl
	On the Town
1945	Up in Central Park
	Carousel
1946	St. Louis Woman

Call Me Mister
Annie Get Your Gun
1947   Street Scene
Finian's Rainbow
Brigadoon
High Button Shoes
Allegro
1948   Make Mine Manhattan
Inside U.S.A.
Love Life
Where's Charley?
As the Girls Go
Lend an Ear
Kiss Me, Kate
1949   South Pacific
Miss Liberty
Lost in the Stars
Regina
Gentlemen Prefer Blondes
1950   Call Me Madam
Guys and Dolls
1951   The King and I
A Tree Grows in Brooklyn
Flahooley
Two on the Aisle
Paint Your Wagon
1952   New Faces of 1952
Wish You Were Here
1953   Wonderful Town
Can-Can
Me and Juliet
Kismet
1954   The Threepenny Opera
The Golden Apple
The Pajama Game
The Boy Friend
Peter Pan

Fanny

House of Flowers

1955   Plain and Fancy

Silk Stockings

Damn Yankees

Pipe Dream

1956   My Fair Lady

The Most Happy Fella

Li'l Abner

Bells Are Ringing

Candide

1957   New Girl in Town

West Side Story

Jamaica

The Music Man

1958   Flower Drum Song

1959   Redhead

Juno

Destry Rides Again

Once upon a Mattress

Gypsy

Take Me Along

The Sound of Music

Little Mary Sunshine

Fiorello!

Saratoga

1960   Greenwillow

Bye Bye Birdie

The Fantasticks

Tenderloin

The Unsinkable Molly Brown

Camelot

Wildcat

Do Re Mi

1961   Carnival

Milk and Honey

How to Succeed in Business without Really Trying

Kwamina
The Gay Life
Subways Are for Sleeping
1962   No Strings
All American
I Can Get It for You Wholesale
A Funny Thing Happened on the Way to the Forum
Stop the World—I Want to Get Off
Mr. President
Little Me
1963   She Loves Me
Here's Love
Oliver!
110 in the Shade
1964   Hello, Dolly!
What Makes Sammy Run?
Funny Girl
Anyone Can Whistle
Fade In–Fade Out
Fiddler on the Roof
Golden Boy
1965   Do I Hear a Waltz?
Flora, the Red Menace
The Roar of the Greasepaint—The Smell of the Crowd
On a Clear Day You Can See Forever
Man of La Mancha
1966   Sweet Charity
It's a Plane, It's a Bird, It's Superman
Mame
The Apple Tree
Cabaret
Man with a Load of Mischief
I Do! I Do!
1967   Hallelujah, Baby!
You're a Good Man, Charlie Brown
1968   Your Own Thing
The Happy Time

Hair
Zorba
Promises, Promises
Dames at Sea
1969 Celebration
Dear World
Oh, Calcutta!
1776
Coco
1970 Purlie
Applause
Company
The Last Sweet Days of Isaac
The Rothschilds
Two by Two
The Me Nobody Knows
1971 Follies
70, Girls, 70
Godspell
Jesus Christ Superstar
The Grass Harp
Two Gentlemen of Verona
1972 Grease
Sugar
Don't Bother Me, I Can't Cope
Pippin
1973 A Little Night Music
Seesaw
Raisin
1974 The Magic Show
Mack and Mabel
1975 The Wiz
Shenandoah
Chicago
A Chorus Line
1976 1600 Pennsylvania Avenue
The Robber Bridegroom

The Baker's Wife
1977   I Love My Wife
Starting Here, Staring Now
Annie
The Act
1978   On the Twentieth Century
Dancin'
The Best Little Whorehouse in Texas
Ain't Misbehavin'
Working
I'm Getting My Act Together and Taking It on the Road
1979   The Grand Tour
They're Playing Our Song
Sweeney Todd, the Demon Barber of Fleet Street
Carmelina
Evita
Sugar Babies
1980   Barnum
42nd Street
1981   Sophisticated Ladies
Woman of the Year
Joseph and the Amazing Technicolor Dreamcoat
Merrily We Roll Along
Dreamgirls
1982   Nine
Little Shop of Horrors
Cats
My One and Only
1983   Dance a Little Closer
La Cage aux Folles
Baby
The Tap Dance Kid
1984   The Rink
Sunday in the Park with George
1985   Big River
The Mystery of Edwin Drood
Nunsense

1986   Me and My Girl
        Rags
1987   Les Misérables
        Into the Woods
1988   The Phantom of the Opera
        Romance, Romance
1989   Black and Blue
        Grand Hotel
        City of Angels
        Closer Than Ever
1990   Once on This Island
        Assassins
1991   Miss Saigon
        The Secret Garden
        The Will Rogers Follies
1992   Crazy for You
        Falsettos
        Jelly's Last Jam

Selected Bibliography

GENERAL WORKS ON THE AMERICAN MUSICAL THEATRE

Albert, Hollis. *Broadway: 125 Years of Musical Theatre*. New York: Arcade Publishers, 1991.

Atkinson, Brooks. *Broadway*. New York: Macmillan Publishing Co., 1974.

Baral, Robert. *Revue: The Great Broadway Period*. New York: Fleet Press Corp., 1962.

The Best Plays, 75 ed. Editors: Garrison Sherwood and John Chapman (1894–1919); Burns Mantle (1919–1947); John Chapman (1947–1952); Louis Kronenberger (1952–1961); Henry Hewes (1961–1964); Otis Guernsey, Jr. (1964–1991). New York: Dodd, Mead & Co., 1894–1991.

Bloom, Ken. *Broadway: An Encyclopedic Guide to the History, People and Places of Times Square*. New York: Facts on File, 1991.

Blum, Daniel, and John Willis. *A Pictorial History of the American Theatre, 1860–1980*, 5th ed. New York: Crown Publishers, 1981.

Bordman, Gerald. *American Musical Comedy: From Adonis to Dreamgirls*. New York: Oxford University Press, 1982.

———. *The American Musical Revue: From The Passing Show to Sugar Babies*. New York: Oxford University Press, 1985.

———. *American Musical Theatre: A Chronicle*, 2nd ed. New York: Oxford University Press, 1992.

———. *American Operetta: From H.M.S. Pinafore to Sweeney Todd*. New York: Oxford University Press, 1981.

———. *The Oxford Companion to the American Theatre*, 2nd ed. New York: Oxford University Press, 1992.

Botto, Louis. *At This Theatre: An Informal History of New York's Legitimate Theatres*. New York: Dodd, Mead & Co., 1984.

Bowers, Dwight Blocker. *American Musical Theatre: Shows, Songs and Stars.* Washington, DC: Smithsonian Press, 1989.

Engel, Lehrman. *The American Musical Theatre: A Consideration.* New York: CBS Legacy Collection Books, 1967.

———. *Their Words Are Music: The Great Theatre Lyricists and Their Lyrics.* New York: Crown Publishers, 1975.

Ewen, David. *American Songwriters.* New York: The H. W. Wilson Co., 1987.

———. *The New Complete Book of the American Musical Theatre.* New York: Henry Holt & Co., 1976.

Ganzl, Kurt, and Andrew Lamb. *Ganzl's Book of the Musical Theatre.* New York: Schirmer Books, 1989.

Gottfried, Martin. *Broadway Musicals.* New York: Harry N. Abrams, 1980.

———. *More Broadway Musicals.* New York: Harry N. Abrams, 1991.

Green, Stanley. *Broadway Musicals of the 1930s.* New York: DaCapo Press, 1971.

———. *Broadway Musicals Show by Show.* Milwaukee: Hal Leonard Books, 1990.

———. *Encyclopedia of the Musical Theatre.* New York: Dodd, Mead & Co., 1976.

———. *The World of Musical Comedy.* New York: A. S. Barnes & Co., 1980.

Guernsey, Otis L. (ed.). *Broadway Song and Story: Playwrights, Lyricists, Composers Discuss Their Hits.* New York: Dodd, Mead & Co., 1985.

———. *Curtain Times: The New York Theatre 1965–1987.* New York: Applause Theatre Book Publishers, 1987.

———. *Playwrights, Lyricists, Composers on Theatre.* New York: Dodd, Mead & Co., 1974.

Henderson, Mary C. *Theatre in America.* New York: Harry N. Abrams, 1986.

Hischak, Thomas S. *Word Crazy: Broadway Lyricists from Cohan to Sondheim.* New York: Praeger Publishers, 1991.

Hubbard, Linda S., and Owen O'Donnell (eds.). *Contemporary Theatre, Film and Television: Who's Who in the Theatre*, Vol. 1–7. Detroit: Gale Research, 1978–1989.

Jackson, Arthur. *The Best Musicals from Show Boat to a Chorus Line.* New York: Crown Publishers, 1977.

Kasha, Al, and Joel Hirschorn. *Notes on Broadway: Conversations with the Great Songwriters.* Chicago: Contemporary Books, 1985.

Laufe, Abe. *Broadway's Greatest Musicals.* New York: Funk and Wagnall, 1969.

Leiter, Samuel L. *The Encyclopedia of the New York Stage, 1920–1930.* (2 vols.) Westport, CT: Greenwood Press, 1985.

———. *The Encyclopedia of the New York Stage, 1930–1940.* Westport, CT: Greenwood Press, 1989.

———. *The Encyclopedia of the New York Stage, 1940–1950.* Westport, CT: Greenwood Press, 1992.

———. *Ten Seasons: New York Theatre in the Seventies.* Westport, CT: Greenwood Press, 1986.

Lerner, Alan Jay. *The Musical Theatre: A Celebration.* New York: McGraw Hill Book Co., 1986.

Lewine, Richard, and Alfred Simon. *Encyclopedia of Theatre Music.* New York: Bonanza Books, 1961.

———. *Songs of the Theatre.* New York: H. W. Wilson Company, 1984.

Mandelbaum, Ken. *Not Since Carrie: Forty Years of Broadway Musical Flops.* New York: St. Martin's Press, 1991.

Mates, Julian. *America's Musical Stage: Two Hundred Years of Musical Theatre.* Westport, CT: Greenwood Press, 1985.

Mordden, Ethan. *Better Foot Forward: A History of American Musical Theatre*. New York: Viking Press, 1976.

———. *Broadway Babies: The People Who Made the American Musical*. New York: Oxford University Press, 1983.

Morehouse, Ward. *Matinee Tomorrow: Fifty Years of Our Theatre*. New York: McGraw Hill, 1949.

Morrow, Lee Alan. *The Tony Award Book*. New York: Abbeville Press, 1987.

Owen, Bobbi. *Costume Design on Broadway: Designers and Their Credits, 1915–1985*. Westport, CT: Greenwood Press, 1987.

———. *Lighting Design on Broadway: Designers and Their Credits, 1915–1990*. Westport, CT: Greenwood Press, 1991.

———. *Scenic Design on Broadway: Designers and Their Credits, 1915–1990*. Westport, CT: Greenwood Press, 1991.

Smith, Cecil, and Glenn Litton. *Musical Comedy in America*. New York: Theatre Arts Books, 1981.

Suskin, Steven. *Opening Night on Broadway: A Critical Quotebook of the Golden Era of the Musical Theatre*. New York: Schirmer Books, 1990.

———. *Show Tunes: 1905–1985*. New York: Dodd, Mead & Co., 1986.

Swain, Joseph P. *The Broadway Musical: A Critical and Musical Survey*. New York: Oxford University Press, 1990.

Theatre World, 46 ed. Editors: Daniel Blum (1944–1964); John Willis (1964–1990). New York: Greenburg, 1944–1957; Philadelphia: Chilton, 1957–1964; New York: Crown Publishers, 1964–1990.

Toll, Robert C. *On with the Show: The First Century of Show Business in America*. New York: Oxford University Press, 1976.

Traubner, Richard. *Operetta: A Theatrical History*. Garden City, NY: Doubleday & Co., 1983.

Woll, Allen. *Black Musical Theatre: From Coontown to Dreamgirls*. Baton Rouge: Louisiana State University Press, 1989.

Index

Page numbers in **bold** refer to individual entries.

About the Author

THOMAS S. HISCHAK is Associate Professor of Theatre History and Criticism at the State University of New York, College at Cortland. He is the author of *Word Crazy: Broadway Lyricists from Cohan to Sondheim* (Praeger, 1991). Twelve of his own plays have been published by Samuel French, Inc., Dramatic Publishing Company, and others.